SAVE 58% OFF
THE COVER PRICE!
THAT'S LIKE GETTING 7 ISSUES FREE!

❑ I want 12 GIANT issues of *Shojo Beat* for $29.95*!

NAME ....

ADDRESS ....

CITY .... STATE .... ZIP ....

EMAIL ADDRESS ....

DATE OF BIRTH ....

❑ **Yes!** Send me via email information, advertising, offers, and promotions related to VIZ Media, *Shojo Beat*, and/or their business partners.
❑ CHECK ENCLOSED (payable to *Shojo Beat*)   ❑ BILL ME LATER
CREDIT CARD: ❑ VISA   ❑ MC
      ACCOUNT #: ....
      EXPIRE DATE: ....
      SIGNATURE ....

CLIP & MAIL TO:
SHOJO BEAT SUBSCRIPTIONS SERVICE DEPT.
P.O. BOX 438
MOUNT MORRIS, IL 61054-0438

P9GNC1

ratings.viz.com   www.viz.com

ou think Beat Manga!

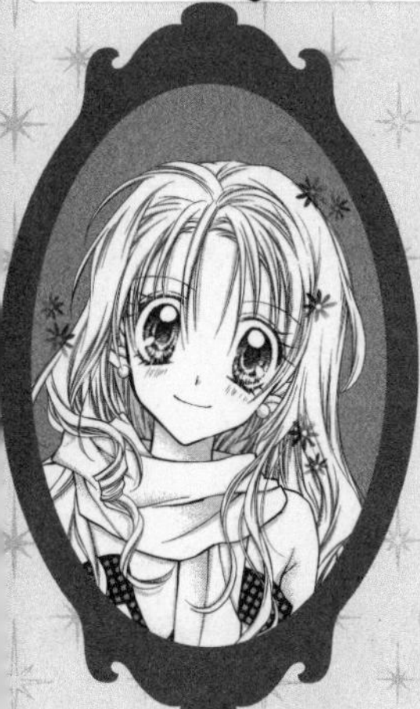

Our survey is now available online. Go to:

shojobeat.com/mangasurvey

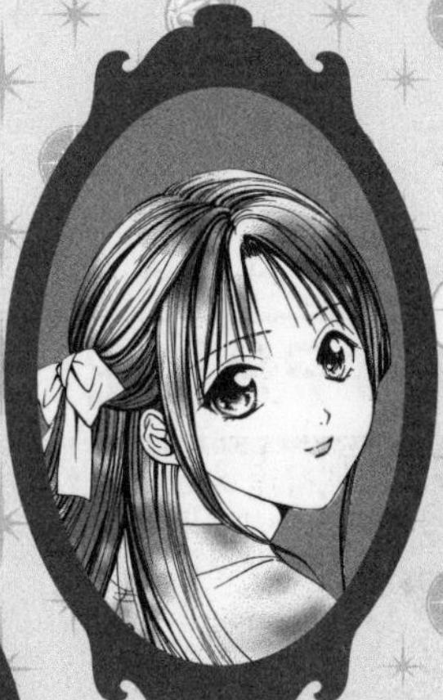

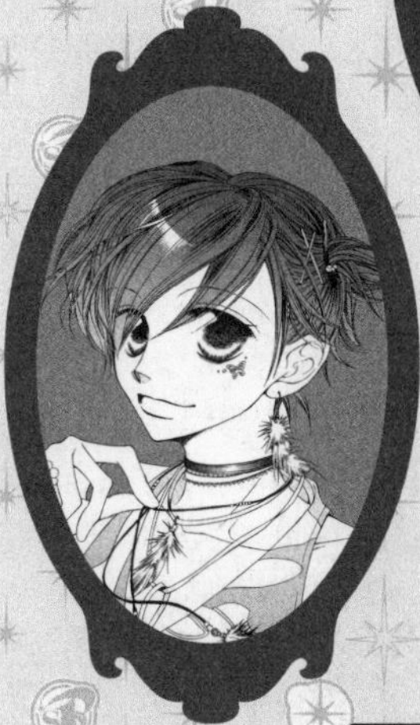

Help us make our product offerings better!

VIZ media

Shojo Beat THE REAL DRAMA BEGINS IN...

MANGA from the HEART

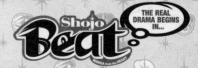

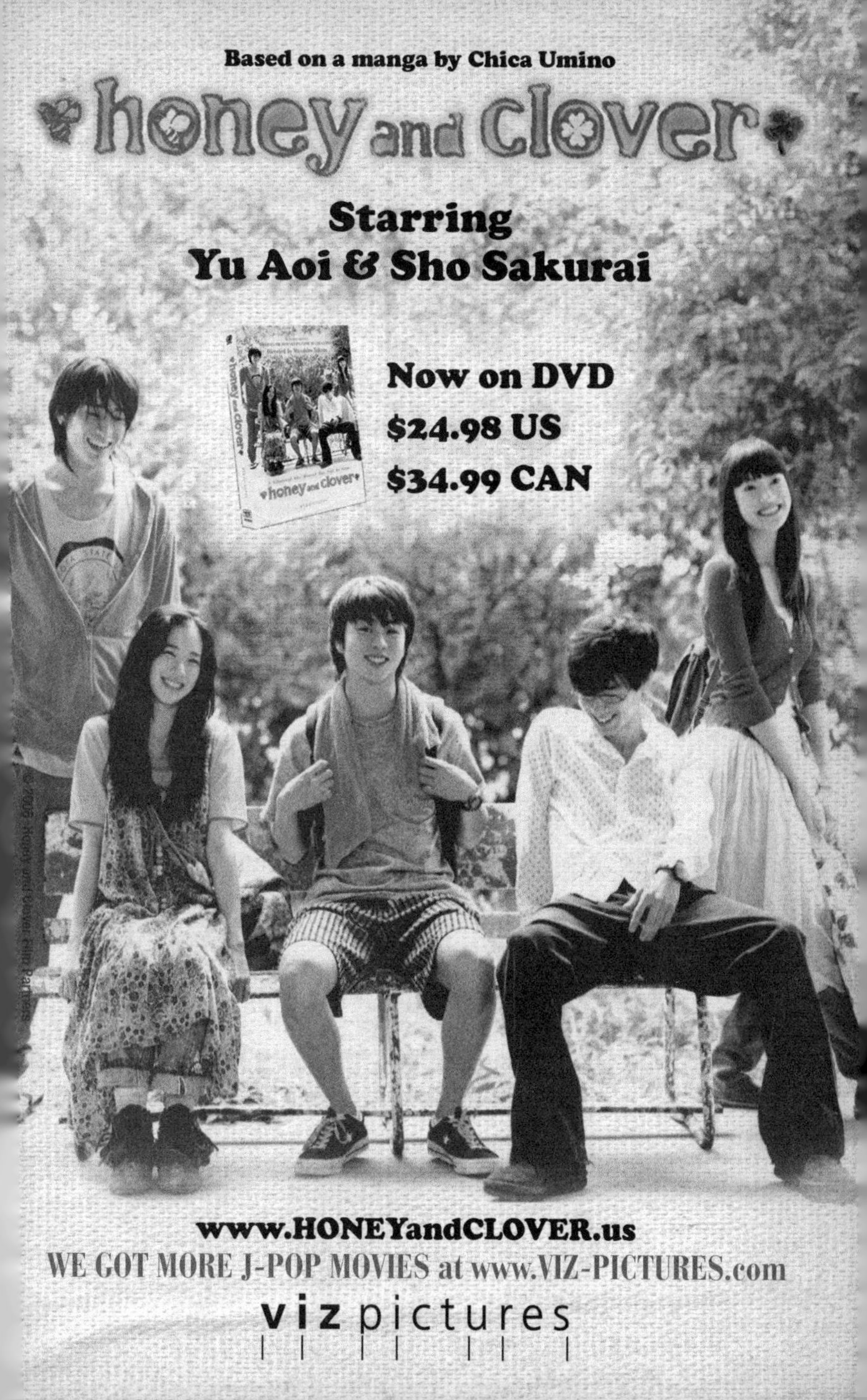
Based on a manga by Chica Umino
honey and clover
Starring
Yu Aoi & Sho Sakurai
honey and clover
Now on DVD
$24.98 US
$34.99 CAN
© 2006 Honey and Clover Film Partners
www.HONEYandCLOVER.us
WE GOT MORE J-POP MOVIES at www.VIZ-PICTURES.com
viz pictures

Shojo Beat

HONEY AND CLOVER
VOL. 6
The Shojo Beat Manga Edition

This manga volume contains material that was originally published in English in *Shojo Beat* magazine, February-April 2009. Artwork in the magazine may have been slightly altered from that presented here.

STORY AND ART BY CHICA UMINO

English Translation & Adaptation/Akemi Wegmuller
Touch-up Art & Lettering/Sabrina Heep
Design/Yukiko Whitley
Editor/Pancha Diaz

Editor in Chief, Books/Alvin Lu
Editor in Chief, Magazines/Marc Weidenbaum
VP, Publishing Licensing/Rika Inouye
VP, Sales & Product Marketing/Gonzalo Ferreyra
VP, Creative/Linda Espinosa
Publisher/Hyoe Narita

Printed in Canada

Published by VIZ Media, LLC
P.O. Box 77010
San Francisco, CA 94107

VIZ media

www.viz.com

Shojo Beat Manga Edition
10 9 8 7 6 5 4 3 2 1
First printing, June 2009

RATED T+ FOR OLDER TEEN

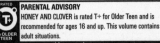

PARENTAL ADVISORY
HONEY AND CLOVER is rated T+ for Older Teen and is recommended for ages 16 and up. This volume contains adult situations.

ratings.viz.com

Shojo Beat

honey and clover

Vol. 6

Story & Art by
Chica Umino

honey and clover

Volume 6
CONTENTS

honey and clover

honey and clover

chapter 35

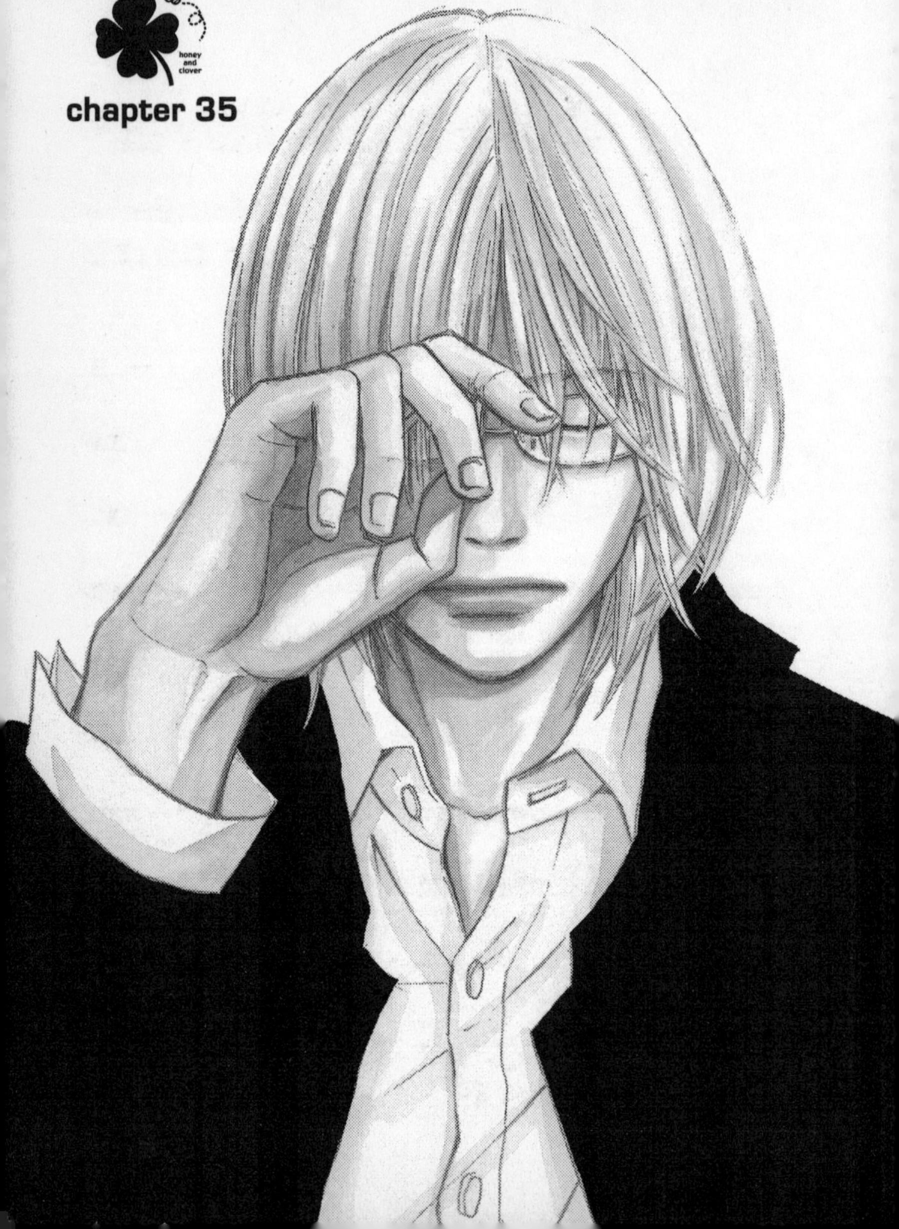

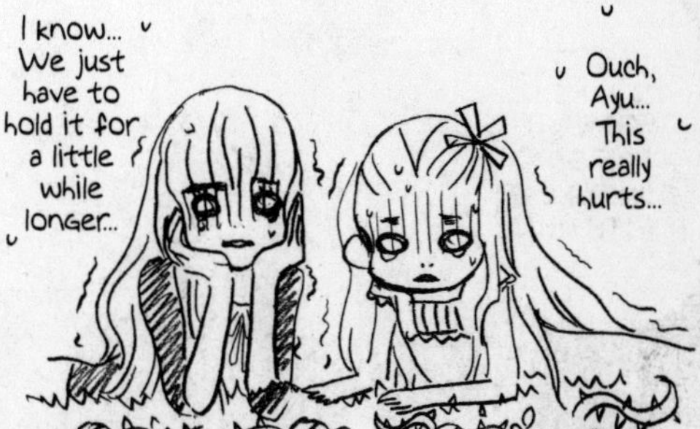
Ouch, Ayu... This really hurts...
I know... We just have to hold it for a little while longer...

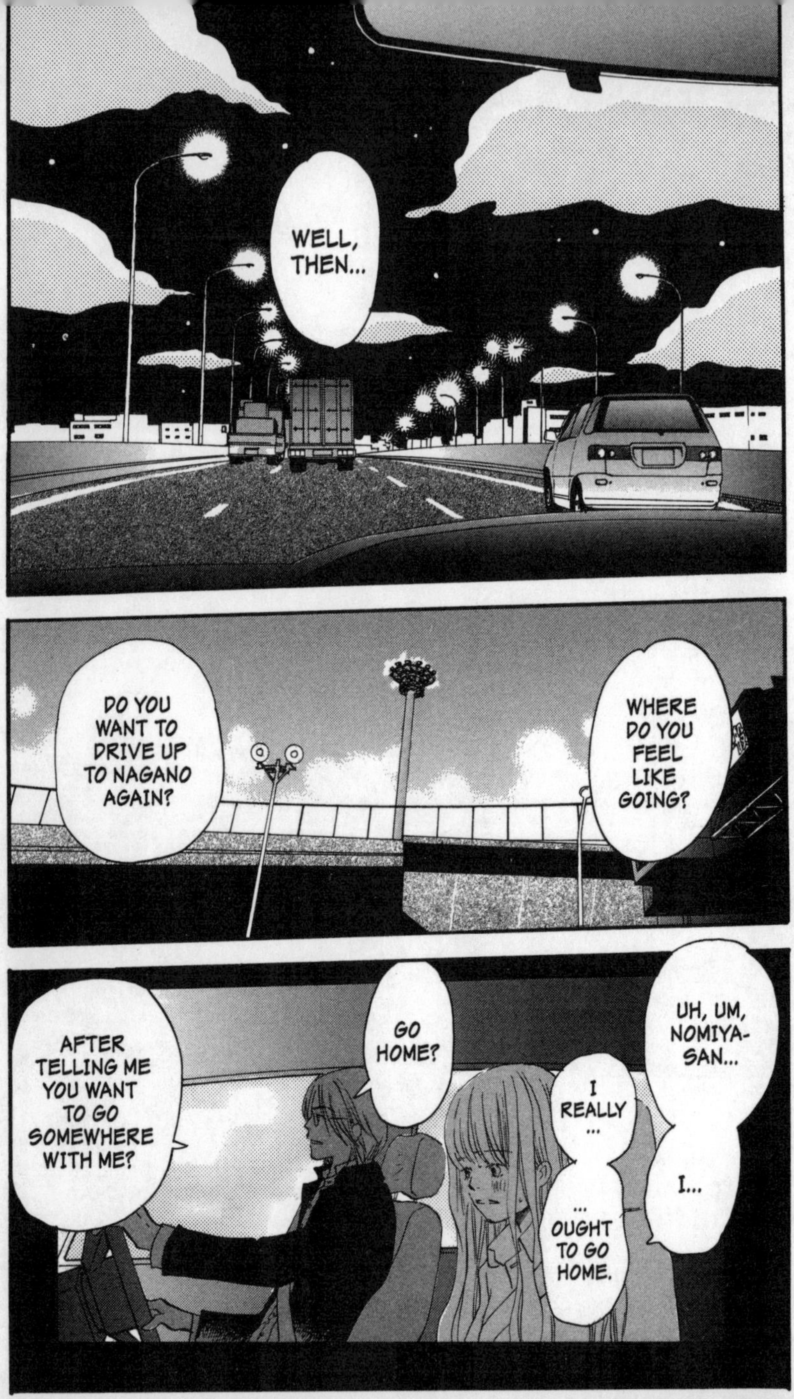
WELL, THEN...
WHERE DO YOU FEEL LIKE GOING?
DO YOU WANT TO DRIVE UP TO NAGANO AGAIN?
UH, UM, NOMIYA-SAN...
I...
I REALLY...
...OUGHT TO GO HOME.
GO HOME?
AFTER TELLING ME YOU WANT TO GO SOMEWHERE WITH ME?

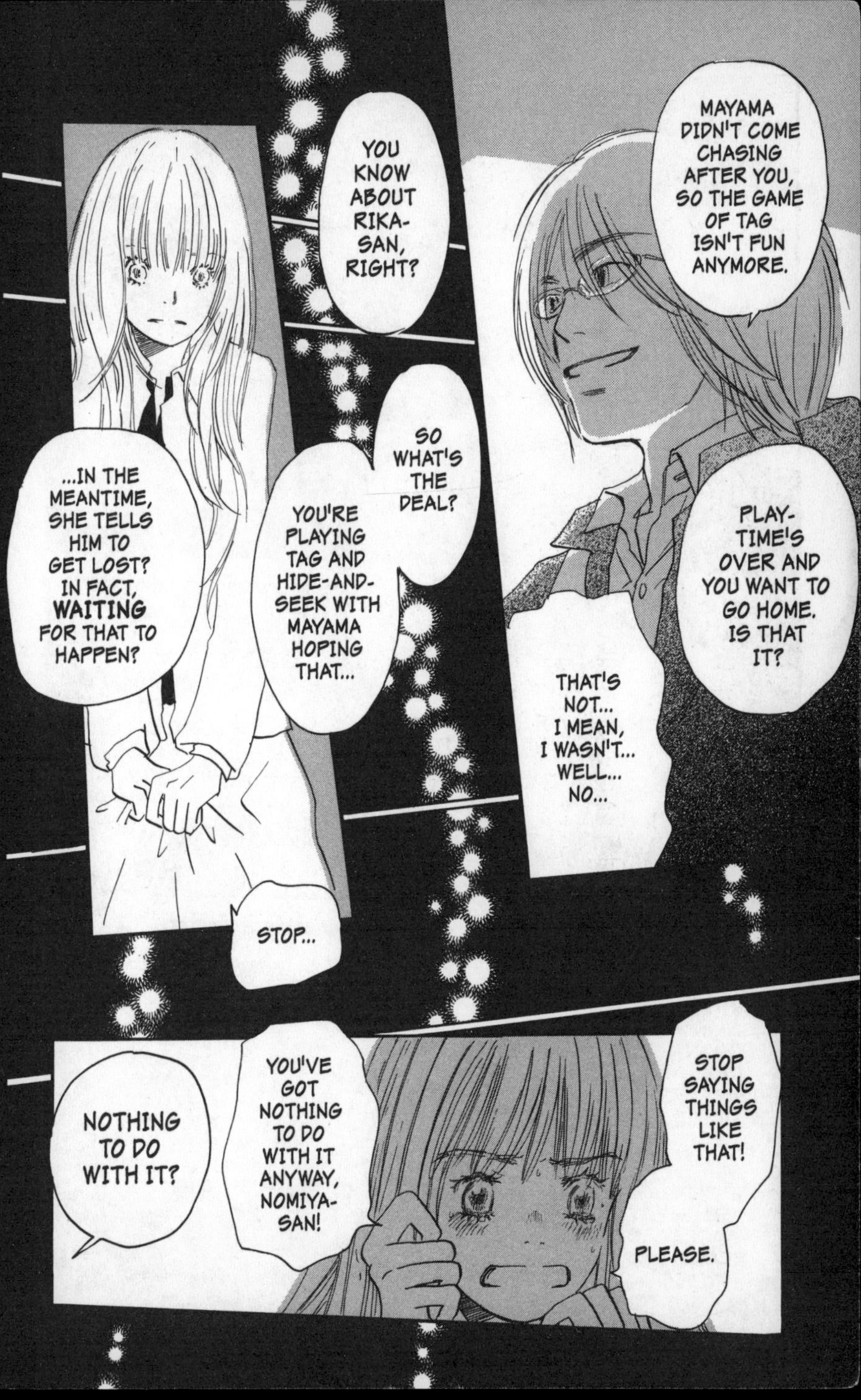
MAYAMA DIDN'T COME CHASING AFTER YOU, SO THE GAME OF TAG ISN'T FUN ANYMORE.
PLAY-TIME'S OVER AND YOU WANT TO GO HOME. IS THAT IT?
THAT'S NOT... I MEAN, I WASN'T... WELL... NO...
YOU KNOW ABOUT RIKA-SAN, RIGHT?
SO WHAT'S THE DEAL?
YOU'RE PLAYING TAG AND HIDE-AND-SEEK WITH MAYAMA HOPING THAT...
...IN THE MEANTIME, SHE TELLS HIM TO GET LOST? IN FACT, **WAITING** FOR THAT TO HAPPEN?
STOP...
STOP SAYING THINGS LIKE THAT!
PLEASE.
YOU'VE GOT NOTHING TO DO WITH IT ANYWAY, NOMIYA-SAN!
NOTHING TO DO WITH IT?

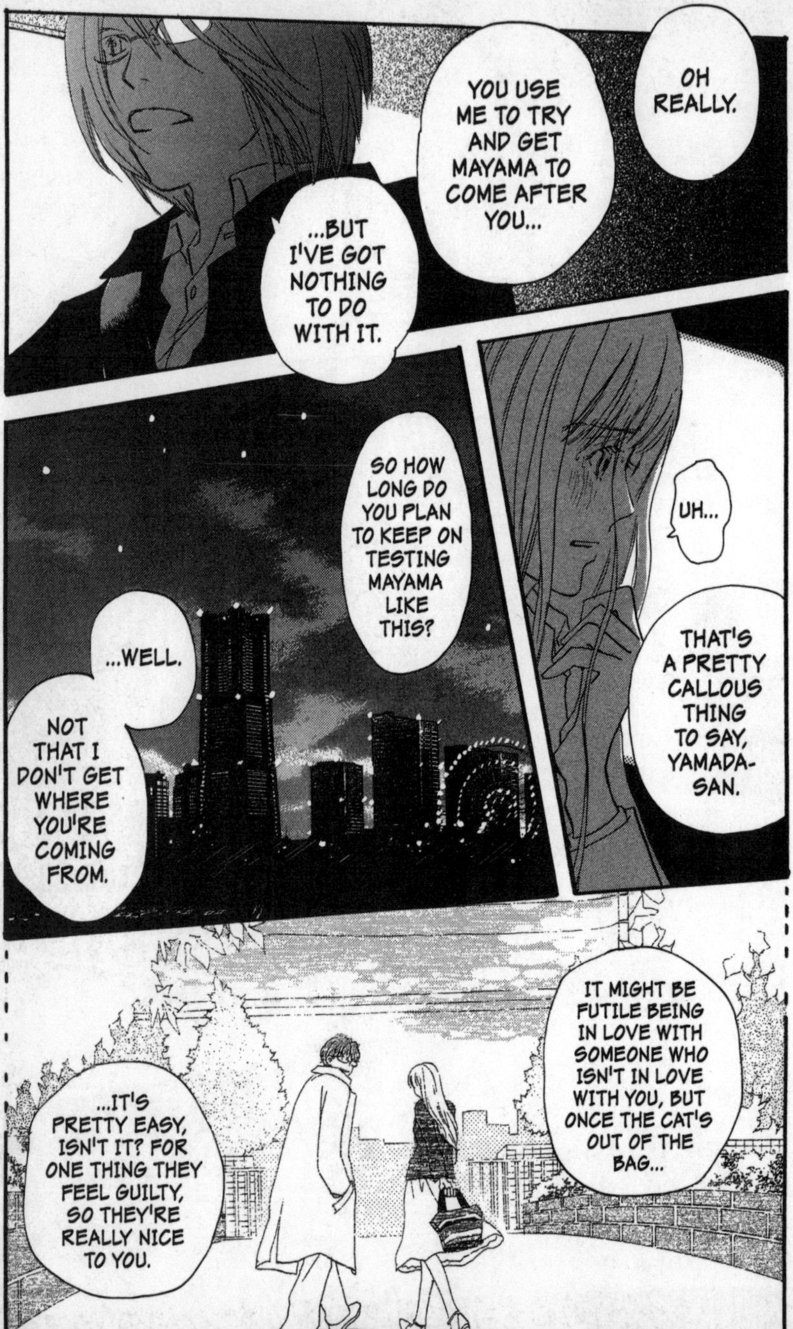
OH REALLY.
YOU USE ME TO TRY AND GET MAYAMA TO COME AFTER YOU...
...BUT I'VE GOT NOTHING TO DO WITH IT.
UH...
THAT'S A PRETTY CALLOUS THING TO SAY, YAMADA-SAN.
SO HOW LONG DO YOU PLAN TO KEEP ON TESTING MAYAMA LIKE THIS?
...WELL.
NOT THAT I DON'T GET WHERE YOU'RE COMING FROM.
IT MIGHT BE FUTILE BEING IN LOVE WITH SOMEONE WHO ISN'T IN LOVE WITH YOU, BUT ONCE THE CAT'S OUT OF THE BAG...
...IT'S PRETTY EASY, ISN'T IT? FOR ONE THING THEY FEEL GUILTY, SO THEY'RE REALLY NICE TO YOU.

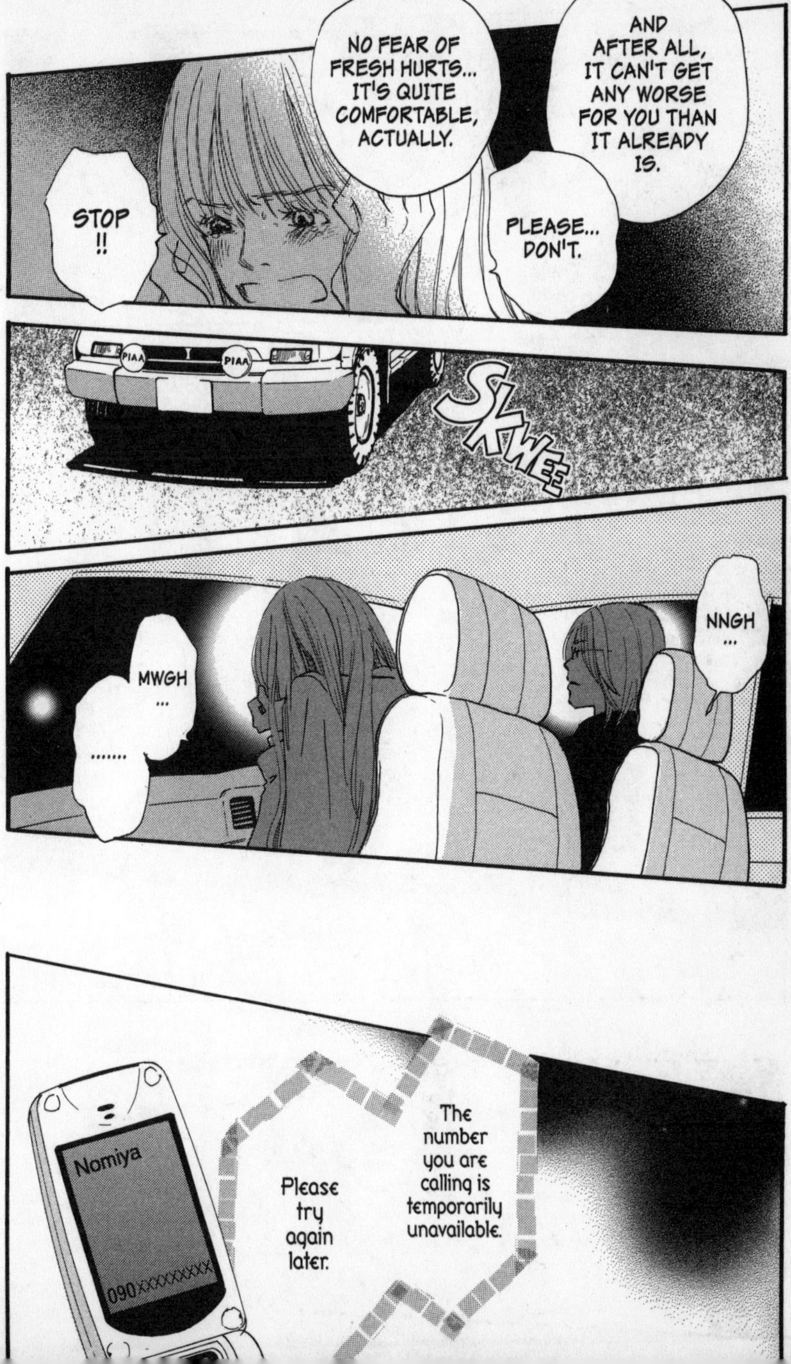
AND AFTER ALL, IT CAN'T GET ANY WORSE FOR YOU THAN IT ALREADY IS.
NO FEAR OF FRESH HURTS... IT'S QUITE COMFORTABLE, ACTUALLY.
PLEASE... DON'T.
STOP !!
SKWEE
PIAA
PIAA
NNGH ...
MWGH ...
....
The number you are calling is temporarily unavailable.
Please try again later.
Nomiya
090XXXXXXXX

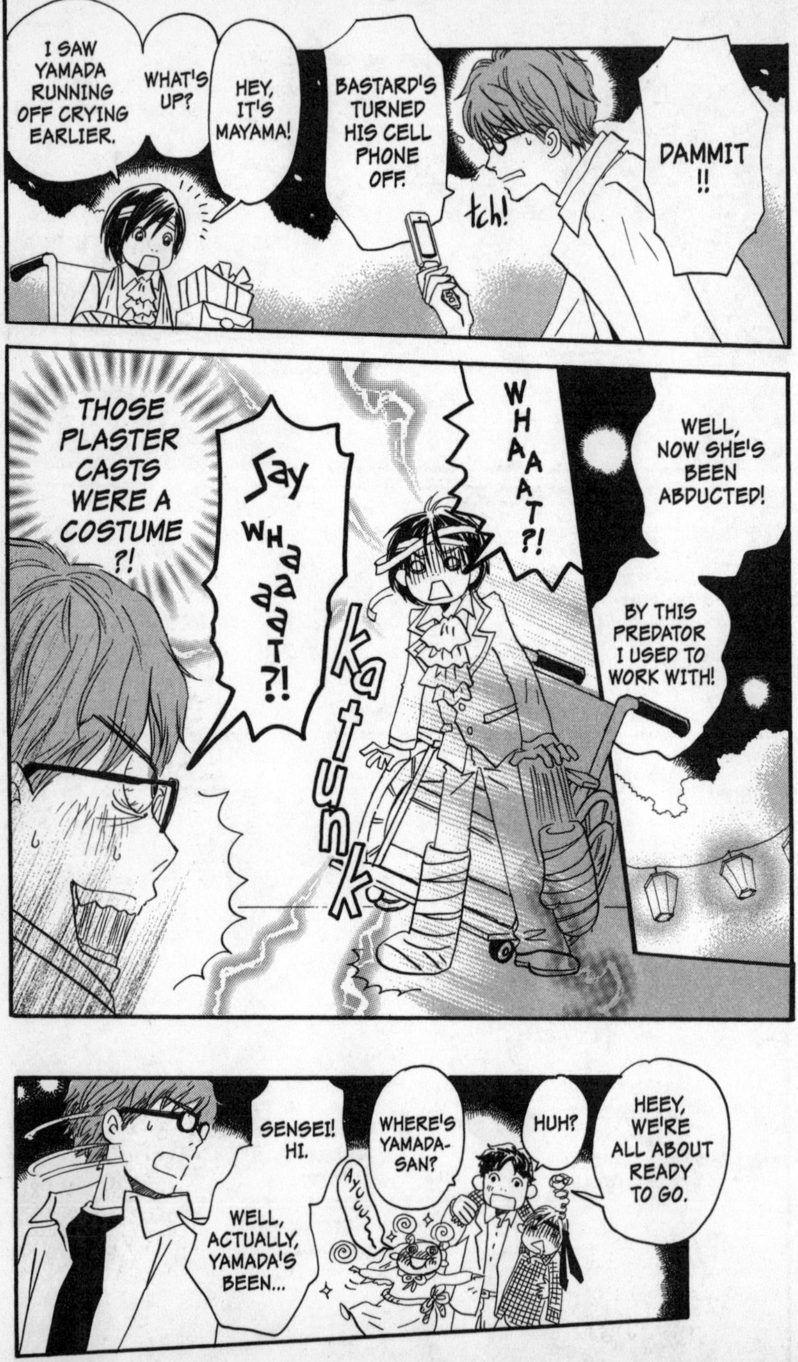
DAMMIT !!
tch!
BASTARD'S TURNED HIS CELL PHONE OFF.
HEY, IT'S MAYAMA!
WHAT'S UP?
I SAW YAMADA RUNNING OFF CRYING EARLIER.
WELL, NOW SHE'S BEEN ABDUCTED!
BY THIS PREDATOR I USED TO WORK WITH!
WHAAAT?!
Say whaaaaT?!
katunk
THOSE PLASTER CASTS WERE A COSTUME ?!
HEEY, WE'RE ALL ABOUT READY TO GO.
HUH?
WHERE'S YAMADA-SAN?
AYUUU...
SENSEI! HI.
WELL, ACTUALLY, YAMADA'S BEEN...

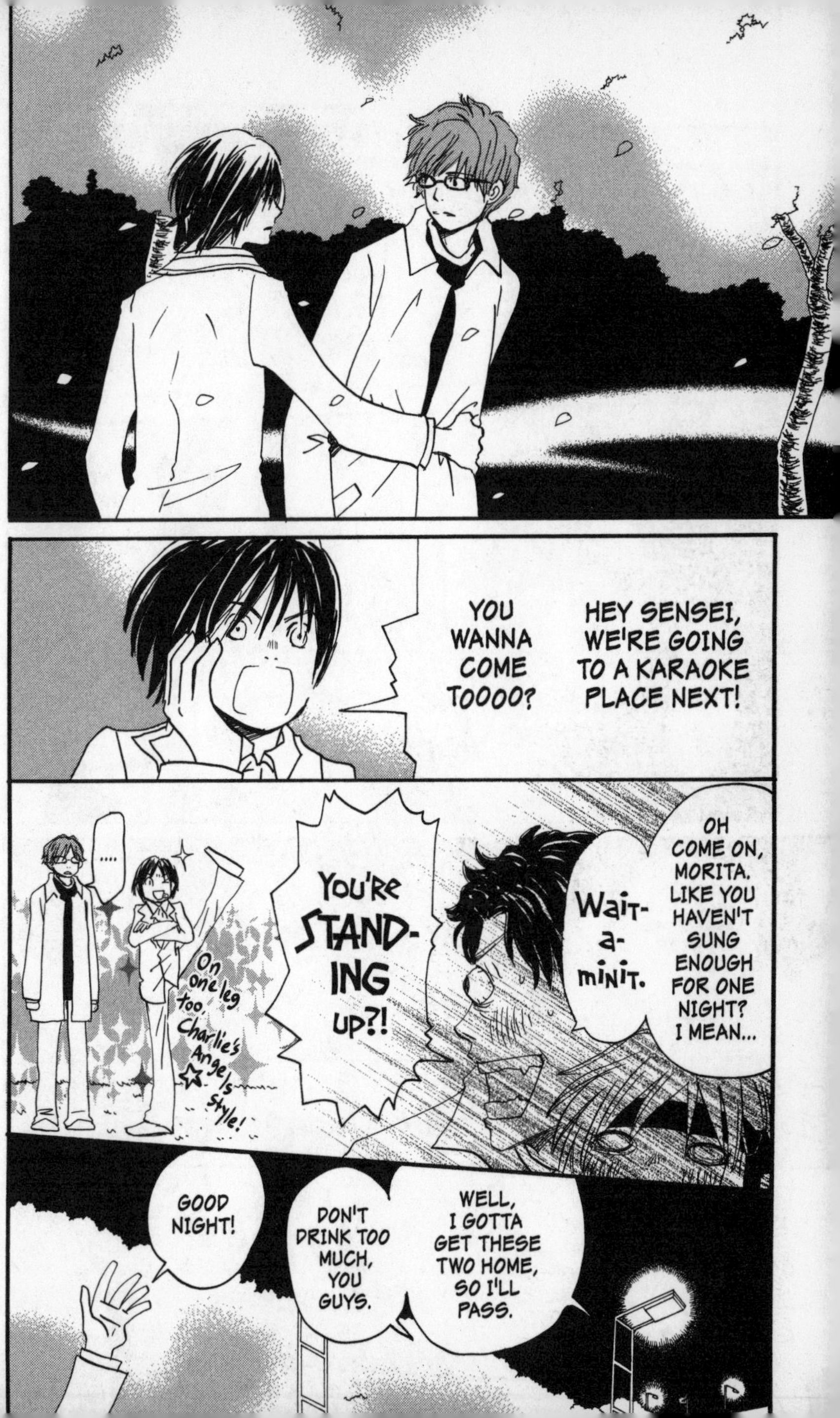
HEY SENSEI, WE'RE GOING TO A KARAOKE PLACE NEXT!
YOU WANNA COME TOOOO?
OH COME ON, MORITA. LIKE YOU HAVEN'T SUNG ENOUGH FOR ONE NIGHT? I MEAN...
Wait-a-minit.
You're STANDING-ING up?!
On one leg too. Charlie's Angels style!
....
WELL, I GOTTA GET THESE TWO HOME, SO I'LL PASS.
DON'T DRINK TOO MUCH, YOU GUYS.
GOOD NIGHT!

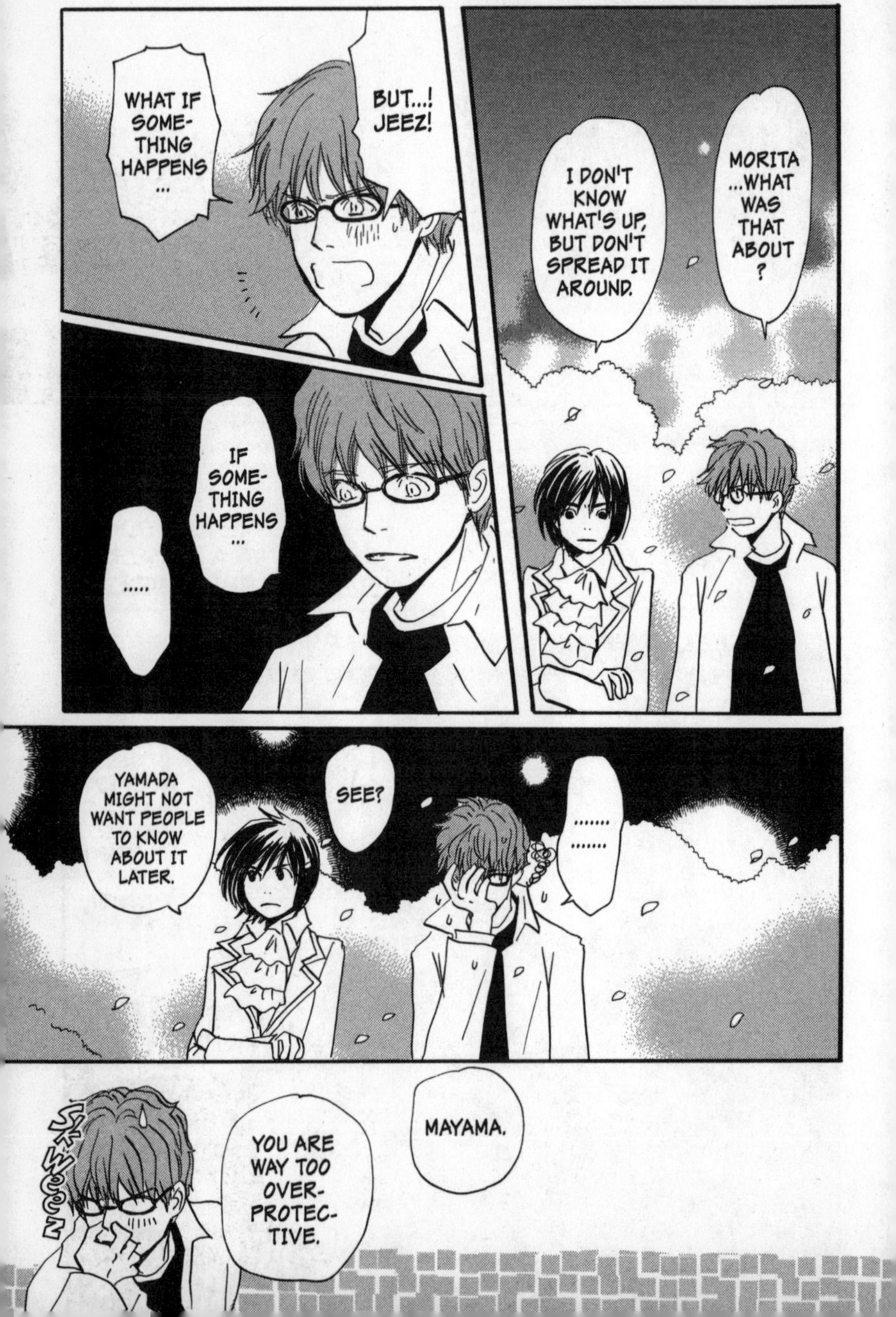
MORITA ...WHAT WAS THAT ABOUT?
I DON'T KNOW WHAT'S UP, BUT DON'T SPREAD IT AROUND.
BUT...! JEEZ!
WHAT IF SOMETHING HAPPENS...
IF SOMETHING HAPPENS...
.....
....
....
SEE?
YAMADA MIGHT NOT WANT PEOPLE TO KNOW ABOUT IT LATER.
MAYAMA.
YOU ARE WAY TOO OVERPROTECTIVE.
SKWEEN

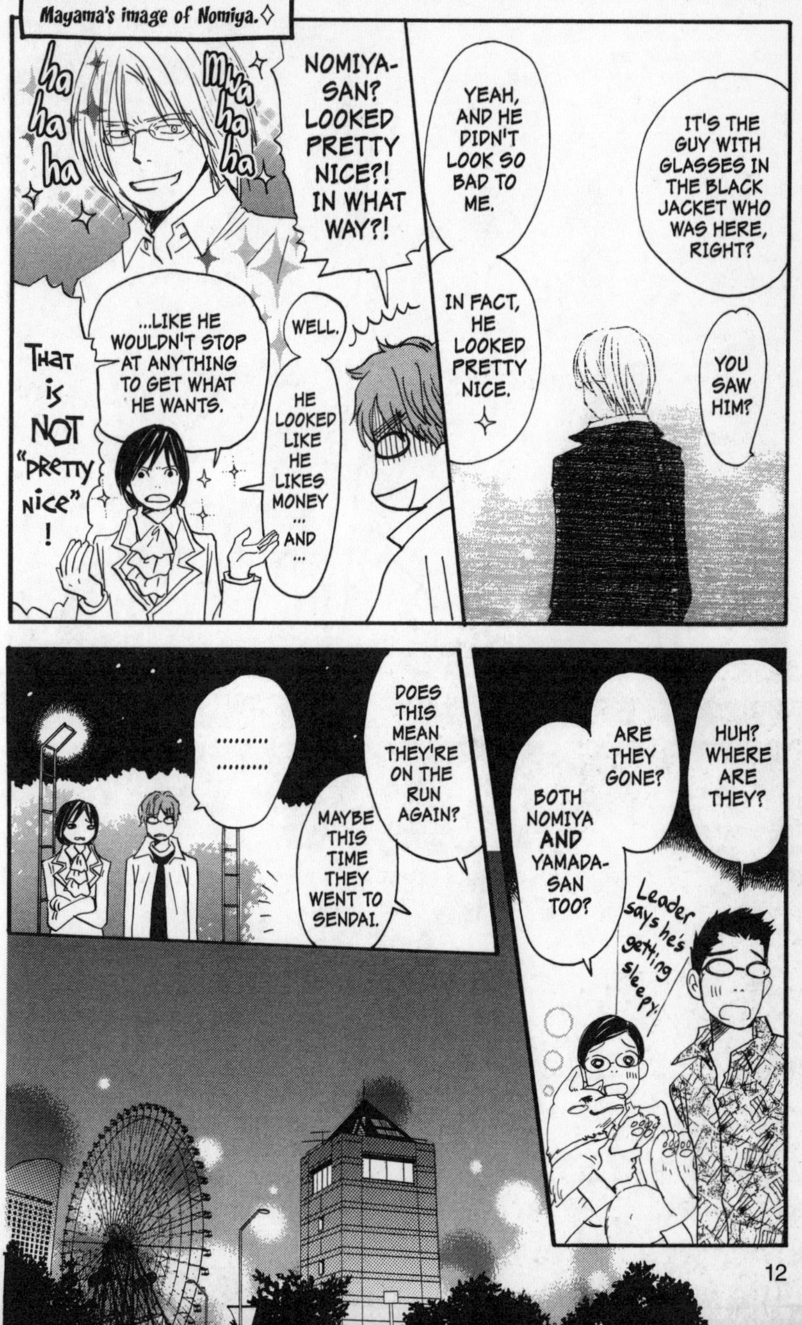
IT'S THE GUY WITH GLASSES IN THE BLACK JACKET WHO WAS HERE, RIGHT?
YOU SAW HIM?
YEAH, AND HE DIDN'T LOOK SO BAD TO ME.
IN FACT, HE LOOKED PRETTY NICE.
Mayama's image of Nomiya.◇
NOMIYA-SAN? LOOKED PRETTY NICE?! IN WHAT WAY?!
Mwa ha ha ha
ha ha ha
WELL.
HE LOOKED LIKE HE LIKES MONEY ... AND ...
...LIKE HE WOULDN'T STOP AT ANYTHING TO GET WHAT HE WANTS.
That is NOT "pretty nice"!
HUH? WHERE ARE THEY?
ARE THEY GONE?
BOTH NOMIYA AND YAMADA-SAN TOO?
Leader says he's getting sleepy.
DOES THIS MEAN THEY'RE ON THE RUN AGAIN?
MAYBE THIS TIME THEY WENT TO SENDAI.
....
....

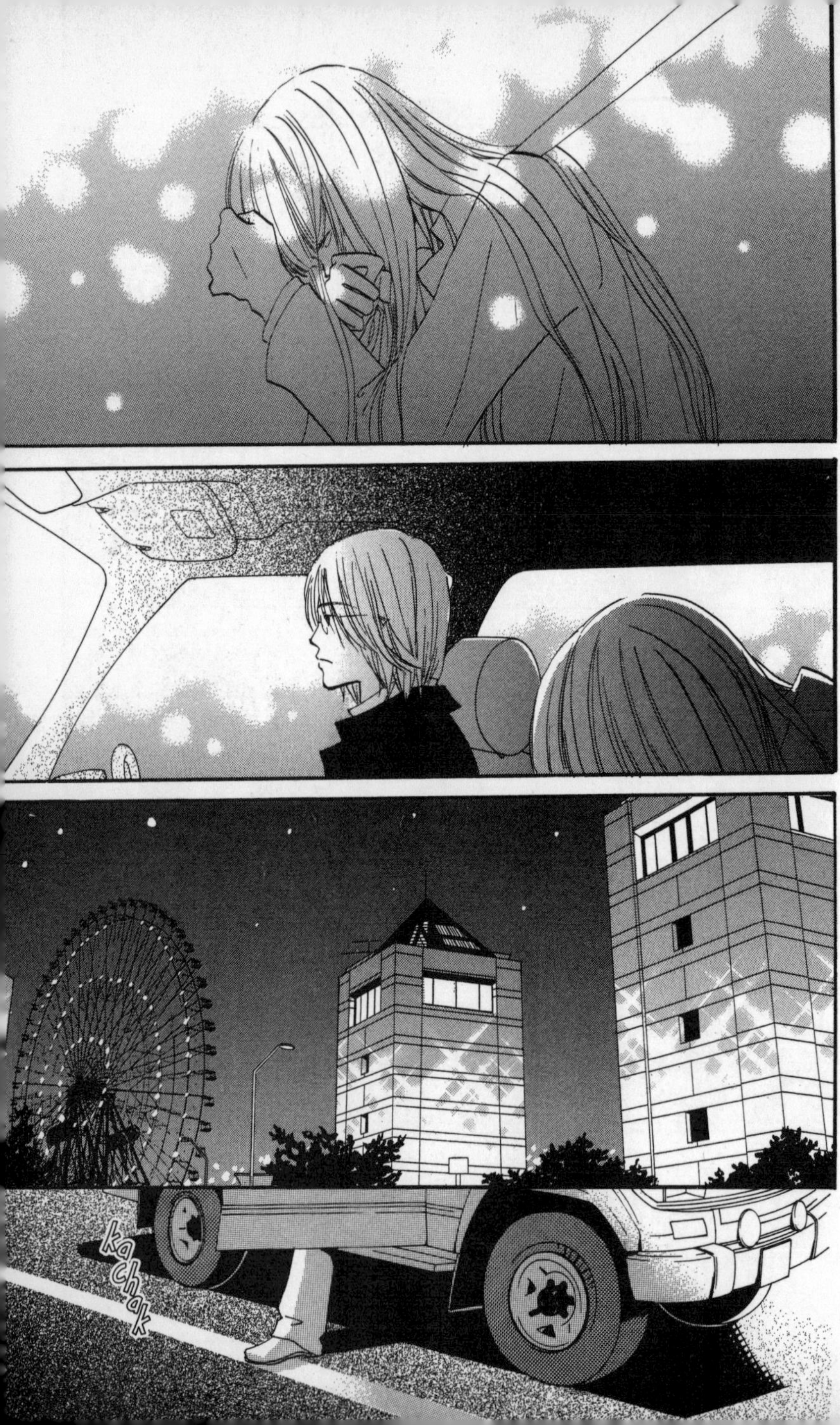
kachak

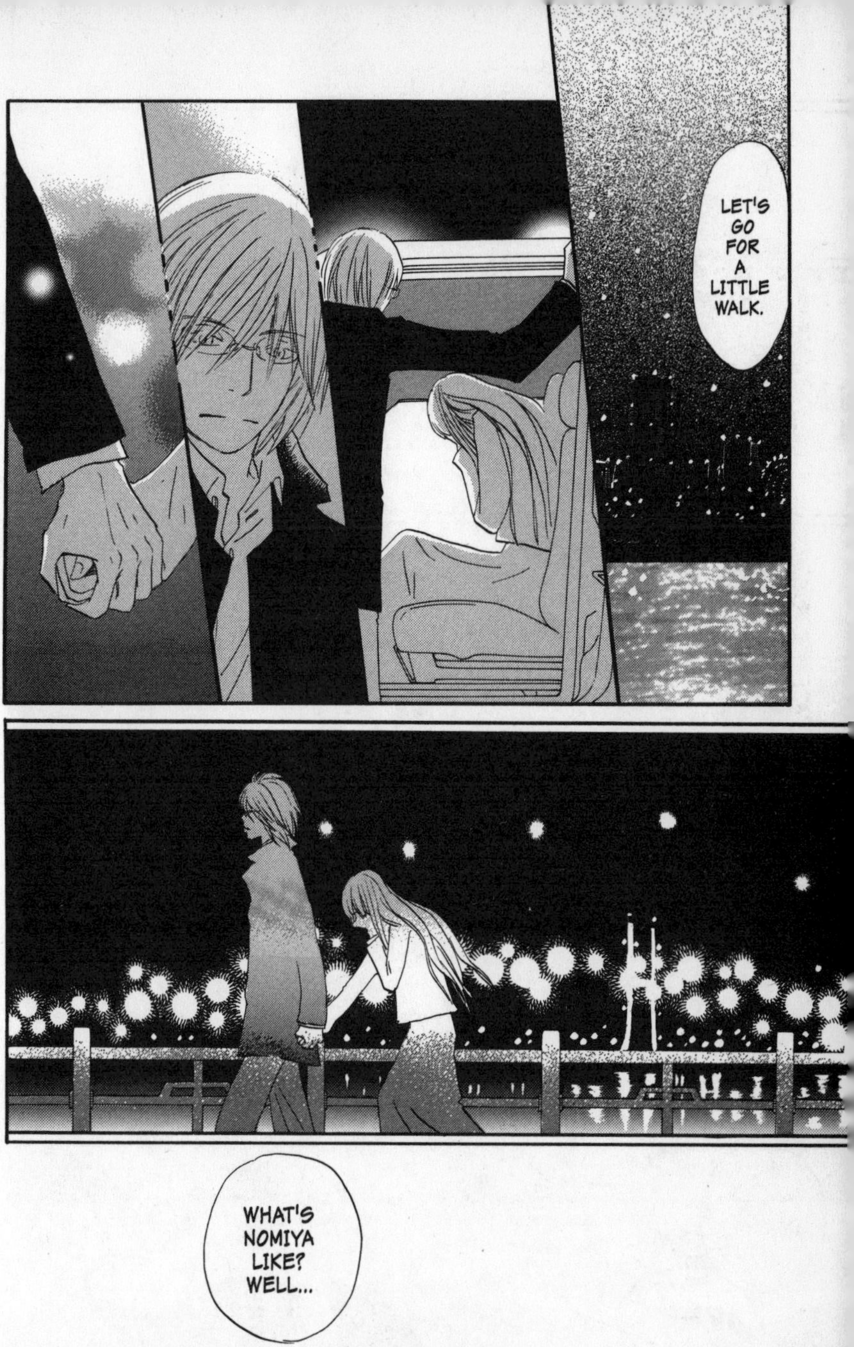
LET'S GO FOR A LITTLE WALK.
WHAT'S NOMIYA LIKE? WELL...

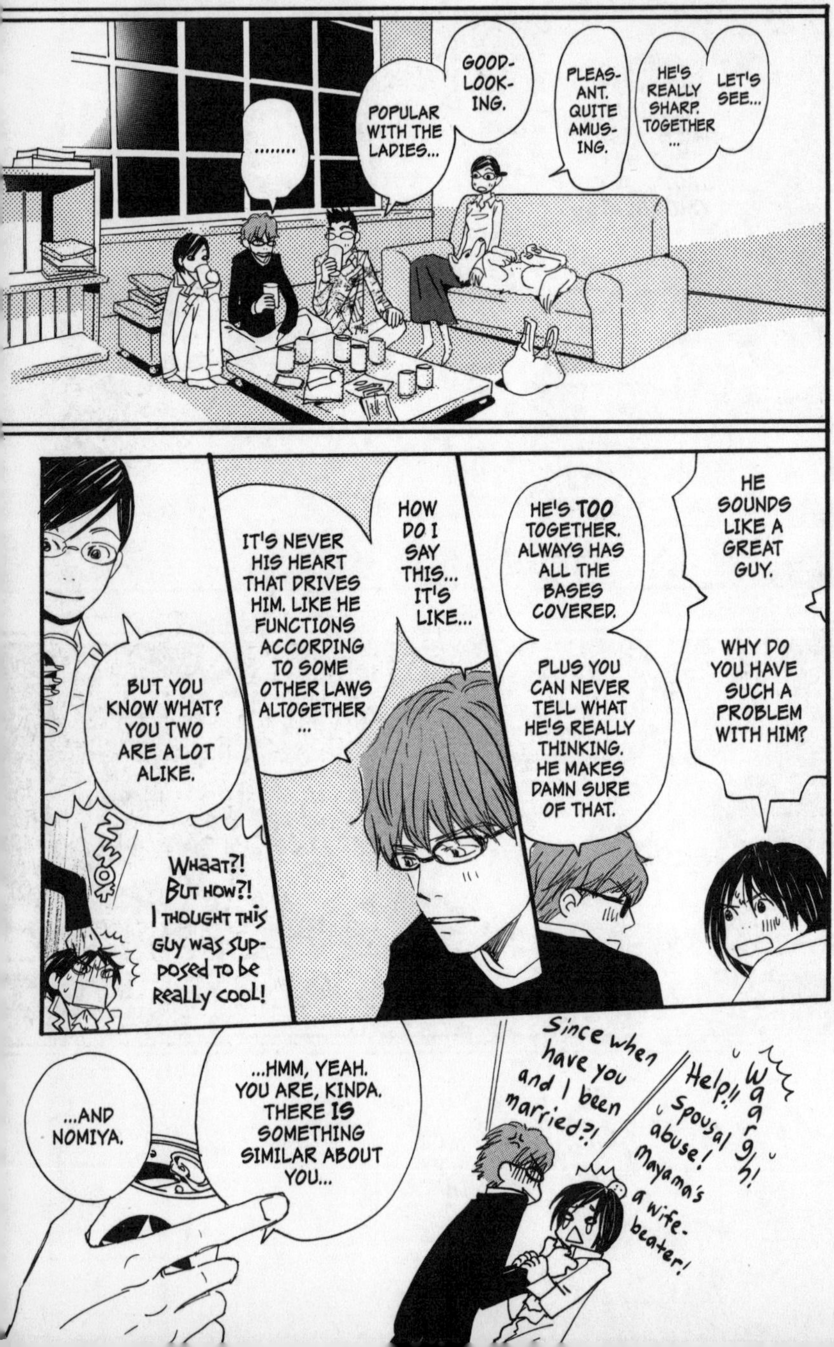
LET'S SEE...
HE'S REALLY SHARP. TOGETHER ...
PLEASANT. QUITE AMUSING.
GOOD-LOOKING.
POPULAR WITH THE LADIES...
....
HE SOUNDS LIKE A GREAT GUY.
WHY DO YOU HAVE SUCH A PROBLEM WITH HIM?
HE'S TOO TOGETHER. ALWAYS HAS ALL THE BASES COVERED.
PLUS YOU CAN NEVER TELL WHAT HE'S REALLY THINKING. HE MAKES DAMN SURE OF THAT.
HOW DO I SAY THIS... IT'S LIKE...
IT'S NEVER HIS HEART THAT DRIVES HIM. LIKE HE FUNCTIONS ACCORDING TO SOME OTHER LAWS ALTOGETHER ...
BUT YOU KNOW WHAT? YOU TWO ARE A LOT ALIKE.
Whaat?! But how?! I thought this guy was supposed to be really cool!
Waargh!
Help!! Spousal abuse! Mayama's a wife-beater!
Since when have you and I been married?!
...HMM, YEAH. YOU ARE, KINDA. THERE IS SOMETHING SIMILAR ABOUT YOU...
...AND NOMIYA.

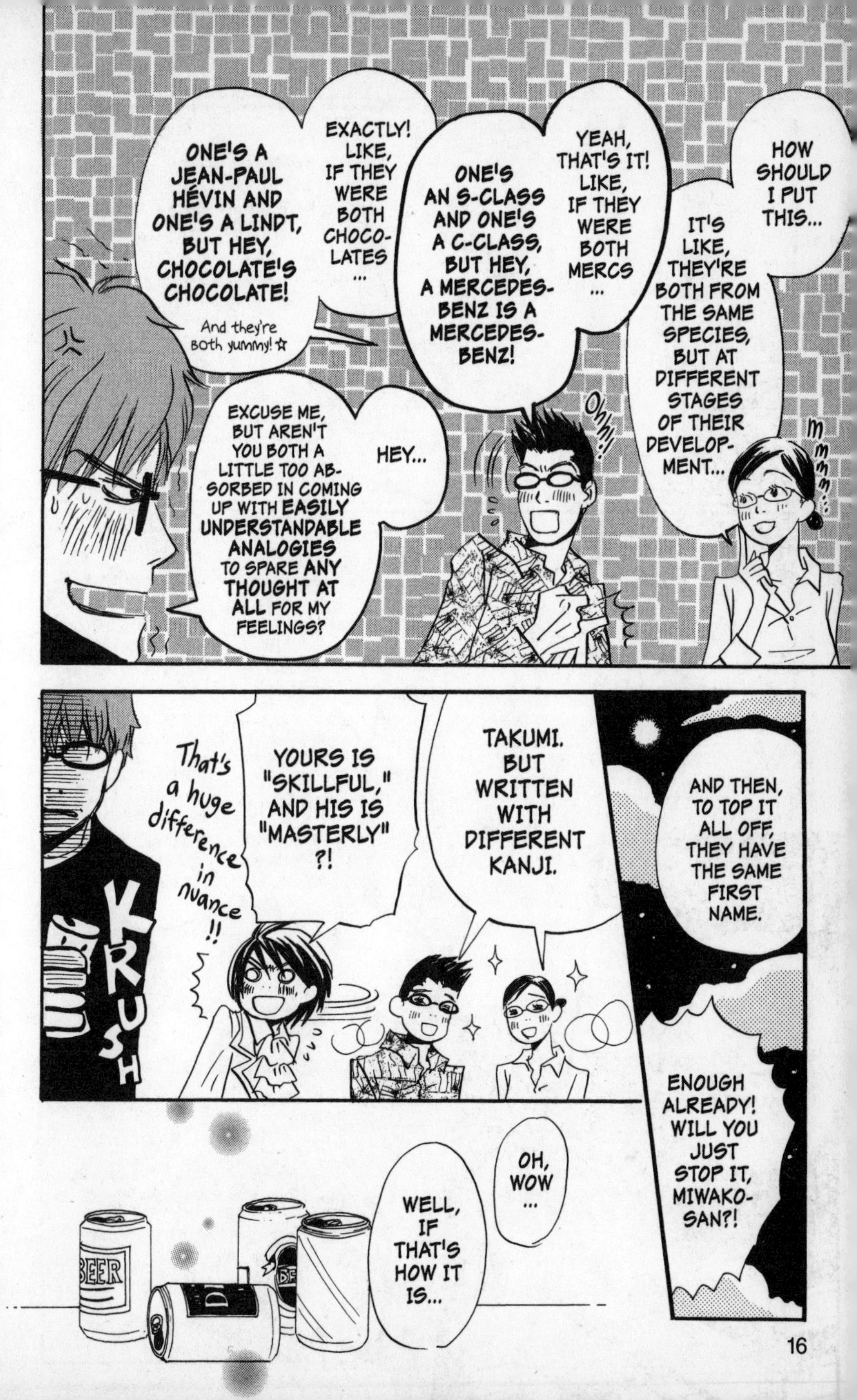
HOW SHOULD I PUT THIS...
IT'S LIKE, THEY'RE BOTH FROM THE SAME SPECIES, BUT AT DIFFERENT STAGES OF THEIR DEVELOPMENT...
Mmmm...
YEAH, THAT'S IT! LIKE, IF THEY WERE BOTH MERCS...
ONE'S AN S-CLASS AND ONE'S A C-CLASS, BUT HEY, A MERCEDES-BENZ IS A MERCEDES-BENZ!
Oh!!
EXACTLY! LIKE, IF THEY WERE BOTH CHOCOLATES...
ONE'S A JEAN-PAUL HÉVIN AND ONE'S A LINDT, BUT HEY, CHOCOLATE'S CHOCOLATE!
And they're both yummy! ☆
HEY...
EXCUSE ME, BUT AREN'T YOU BOTH A LITTLE TOO ABSORBED IN COMING UP WITH EASILY UNDERSTANDABLE ANALOGIES TO SPARE ANY THOUGHT AT ALL FOR MY FEELINGS?
AND THEN, TO TOP IT ALL OFF, THEY HAVE THE SAME FIRST NAME.
ENOUGH ALREADY! WILL YOU JUST STOP IT, MIWAKO-SAN?!
TAKUMI. BUT WRITTEN WITH DIFFERENT KANJI.
YOURS IS "SKILLFUL," AND HIS IS "MASTERLY"?!
That's a huge difference in nuance!!
KRUSH
OH, WOW...
WELL, IF THAT'S HOW IT IS...

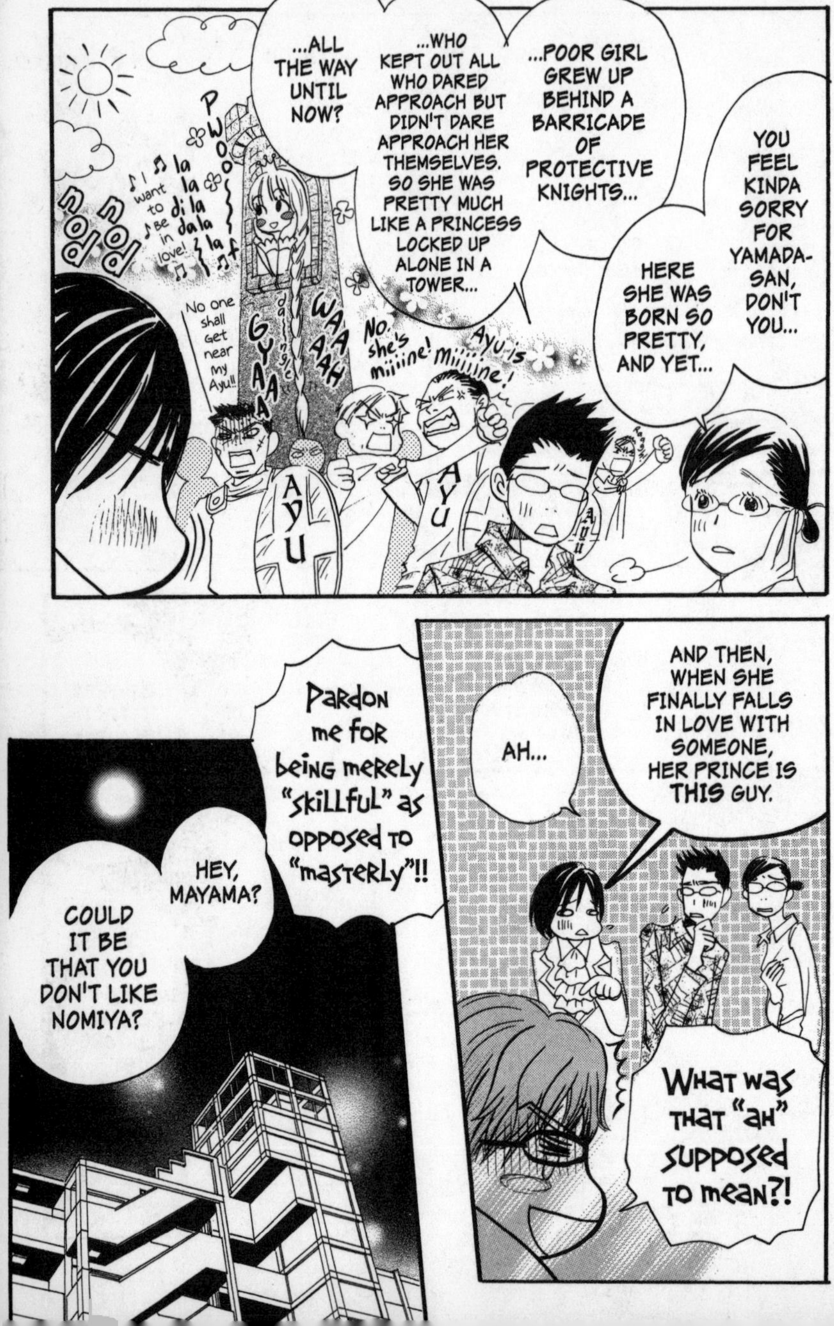
YOU FEEL KINDA SORRY FOR YAMADA-SAN, DON'T YOU...
HERE SHE WAS BORN SO PRETTY, AND YET...
...POOR GIRL GREW UP BEHIND A BARRICADE OF PROTECTIVE KNIGHTS...
...WHO KEPT OUT ALL WHO DARED APPROACH BUT DIDN'T DARE APPROACH HER THEMSELVES. SO SHE WAS PRETTY MUCH LIKE A PRINCESS LOCKED UP ALONE IN A TOWER...
...ALL THE WAY UNTIL NOW?
Pwoo~f
pon pon
I want to be in love!
la la di la da la la
Ayu is miiiine!
No, she's miiiine!
WAAAAH
GYAAA
No one shall get near my Ayu!!
AYU
AYU
AYU
AND THEN, WHEN SHE FINALLY FALLS IN LOVE WITH SOMEONE, HER PRINCE IS THIS GUY.
AH...
What was that "ah" supposed to mean?!
Pardon me for being merely "skillful" as opposed to "masterly"!!
HEY, MAYAMA?
COULD IT BE THAT YOU DON'T LIKE NOMIYA?

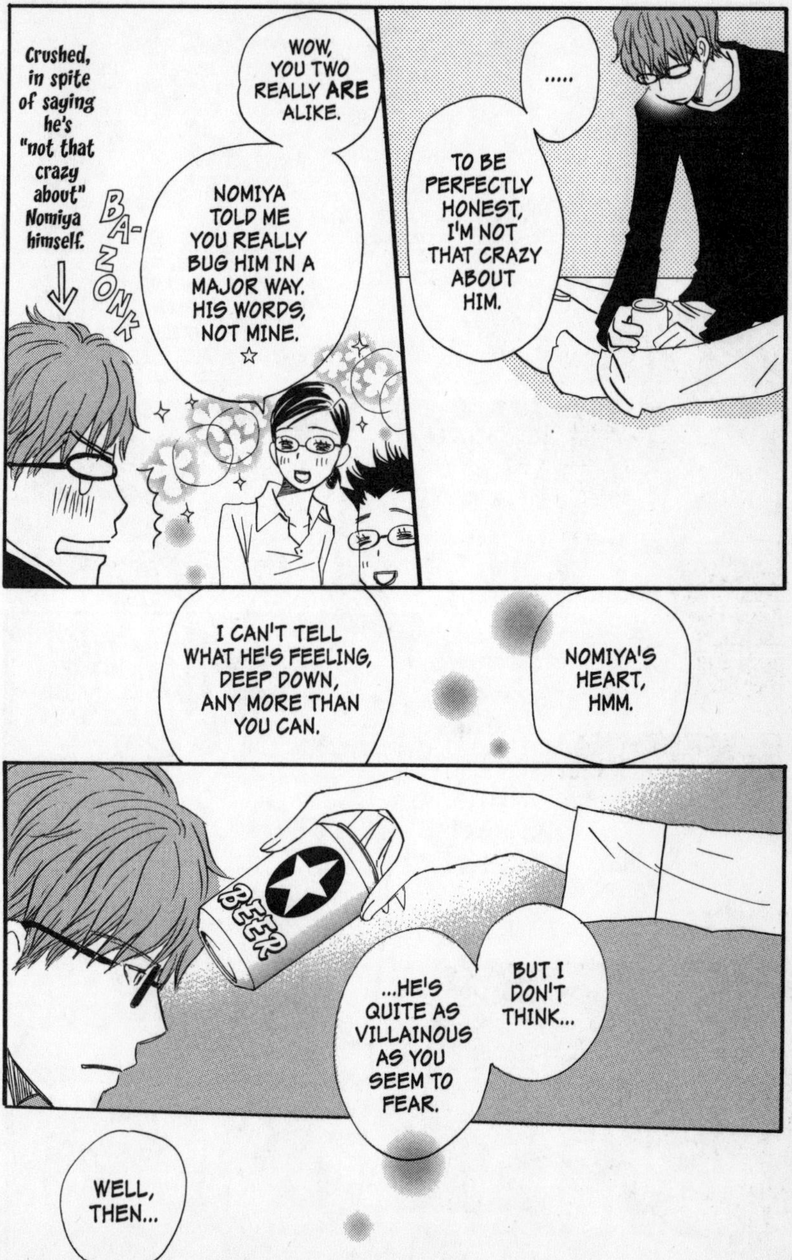
.....
TO BE PERFECTLY HONEST, I'M NOT THAT CRAZY ABOUT HIM.
WOW, YOU TWO REALLY **ARE** ALIKE.
NOMIYA TOLD ME YOU REALLY BUG HIM IN A MAJOR WAY. HIS WORDS, NOT MINE. ☆
Crushed, in spite of saying he's "not that crazy about" Nomiya himself.
BA-ZONK
NOMIYA'S HEART, HMM.
I CAN'T TELL WHAT HE'S FEELING, DEEP DOWN, ANY MORE THAN YOU CAN.
BEER
BUT I DON'T THINK...
...HE'S QUITE AS VILLAINOUS AS YOU SEEM TO FEAR.
WELL, THEN...

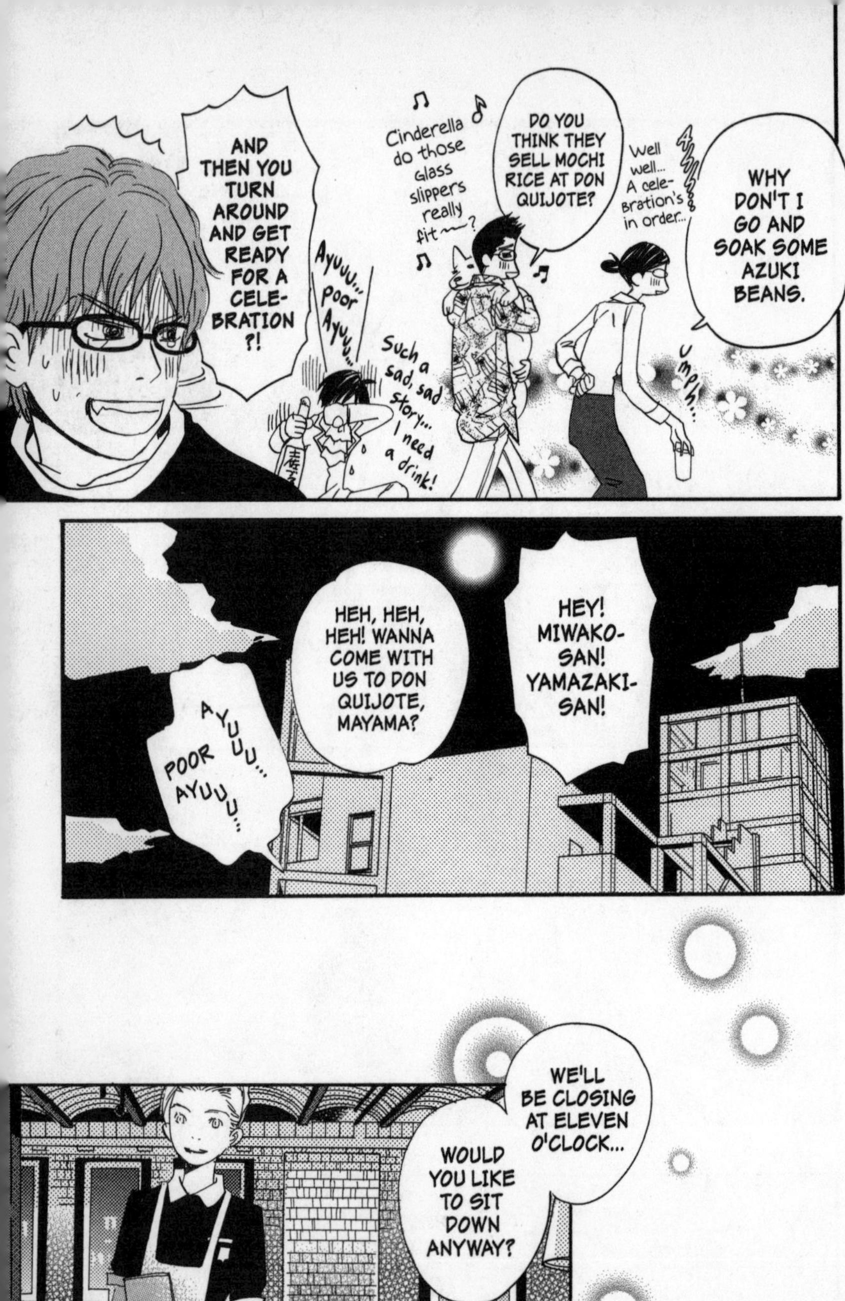
WHY DON'T I GO AND SOAK SOME AZUKI BEANS.
Well well... A celebration's in order...
Umph...
DO YOU THINK THEY SELL MOCHI RICE AT DON QUIJOTE?
Cinderella do those Glass slippers really fit~~?
Such a sad, sad story... I need a drink!
Ayuuu... Poor Ayuuu...
AND THEN YOU TURN AROUND AND GET READY FOR A CELEBRATION?!
HEY! MIWAKO-SAN! YAMAZAKI-SAN!
HEH, HEH, HEH! WANNA COME WITH US TO DON QUIJOTE, MAYAMA?
AYUUU... POOR AYUUU...
WE'LL BE CLOSING AT ELEVEN O'CLOCK...
WOULD YOU LIKE TO SIT DOWN ANYWAY?

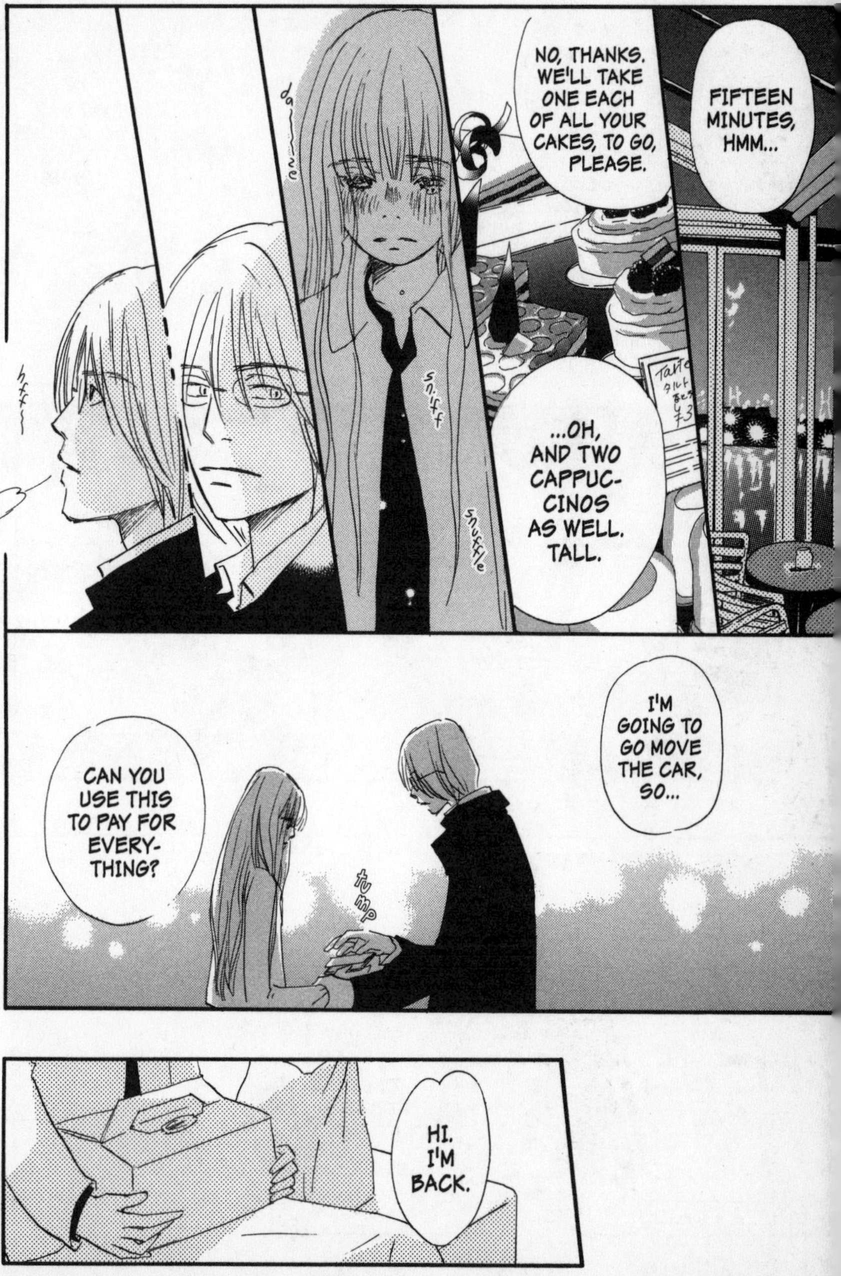
FIFTEEN MINUTES, HMM...
NO, THANKS. WE'LL TAKE ONE EACH OF ALL YOUR CAKES, TO GO, PLEASE.
...OH, AND TWO CAPPUC-CINOS AS WELL. TALL.
snuffle
sniff
hff~
I'M GOING TO GO MOVE THE CAR, SO...
CAN YOU USE THIS TO PAY FOR EVERY-THING?
tump
HI. I'M BACK.

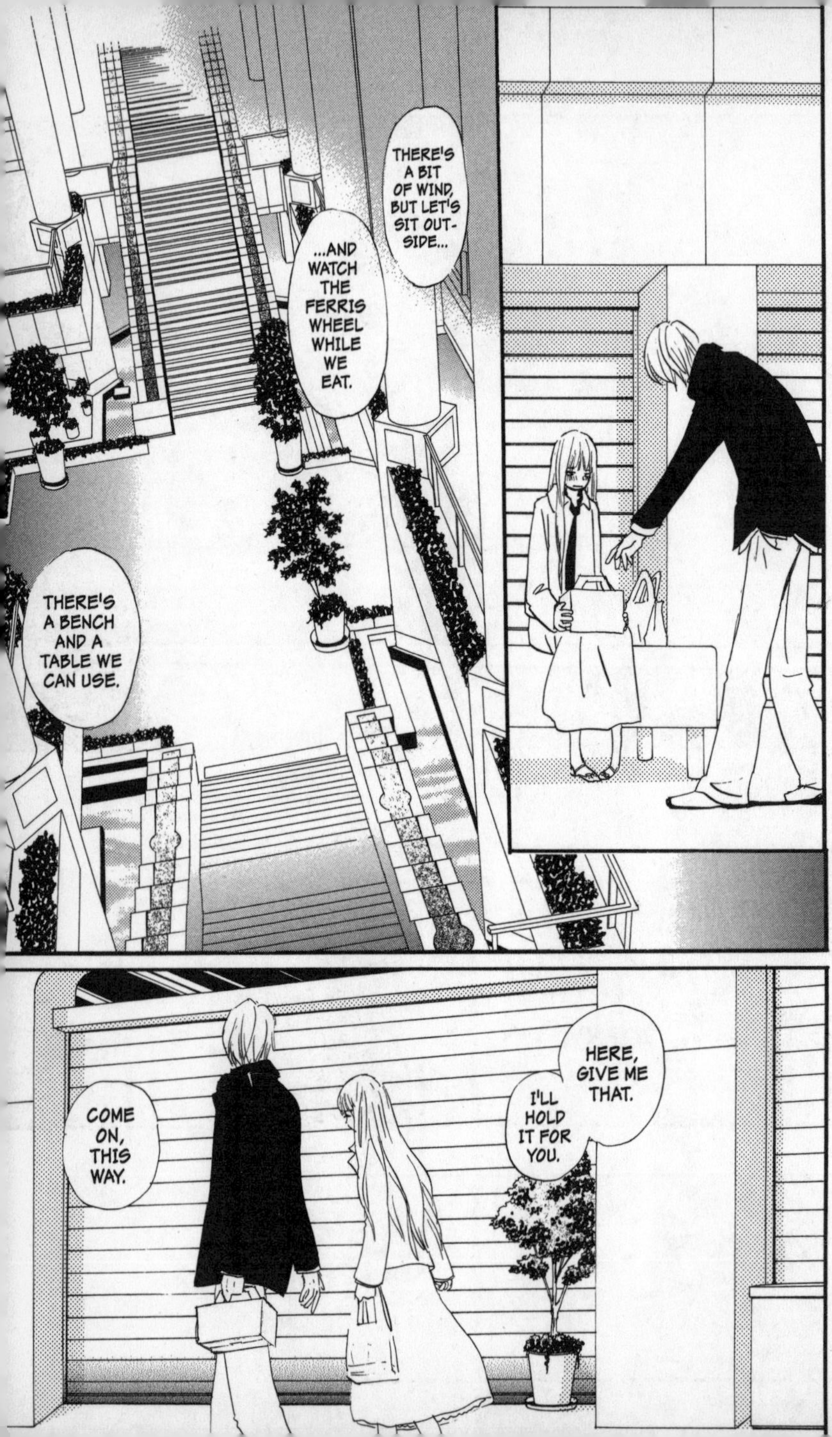
THERE'S A BIT OF WIND, BUT LET'S SIT OUT-SIDE...
...AND WATCH THE FERRIS WHEEL WHILE WE EAT.
THERE'S A BENCH AND A TABLE WE CAN USE.
HERE, GIVE ME THAT.
I'LL HOLD IT FOR YOU.
COME ON, THIS WAY.

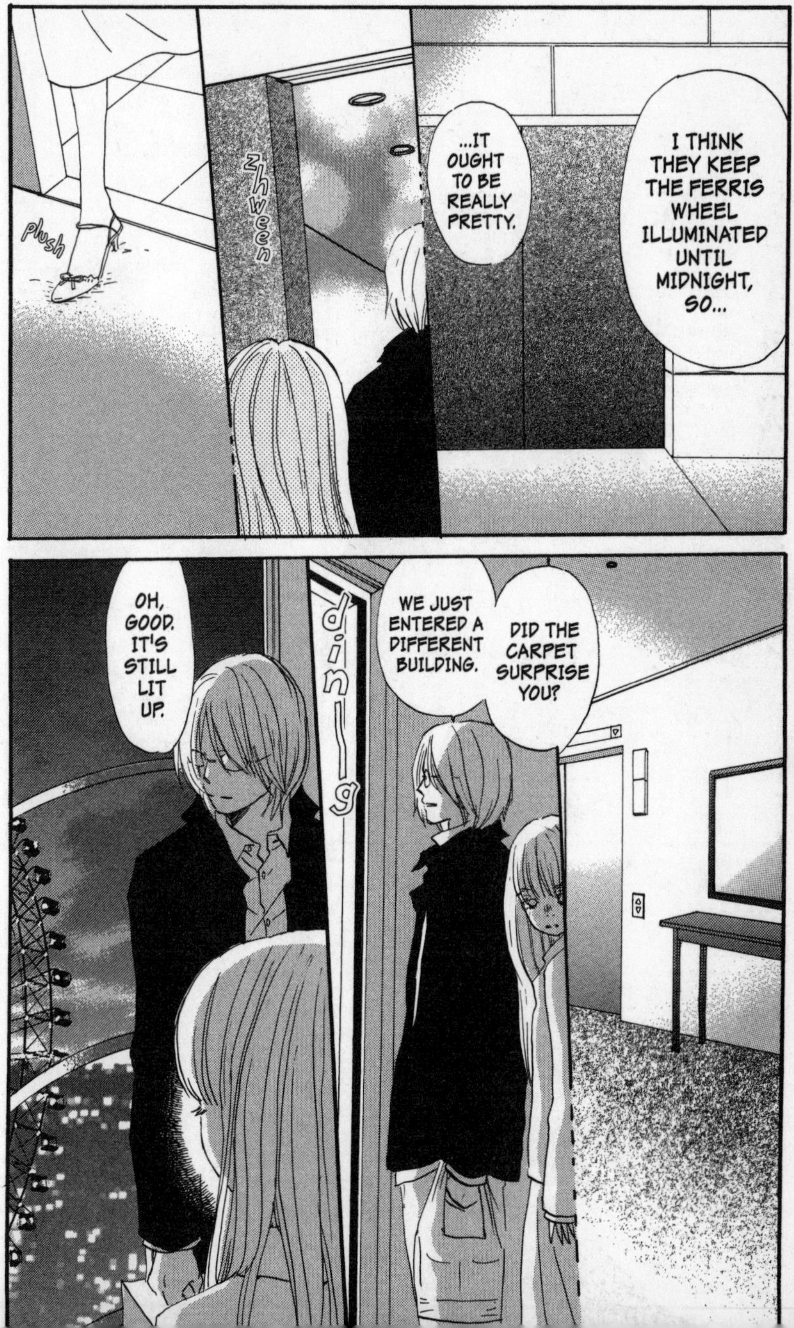
I THINK THEY KEEP THE FERRIS WHEEL ILLUMINATED UNTIL MIDNIGHT, SO...
...IT OUGHT TO BE REALLY PRETTY.
zhween
plush
DID THE CARPET SURPRISE YOU?
WE JUST ENTERED A DIFFERENT BUILDING.
ding
OH, GOOD. IT'S STILL LIT UP.

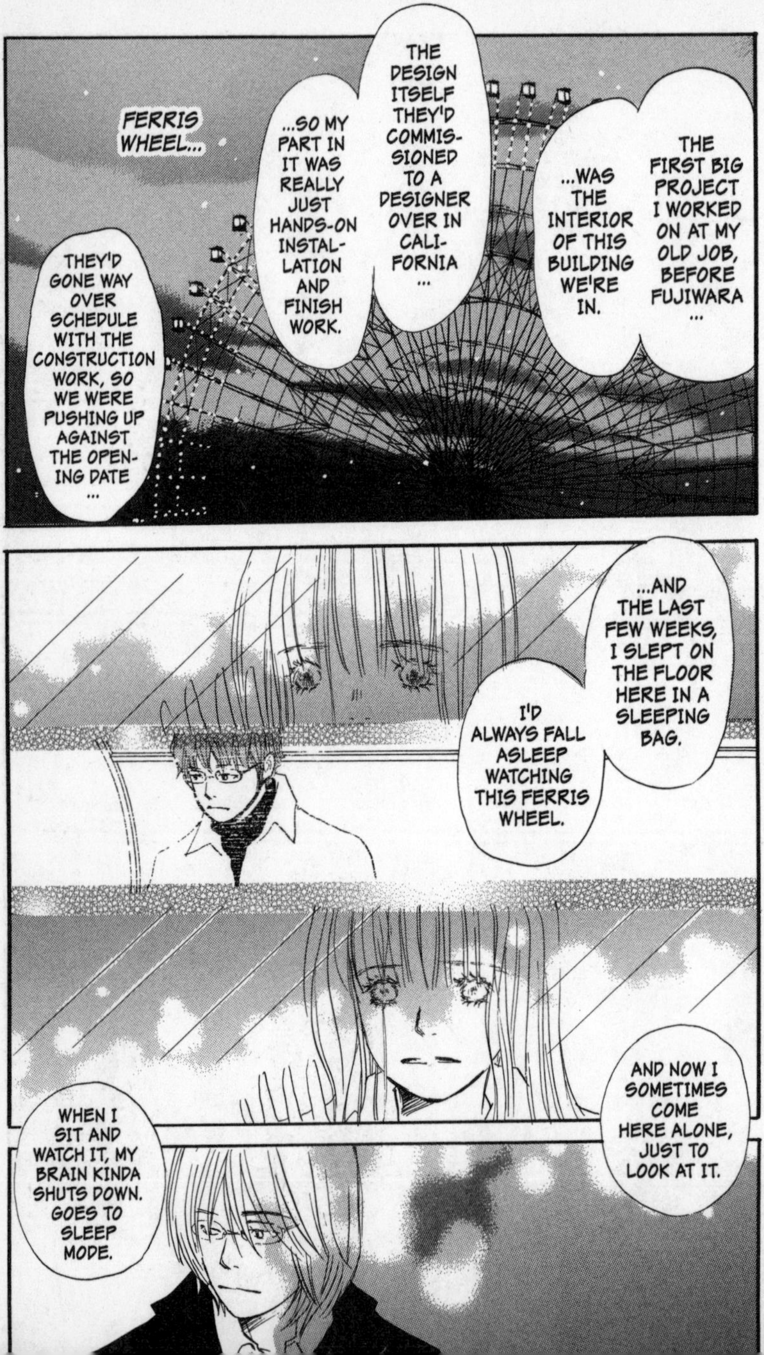
THE FIRST BIG PROJECT I WORKED ON AT MY OLD JOB, BEFORE FUJIWARA...
...WAS THE INTERIOR OF THIS BUILDING WE'RE IN.
THE DESIGN ITSELF THEY'D COMMISSIONED TO A DESIGNER OVER IN CALIFORNIA...
...SO MY PART IN IT WAS REALLY JUST HANDS-ON INSTALLATION AND FINISH WORK.
FERRIS WHEEL...
THEY'D GONE WAY OVER SCHEDULE WITH THE CONSTRUCTION WORK, SO WE WERE PUSHING UP AGAINST THE OPENING DATE...
...AND THE LAST FEW WEEKS, I SLEPT ON THE FLOOR HERE IN A SLEEPING BAG.
I'D ALWAYS FALL ASLEEP WATCHING THIS FERRIS WHEEL.
AND NOW I SOMETIMES COME HERE ALONE, JUST TO LOOK AT IT.
WHEN I SIT AND WATCH IT, MY BRAIN KINDA SHUTS DOWN. GOES TO SLEEP MODE.

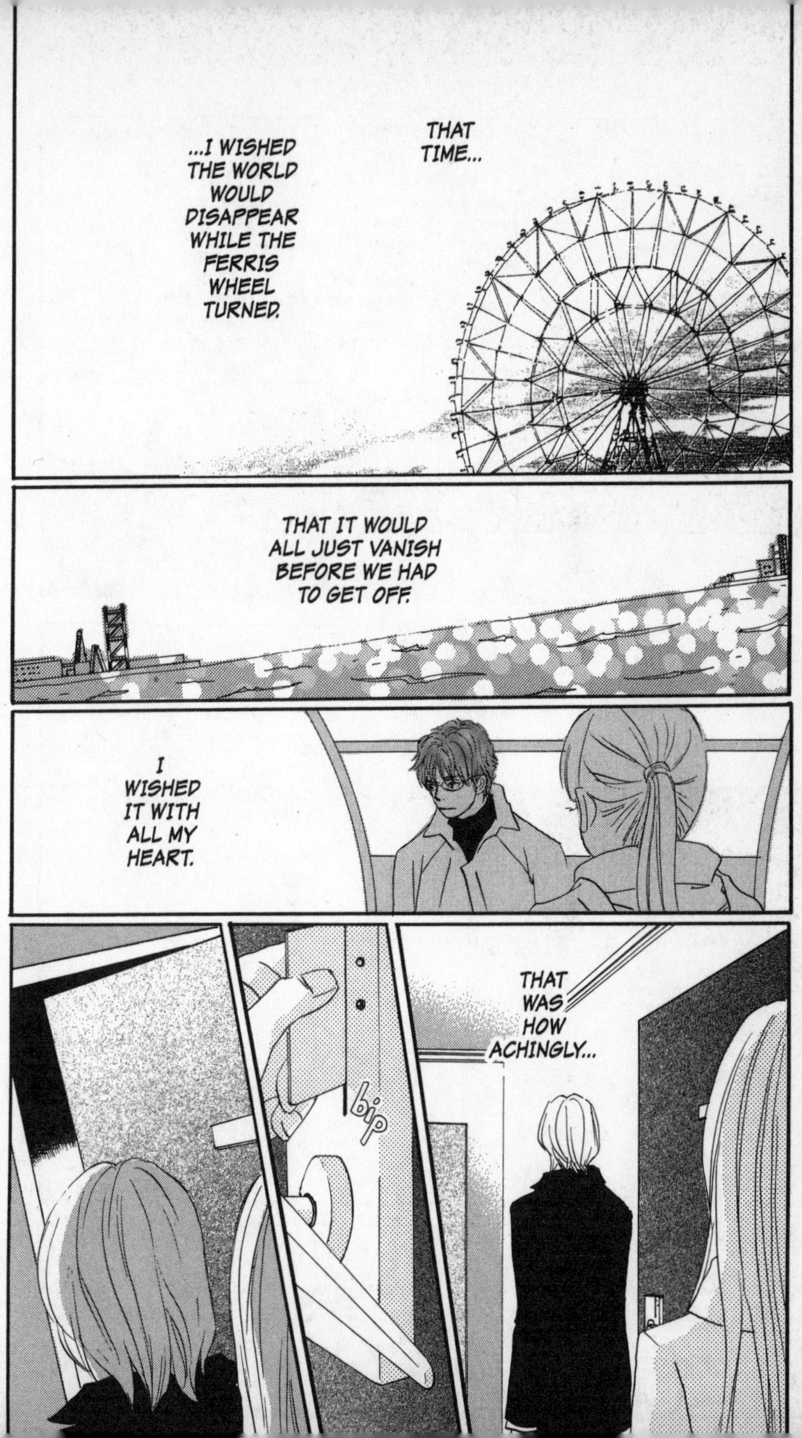
THAT TIME...
...I WISHED THE WORLD WOULD DISAPPEAR WHILE THE FERRIS WHEEL TURNED.
THAT IT WOULD ALL JUST VANISH BEFORE WE HAD TO GET OFF.
I WISHED IT WITH ALL MY HEART.
THAT WAS HOW ACHINGLY...
bip

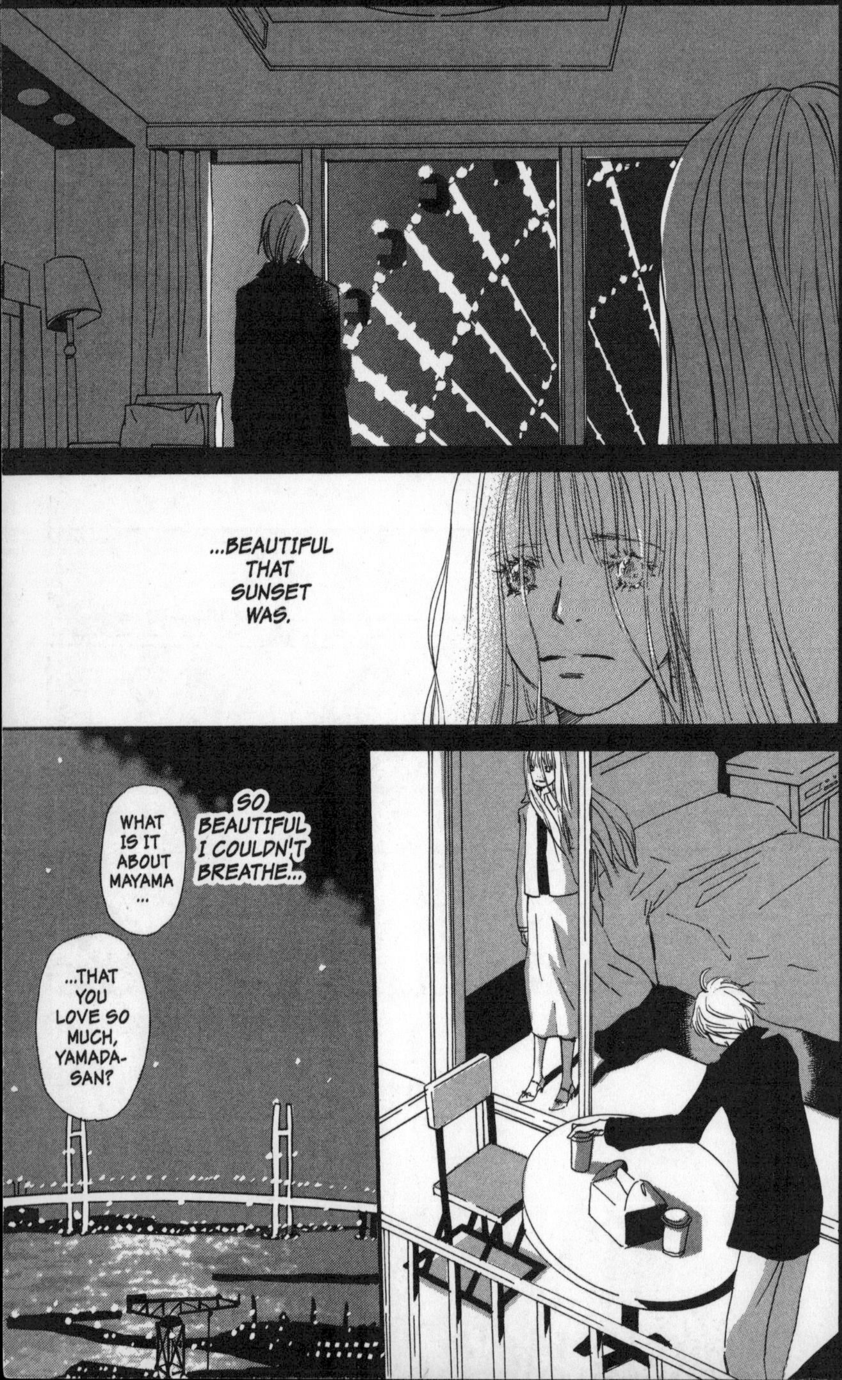
...BEAUTIFUL THAT SUNSET WAS.
SO BEAUTIFUL I COULDN'T BREATHE...
WHAT IS IT ABOUT MAYAMA ...
...THAT YOU LOVE SO MUCH, YAMADA-SAN?

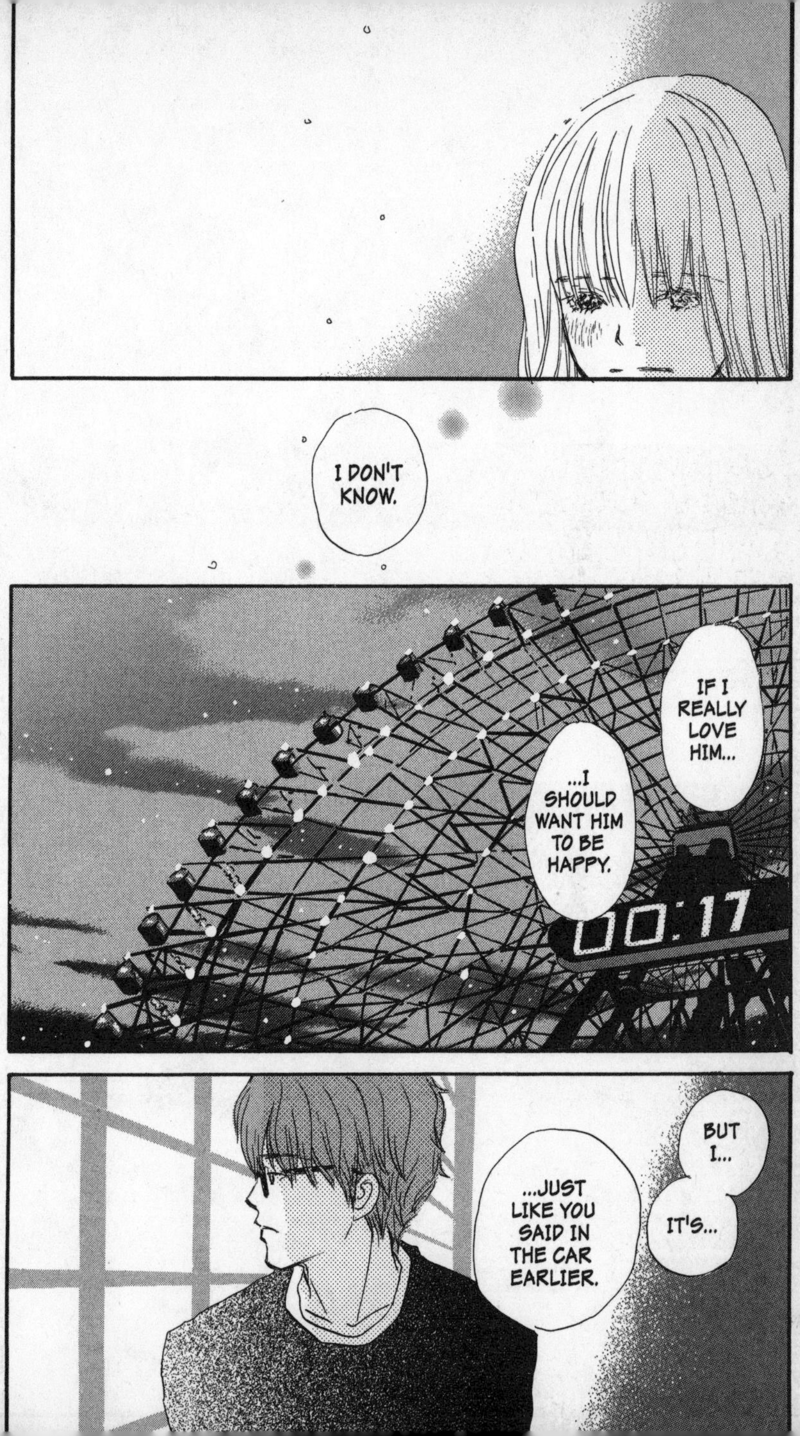
I DON'T KNOW.
IF I REALLY LOVE HIM...
...I SHOULD WANT HIM TO BE HAPPY.
00:17
BUT I...
IT'S...
...JUST LIKE YOU SAID IN THE CAR EARLIER.

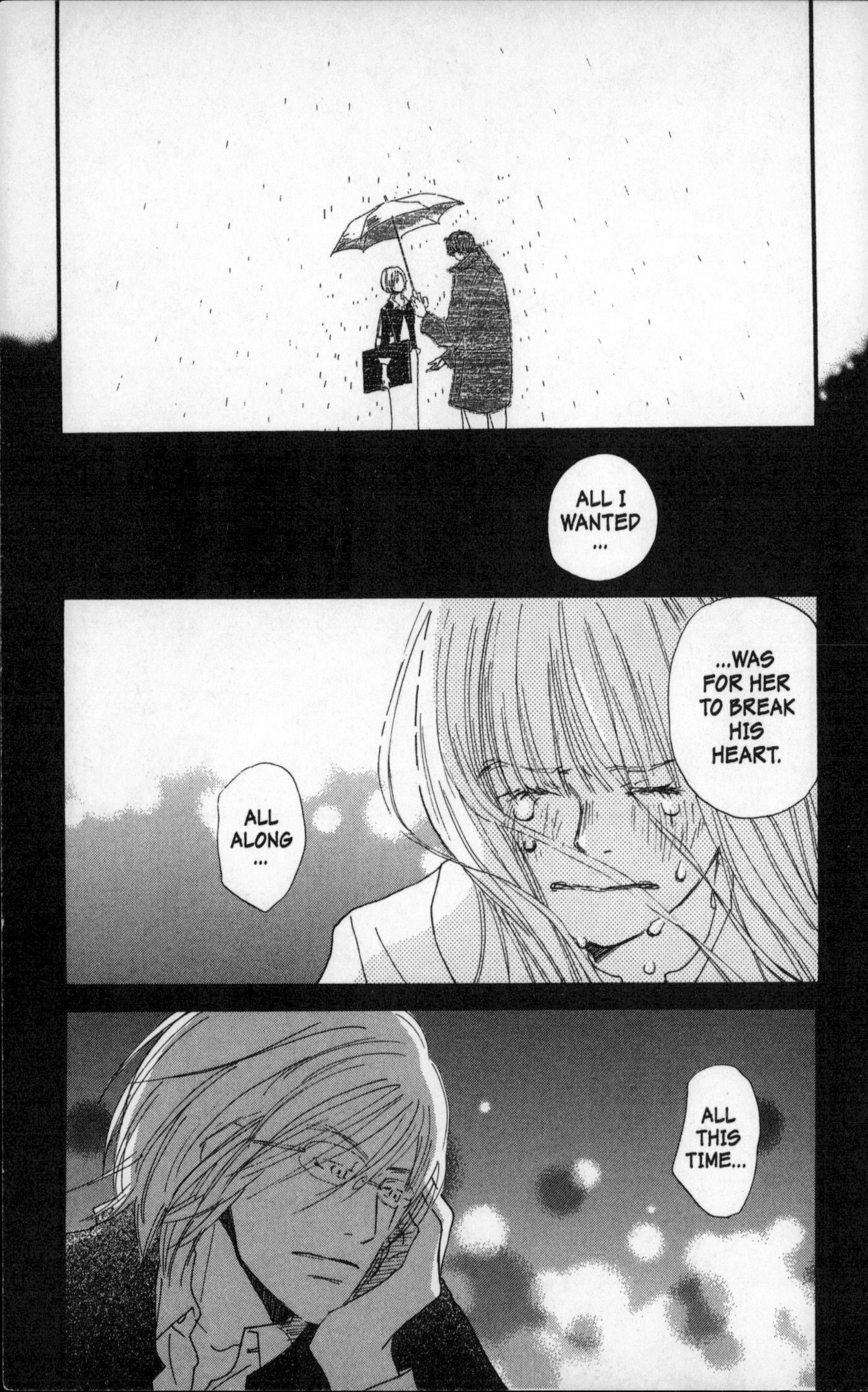
ALL I WANTED ...
...WAS FOR HER TO BREAK HIS HEART.
ALL ALONG ...
ALL THIS TIME...

YEAH
...

YEAH.

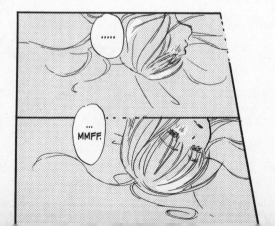

.....

...
MMFF.

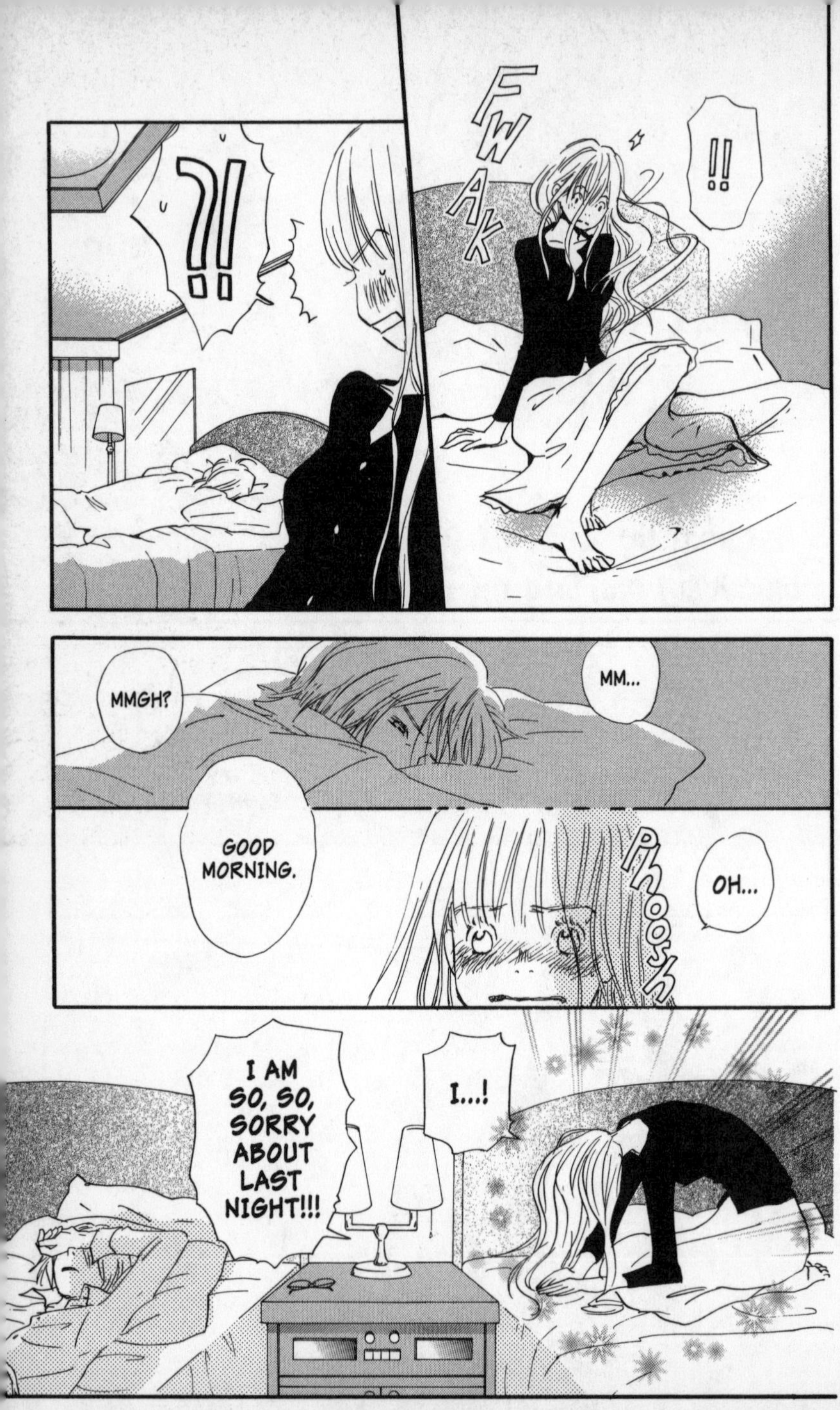
!!
FWAK
?!!
MM...
MMGH?
OH...
Phoosh
GOOD MORNING.
I...!
I AM SO, SO, SORRY ABOUT LAST NIGHT!!!

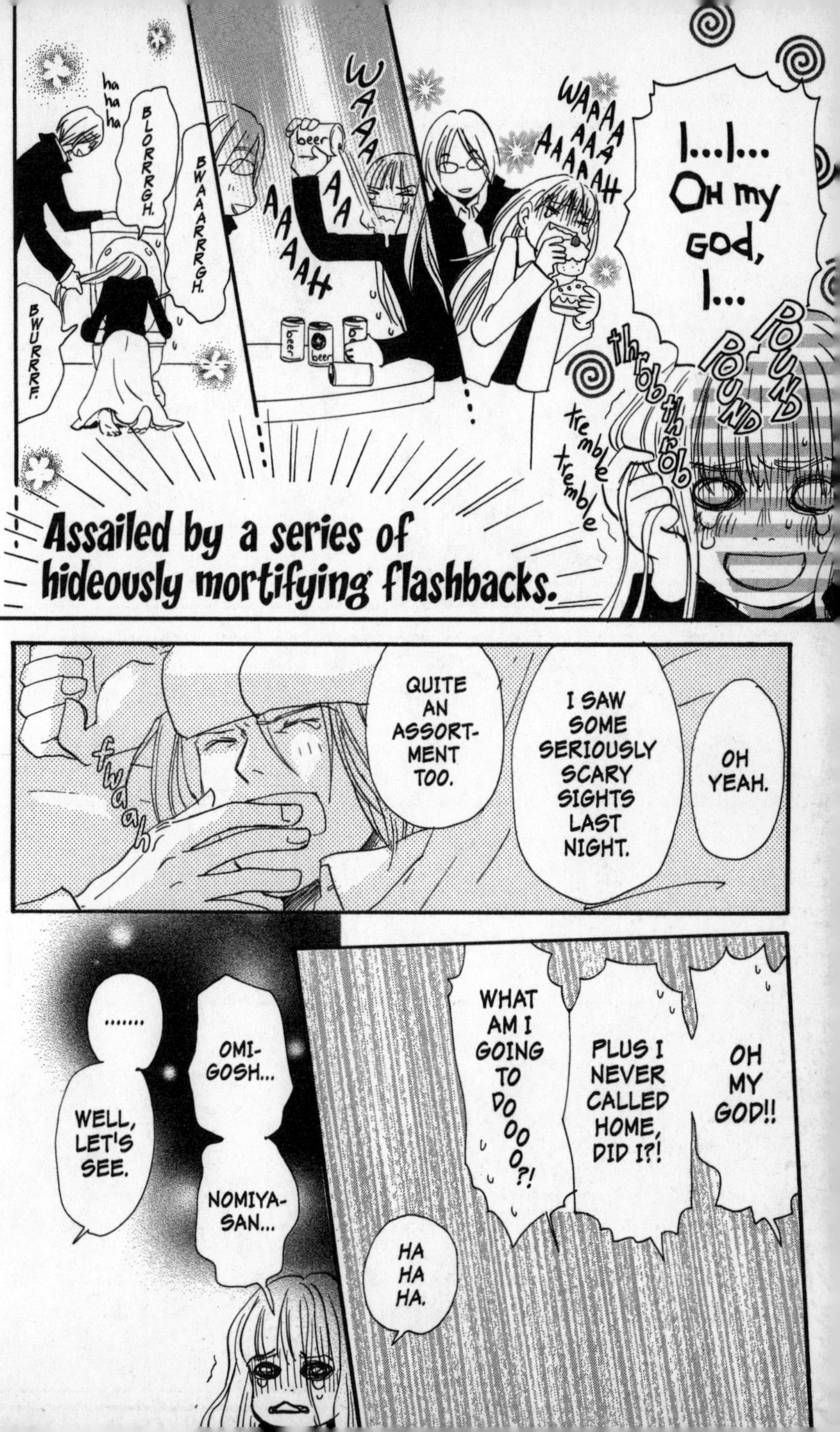
I...I... OH my GOD, I...
POUND POUND
throb throb
tremble tremble
WAAAAAAAAAAAAAH
WAAAAAAAAAAAH
beer
beer
beer
BWAAAARRRGH.
BLORRRGH.
ha ha ha
BWURRRF.
Assailed by a series of hideously mortifying flashbacks.
OH YEAH.
I SAW SOME SERIOUSLY SCARY SIGHTS LAST NIGHT.
QUITE AN ASSORTMENT TOO.
fwaah
OH MY GOD!!
PLUS I NEVER CALLED HOME, DID I?!
WHAT AM I GOING TO DOOOOO?!
HA HA HA.
OMI-GOSH... NOMIYA-SAN...
.... WELL, LET'S SEE.

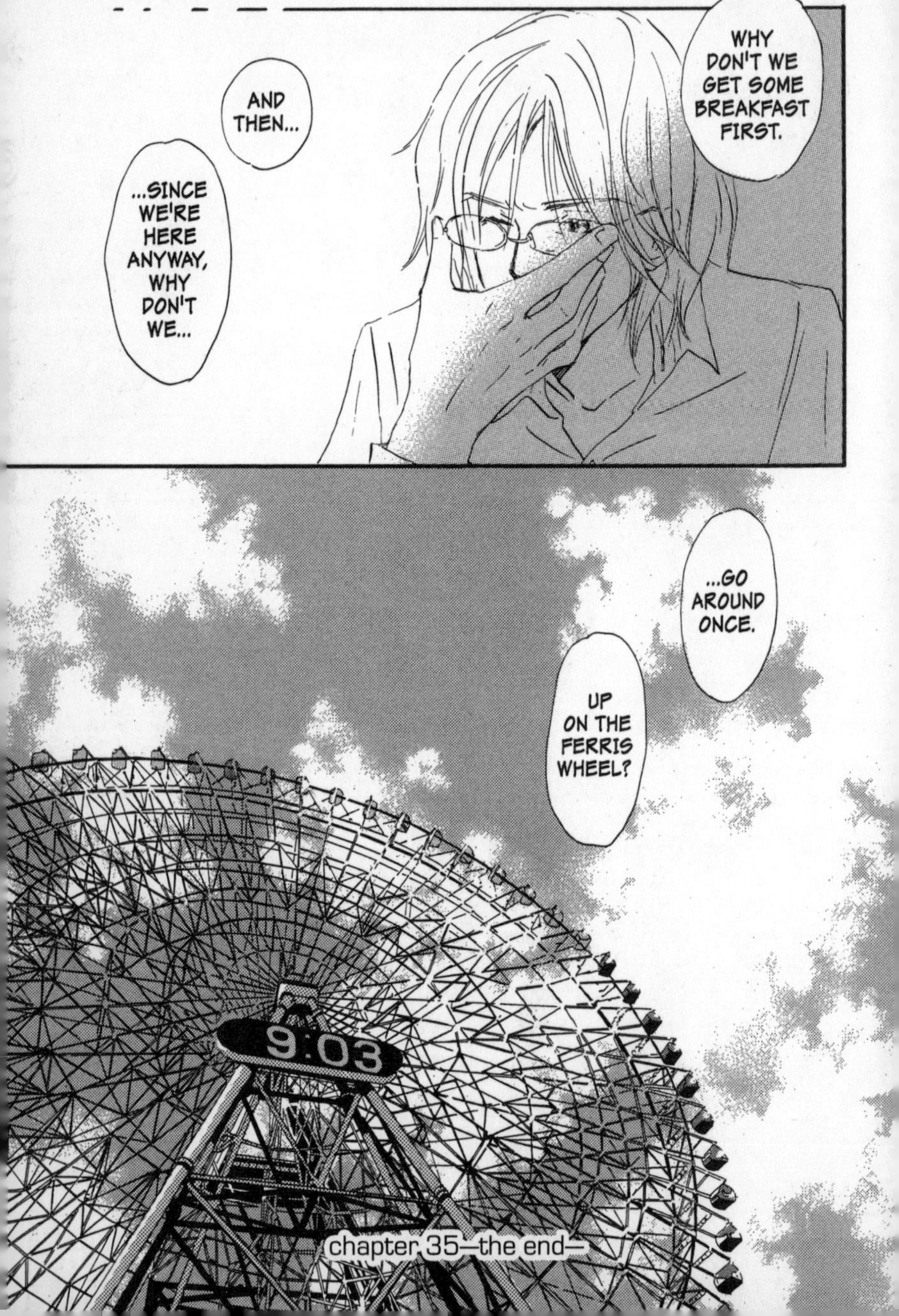
WHY DON'T WE GET SOME BREAKFAST FIRST.
AND THEN...
...SINCE WE'RE HERE ANYWAY, WHY DON'T WE...
...GO AROUND ONCE.
UP ON THE FERRIS WHEEL?
9:03
chapter 35—the end—

Pink custom-ordered blouse with five rows of frills

→ ¥48,000

Powder-blue high-waisted sailor pants with flared legs

→ ¥69,000

Glossy white enamel boots with 15cm heels

→ ¥72,000

The exultation you feel when you wear these together...

→ Priceless

honey and clover

chapter 36

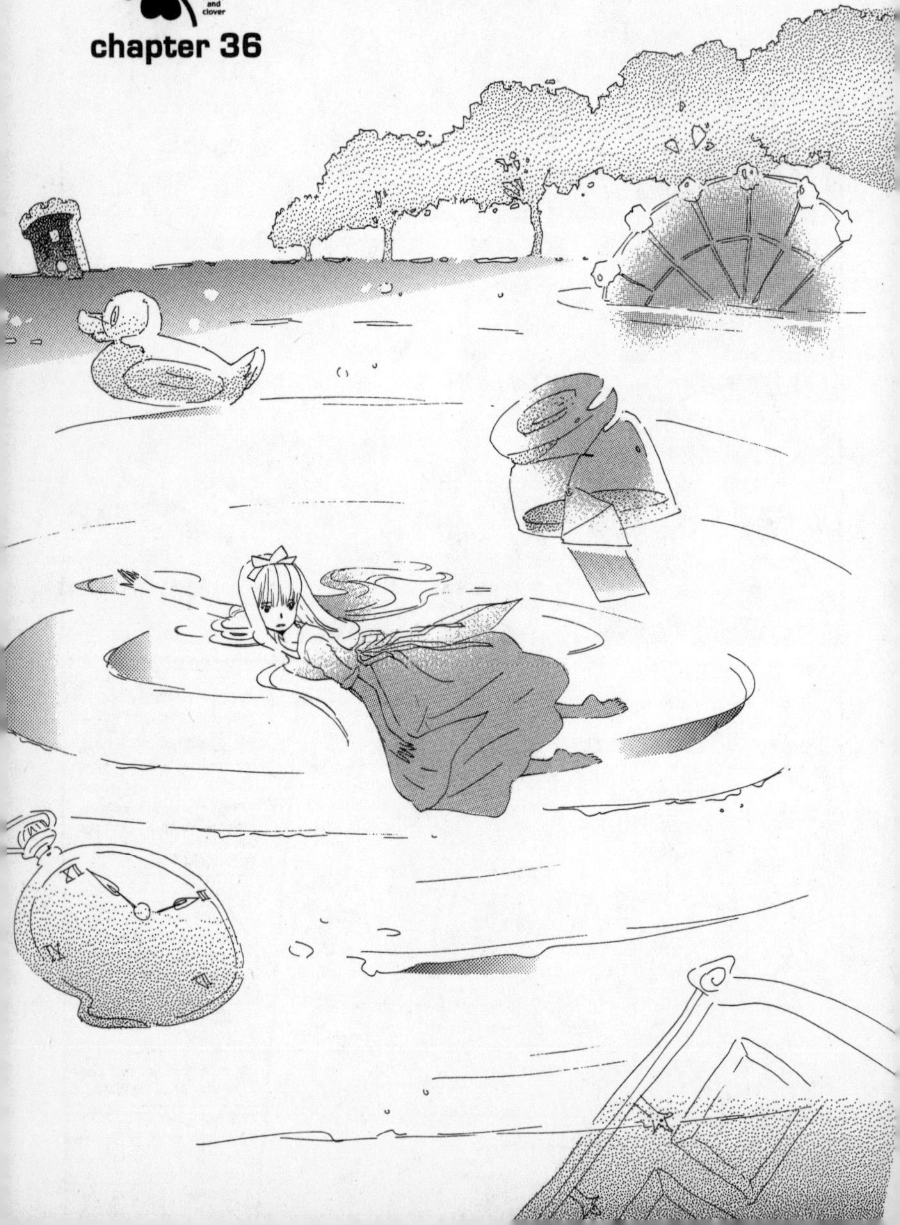

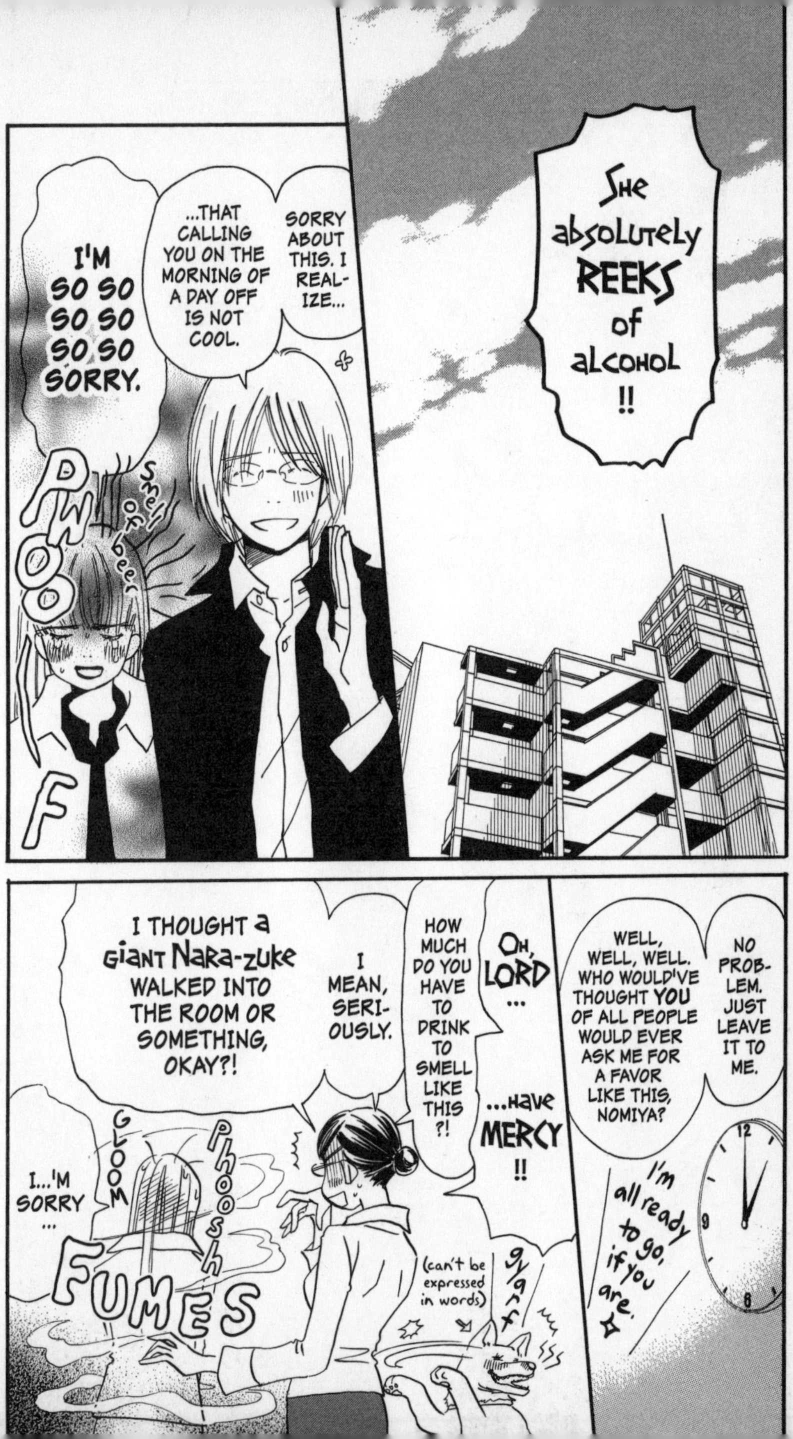
She absolutely REEKS of alcohol !!
SORRY ABOUT THIS. I REAL-IZE...
...THAT CALLING YOU ON THE MORNING OF A DAY OFF IS NOT COOL.
I'M SO SO SO SO SO SO SORRY.
Smell of beer
PWOOOF
NO PROB-LEM. JUST LEAVE IT TO ME.
WELL, WELL, WELL. WHO WOULD'VE THOUGHT YOU OF ALL PEOPLE WOULD EVER ASK ME FOR A FAVOR LIKE THIS, NOMIYA?
I'm all ready to go, if you are.
OH, LORD...
...Have MERCY !!
HOW MUCH DO YOU HAVE TO DRINK TO SMELL LIKE THIS ?!
I MEAN, SERI-OUSLY.
I THOUGHT a giant Nara-zuke WALKED INTO THE ROOM OR SOMETHING, OKAY?!
I...'M SORRY...
GLOOM
Phooosh
FUMES
(can't be expressed in words)
gyarf

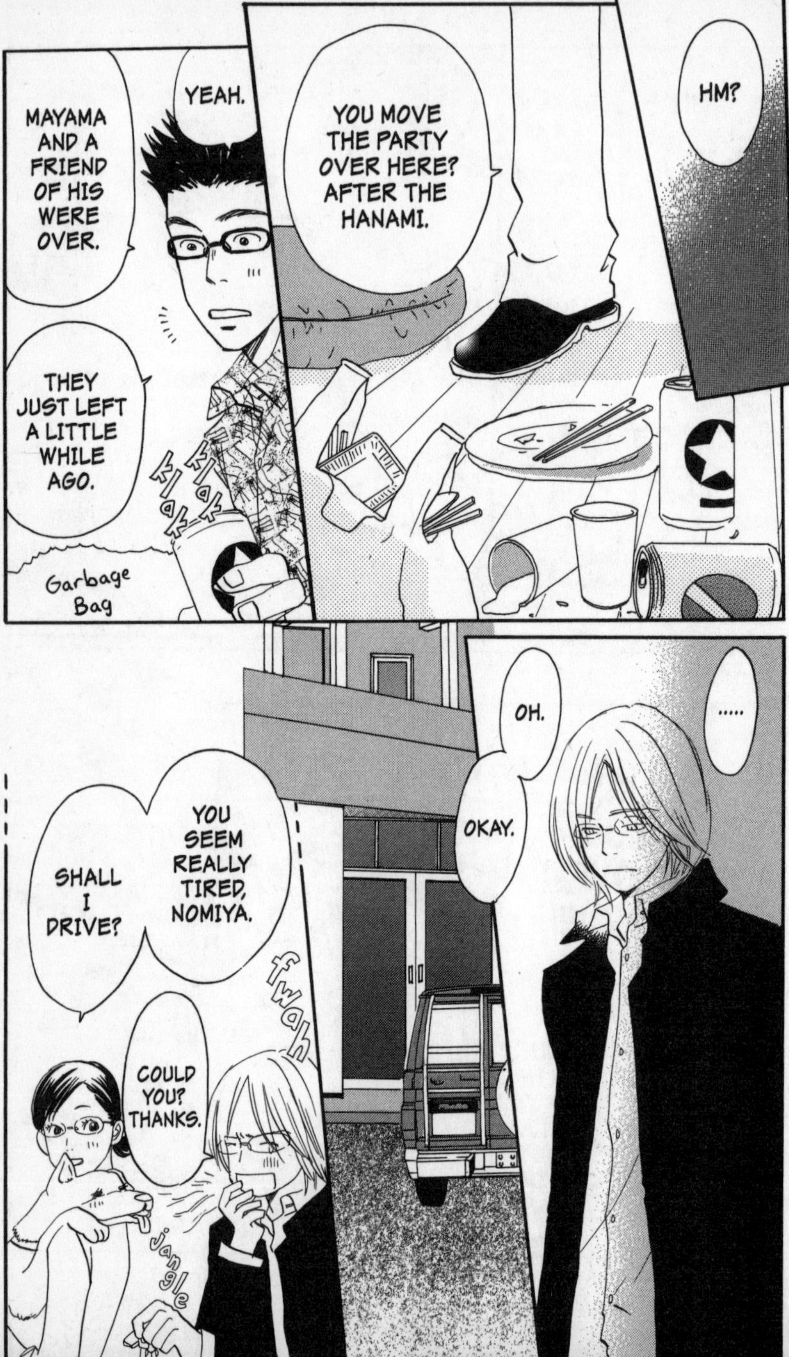

HM?
YOU MOVE THE PARTY OVER HERE? AFTER THE HANAMI.
YEAH.
MAYAMA AND A FRIEND OF HIS WERE OVER.
THEY JUST LEFT A LITTLE WHILE AGO.
klak klak
Garbage Bag
.....
OH.
OKAY.
YOU SEEM REALLY TIRED, NOMIYA.
SHALL I DRIVE?
fwah
COULD YOU? THANKS.
jangle

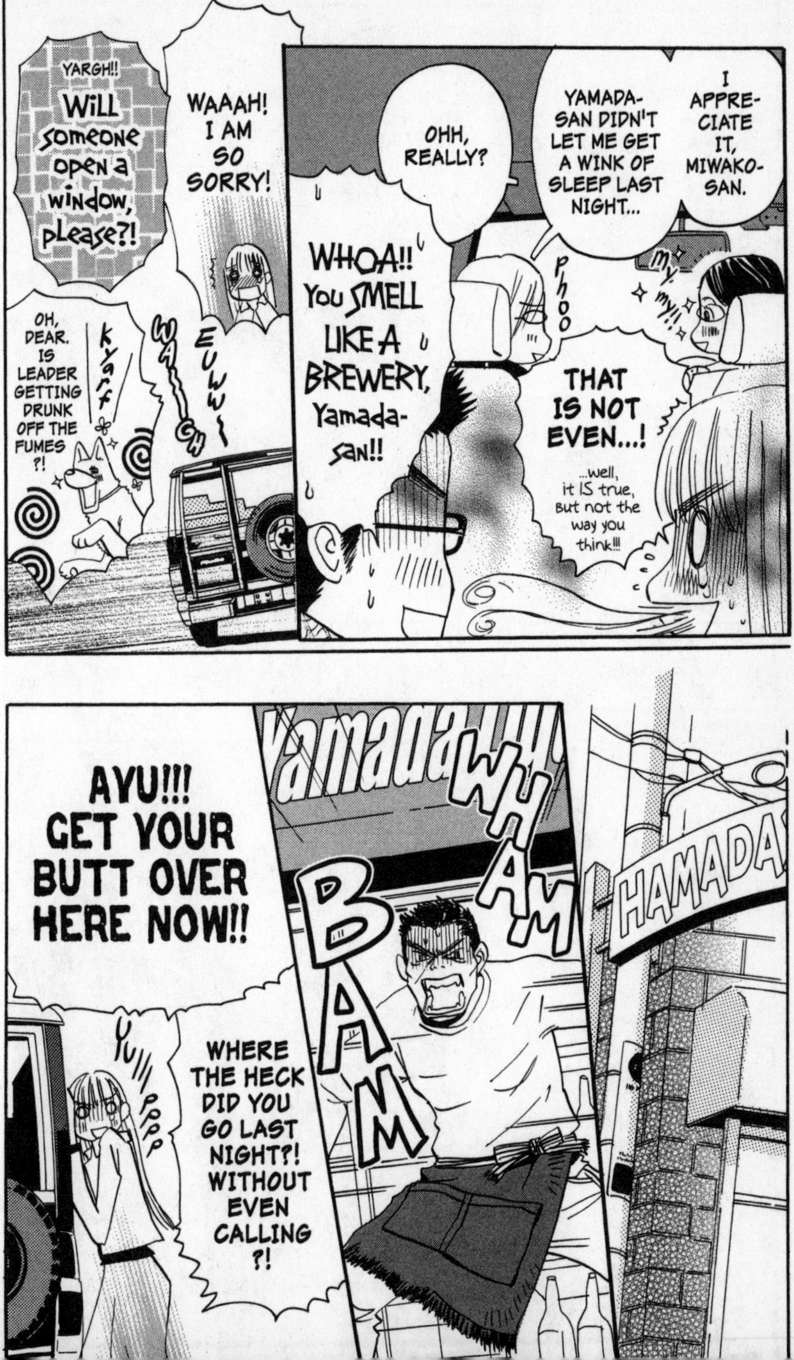
I APPRECIATE IT, MIWAKO-SAN.
YAMADA-SAN DIDN'T LET ME GET A WINK OF SLEEP LAST NIGHT...
OHH, REALLY?
my, my!!
phoo
THAT IS NOT EVEN...!
...well, it IS true, but not the way you think!!!
WHOA!! You SMELL LIKE A BREWERY, Yamada-san!!
WAAAH! I AM SO SORRY!
YARGH!! Will someone open a window, please?!
EUWWW
WAAGH
kyarf
OH, DEAR. IS LEADER GETTING DRUNK OFF THE FUMES?!
HAMADA
Yamada
WHAM
BAM
AYU!!! GET YOUR BUTT OVER HERE NOW!!
WHERE THE HECK DID YOU GO LAST NIGHT?! WITHOUT EVEN CALLING?!

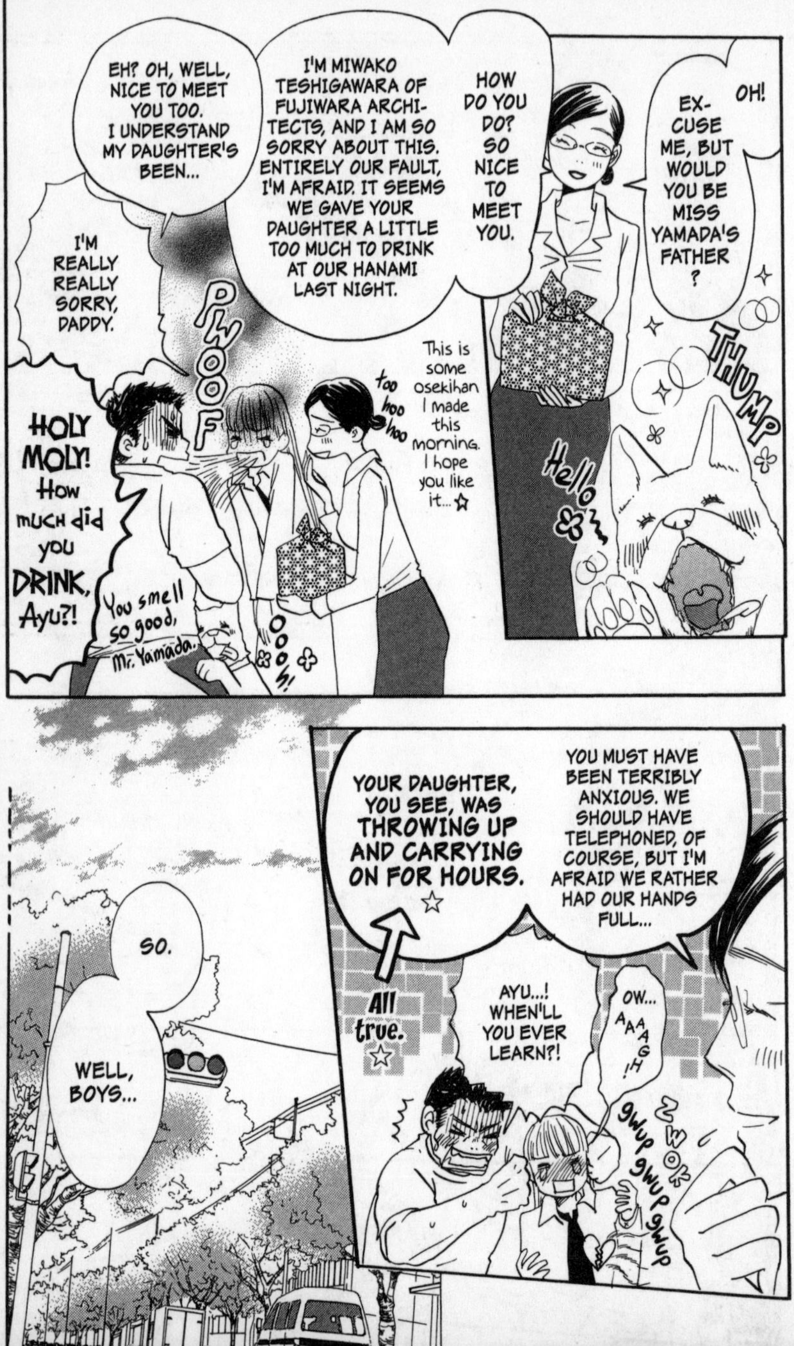
OH!
EX-CUSE ME, BUT WOULD YOU BE MISS YAMADA'S FATHER?
THUMP
Hello
HOW DO YOU DO? SO NICE TO MEET YOU.
I'M MIWAKO TESHIGAWARA OF FUJIWARA ARCHI-TECTS, AND I AM SO SORRY ABOUT THIS. ENTIRELY OUR FAULT, I'M AFRAID. IT SEEMS WE GAVE YOUR DAUGHTER A LITTLE TOO MUCH TO DRINK AT OUR HANAMI LAST NIGHT.
This is some osekihan I made this morning. I hope you like it...☆
too hoo hoo
EH? OH, WELL, NICE TO MEET YOU TOO. I UNDERSTAND MY DAUGHTER'S BEEN...
I'M REALLY REALLY SORRY, DADDY.
PWOOF
Ooooh!
HOLY MOLY! How much did you DRINK, Ayu?!
You smell so good, Mr. Yamada.
YOU MUST HAVE BEEN TERRIBLY ANXIOUS. WE SHOULD HAVE TELEPHONED, OF COURSE, BUT I'M AFRAID WE RATHER HAD OUR HANDS FULL...
YOUR DAUGHTER, YOU SEE, WAS THROWING UP AND CARRYING ON FOR HOURS. ☆
All true. ☆
OW... AAAAGH!
AYU...! WHEN'LL YOU EVER LEARN?!
ZWOK
gwup gwup gwup gwup
SO.
WELL, BOYS...

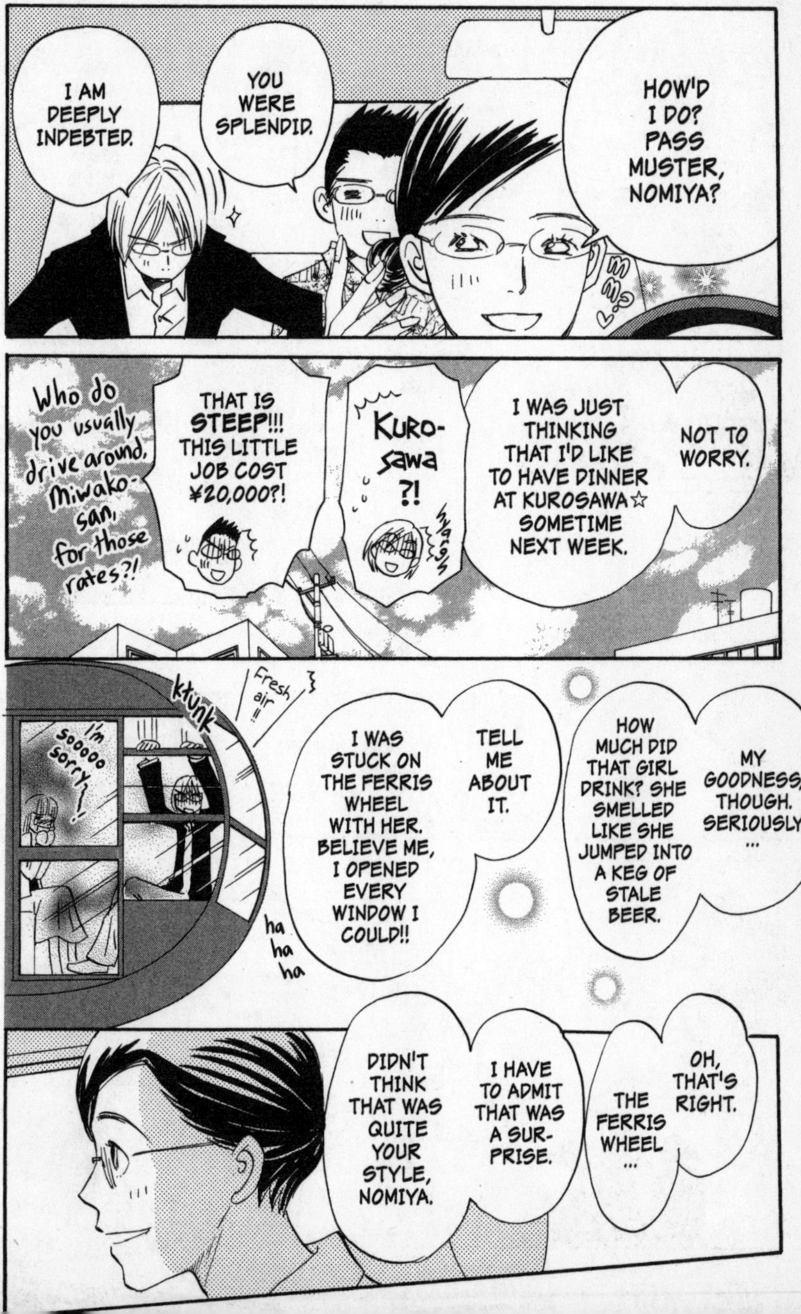
HOW'D I DO? PASS MUSTER, NOMIYA?
YOU WERE SPLENDID.
I AM DEEPLY INDEBTED.
NOT TO WORRY.
I WAS JUST THINKING THAT I'D LIKE TO HAVE DINNER AT KUROSAWA☆ SOMETIME NEXT WEEK.
KURO-SAWA ?!
THAT IS STEEP!!! THIS LITTLE JOB COST ¥20,000?!
Who do you usually drive around, Miwako-san, for those rates?!
MY GOODNESS, THOUGH. SERIOUSLY ...
HOW MUCH DID THAT GIRL DRINK? SHE SMELLED LIKE SHE JUMPED INTO A KEG OF STALE BEER.
TELL ME ABOUT IT.
I WAS STUCK ON THE FERRIS WHEEL WITH HER. BELIEVE ME, I OPENED EVERY WINDOW I COULD!!
ha ha ha
Fresh air !!
ktunk
I'm sooooo sorry!
OH, THAT'S RIGHT.
THE FERRIS WHEEL ...
I HAVE TO ADMIT THAT WAS A SUR-PRISE.
DIDN'T THINK THAT WAS QUITE YOUR STYLE, NOMIYA.

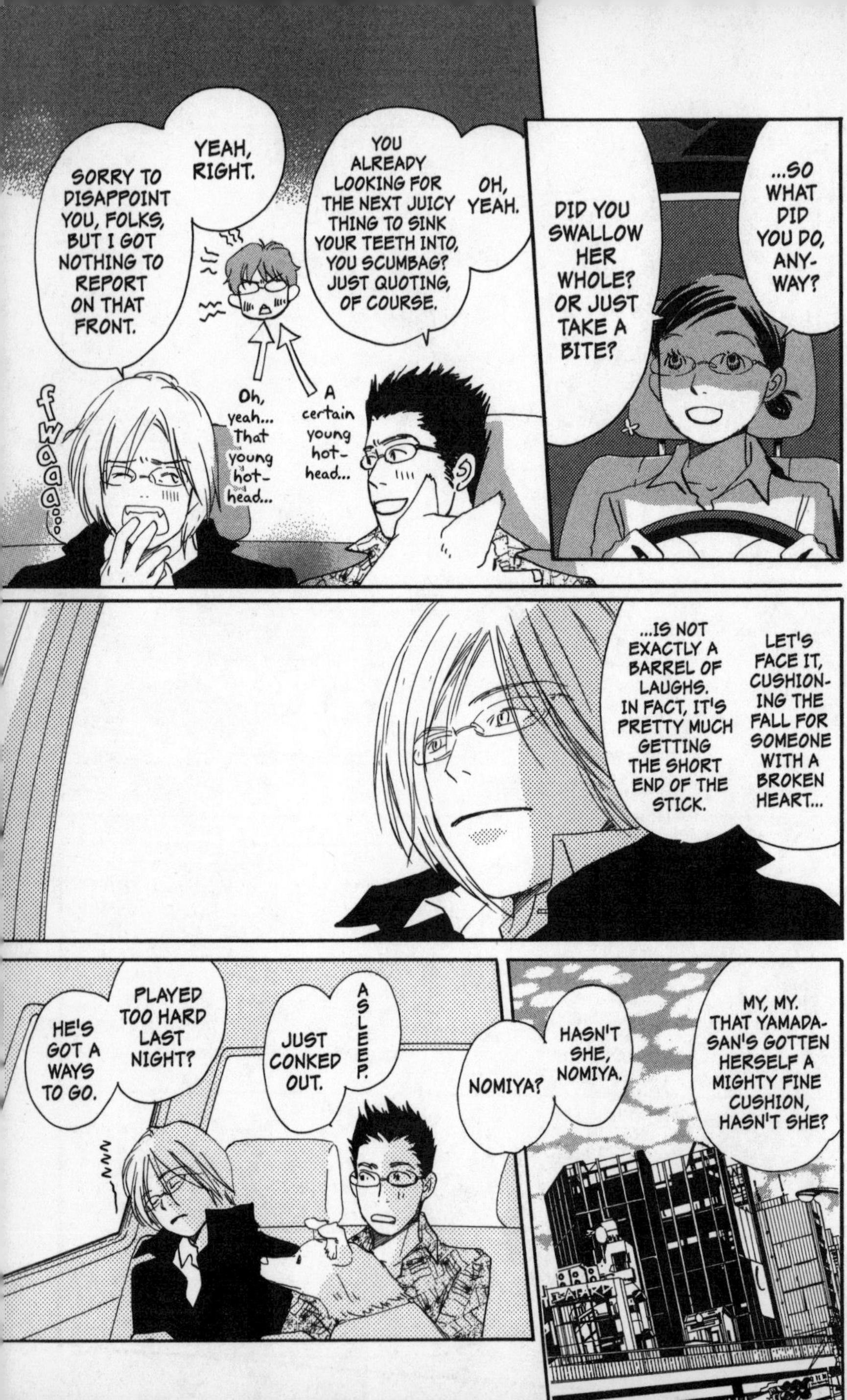
...SO WHAT DID YOU DO, ANYWAY?
DID YOU SWALLOW HER WHOLE? OR JUST TAKE A BITE?
OH, YEAH.
YOU ALREADY LOOKING FOR THE NEXT JUICY THING TO SINK YOUR TEETH INTO, YOU SCUMBAG? JUST QUOTING, OF COURSE.
YEAH, RIGHT.
SORRY TO DISAPPOINT YOU, FOLKS, BUT I GOT NOTHING TO REPORT ON THAT FRONT.
A certain young hot-head...
Oh, yeah... That young hot-head...
fwaaaa...
LET'S FACE IT, CUSHIONING THE FALL FOR SOMEONE WITH A BROKEN HEART...
...IS NOT EXACTLY A BARREL OF LAUGHS. IN FACT, IT'S PRETTY MUCH GETTING THE SHORT END OF THE STICK.
MY, MY. THAT YAMADA-SAN'S GOTTEN HERSELF A MIGHTY FINE CUSHION, HASN'T SHE?
HASN'T SHE, NOMIYA.
NOMIYA?
ASLEEP.
JUST CONKED OUT.
PLAYED TOO HARD LAST NIGHT?
HE'S GOT A WAYS TO GO.

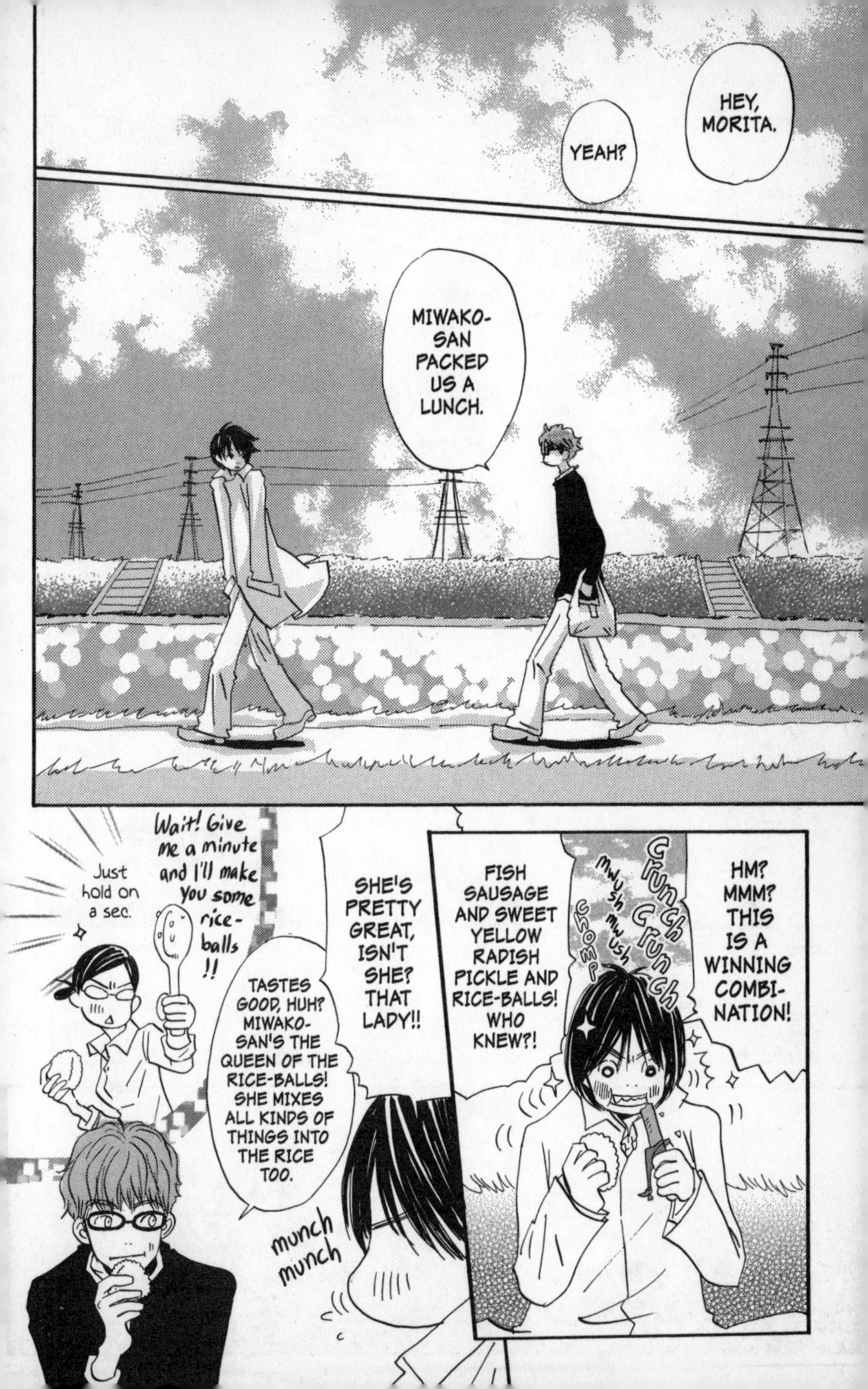
HEY, MORITA.
YEAH?
MIWAKO-SAN PACKED US A LUNCH.
HM? MMM? THIS IS A WINNING COMBINATION!
FISH SAUSAGE AND SWEET YELLOW RADISH PICKLE AND RICE-BALLS! WHO KNEW?!
Crunch Crunch
mwush mwush
chomp
SHE'S PRETTY GREAT, ISN'T SHE? THAT LADY!!
TASTES GOOD, HUH? MIWAKO-SAN'S THE QUEEN OF THE RICE-BALLS! SHE MIXES ALL KINDS OF THINGS INTO THE RICE TOO.
munch munch
Wait! Give me a minute and I'll make you some rice-balls!!
Just hold on a sec.

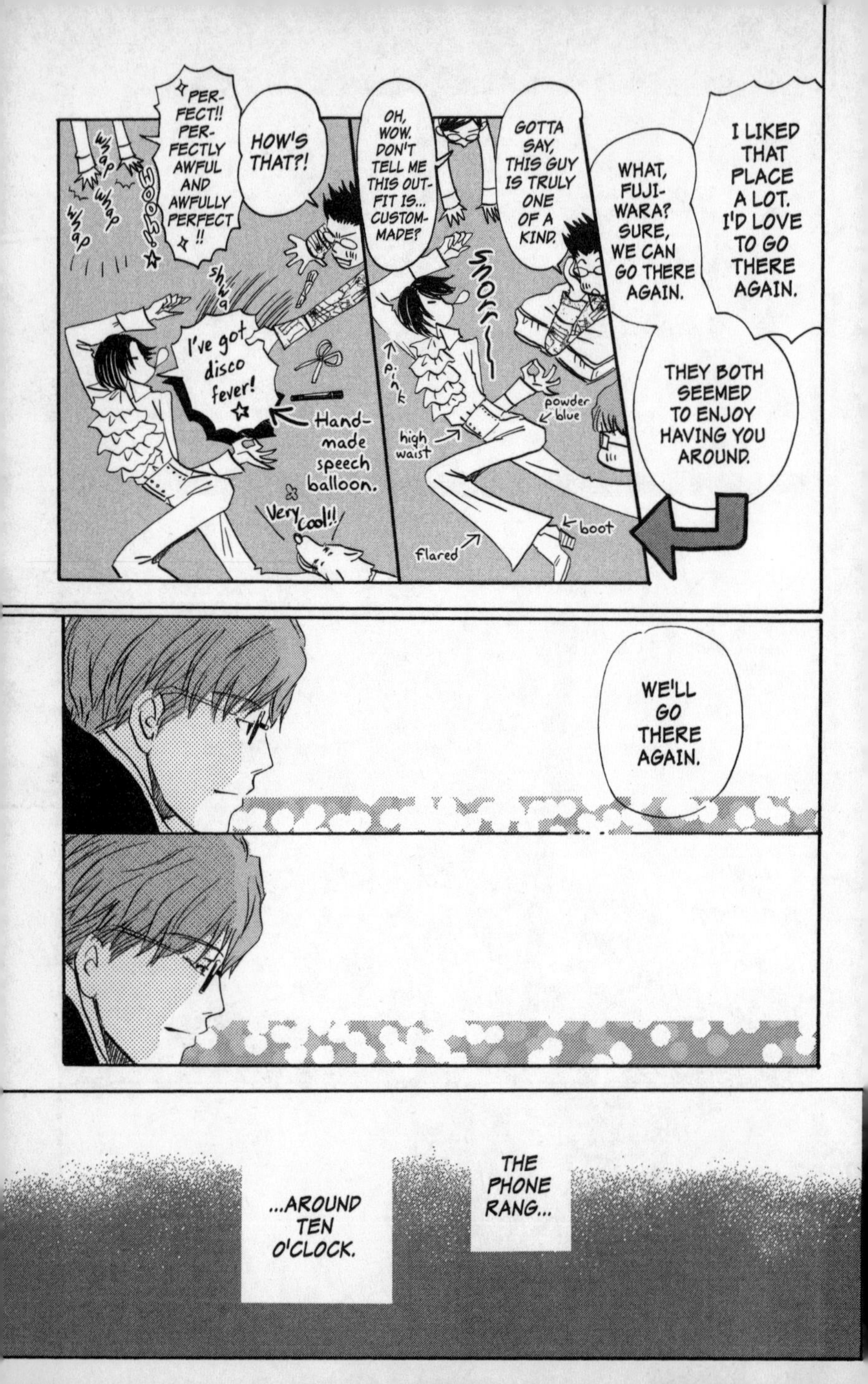
I LIKED THAT PLACE A LOT. I'D LOVE TO GO THERE AGAIN.
THEY BOTH SEEMED TO ENJOY HAVING YOU AROUND.
WHAT, FUJI-WARA? SURE, WE CAN GO THERE AGAIN.
GOTTA SAY, THIS GUY IS TRULY ONE OF A KIND.
OH, WOW. DON'T TELL ME THIS OUT-FIT IS... CUSTOM-MADE?
snorr~
pink
powder blue
high waist
boot
flared
HOW'S THAT?!
PER-FECT!! PER-FECTLY AWFUL AND AWFULLY PERFECT!!
Hooh!
whap whap whap
shwa
I've got disco fever!
Hand-made speech balloon.
Very cool!!
WE'LL GO THERE AGAIN.
THE PHONE RANG...
...AROUND TEN O'CLOCK.

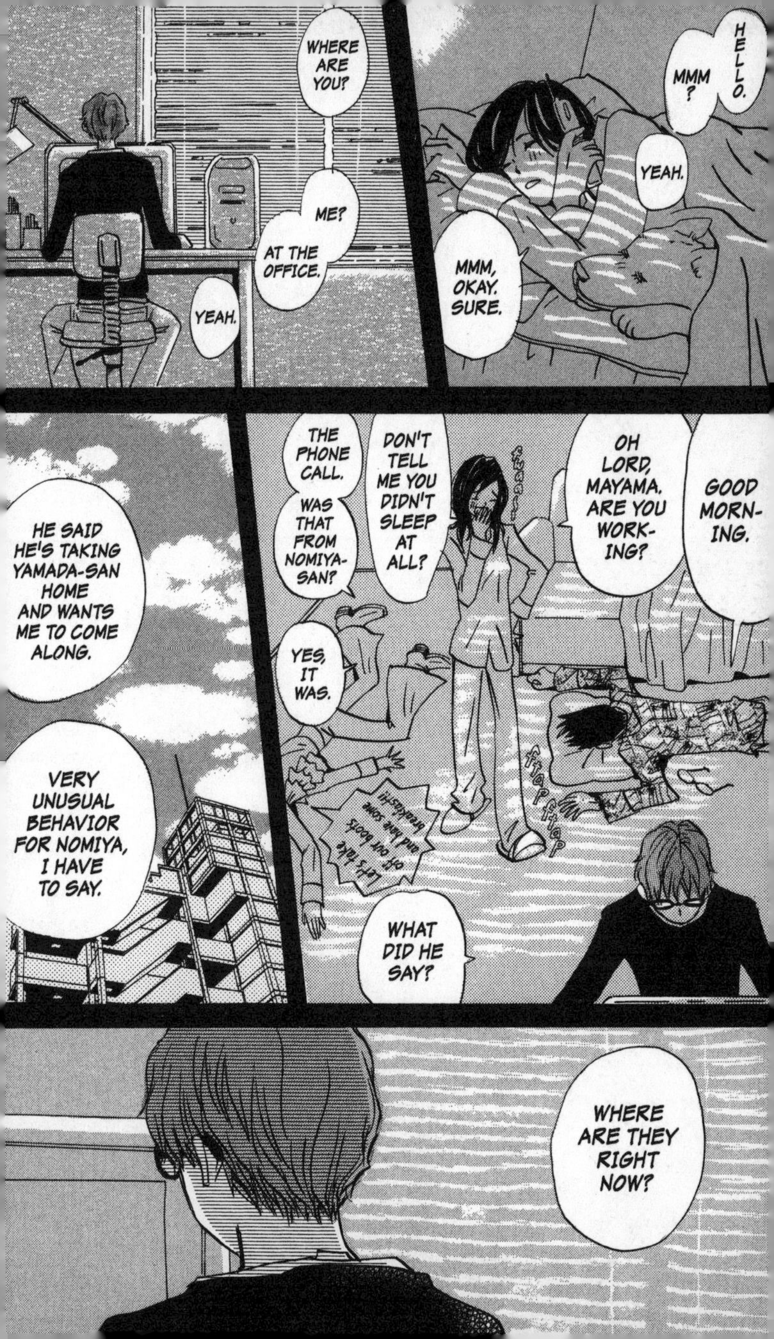
HELLO.
MMM?
YEAH.
MMM, OKAY. SURE.
WHERE ARE YOU?
ME?
AT THE OFFICE.
YEAH.
GOOD MORNING.
OH LORD, MAYAMA. ARE YOU WORKING?
DON'T TELL ME YOU DIDN'T SLEEP AT ALL?
THE PHONE CALL.
WAS THAT FROM NOMIYA-SAN?
YES, IT WAS.
flop flop
Let's take off our boots and have some breakfast!!
WHAT DID HE SAY?
HE SAID HE'S TAKING YAMADA-SAN HOME AND WANTS ME TO COME ALONG.
VERY UNUSUAL BEHAVIOR FOR NOMIYA, I HAVE TO SAY.
WHERE ARE THEY RIGHT NOW?

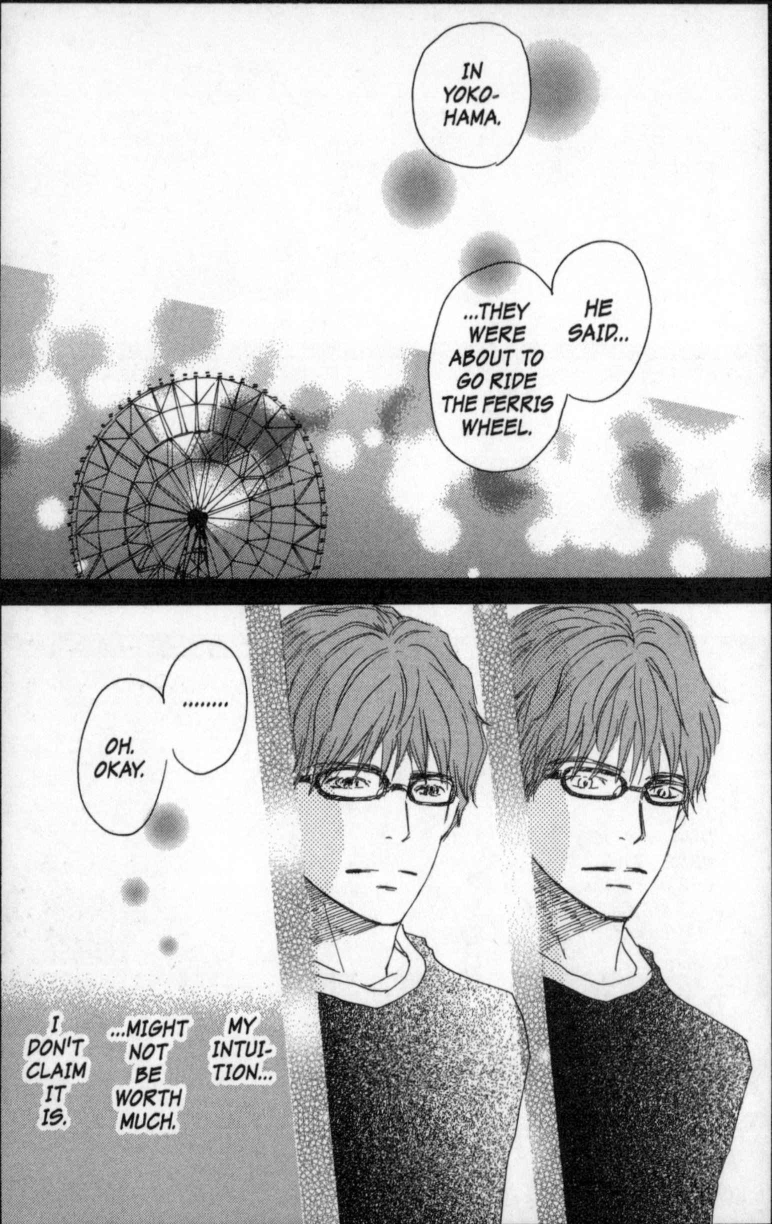
IN YOKO-HAMA.
HE SAID...
...THEY WERE ABOUT TO GO RIDE THE FERRIS WHEEL.
....
OH. OKAY.
MY INTUI-TION...
...MIGHT NOT BE WORTH MUCH.
I DON'T CLAIM IT IS.

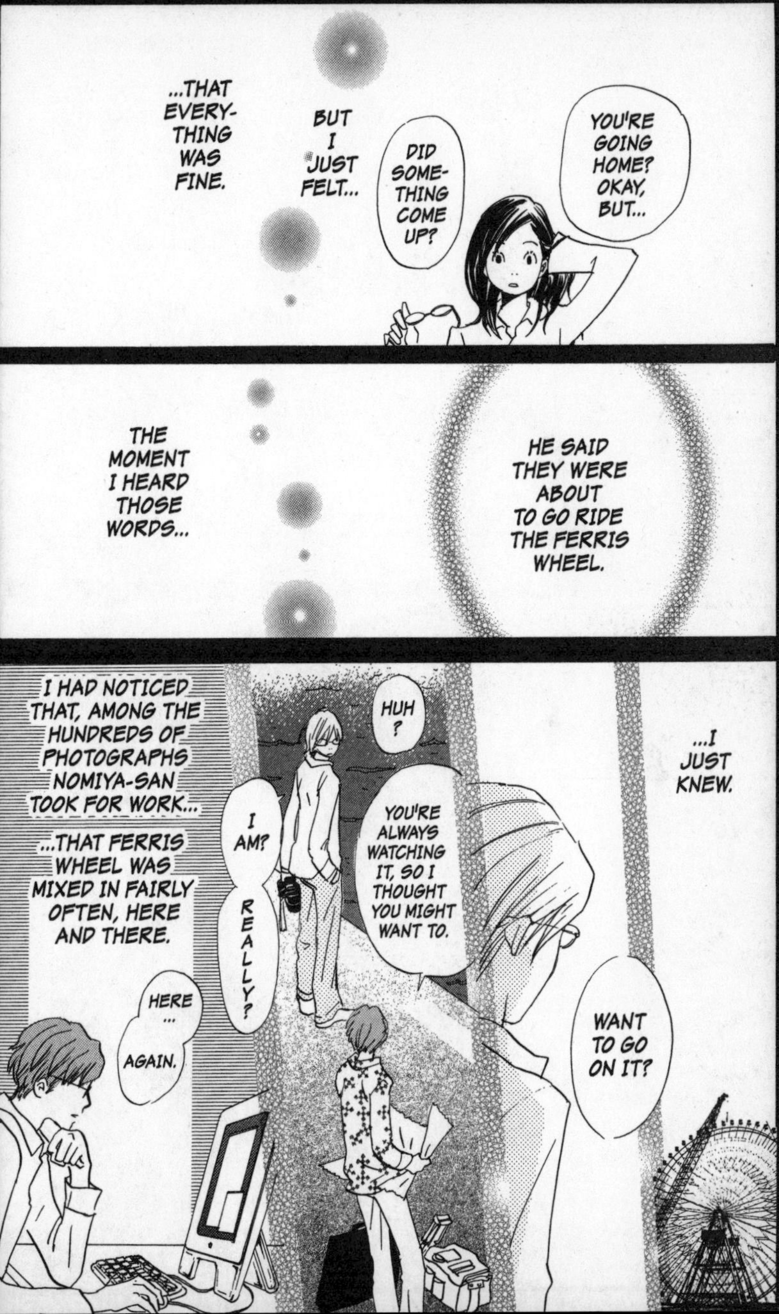

YOU'RE GOING HOME? OKAY, BUT...
DID SOMETHING COME UP?
BUT I JUST FELT...
...THAT EVERYTHING WAS FINE.
HE SAID THEY WERE ABOUT TO GO RIDE THE FERRIS WHEEL.
THE MOMENT I HEARD THOSE WORDS...
...I JUST KNEW.
WANT TO GO ON IT?
HUH?
YOU'RE ALWAYS WATCHING IT, SO I THOUGHT YOU MIGHT WANT TO.
I AM?
REALLY?
I HAD NOTICED THAT, AMONG THE HUNDREDS OF PHOTOGRAPHS NOMIYA-SAN TOOK FOR WORK...
...THAT FERRIS WHEEL WAS MIXED IN FAIRLY OFTEN, HERE AND THERE.
HERE...
AGAIN.

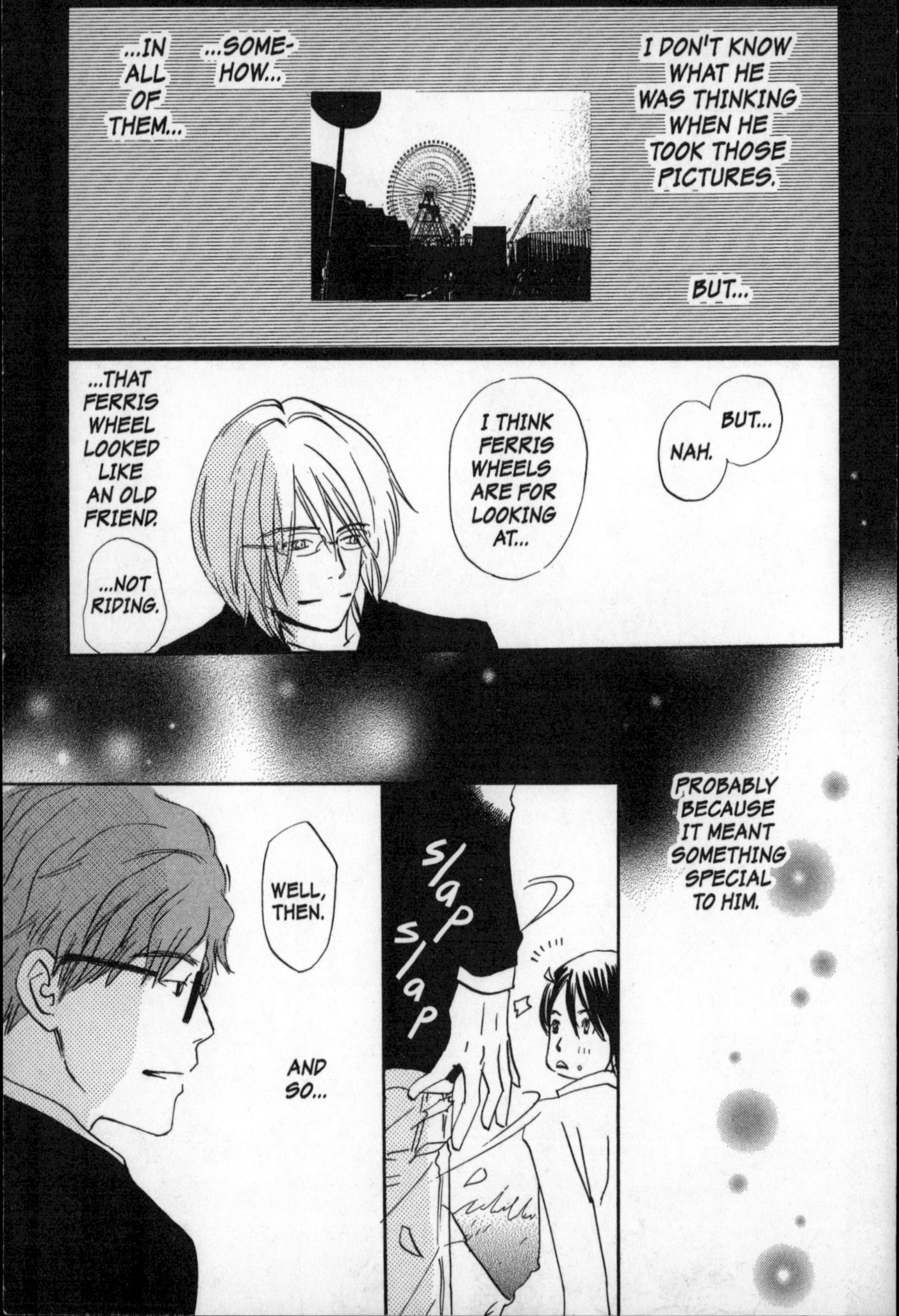
I DON'T KNOW WHAT HE WAS THINKING WHEN HE TOOK THOSE PICTURES.
BUT...
...SOME-HOW...
...IN ALL OF THEM...
BUT... NAH.
I THINK FERRIS WHEELS ARE FOR LOOKING AT...
...THAT FERRIS WHEEL LOOKED LIKE AN OLD FRIEND.
...NOT RIDING.
PROBABLY BECAUSE IT MEANT SOMETHING SPECIAL TO HIM.
slap slap
WELL, THEN.
AND SO...

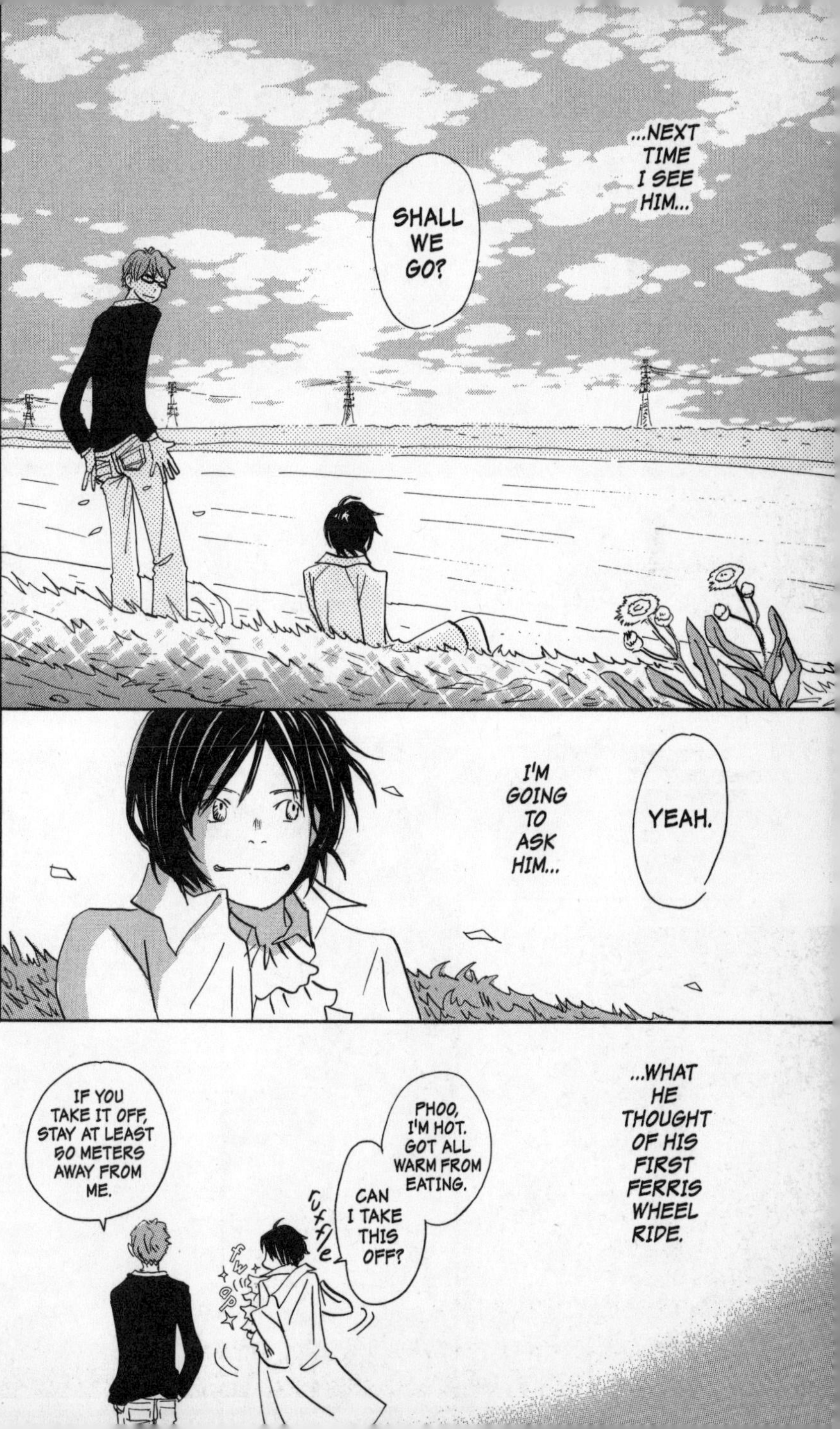
...NEXT TIME I SEE HIM...
SHALL WE GO?
YEAH.
I'M GOING TO ASK HIM...
...WHAT HE THOUGHT OF HIS FIRST FERRIS WHEEL RIDE.
PHOO, I'M HOT. GOT ALL WARM FROM EATING.
CAN I TAKE THIS OFF?
ruffle
fwap
IF YOU TAKE IT OFF, STAY AT LEAST 50 METERS AWAY FROM ME.

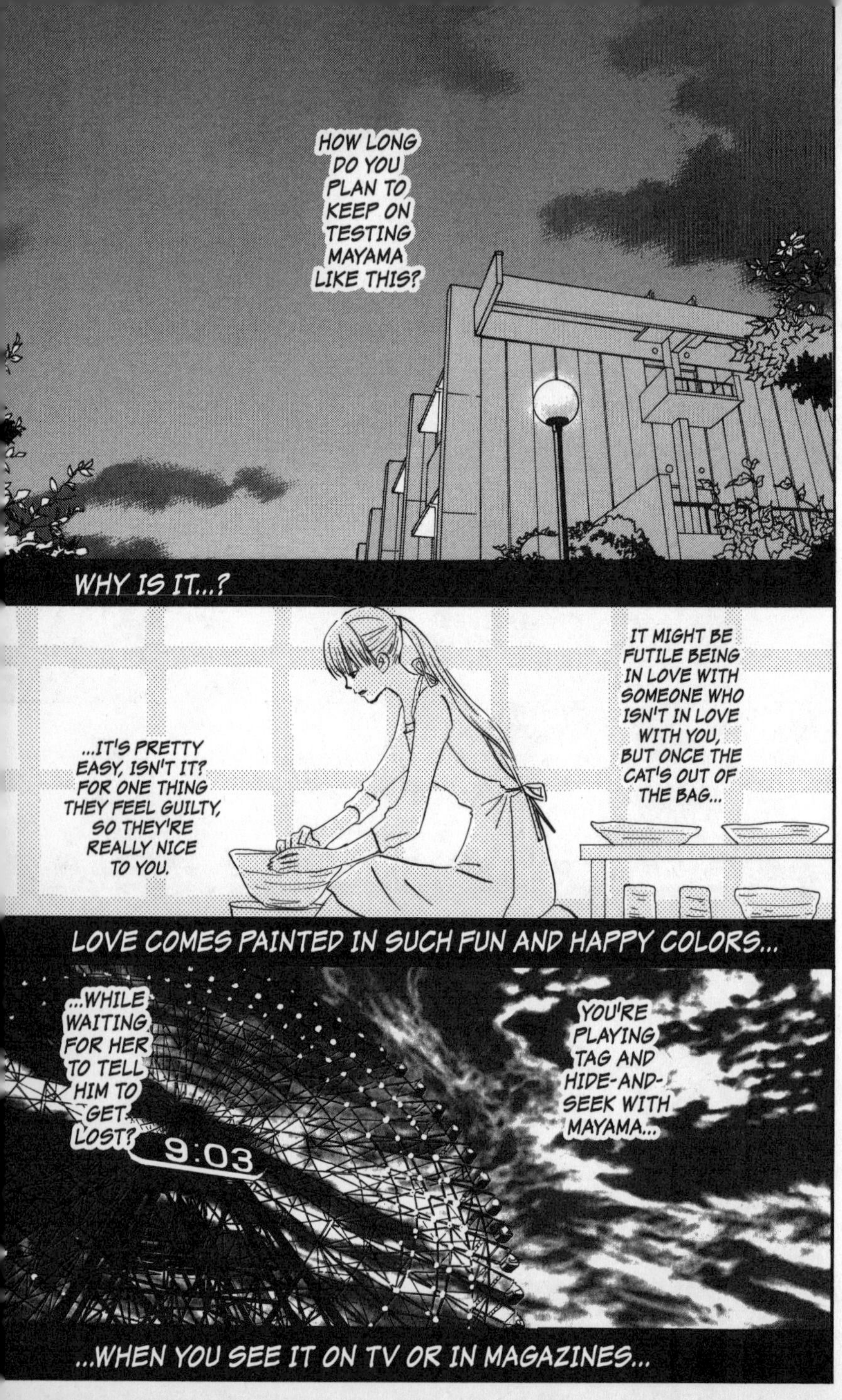
HOW LONG DO YOU PLAN TO KEEP ON TESTING MAYAMA LIKE THIS?
WHY IS IT...?
IT MIGHT BE FUTILE BEING IN LOVE WITH SOMEONE WHO ISN'T IN LOVE WITH YOU, BUT ONCE THE CAT'S OUT OF THE BAG...
...IT'S PRETTY EASY, ISN'T IT? FOR ONE THING THEY FEEL GUILTY, SO THEY'RE REALLY NICE TO YOU.
LOVE COMES PAINTED IN SUCH FUN AND HAPPY COLORS...
YOU'RE PLAYING TAG AND HIDE-AND-SEEK WITH MAYAMA...
...WHILE WAITING FOR HER TO TELL HIM TO GET LOST?
9:03
...WHEN YOU SEE IT ON TV OR IN MAGAZINES...

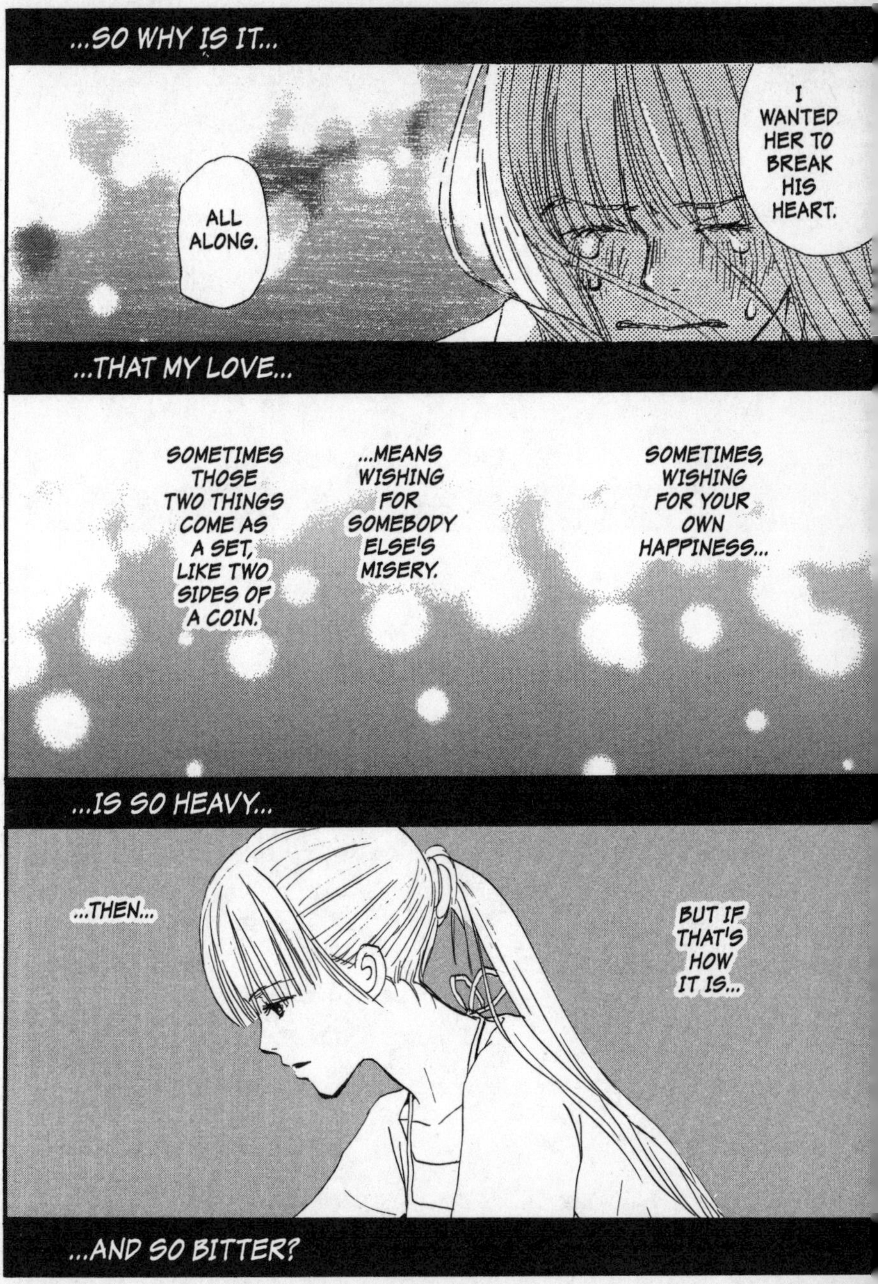
...SO WHY IS IT...
I WANTED HER TO BREAK HIS HEART.
ALL ALONG.
...THAT MY LOVE...
SOMETIMES, WISHING FOR YOUR OWN HAPPINESS...
...MEANS WISHING FOR SOMEBODY ELSE'S MISERY.
SOMETIMES THOSE TWO THINGS COME AS A SET, LIKE TWO SIDES OF A COIN.
...IS SO HEAVY...
BUT IF THAT'S HOW IT IS...
...THEN...
...AND SO BITTER?

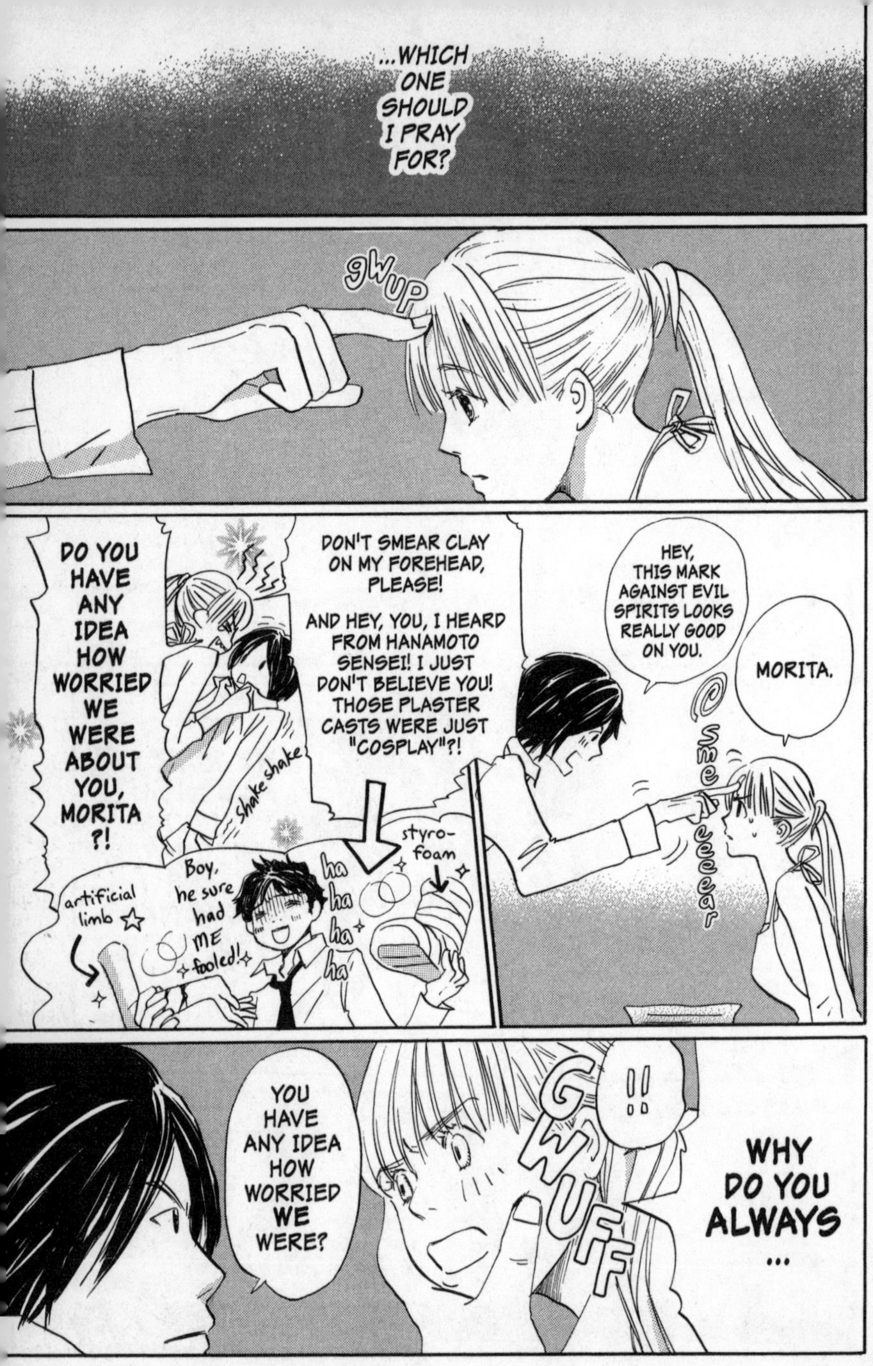
...WHICH ONE SHOULD I PRAY FOR?
gWUP
MORITA.
HEY, THIS MARK AGAINST EVIL SPIRITS LOOKS REALLY GOOD ON YOU.
smeeeeeear
DON'T SMEAR CLAY ON MY FOREHEAD, PLEASE!
AND HEY, YOU, I HEARD FROM HANAMOTO SENSEI! I JUST DON'T BELIEVE YOU! THOSE PLASTER CASTS WERE JUST "COSPLAY"?!
DO YOU HAVE ANY IDEA HOW WORRIED WE WERE ABOUT YOU, MORITA?!
shakeshake
styro-foam
ha ha ha ha
Boy, he sure had ME fooled!
artificial limb
WHY DO YOU ALWAYS ...
!!
GWUFF
YOU HAVE ANY IDEA HOW WORRIED WE WERE?

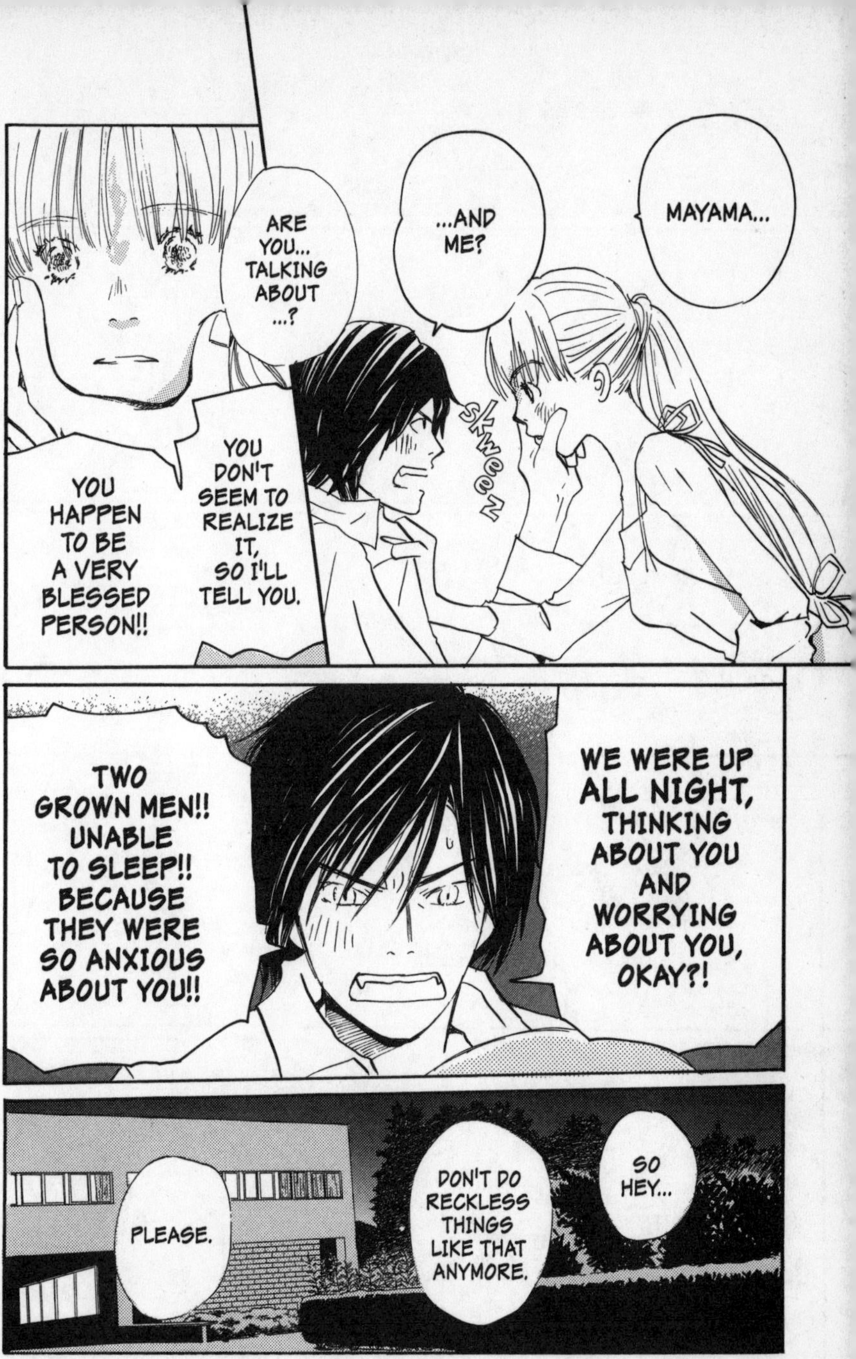
MAYAMA...
...AND ME?
ARE YOU... TALKING ABOUT ...?
skweeZ
YOU DON'T SEEM TO REALIZE IT, SO I'LL TELL YOU.
YOU HAPPEN TO BE A VERY BLESSED PERSON!!
WE WERE UP ALL NIGHT, THINKING ABOUT YOU AND WORRYING ABOUT YOU, OKAY?!
TWO GROWN MEN!! UNABLE TO SLEEP!! BECAUSE THEY WERE SO ANXIOUS ABOUT YOU!!
SO HEY...
DON'T DO RECKLESS THINGS LIKE THAT ANYMORE.
PLEASE.

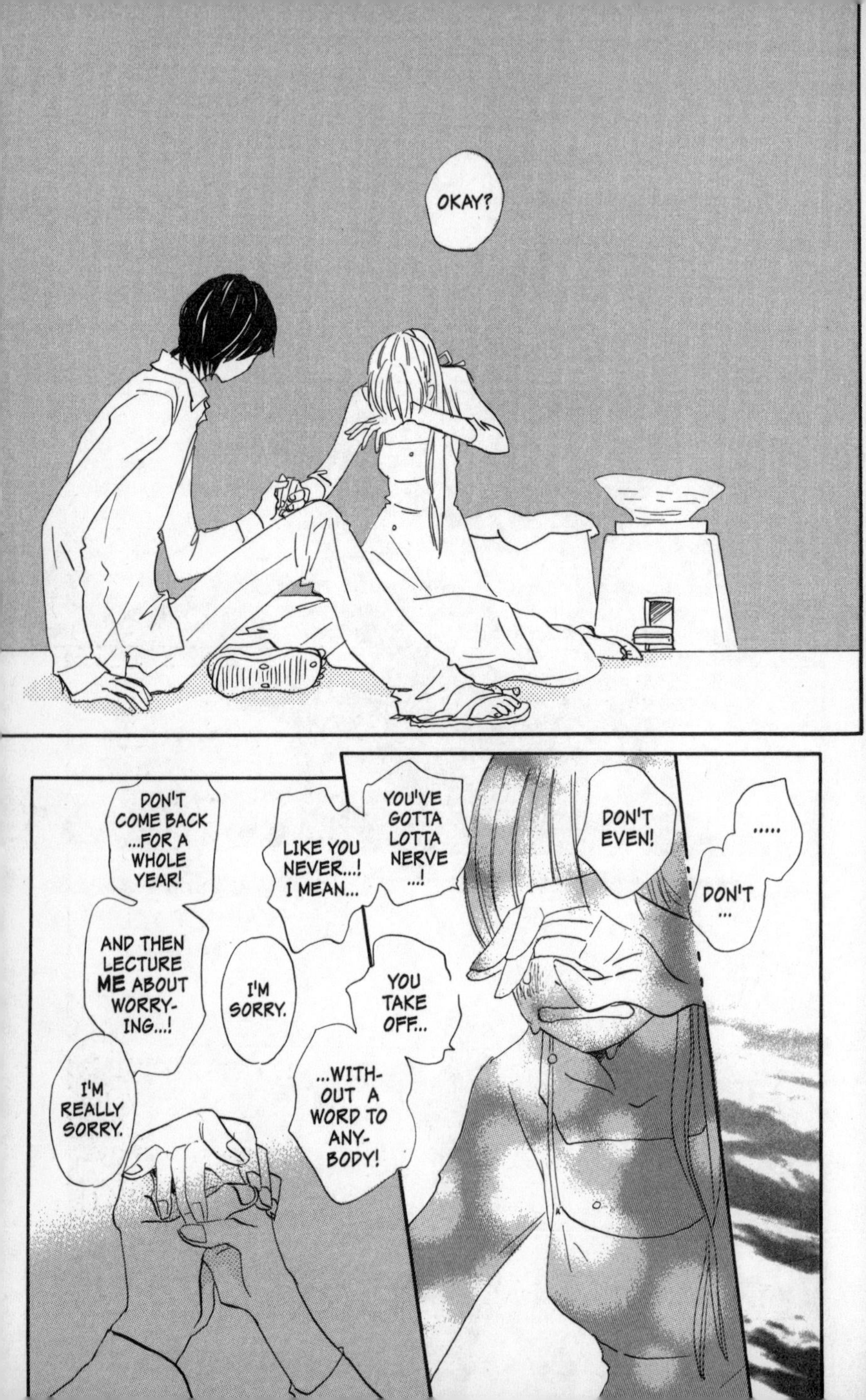
OKAY?
.....
DON'T ...
DON'T EVEN!
YOU'VE GOTTA LOTTA NERVE ...!
LIKE YOU NEVER...! I MEAN...
DON'T COME BACK ...FOR A WHOLE YEAR!
YOU TAKE OFF...
...WITH-OUT A WORD TO ANY-BODY!
I'M SORRY.
AND THEN LECTURE ME ABOUT WORRY-ING...!
I'M REALLY SORRY.

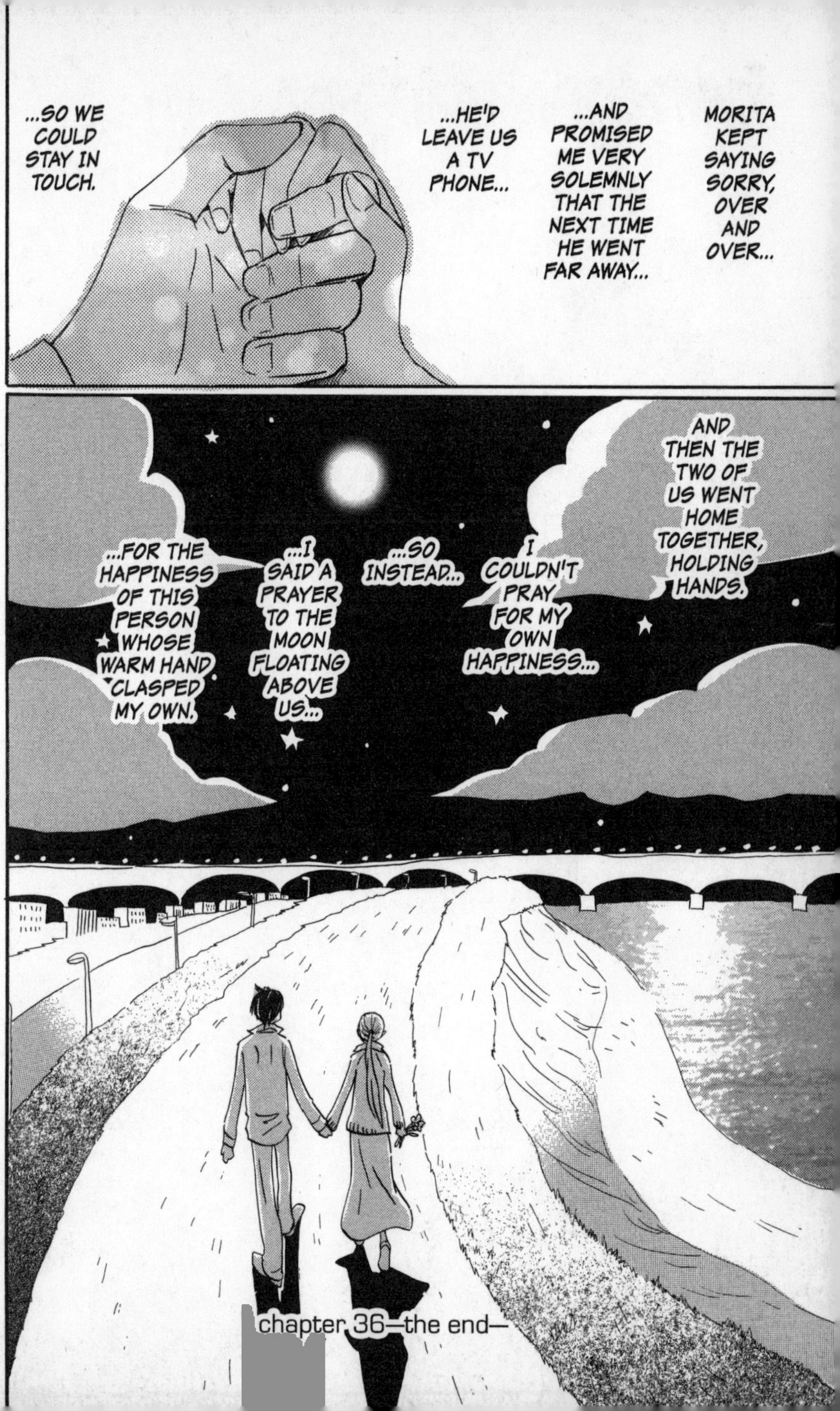
MORITA KEPT SAYING SORRY, OVER AND OVER...
...AND PROMISED ME VERY SOLEMNLY THAT THE NEXT TIME HE WENT FAR AWAY...
...HE'D LEAVE US A TV PHONE...
...SO WE COULD STAY IN TOUCH.
AND THEN THE TWO OF US WENT HOME TOGETHER, HOLDING HANDS.
I COULDN'T PRAY FOR MY OWN HAPPINESS...
...SO INSTEAD...
...I SAID A PRAYER TO THE MOON FLOATING ABOVE US...
...FOR THE HAPPINESS OF THIS PERSON WHOSE WARM HAND CLASPED MY OWN.
chapter 36—the end—

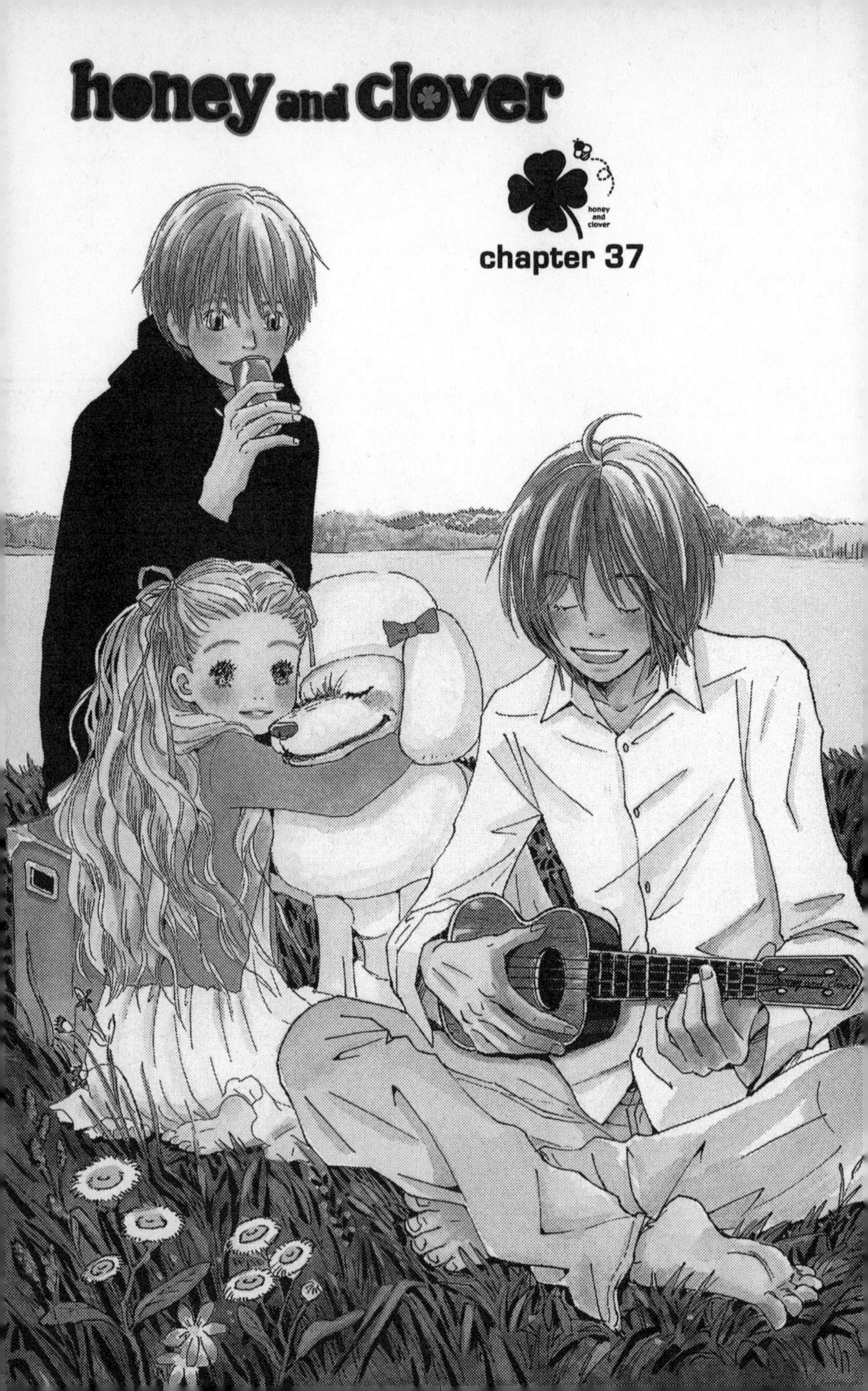
honey and clover
honey
and
clover
chapter 37

Lindt vs. Jean-Paul Hévin Part 1

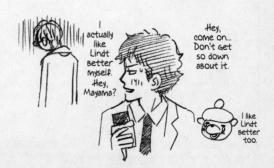

Hey, come on... Don't get so down about it.
I actually like Lindt better myself. Hey, Mayama?
I like Lindt better too.

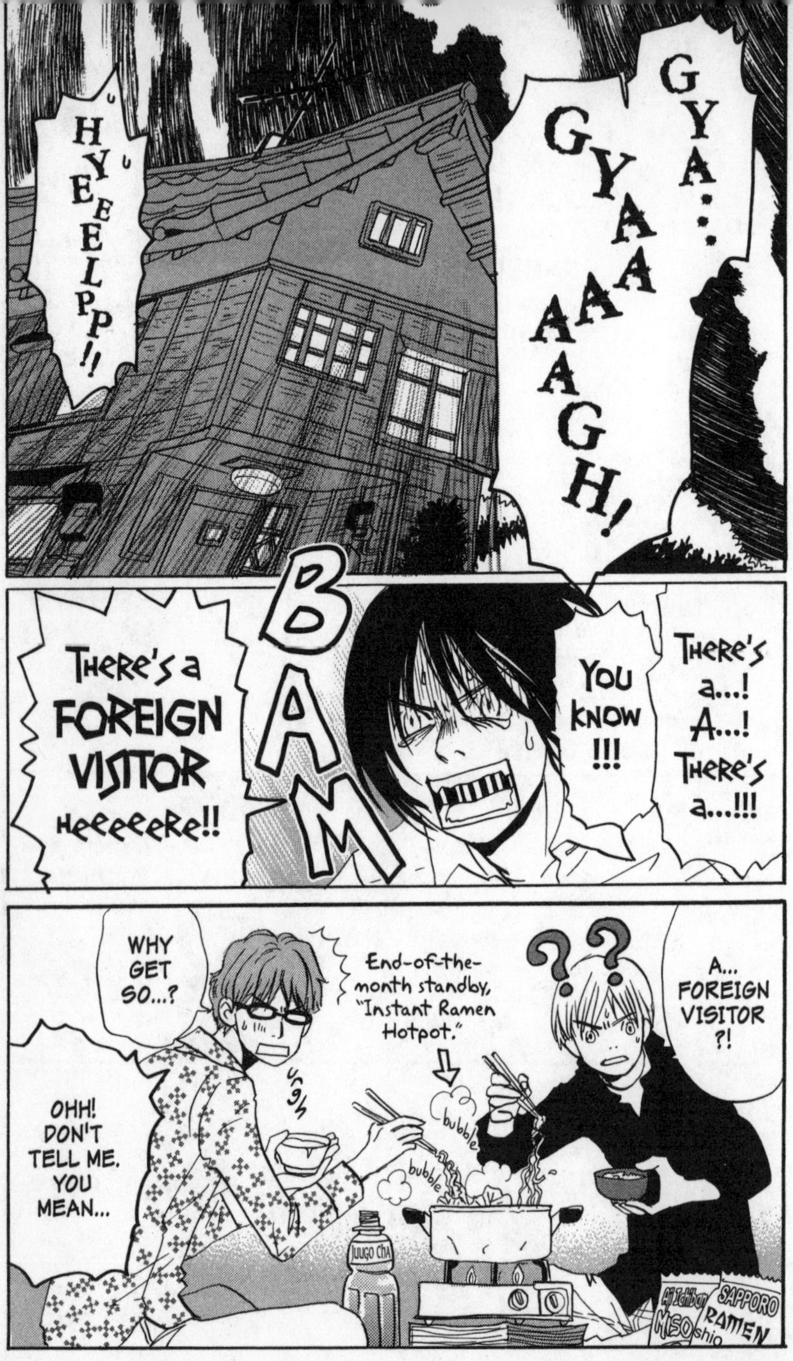

GYA... GYAAAAAGH!
HYEEELPP!!
There's a...! A...! There's a...!!!
YOU KNOW!!!
BAM
There's a FOREIGN VISITOR Heeeeere!!
A... FOREIGN VISITOR?!
End-of-the-month standby, "Instant Ramen Hotpot."
WHY GET SO...?
urgh
bubble
bubble
OHH! DON'T TELL ME. YOU MEAN...
JUUGO CHA
SAPPORO RAMEN

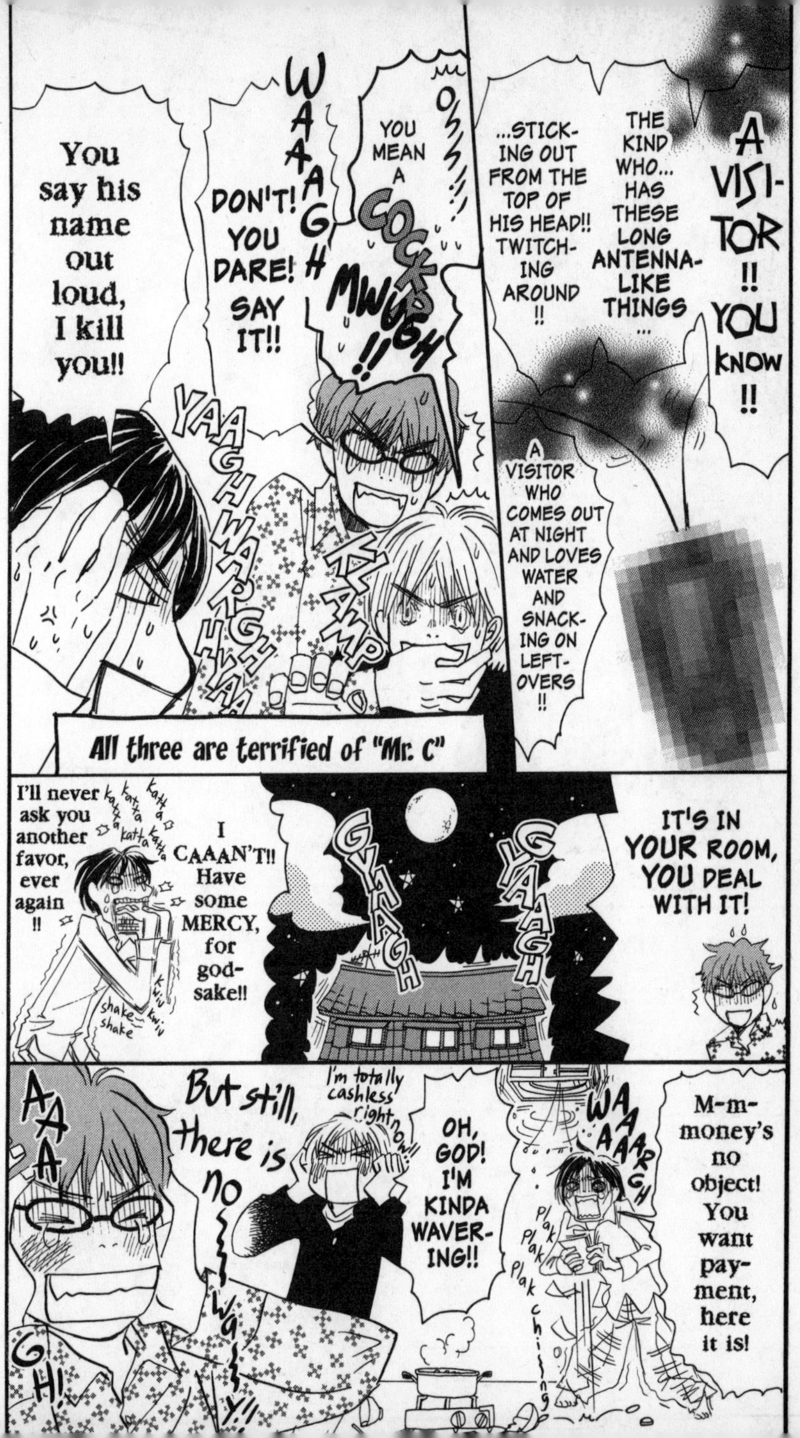
A VISITOR!! YOU KNOW!!
THE KIND WHO... HAS THESE LONG ANTENNA-LIKE THINGS...
...STICKING OUT FROM THE TOP OF HIS HEAD!! TWITCHING AROUND!!
A VISITOR WHO COMES OUT AT NIGHT AND LOVES WATER AND SNACKING ON LEFTOVERS!!
O...!!
YOU MEAN A COCKR
MWUGH!!
WAAAAGH
DON'T! YOU DARE! SAY IT!!
You say his name out loud, I kill you!!
YAAGHWARGHYAA
KLAMP
All three are terrified of "Mr. C"
IT'S IN YOUR ROOM, YOU DEAL WITH IT!
GYAAAGH
GYAAAGH
I CAAAN'T!! Have some MERCY, for god-sake!!
I'll never ask you another favor, ever again!!
katta katta katta katta
kwiv kwiv
shake shake
M-m-money's no object! You want payment, here it is!
WAAAARGH
Plak Plak Plak
chiiing
OH, GOD! I'M KINDA WAVERING!!
I'm totally cashless right now!!
But still, there is no wayyy!!
AAAGH!

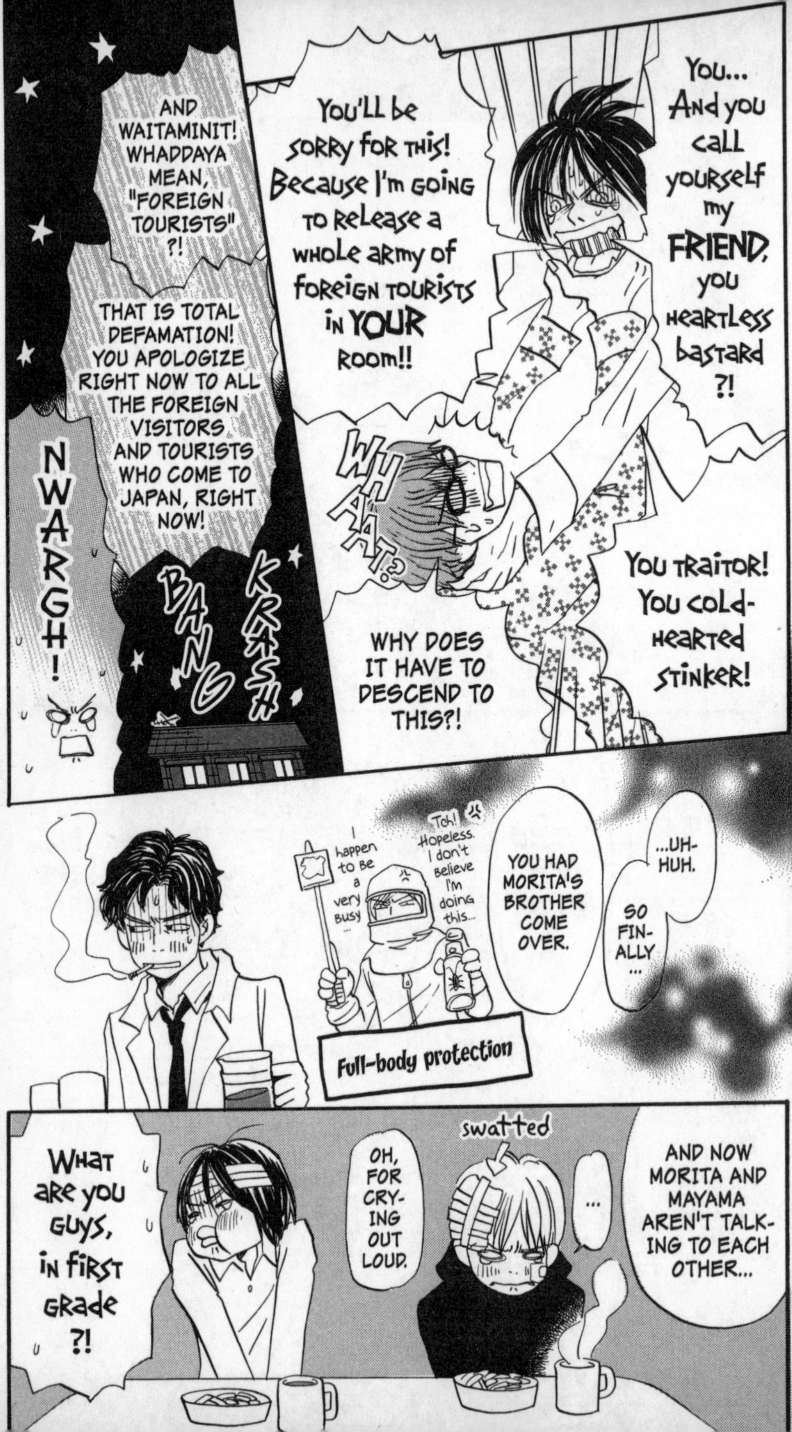
You... And you call yourself my FRIEND, you heartless bastard?!
You'll be sorry for this! Because I'm going to release a whole army of foreign tourists in YOUR room!!
WHAAAT?
You traitor! You cold-hearted stinker!
WHY DOES IT HAVE TO DESCEND TO THIS?!
AND WAITAMINIT! WHADDAYA MEAN, "FOREIGN TOURISTS"?!
THAT IS TOTAL DEFAMATION! YOU APOLOGIZE RIGHT NOW TO ALL THE FOREIGN VISITORS AND TOURISTS WHO COME TO JAPAN, RIGHT NOW!
KRASH
BANG
NWARGH!
...UH-HUH.
SO FIN-ALLY...
YOU HAD MORITA'S BROTHER COME OVER.
Tch! Hopeless. I don't believe I'm doing this...
I happen to be a very busy...
Full-body protection
AND NOW MORITA AND MAYAMA AREN'T TALK-ING TO EACH OTHER...
...
swatted
OH, FOR CRY-ING OUT LOUD.
What are you guys, in first grade?!

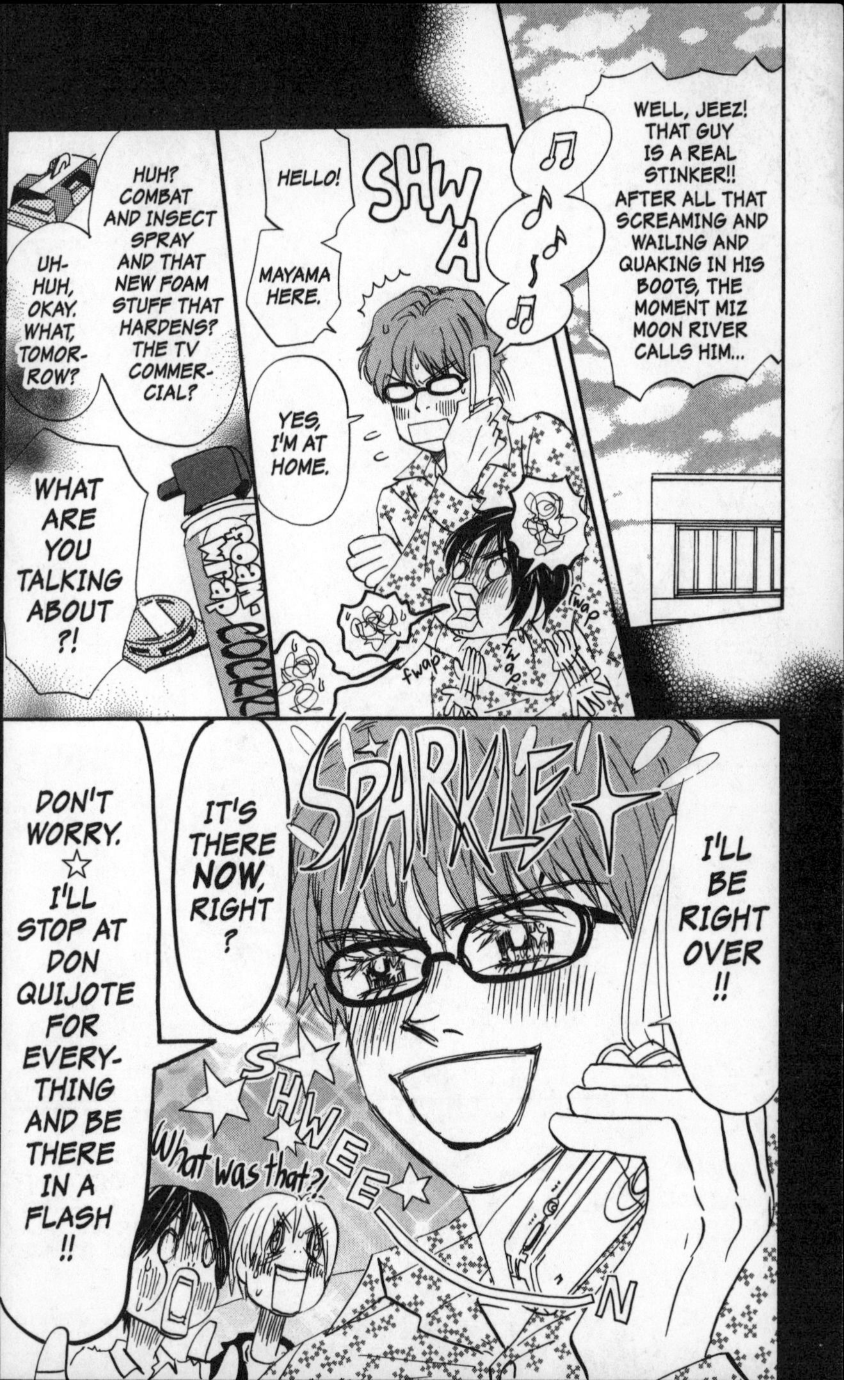
WELL, JEEZ! THAT GUY IS A REAL STINKER!! AFTER ALL THAT SCREAMING AND WAILING AND QUAKING IN HIS BOOTS, THE MOMENT MIZ MOON RIVER CALLS HIM...
SHWA
HELLO!
MAYAMA HERE.
YES, I'M AT HOME.
fwap
fwap
fwap
HUH? COMBAT AND INSECT SPRAY AND THAT NEW FOAM STUFF THAT HARDENS? THE TV COMMERCIAL?
UH-HUH, OKAY. WHAT, TOMORROW?
WHAT ARE YOU TALKING ABOUT?!
Foam Wrap
SPARKLE
I'LL BE RIGHT OVER!!
IT'S THERE NOW, RIGHT?
DON'T WORRY. ☆ I'LL STOP AT DON QUIJOTE FOR EVERYTHING AND BE THERE IN A FLASH!!
SHWEEEN
What was that?!

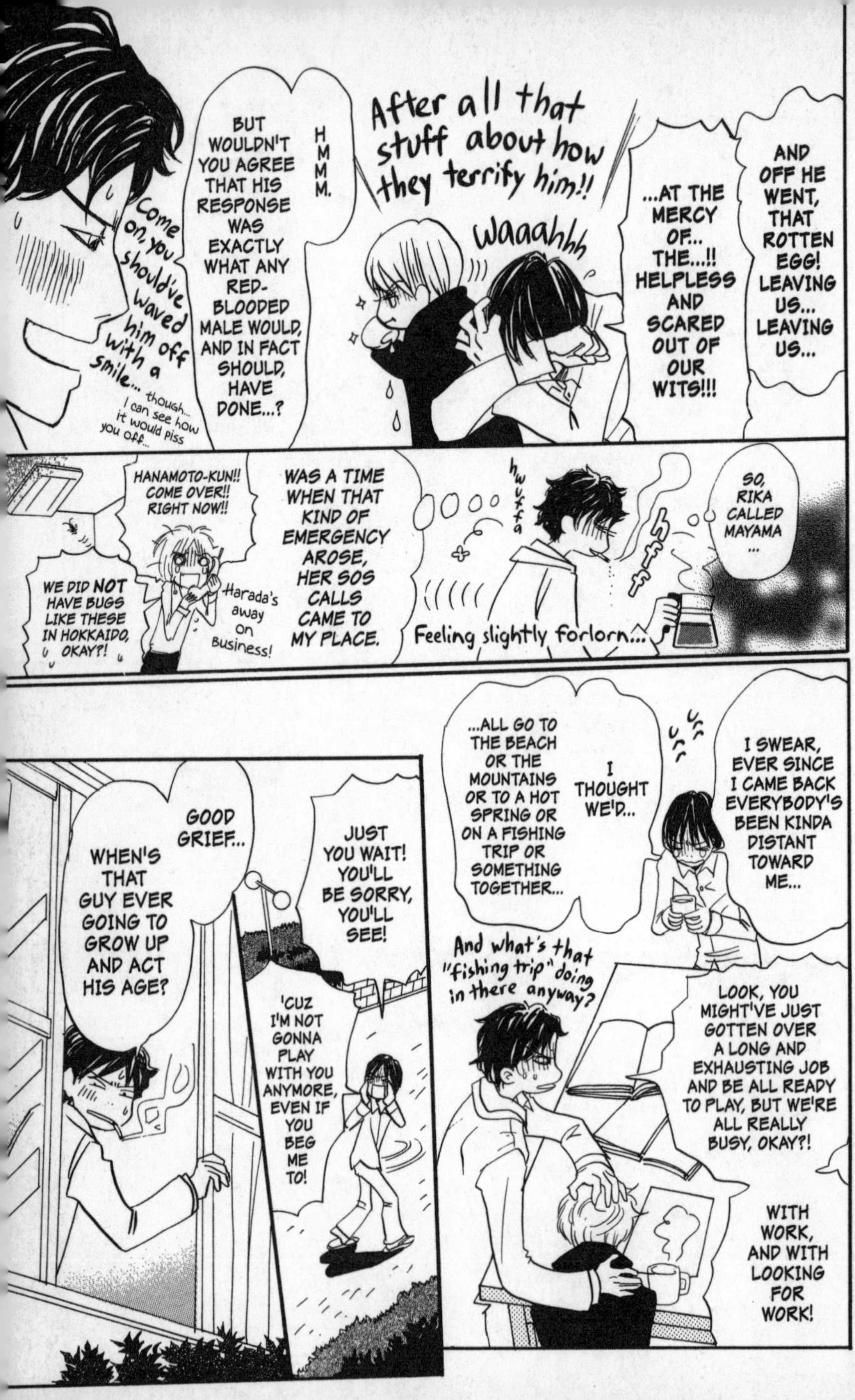
AND OFF HE WENT, THAT ROTTEN EGG! LEAVING US... LEAVING US...
...AT THE MERCY OF... THE...!! HELPLESS AND SCARED OUT OF OUR WITS!!!
Waaahhh
After all that stuff about how they terrify him!!
HMMM.
BUT WOULDN'T YOU AGREE THAT HIS RESPONSE WAS EXACTLY WHAT ANY RED-BLOODED MALE WOULD, AND IN FACT SHOULD, HAVE DONE...?
Come on, you should've waved him off with a smile...
though... I can see how it would piss you off...
SO, RIKA CALLED MAYAMA ...
hwuffa
huff
Feeling slightly forlorn...
WAS A TIME WHEN THAT KIND OF EMERGENCY AROSE, HER SOS CALLS CAME TO MY PLACE.
HANAMOTO-KUN!! COME OVER!! RIGHT NOW!!
Harada's away on Business!
WE DID NOT HAVE BUGS LIKE THESE IN HOKKAIDO, OKAY?!
I SWEAR, EVER SINCE I CAME BACK EVERYBODY'S BEEN KINDA DISTANT TOWARD ME...
urr urr
I THOUGHT WE'D...
...ALL GO TO THE BEACH OR THE MOUNTAINS OR TO A HOT SPRING OR ON A FISHING TRIP OR SOMETHING TOGETHER...
And what's that "fishing trip" doing in there anyway?
LOOK, YOU MIGHT'VE JUST GOTTEN OVER A LONG AND EXHAUSTING JOB AND BE ALL READY TO PLAY, BUT WE'RE ALL REALLY BUSY, OKAY?!
WITH WORK, AND WITH LOOKING FOR WORK!
JUST YOU WAIT! YOU'LL BE SORRY, YOU'LL SEE!
'CUZ I'M NOT GONNA PLAY WITH YOU ANYMORE, EVEN IF YOU BEG ME TO!
GOOD GRIEF...
WHEN'S THAT GUY EVER GOING TO GROW UP AND ACT HIS AGE?

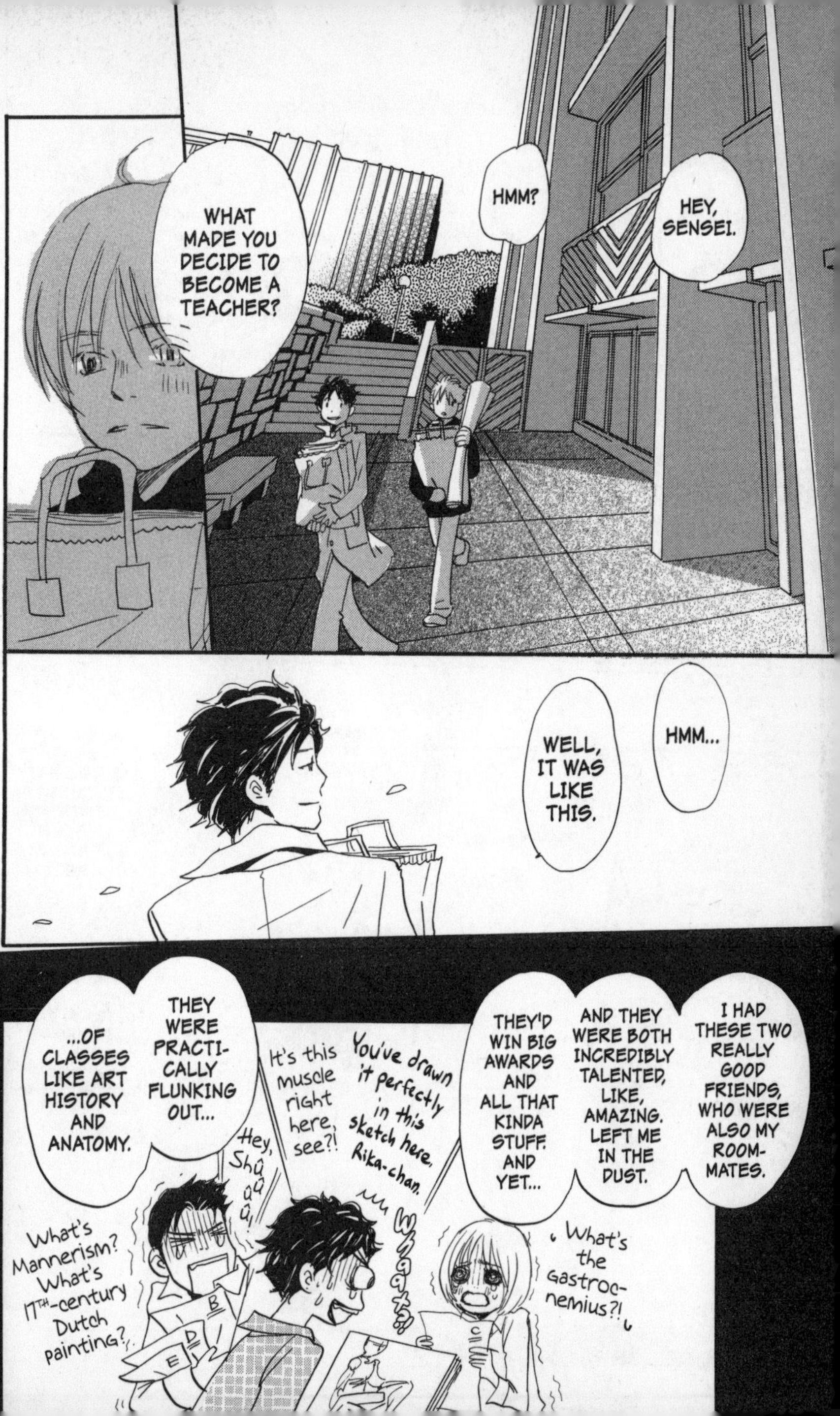
HEY, SENSEI.
HMM?
WHAT MADE YOU DECIDE TO BECOME A TEACHER?
HMM...
WELL, IT WAS LIKE THIS.
I HAD THESE TWO REALLY GOOD FRIENDS, WHO WERE ALSO MY ROOM-MATES.
AND THEY WERE BOTH INCREDIBLY TALENTED, LIKE, AMAZING. LEFT ME IN THE DUST.
THEY'D WIN BIG AWARDS AND ALL THAT KINDA STUFF. AND YET...
What's the Gastroc-nemius?!
Whaaat?!
You've drawn it perfectly in this sketch here, Rika-chan.
It's this muscle right here, see?!
THEY WERE PRACTI-CALLY FLUNKING OUT...
...OF CLASSES LIKE ART HISTORY AND ANATOMY.
Hey, Shûûûû!
What's Mannerism? What's 17TH-century Dutch painting?

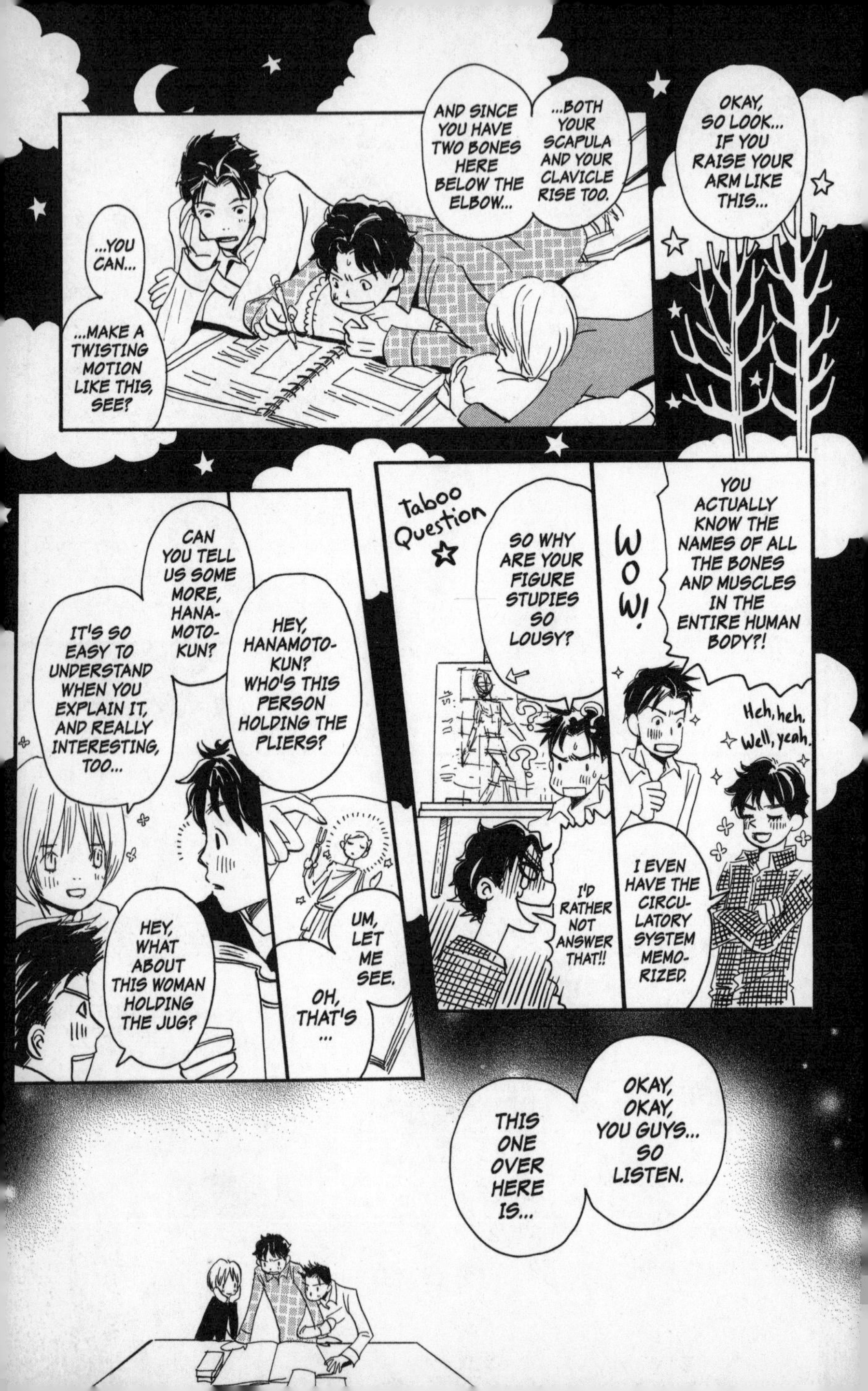
OKAY, SO LOOK... IF YOU RAISE YOUR ARM LIKE THIS...
...BOTH YOUR SCAPULA AND YOUR CLAVICLE RISE TOO.
AND SINCE YOU HAVE TWO BONES HERE BELOW THE ELBOW...
...YOU CAN...
...MAKE A TWISTING MOTION LIKE THIS, SEE?
YOU ACTUALLY KNOW THE NAMES OF ALL THE BONES AND MUSCLES IN THE ENTIRE HUMAN BODY?!
WOW!
Heh, heh. Well, yeah.
I EVEN HAVE THE CIRCULATORY SYSTEM MEMORIZED.
Taboo Question
SO WHY ARE YOUR FIGURE STUDIES SO LOUSY?
I'D RATHER NOT ANSWER THAT!!
HEY, HANAMOTO-KUN? WHO'S THIS PERSON HOLDING THE PLIERS?
UM, LET ME SEE.
OH, THAT'S ...
CAN YOU TELL US SOME MORE, HANAMOTO-KUN?
IT'S SO EASY TO UNDERSTAND WHEN YOU EXPLAIN IT, AND REALLY INTERESTING, TOO...
HEY, WHAT ABOUT THIS WOMAN HOLDING THE JUG?
OKAY, OKAY, YOU GUYS... SO LISTEN.
THIS ONE OVER HERE IS...

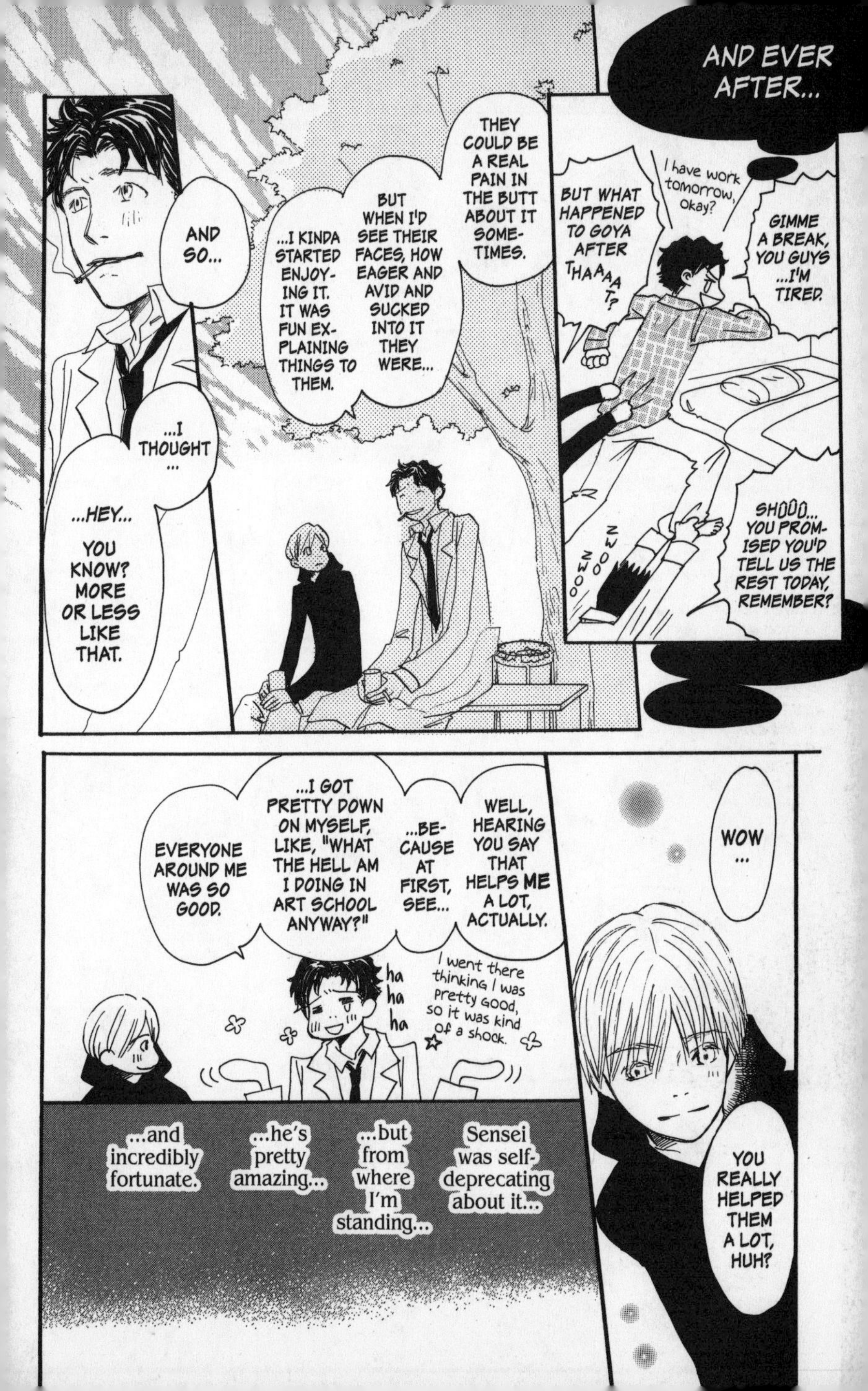
AND EVER AFTER...
GIMME A BREAK, YOU GUYS ...I'M TIRED.
I have work tomorrow, okay?
BUT WHAT HAPPENED TO GOYA AFTER THAAAAT?
SHOOO... YOU PROMISED YOU'D TELL US THE REST TODAY, REMEMBER?
ZWOO ZWOO
THEY COULD BE A REAL PAIN IN THE BUTT ABOUT IT SOMETIMES.
BUT WHEN I'D SEE THEIR FACES, HOW EAGER AND AVID AND SUCKED INTO IT THEY WERE...
...I KINDA STARTED ENJOYING IT. IT WAS FUN EXPLAINING THINGS TO THEM.
AND SO...
...I THOUGHT...
...HEY... YOU KNOW? MORE OR LESS LIKE THAT.
WOW...
YOU REALLY HELPED THEM A LOT, HUH?
WELL, HEARING YOU SAY THAT HELPS ME A LOT, ACTUALLY.
...BECAUSE AT FIRST, SEE...
...I GOT PRETTY DOWN ON MYSELF, LIKE, "WHAT THE HELL AM I DOING IN ART SCHOOL ANYWAY?"
EVERYONE AROUND ME WAS SO GOOD.
I went there thinking I was pretty good, so it was kind of a shock.
ha ha ha
Sensei was self-deprecating about it...
...but from where I'm standing...
...he's pretty amazing...
...and incredibly fortunate.

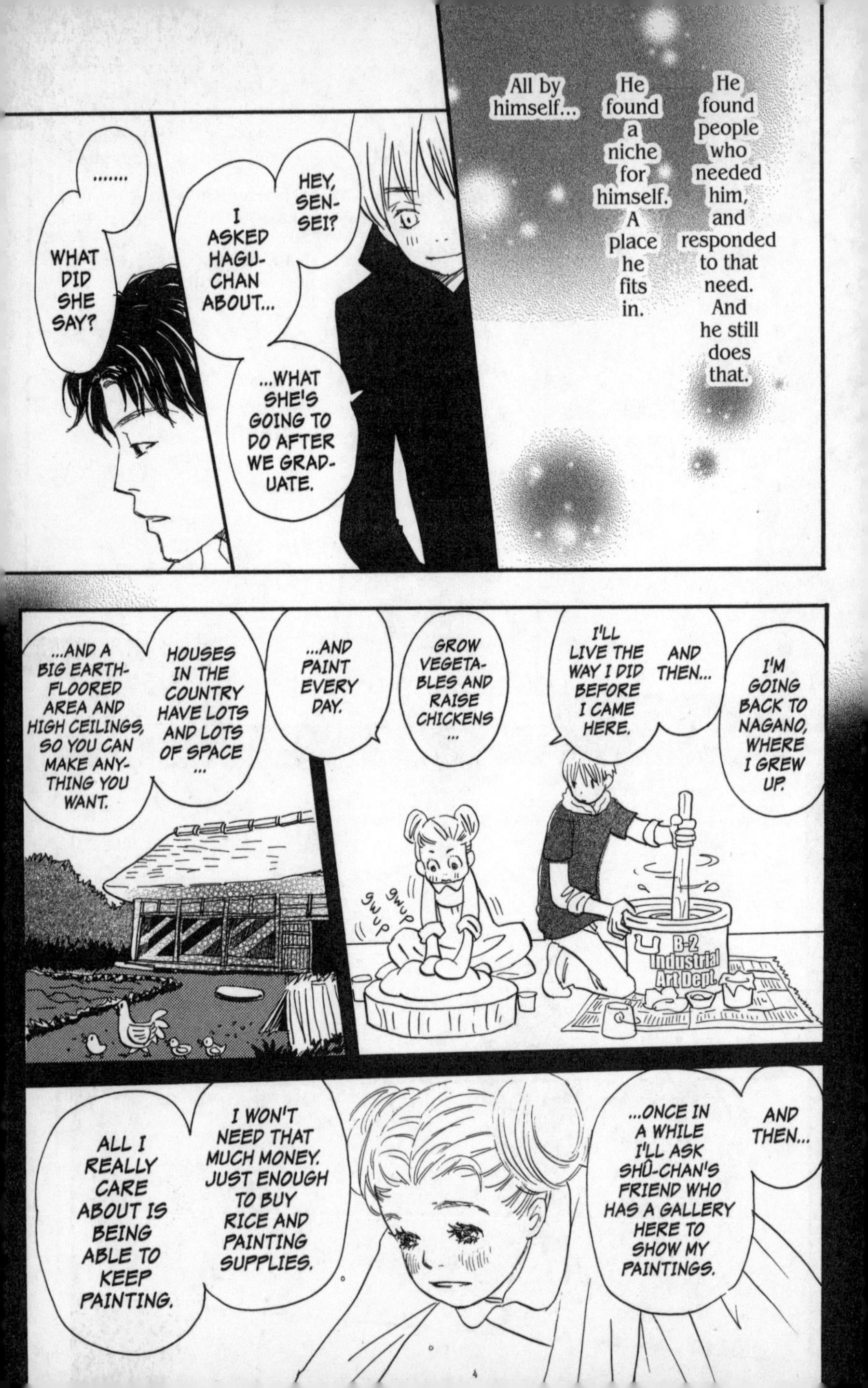
He found people who needed him, and responded to that need. And he still does that.
He found a niche for himself. A place he fits in.
All by himself...
HEY, SENSEI?
I ASKED HAGU-CHAN ABOUT...
...WHAT SHE'S GOING TO DO AFTER WE GRADUATE.
....
WHAT DID SHE SAY?
I'M GOING BACK TO NAGANO, WHERE I GREW UP.
AND THEN...
I'LL LIVE THE WAY I DID BEFORE I CAME HERE.
GROW VEGETABLES AND RAISE CHICKENS...
...AND PAINT EVERY DAY.
B-2 Industrial Art Dept.
gwup gwup
HOUSES IN THE COUNTRY HAVE LOTS AND LOTS OF SPACE...
...AND A BIG EARTH-FLOORED AREA AND HIGH CEILINGS, SO YOU CAN MAKE ANYTHING YOU WANT.
AND THEN...
...ONCE IN A WHILE I'LL ASK SHÛ-CHAN'S FRIEND WHO HAS A GALLERY HERE TO SHOW MY PAINTINGS.
I WON'T NEED THAT MUCH MONEY. JUST ENOUGH TO BUY RICE AND PAINTING SUPPLIES.
ALL I REALLY CARE ABOUT IS BEING ABLE TO KEEP PAINTING.

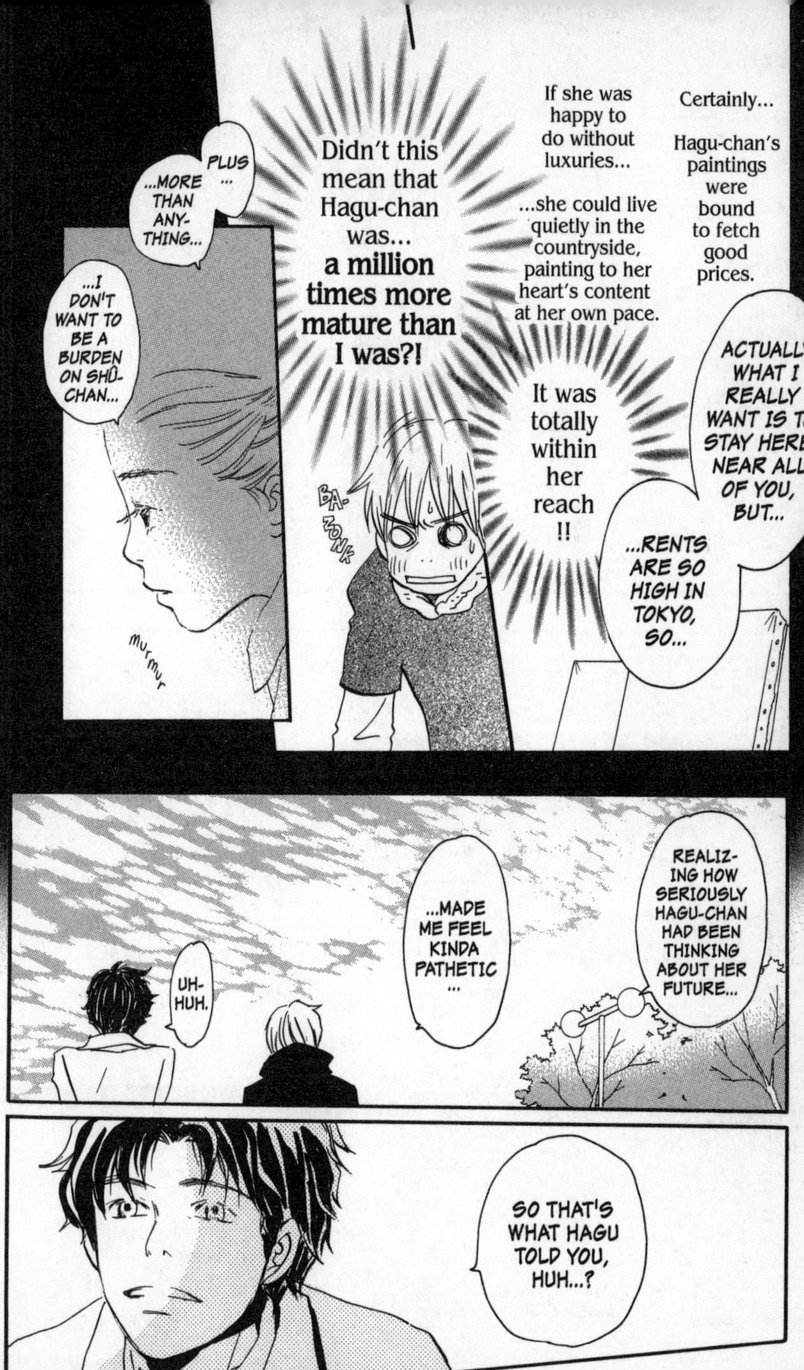
Certainly...
Hagu-chan's paintings were bound to fetch good prices.
If she was happy to do without luxuries...
...she could live quietly in the countryside, painting to her heart's content at her own pace.
ACTUALLY, WHAT I REALLY WANT IS TO STAY HERE NEAR ALL OF YOU, BUT...
...RENTS ARE SO HIGH IN TOKYO, SO...
It was totally within her reach !!
Didn't this mean that Hagu-chan was... **a million times more mature than I was?!**
BA-ZONK
PLUS...
...MORE THAN ANYTHING...
...I DON'T WANT TO BE A BURDEN ON SHÛ-CHAN...
Murmur
REALIZING HOW SERIOUSLY HAGU-CHAN HAD BEEN THINKING ABOUT HER FUTURE...
...MADE ME FEEL KINDA PATHETIC...
UH-HUH.
SO THAT'S WHAT HAGU TOLD YOU, HUH...?

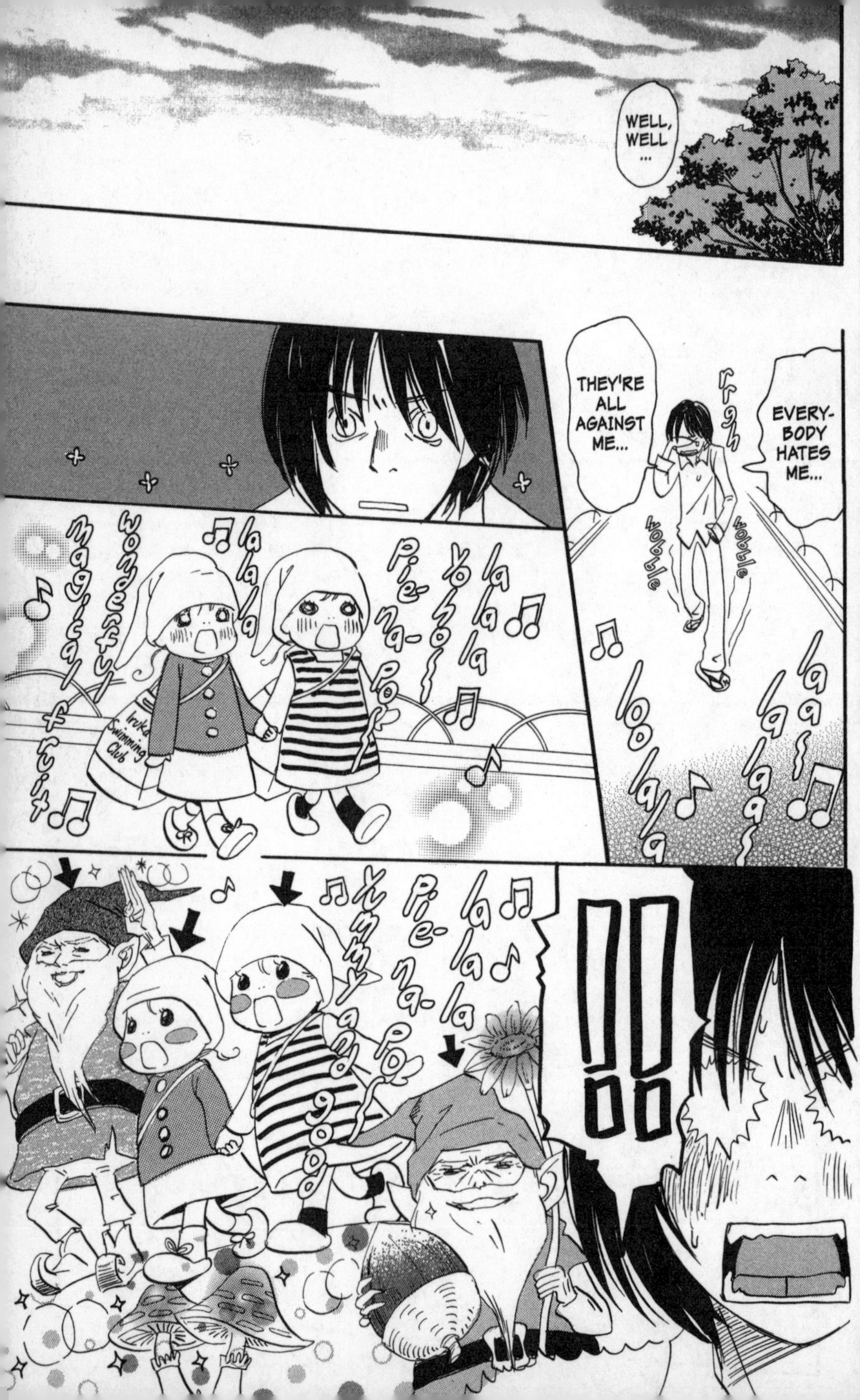
WELL, WELL ...
EVERY-BODY HATES ME...
rrgh
THEY'RE ALL AGAINST ME...
wobble
wobble
la~ la la~ las~
loo lala
la la la
Yo ho~!
Pie-na-po~
la la la
wonderful
magical fruit
!!
la la la
Pie-na-la
Yummy and po~
good
Iruka Swimming Club

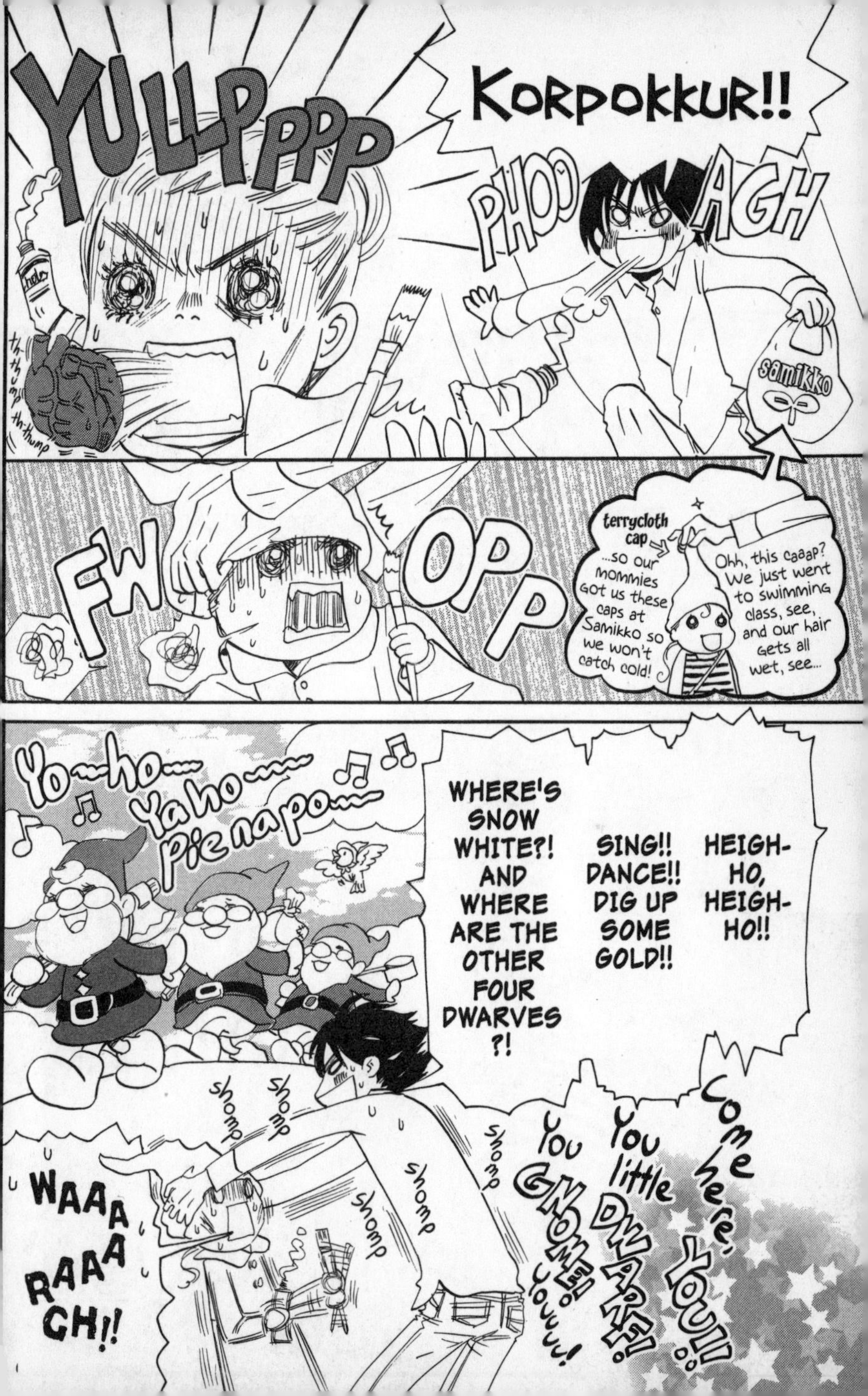
Korpokkur!!
PHOOAGH
YULLPPPP
th-thump th-thump
samikko
Ohh, this caaap? We just went to swimming class, see, and our hair gets all wet, see...
terrycloth cap
...so our mommies got us these caps at Samikko so we won't catch cold!
FWOPP
HEIGH-HO, HEIGH-HO!!
SING!! DANCE!! DIG UP SOME GOLD!!
WHERE'S SNOW WHITE?! AND WHERE ARE THE OTHER FOUR DWARVES?!
Yo~ho~ Ya ho~ Pie na po~
Come here, YOU!!
You little DWARF!!
You GNOME!! Youuuu!
shomp shomp
shomp shomp shomp
WAAAARAAAAGH!!

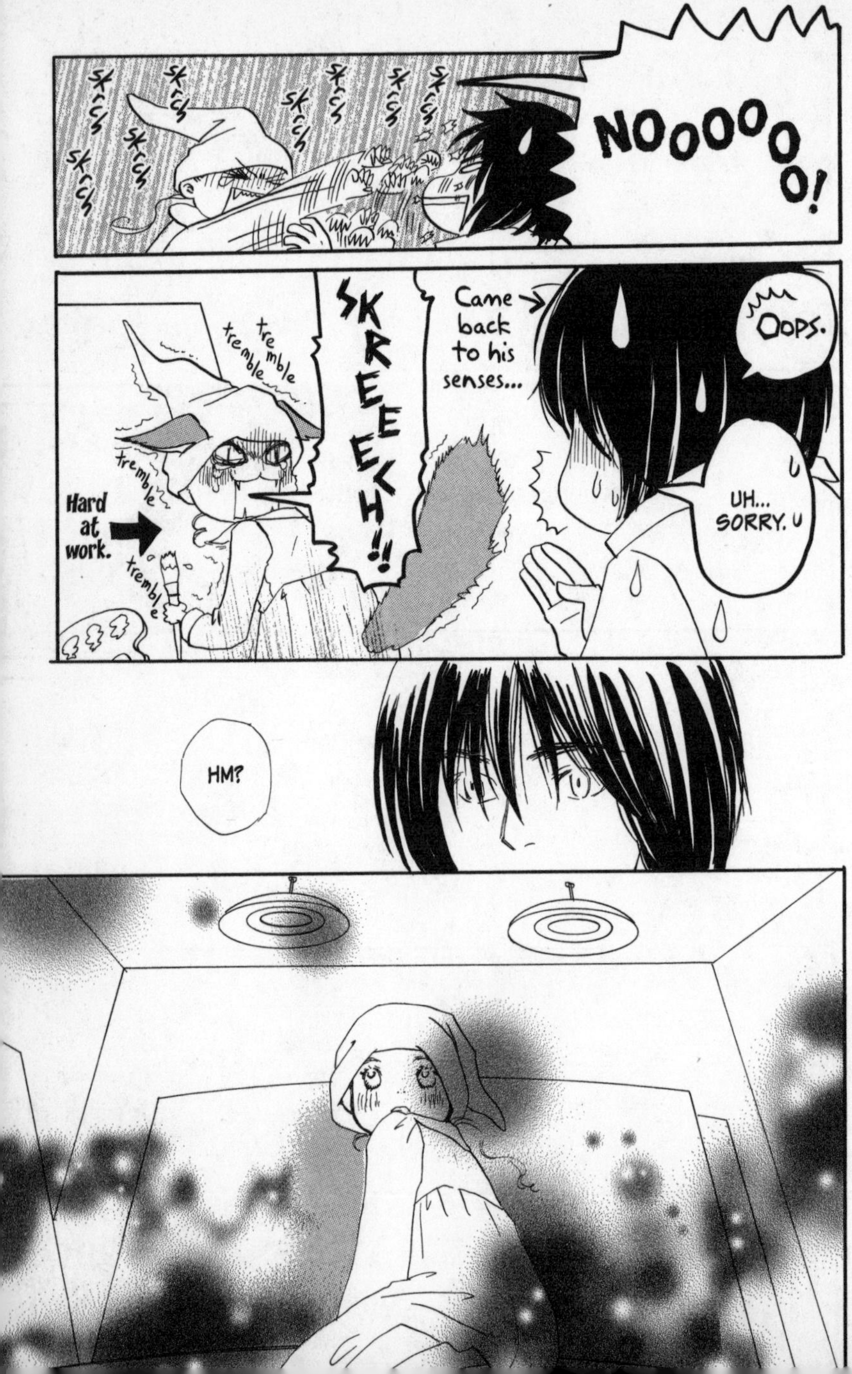
NOOOOOO!
skrch skrch skrch skrch skrch skrch skrch
OOPS.
UH... SORRY.
Came back to his senses...
SKREEEECH!!
tremble tremble
tremble
tremble
Hard at work.
HM?

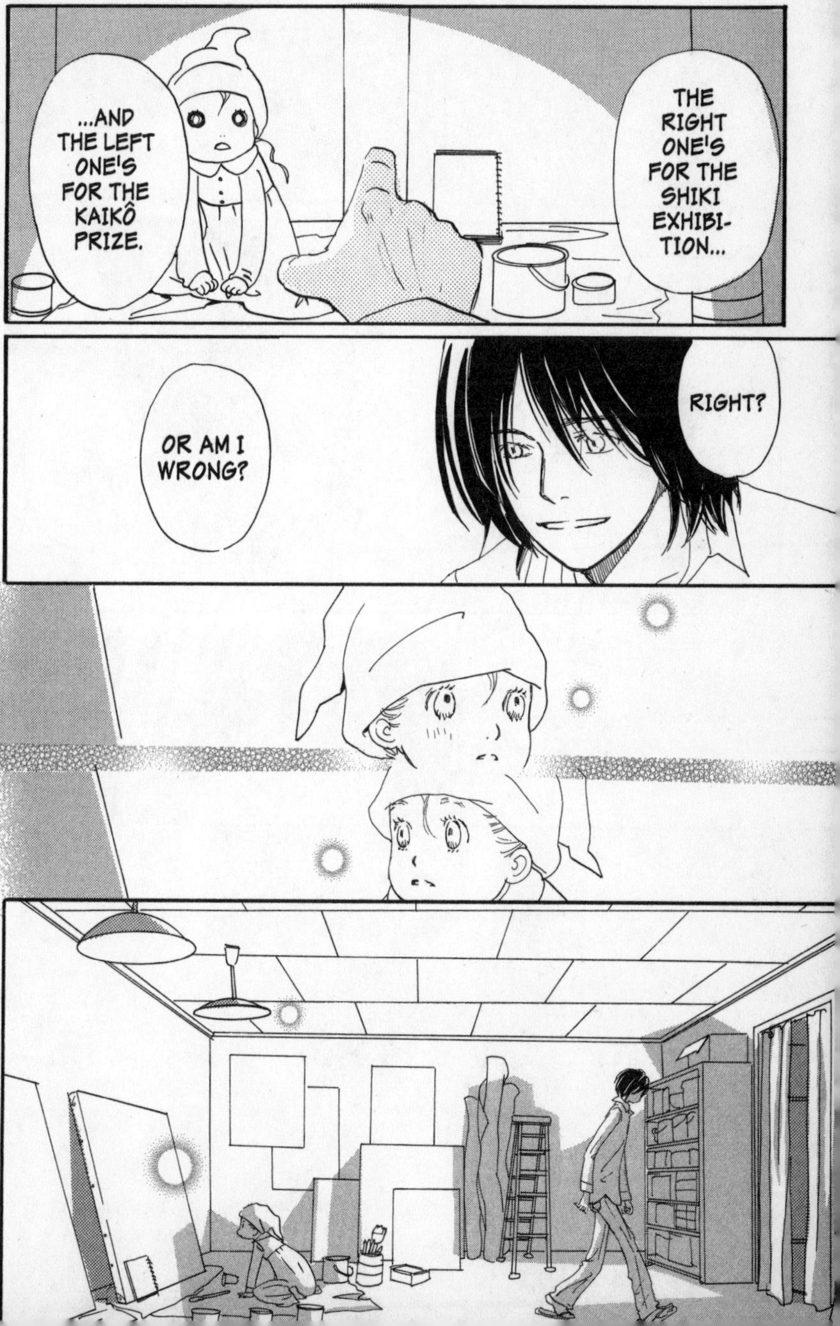
THE RIGHT ONE'S FOR THE SHIKI EXHIBI- TION...
...AND THE LEFT ONE'S FOR THE KAIKÔ PRIZE.
RIGHT?
OR AM I WRONG?

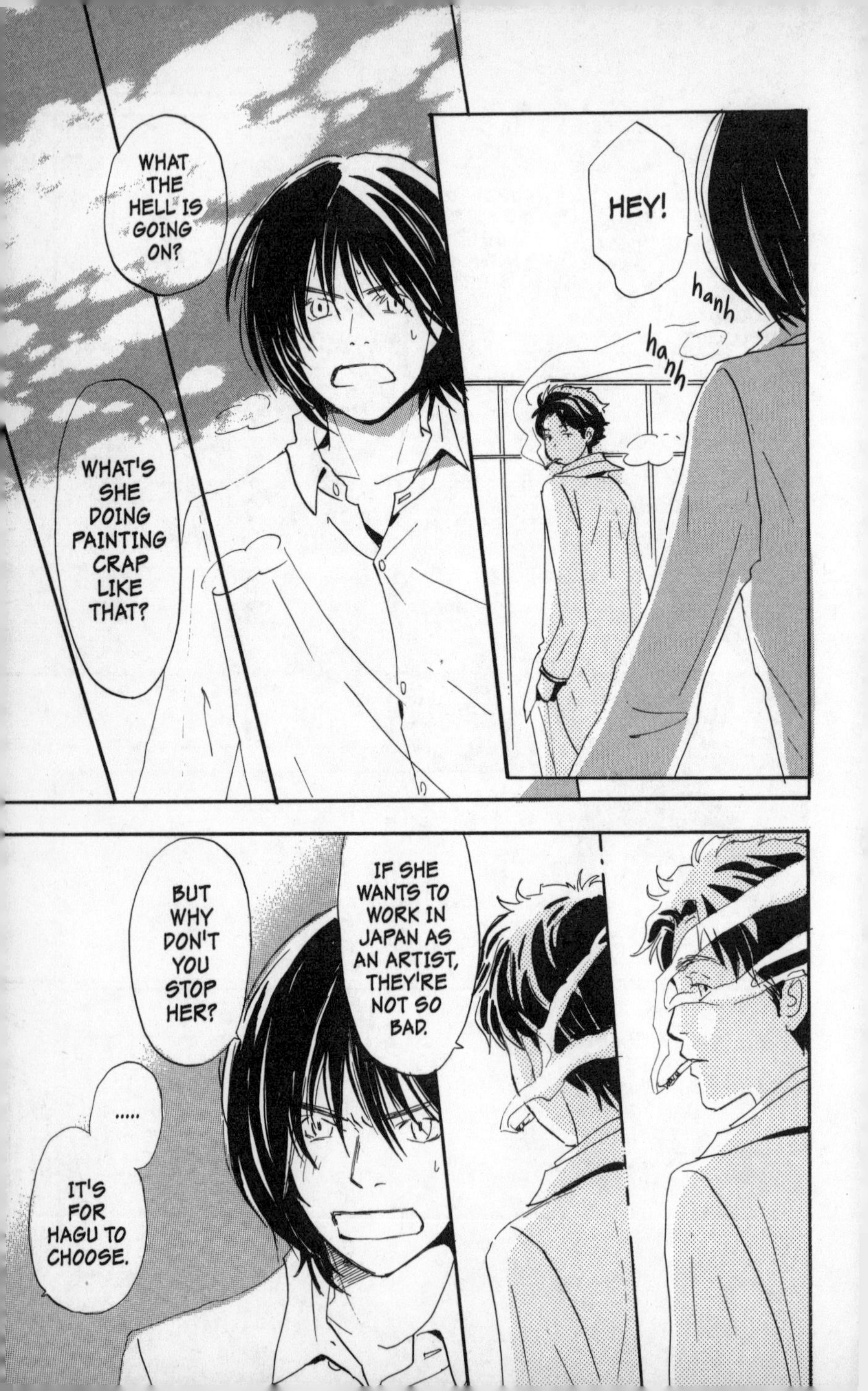
HEY!
hanh hanh
WHAT THE HELL IS GOING ON?
WHAT'S SHE DOING PAINTING CRAP LIKE THAT?
IF SHE WANTS TO WORK IN JAPAN AS AN ARTIST, THEY'RE NOT SO BAD.
BUT WHY DON'T YOU STOP HER?
.....
IT'S FOR HAGU TO CHOOSE.

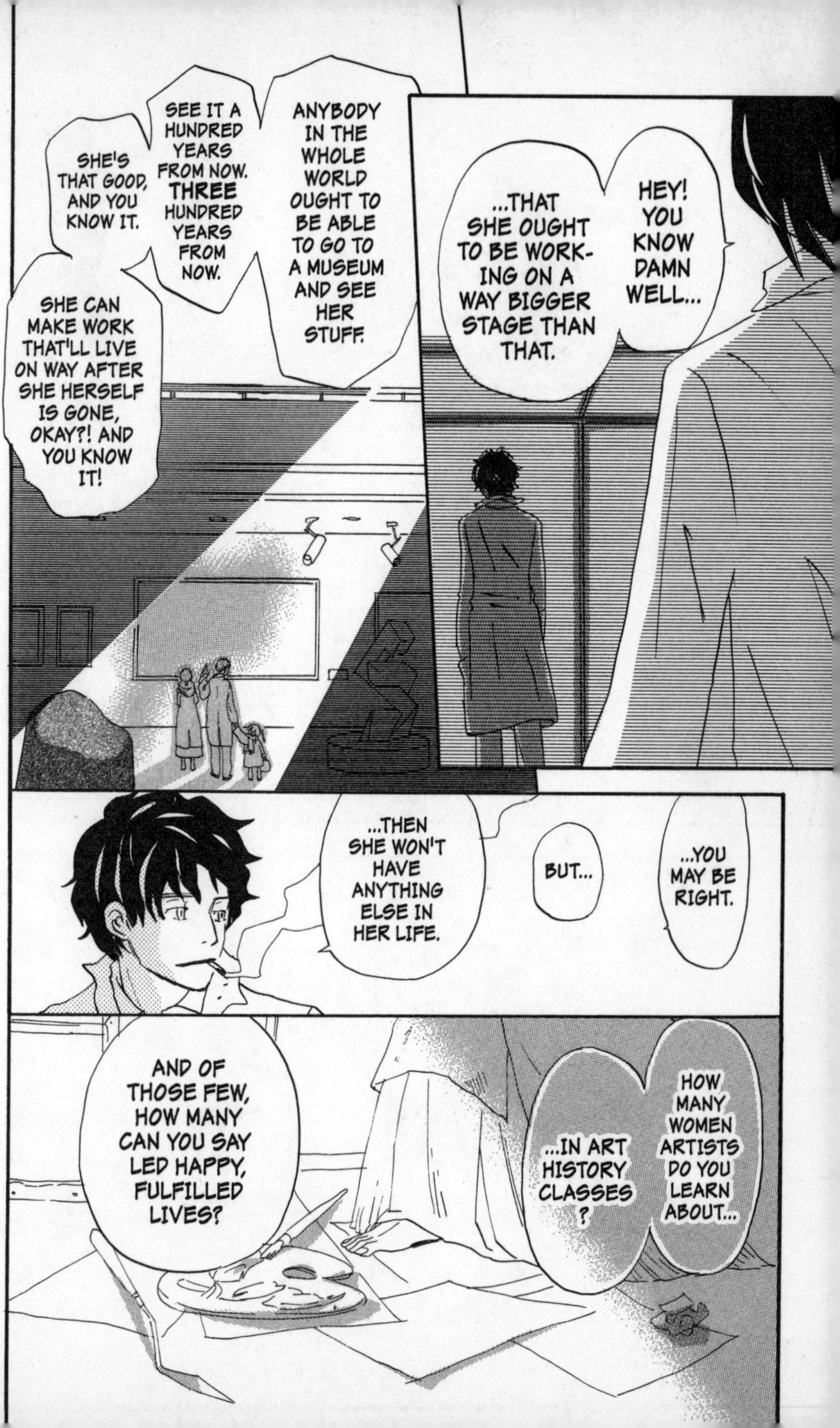
HEY! YOU KNOW DAMN WELL...
...THAT SHE OUGHT TO BE WORK-ING ON A WAY BIGGER STAGE THAN THAT.
ANYBODY IN THE WHOLE WORLD OUGHT TO BE ABLE TO GO TO A MUSEUM AND SEE HER STUFF.
SEE IT A HUNDRED YEARS FROM NOW. THREE HUNDRED YEARS FROM NOW.
SHE'S THAT GOOD, AND YOU KNOW IT.
SHE CAN MAKE WORK THAT'LL LIVE ON WAY AFTER SHE HERSELF IS GONE, OKAY?! AND YOU KNOW IT!
...YOU MAY BE RIGHT.
BUT...
...THEN SHE WON'T HAVE ANYTHING ELSE IN HER LIFE.
HOW MANY WOMEN ARTISTS DO YOU LEARN ABOUT...
...IN ART HISTORY CLASSES?
AND OF THOSE FEW, HOW MANY CAN YOU SAY LED HAPPY, FULFILLED LIVES?

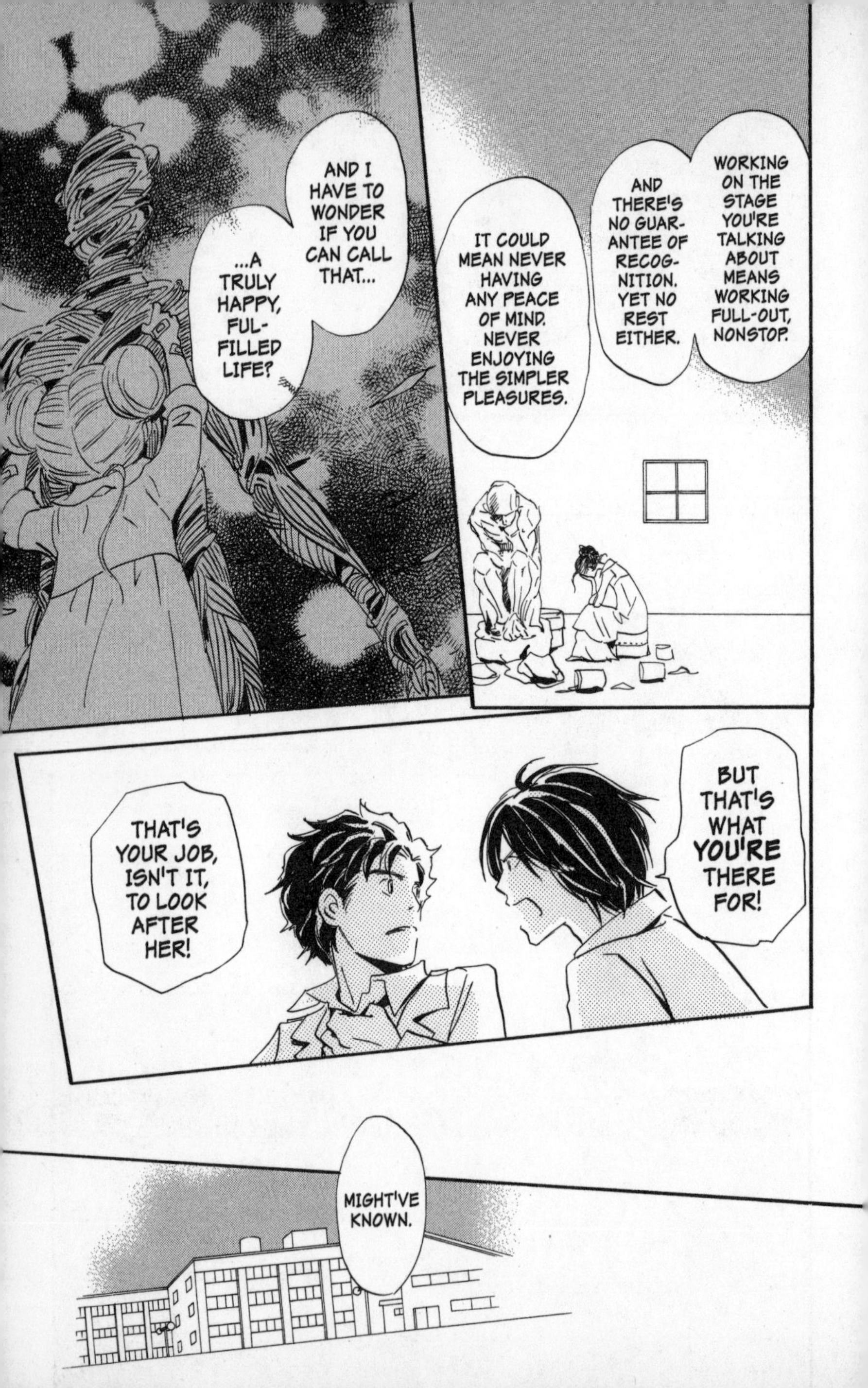
WORKING ON THE STAGE YOU'RE TALKING ABOUT MEANS WORKING FULL-OUT, NONSTOP.
AND THERE'S NO GUAR-ANTEE OF RECOG-NITION. YET NO REST EITHER.
IT COULD MEAN NEVER HAVING ANY PEACE OF MIND. NEVER ENJOYING THE SIMPLER PLEASURES.
AND I HAVE TO WONDER IF YOU CAN CALL THAT...
...A TRULY HAPPY, FUL-FILLED LIFE?
BUT THAT'S WHAT **YOU'RE** THERE FOR!
THAT'S YOUR JOB, ISN'T IT, TO LOOK AFTER HER!
MIGHT'VE KNOWN.

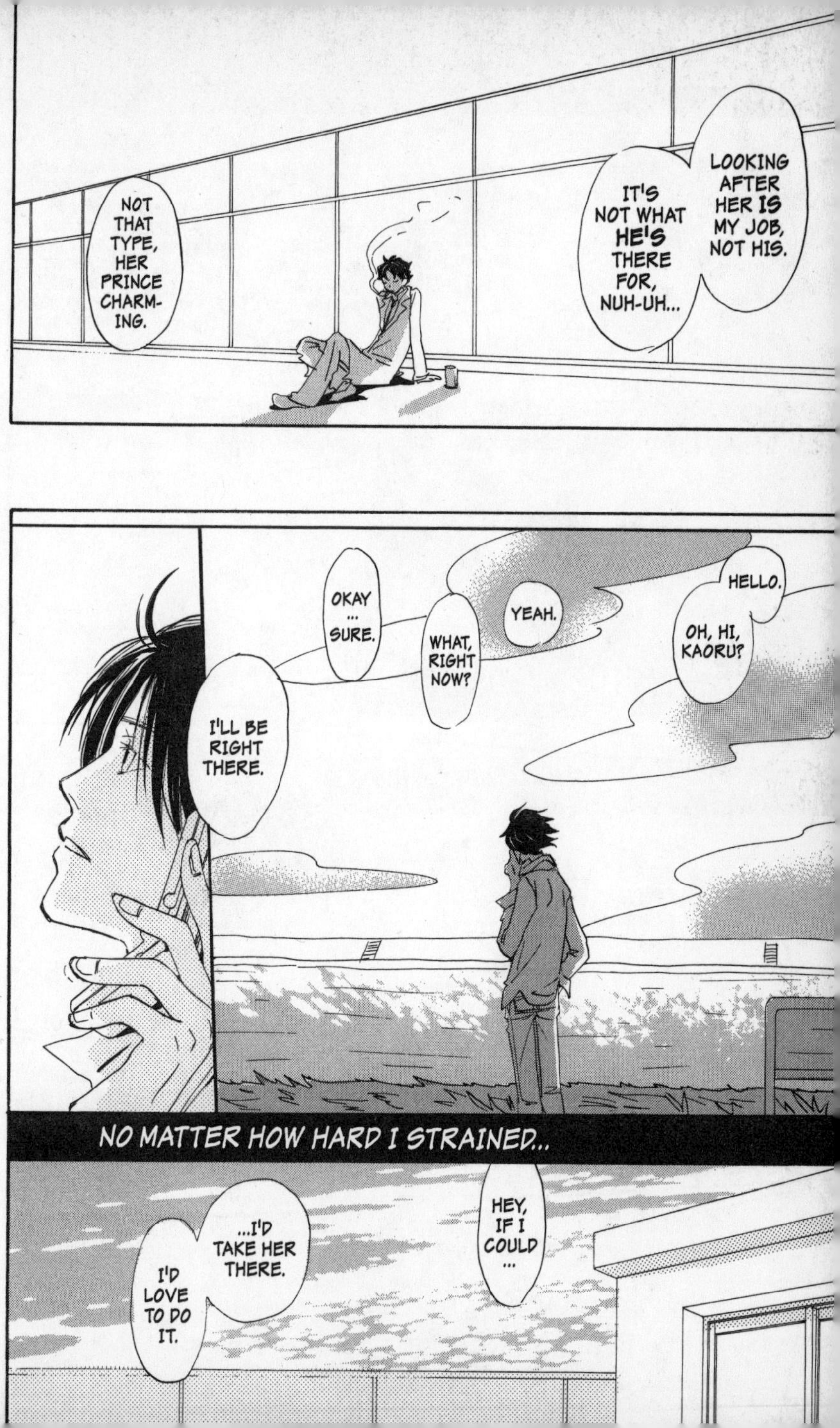
LOOKING AFTER HER IS MY JOB, NOT HIS.
IT'S NOT WHAT HE'S THERE FOR, NUH-UH...
NOT THAT TYPE, HER PRINCE CHARMING.
HELLO.
OH, HI, KAORU?
YEAH.
WHAT, RIGHT NOW?
OKAY ... SURE.
I'LL BE RIGHT THERE.
NO MATTER HOW HARD I STRAINED...
HEY, IF I COULD ...
...I'D TAKE HER THERE.
I'D LOVE TO DO IT.

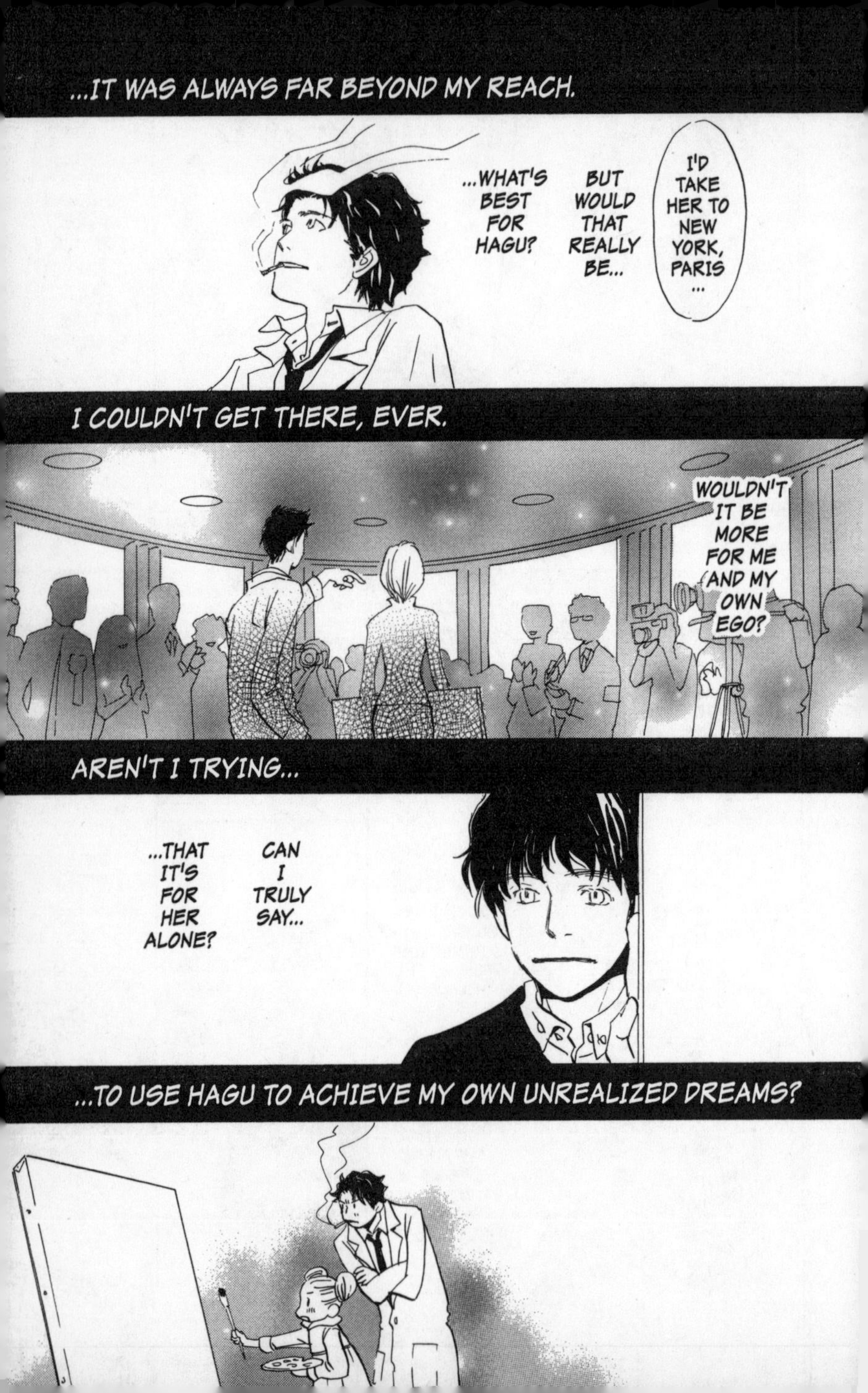
...IT WAS ALWAYS FAR BEYOND MY REACH.
I'D TAKE HER TO NEW YORK, PARIS ...
BUT WOULD THAT REALLY BE...
...WHAT'S BEST FOR HAGU?
I COULDN'T GET THERE, EVER.
WOULDN'T IT BE MORE FOR ME AND MY OWN EGO?
AREN'T I TRYING...
CAN I TRULY SAY...
...THAT IT'S FOR HER ALONE?
...TO USE HAGU TO ACHIEVE MY OWN UNREALIZED DREAMS?

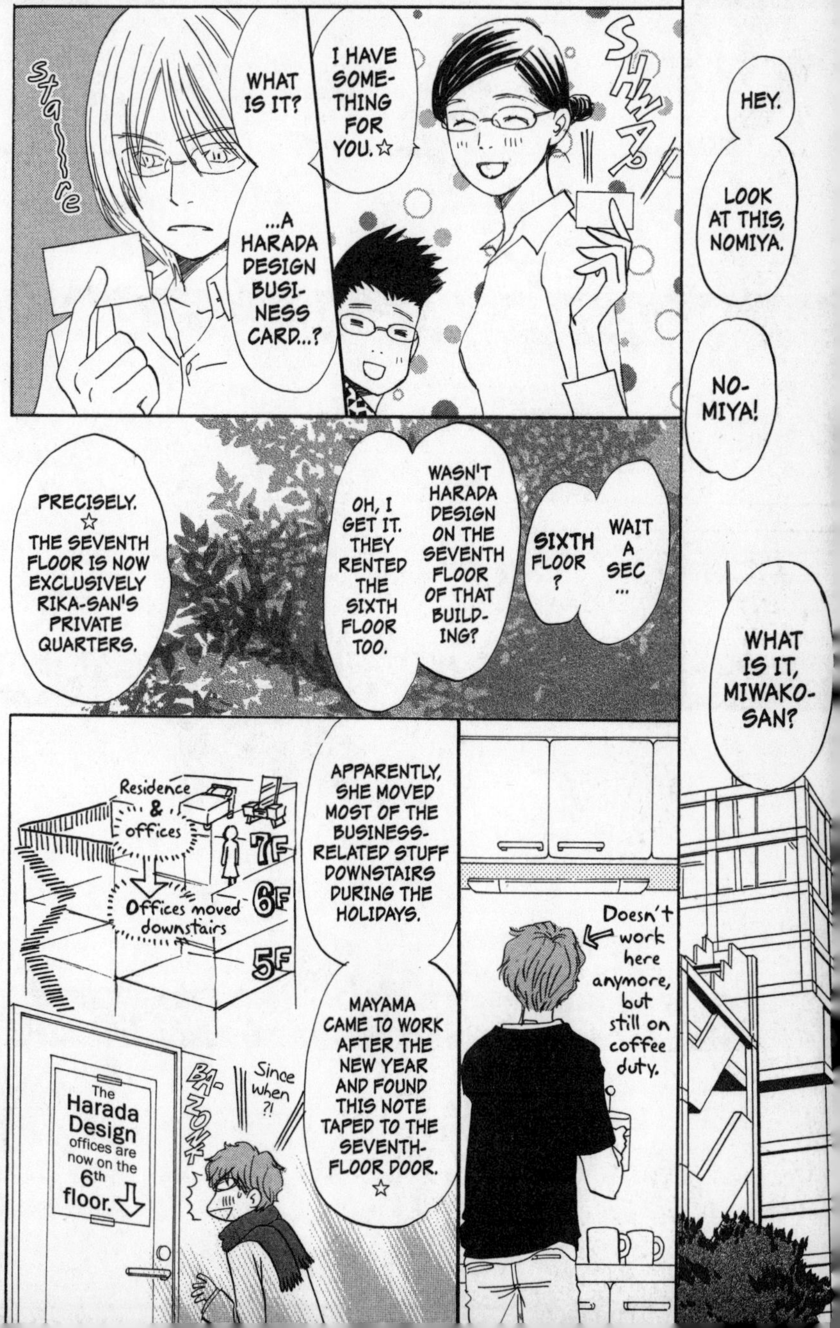
HEY.
LOOK AT THIS, NOMIYA.
NO-MIYA!
WHAT IS IT, MIWAKO-SAN?
SHWAP
I HAVE SOME-THING FOR YOU.☆
WHAT IS IT?
...A HARADA DESIGN BUSI-NESS CARD...?
Sta~~re
WAIT A SEC...
SIXTH FLOOR?
WASN'T HARADA DESIGN ON THE SEVENTH FLOOR OF THAT BUILD-ING?
OH, I GET IT. THEY RENTED THE SIXTH FLOOR TOO.
PRECISELY.☆ THE SEVENTH FLOOR IS NOW EXCLUSIVELY RIKA-SAN'S PRIVATE QUARTERS.
APPARENTLY, SHE MOVED MOST OF THE BUSINESS-RELATED STUFF DOWNSTAIRS DURING THE HOLIDAYS.
Doesn't work here anymore, but still on coffee duty.
Residence & offices
7F
6F
5F
Offices moved downstairs
MAYAMA CAME TO WORK AFTER THE NEW YEAR AND FOUND THIS NOTE TAPED TO THE SEVENTH-FLOOR DOOR.☆
The Harada Design offices are now on the 6th floor.
BA-ZONK
Since when?!

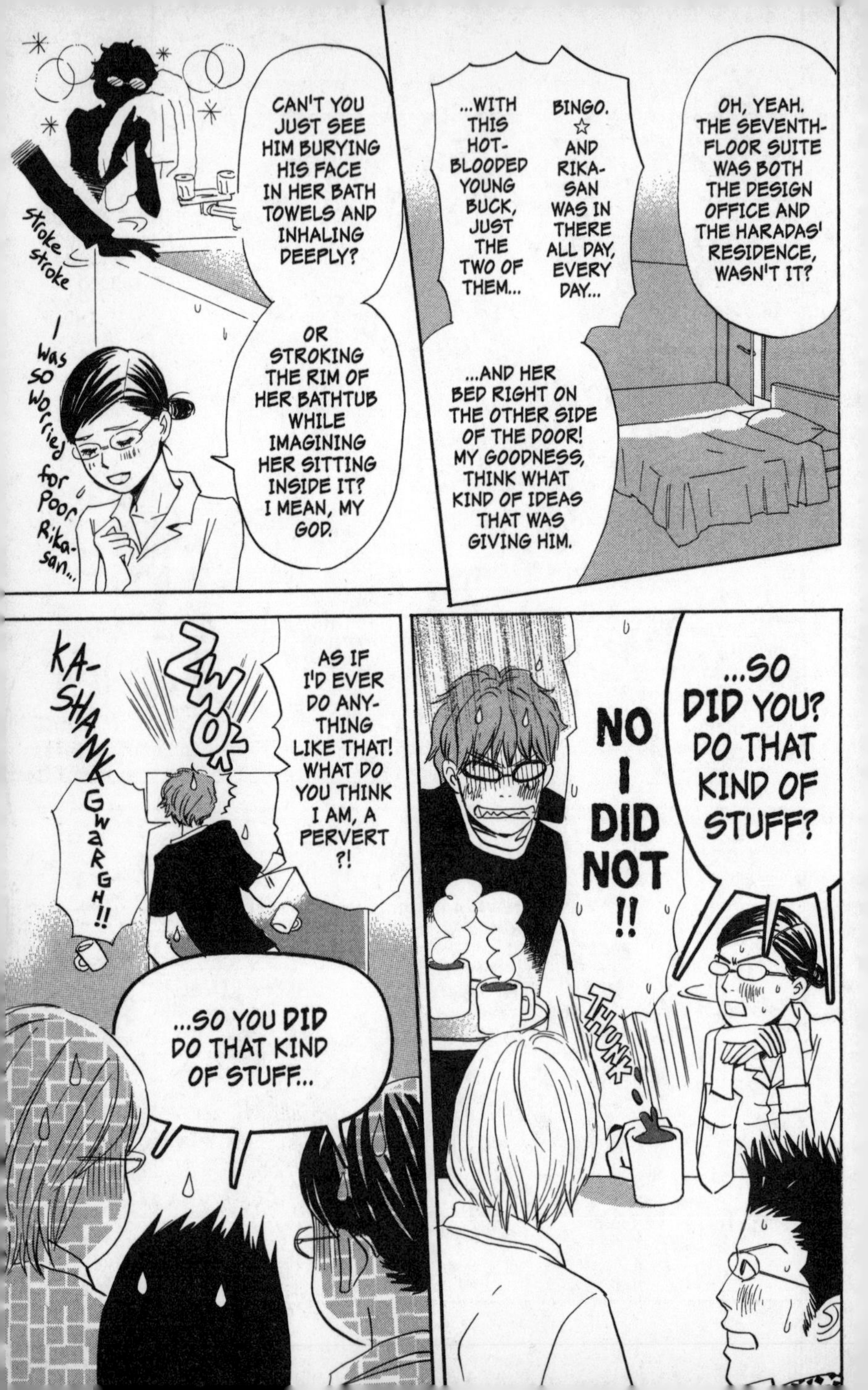
OH, YEAH. THE SEVENTH-FLOOR SUITE WAS BOTH THE DESIGN OFFICE AND THE HARADAS' RESIDENCE, WASN'T IT?
BINGO. ☆ AND RIKA-SAN WAS IN THERE ALL DAY, EVERY DAY...
...WITH THIS HOT-BLOODED YOUNG BUCK, JUST THE TWO OF THEM...
...AND HER BED RIGHT ON THE OTHER SIDE OF THE DOOR! MY GOODNESS, THINK WHAT KIND OF IDEAS THAT WAS GIVING HIM.
CAN'T YOU JUST SEE HIM BURYING HIS FACE IN HER BATH TOWELS AND INHALING DEEPLY?
stroke stroke
OR STROKING THE RIM OF HER BATHTUB WHILE IMAGINING HER SITTING INSIDE IT? I MEAN, MY GOD.
I was so worried for Poor Rika-san...
...SO DID YOU? DO THAT KIND OF STUFF?
NO I DID NOT!!
THUNK
ZWOK
AS IF I'D EVER DO ANYTHING LIKE THAT! WHAT DO YOU THINK I AM, A PERVERT?!
KA-SHANK
GWARGH!!
...SO YOU DID DO THAT KIND OF STUFF...

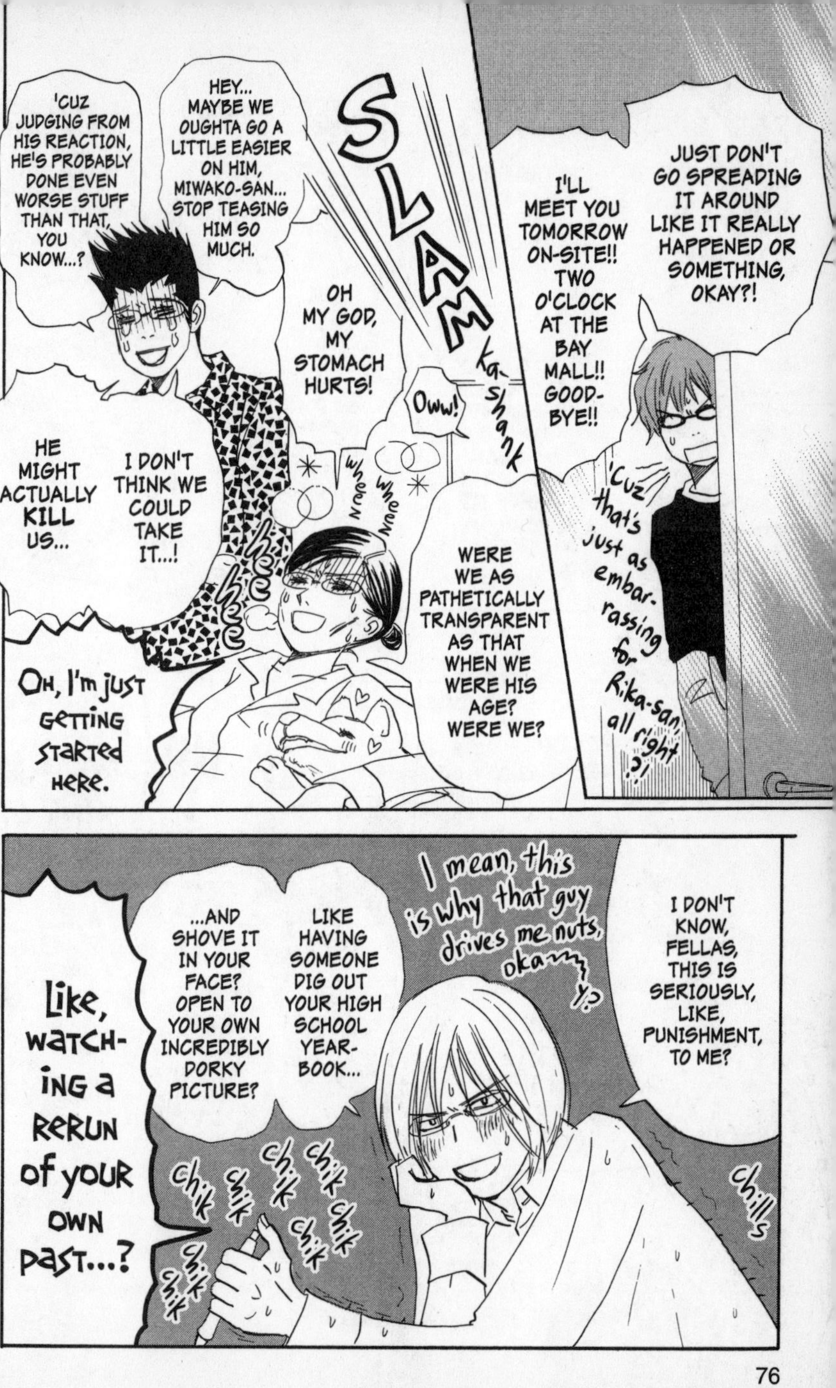
JUST DON'T GO SPREADING IT AROUND LIKE IT REALLY HAPPENED OR SOMETHING, OKAY?!
I'LL MEET YOU TOMORROW ON-SITE!! TWO O'CLOCK AT THE BAY MALL!! GOOD-BYE!!
'Cuz that's just as embar-rassing for Rika-san, all right?!
SLAM
ka-shank
HEY... MAYBE WE OUGHTA GO A LITTLE EASIER ON HIM, MIWAKO-SAN... STOP TEASING HIM SO MUCH.
'CUZ JUDGING FROM HIS REACTION, HE'S PROBABLY DONE EVEN WORSE STUFF THAN THAT, YOU KNOW...?
OH MY GOD, MY STOMACH HURTS!
Oww!
wheeen wheeen
WERE WE AS PATHETICALLY TRANSPARENT AS THAT WHEN WE WERE HIS AGE? WERE WE?
I DON'T THINK WE COULD TAKE IT...!
HE MIGHT ACTUALLY KILL US...
heheehee
Oh, I'm just getting started here.
I DON'T KNOW, FELLAS, THIS IS SERIOUSLY, LIKE, PUNISHMENT, TO ME?
I mean, this is why that guy drives me nuts, okay?
LIKE HAVING SOMEONE DIG OUT YOUR HIGH SCHOOL YEAR-BOOK...
...AND SHOVE IT IN YOUR FACE? OPEN TO YOUR OWN INCREDIBLY DORKY PICTURE?
Like, watch-ing a rerun of your own past...?
chills
chik chik chik chik chik chik chik chik chik

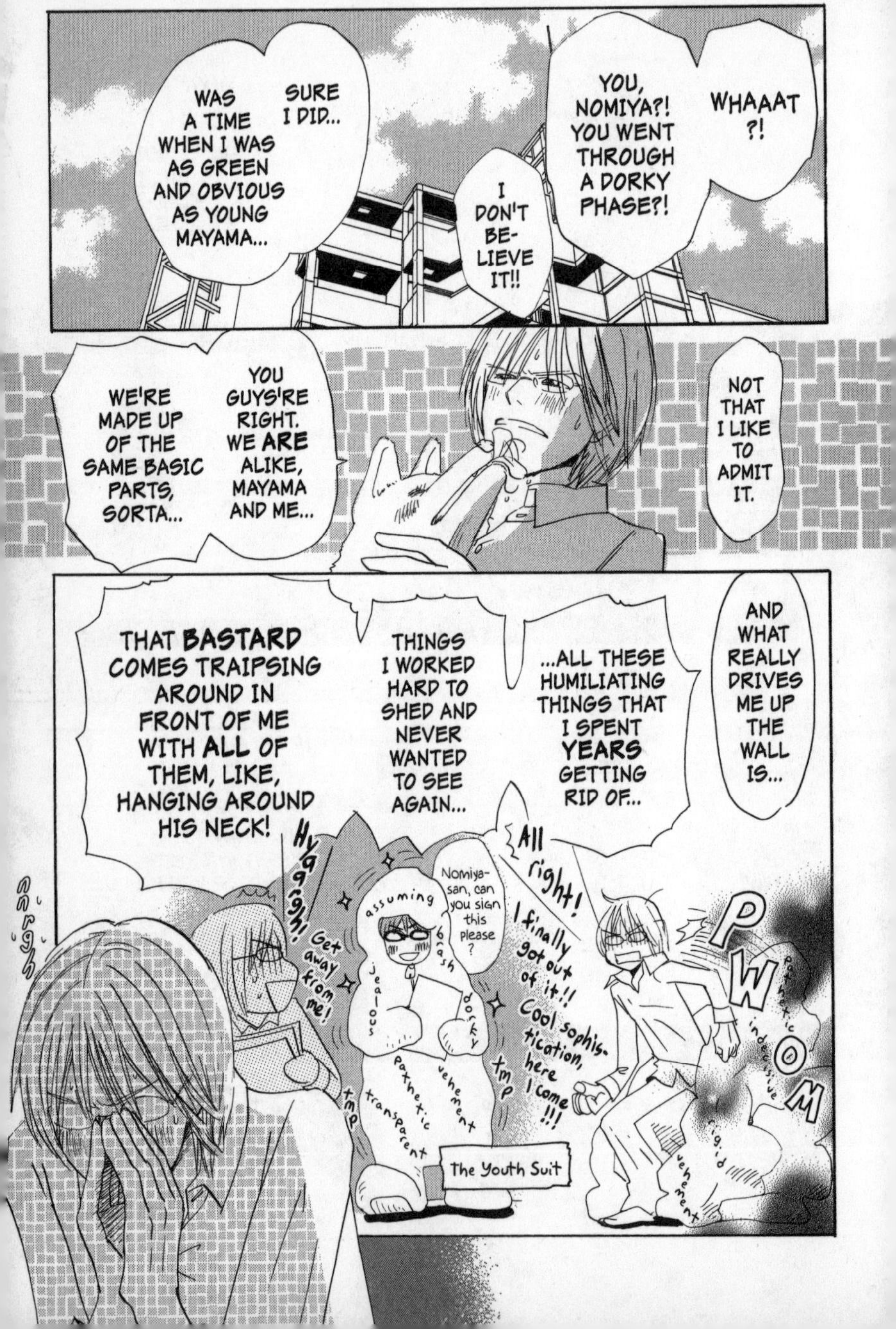
WHAAAT ?!
YOU, NOMIYA?! YOU WENT THROUGH A DORKY PHASE?!
I DON'T BE-LIEVE IT!!
SURE I DID...
WAS A TIME WHEN I WAS AS GREEN AND OBVIOUS AS YOUNG MAYAMA...
NOT THAT I LIKE TO ADMIT IT.
YOU GUYS'RE RIGHT. WE ARE ALIKE, MAYAMA AND ME...
WE'RE MADE UP OF THE SAME BASIC PARTS, SORTA...
AND WHAT REALLY DRIVES ME UP THE WALL IS...
...ALL THESE HUMILIATING THINGS THAT I SPENT YEARS GETTING RID OF...
THINGS I WORKED HARD TO SHED AND NEVER WANTED TO SEE AGAIN...
THAT BASTARD COMES TRAIPSING AROUND IN FRONT OF ME WITH ALL OF THEM, LIKE, HANGING AROUND HIS NECK!
PWOM
pathetic
indecisive
rigid
vehement
All right! I finally got out of it!! Cool sophis-tication, here I come!!!
Nomiya-san, can you sign this please?
assuming
brash
dorky
jealous
vehement
pathetic
transparent
tmp
tmp
The Youth Suit
Hyaargh!
Get away from me!
ergh

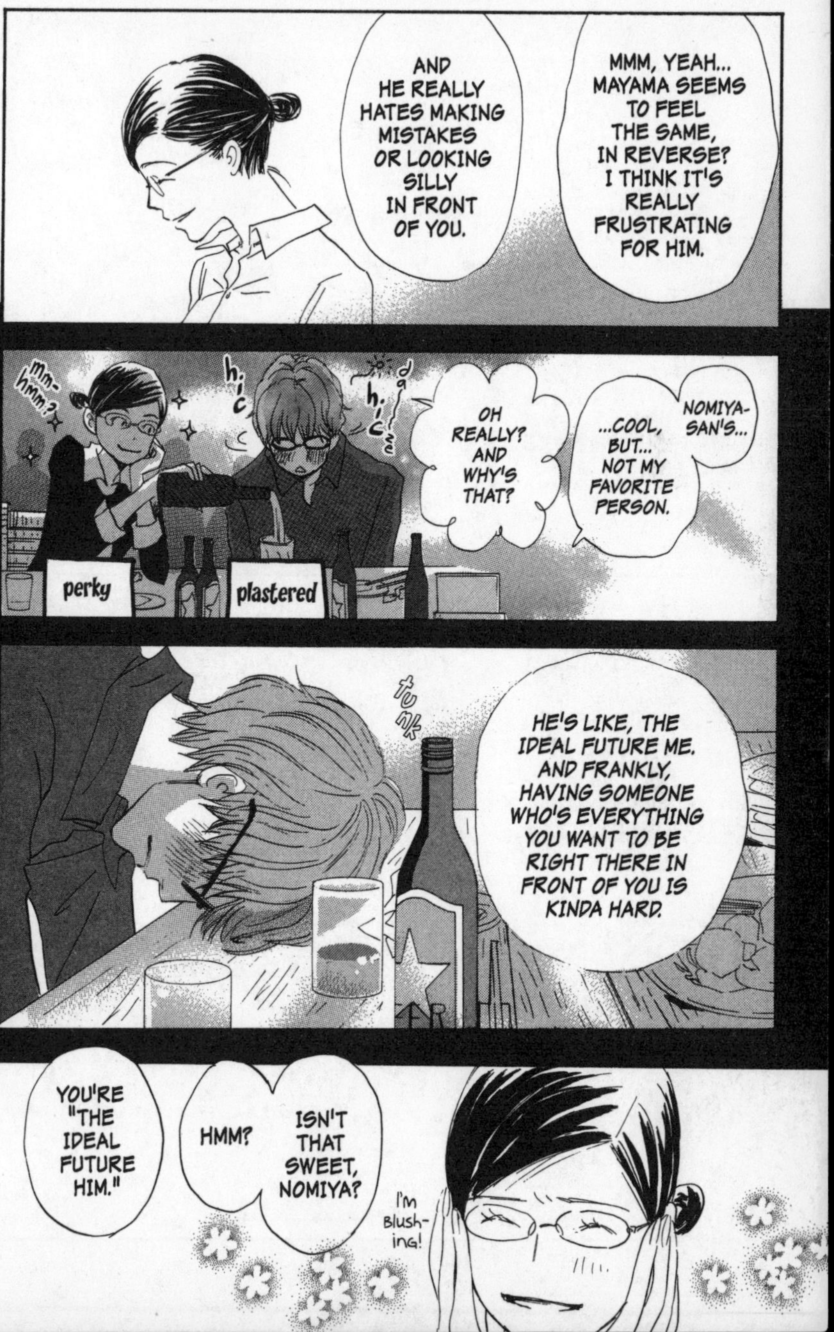
MMM, YEAH... MAYAMA SEEMS TO FEEL THE SAME, IN REVERSE? I THINK IT'S REALLY FRUSTRATING FOR HIM.
AND HE REALLY HATES MAKING MISTAKES OR LOOKING SILLY IN FRONT OF YOU.
NOMIYA-SAN'S...
...COOL, BUT... NOT MY FAVORITE PERSON.
OH REALLY? AND WHY'S THAT?
dazzle
hic
hic
mm-hmm?
plastered
perky
tunk
HE'S LIKE, THE IDEAL FUTURE ME. AND FRANKLY, HAVING SOMEONE WHO'S EVERYTHING YOU WANT TO BE RIGHT THERE IN FRONT OF YOU IS KINDA HARD.
I'm Blushing!
ISN'T THAT SWEET, NOMIYA?
HMM?
YOU'RE "THE IDEAL FUTURE HIM."

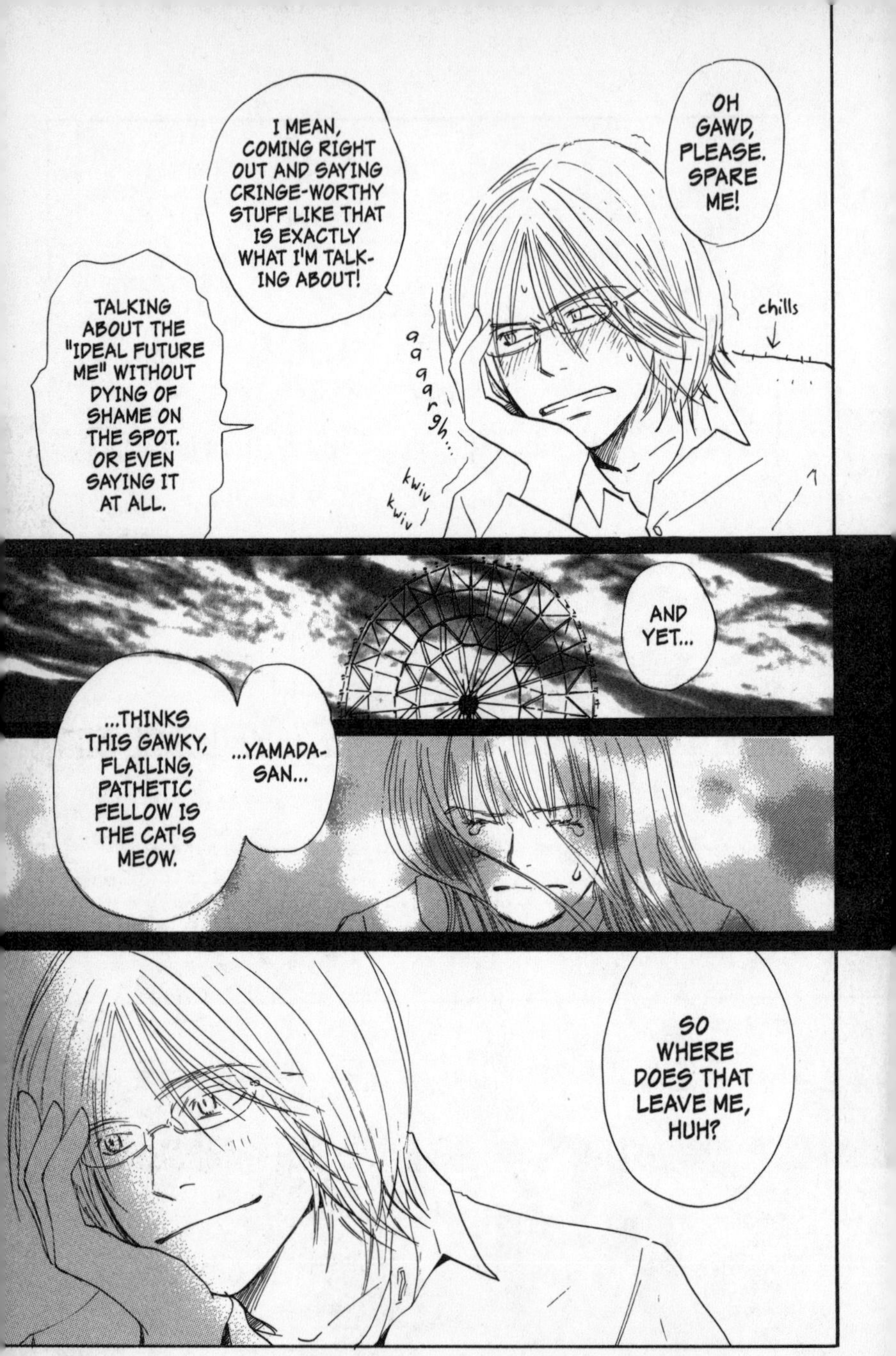
OH GAWD, PLEASE. SPARE ME!
chills
I MEAN, COMING RIGHT OUT AND SAYING CRINGE-WORTHY STUFF LIKE THAT IS EXACTLY WHAT I'M TALK-ING ABOUT!
aaaargh...
kwiv kwiv
TALKING ABOUT THE "IDEAL FUTURE ME" WITHOUT DYING OF SHAME ON THE SPOT. OR EVEN SAYING IT AT ALL.
AND YET...
...YAMADA-SAN...
...THINKS THIS GAWKY, FLAILING, PATHETIC FELLOW IS THE CAT'S MEOW.
SO WHERE DOES THAT LEAVE ME, HUH?

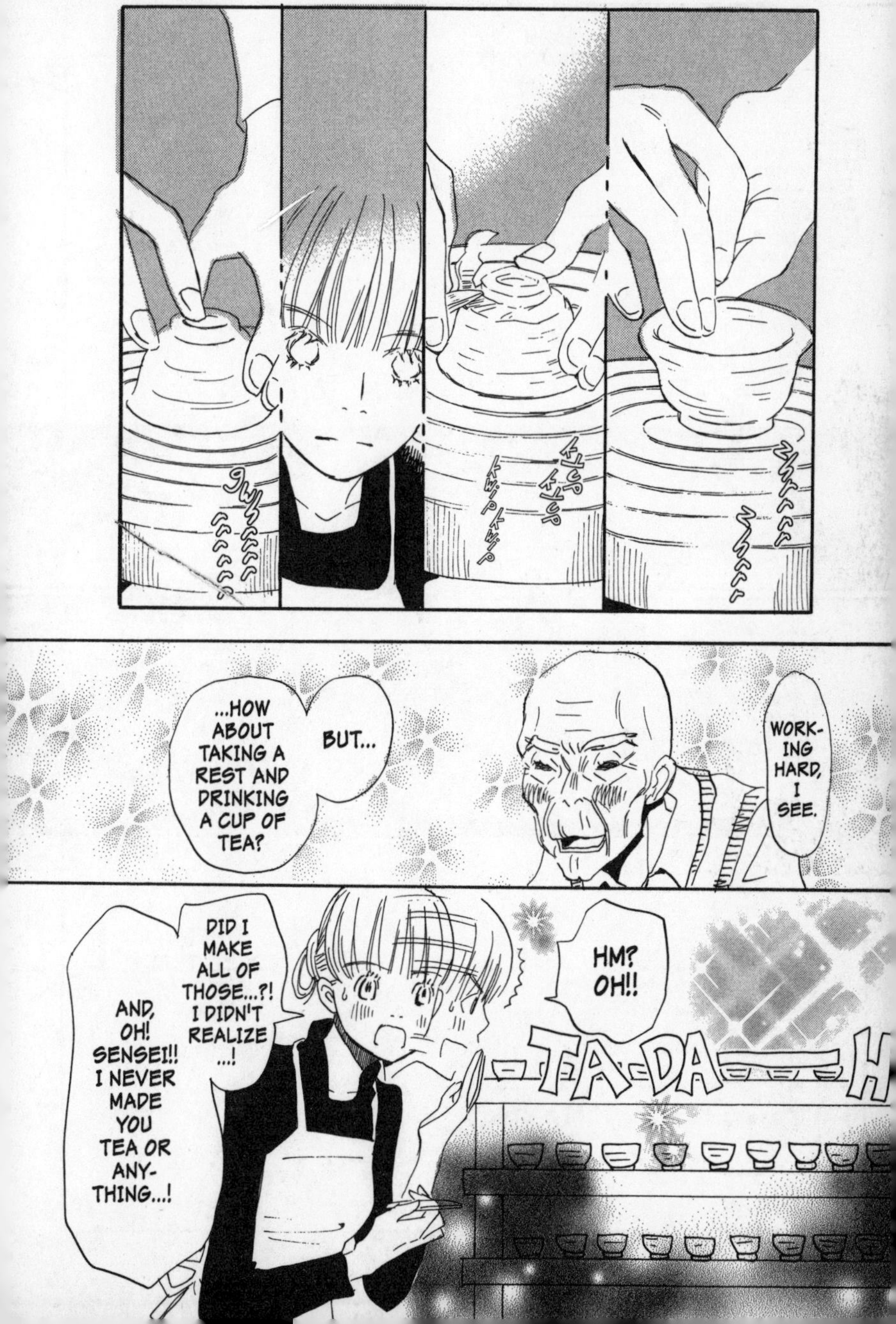
zhrrrrr
zhrrrr
kyup kyup
kwip kwip
gwhrrrrr
rrrrrrr
WORK-ING HARD, I SEE.
BUT...
...HOW ABOUT TAKING A REST AND DRINKING A CUP OF TEA?
HM? OH!!
TA-DA—H
DID I MAKE ALL OF THOSE...?! I DIDN'T REALIZE ...!
AND, OH! SENSEI!! I NEVER MADE YOU TEA OR ANY-THING...!

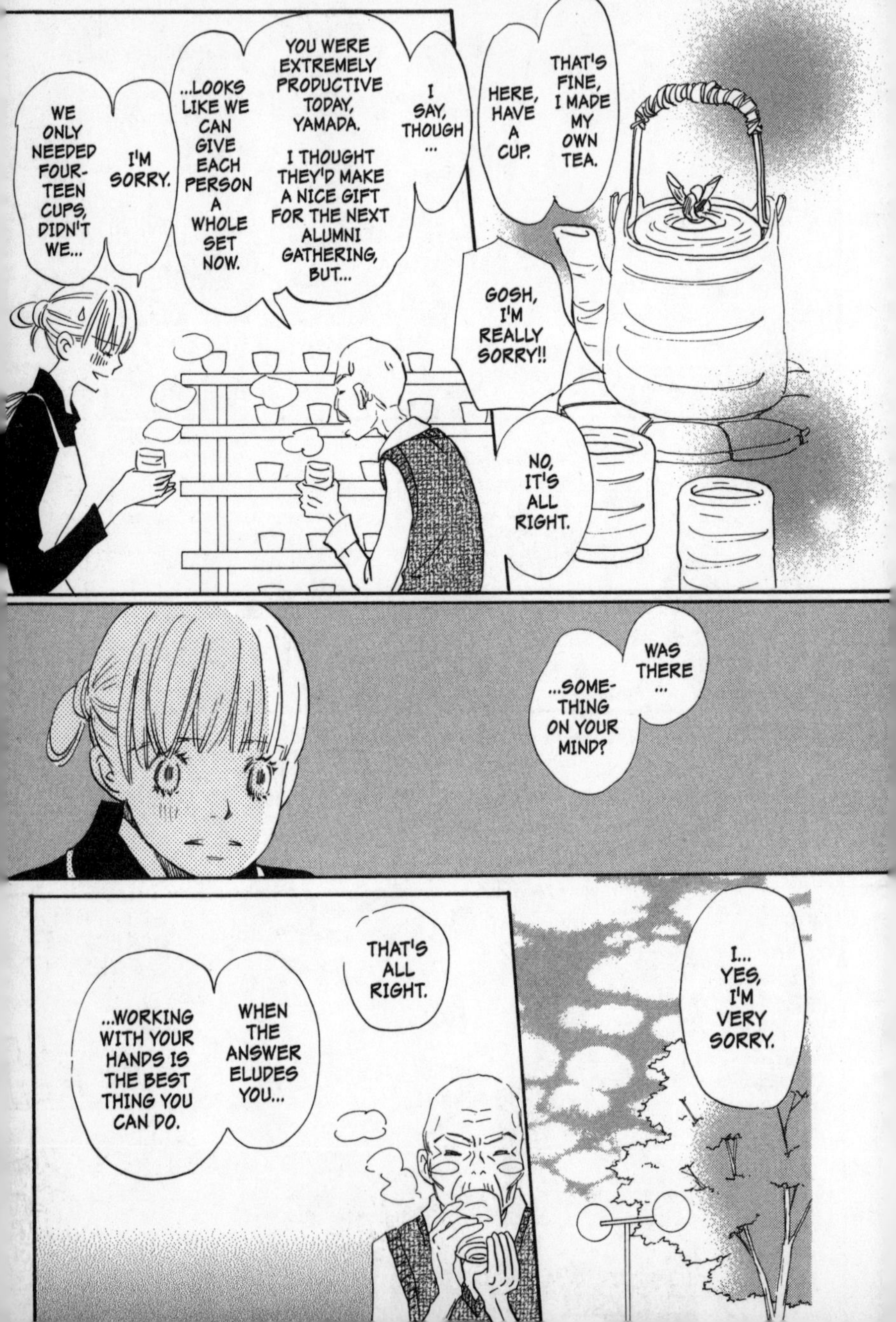
THAT'S FINE, I MADE MY OWN TEA.
HERE, HAVE A CUP.
I SAY, THOUGH ...
YOU WERE EXTREMELY PRODUCTIVE TODAY, YAMADA.
I THOUGHT THEY'D MAKE A NICE GIFT FOR THE NEXT ALUMNI GATHERING, BUT...
...LOOKS LIKE WE CAN GIVE EACH PERSON A WHOLE SET NOW.
I'M SORRY.
WE ONLY NEEDED FOURTEEN CUPS, DIDN'T WE...
GOSH, I'M REALLY SORRY!!
NO, IT'S ALL RIGHT.
WAS THERE ...
...SOMETHING ON YOUR MIND?
I... YES, I'M VERY SORRY.
THAT'S ALL RIGHT.
WHEN THE ANSWER ELUDES YOU...
...WORKING WITH YOUR HANDS IS THE BEST THING YOU CAN DO.

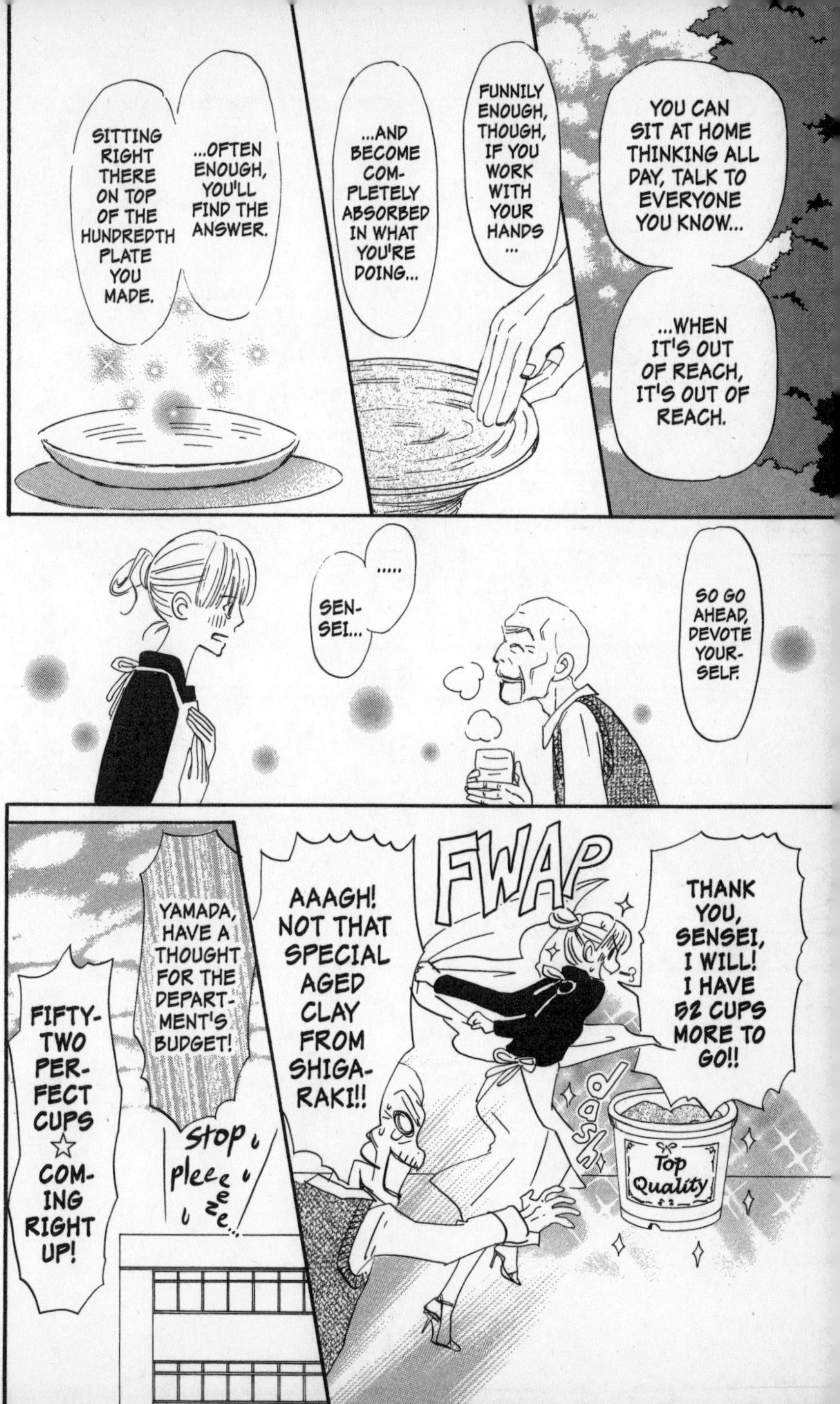
YOU CAN SIT AT HOME THINKING ALL DAY, TALK TO EVERYONE YOU KNOW...
...WHEN IT'S OUT OF REACH, IT'S OUT OF REACH.
FUNNILY ENOUGH, THOUGH, IF YOU WORK WITH YOUR HANDS...
...AND BECOME COM-PLETELY ABSORBED IN WHAT YOU'RE DOING...
...OFTEN ENOUGH, YOU'LL FIND THE ANSWER.
SITTING RIGHT THERE ON TOP OF THE HUNDREDTH PLATE YOU MADE.
SO GO AHEAD, DEVOTE YOUR-SELF.
......
SEN-SEI...
THANK YOU, SENSEI, I WILL! I HAVE 52 CUPS MORE TO GO!!
FWAP
dash
Top Quality
AAAGH! NOT THAT SPECIAL AGED CLAY FROM SHIGA-RAKI!!
YAMADA, HAVE A THOUGHT FOR THE DEPART-MENT'S BUDGET!
Stop pleeeeze...
FIFTY-TWO PER-FECT CUPS ☆ COM-ING RIGHT UP!

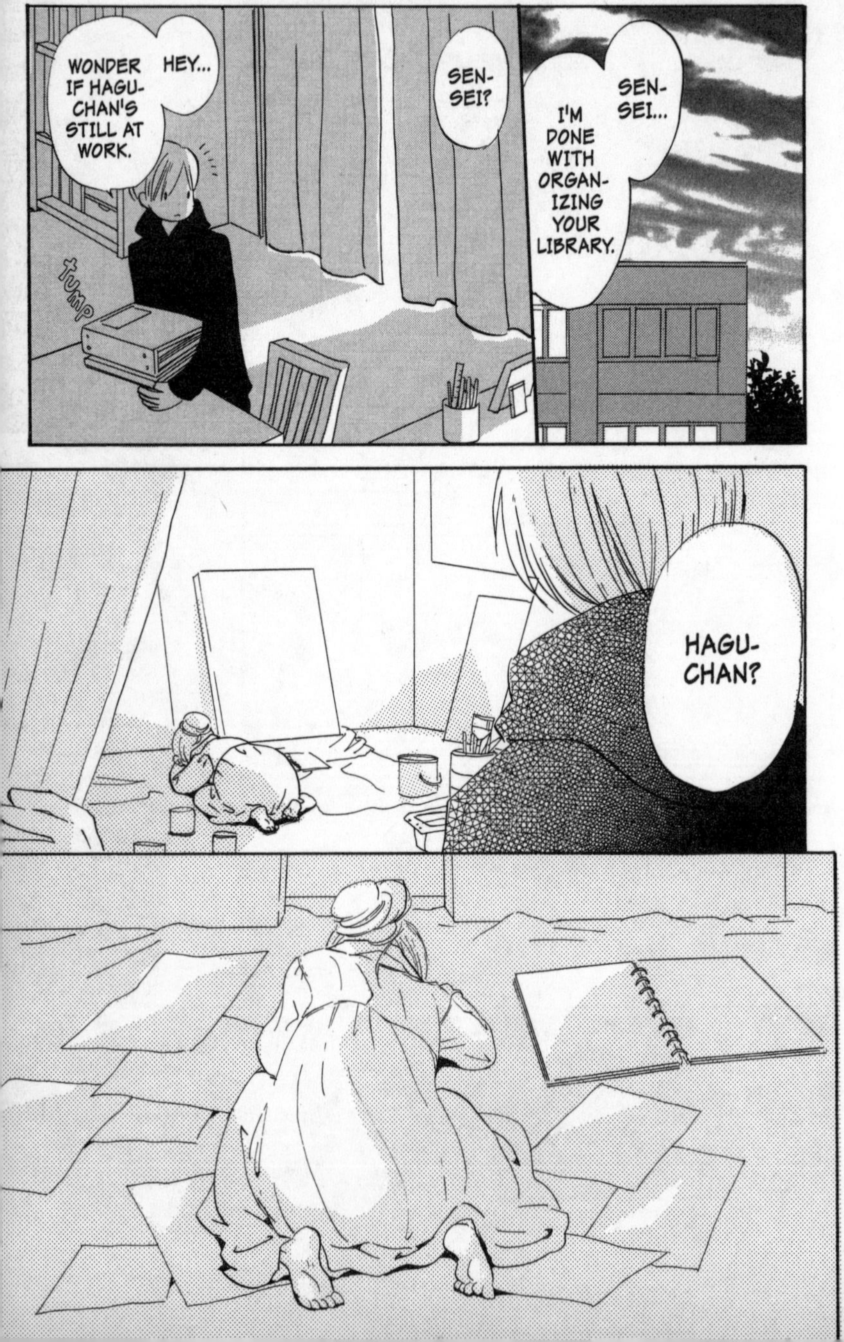
SEN-SEI...
I'M DONE WITH ORGANIZING YOUR LIBRARY.
SEN-SEI?
HEY...
WONDER IF HAGU-CHAN'S STILL AT WORK.
TUMP
HAGU-CHAN?

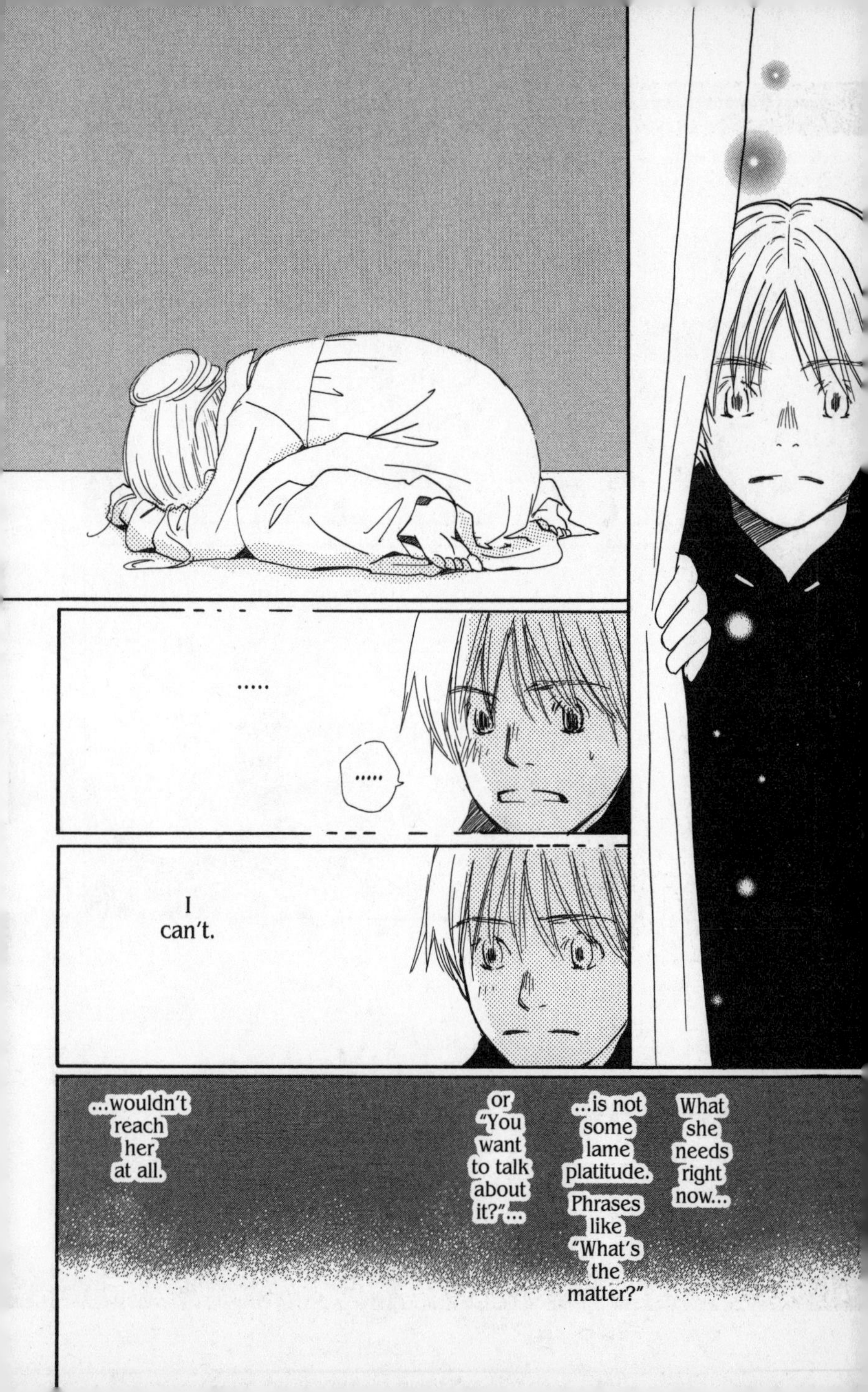
.....
.....
I can't.
What she needs right now...
...is not some lame platitude.
Phrases like "What's the matter?"
or "You want to talk about it?"...
...wouldn't reach her at all.

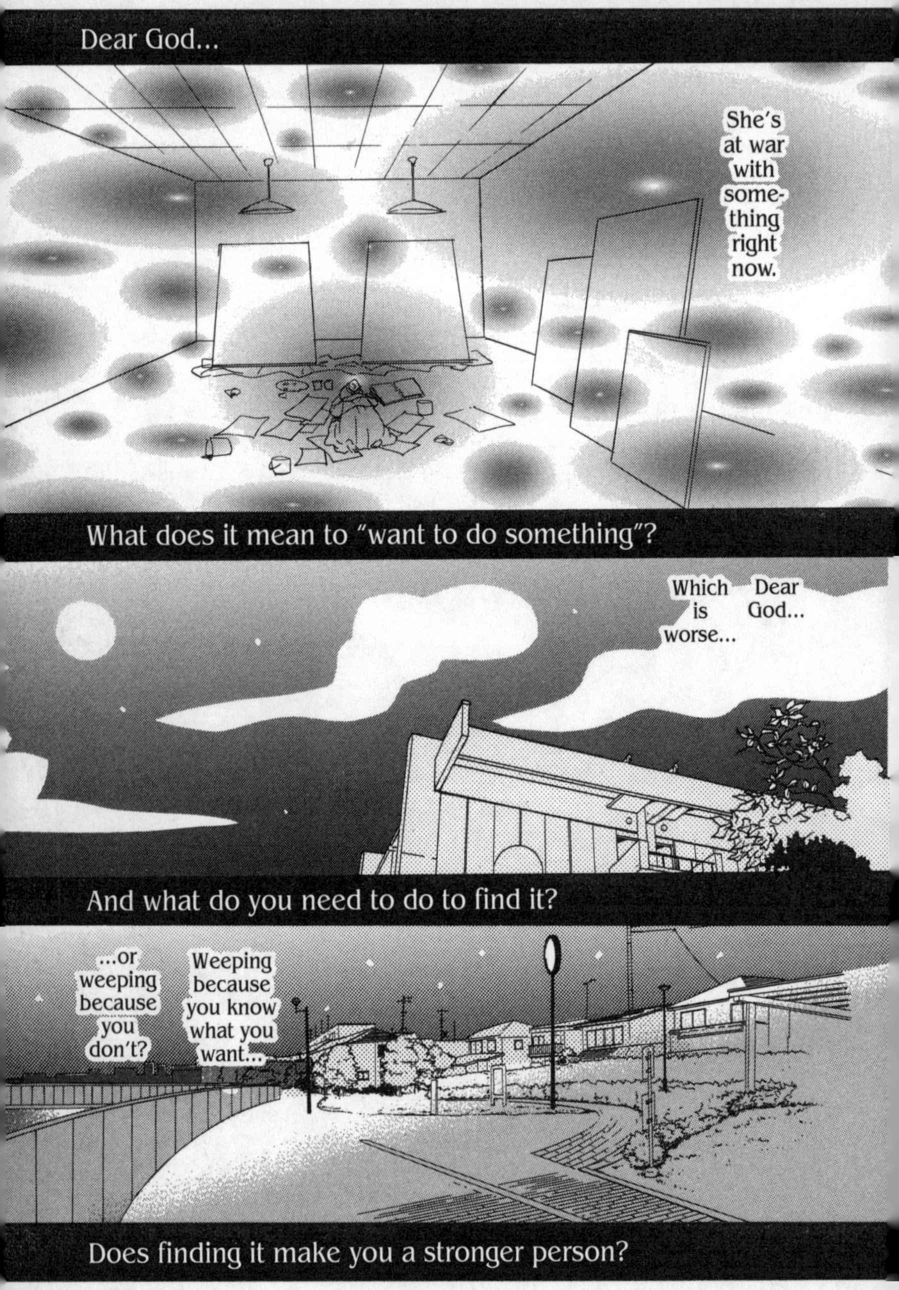
Dear God...
She's at war with something right now.
What does it mean to "want to do something"?
Dear God...
Which is worse...
And what do you need to do to find it?
Weeping because you know what you want...
...or weeping because you don't?
Does finding it make you a stronger person?

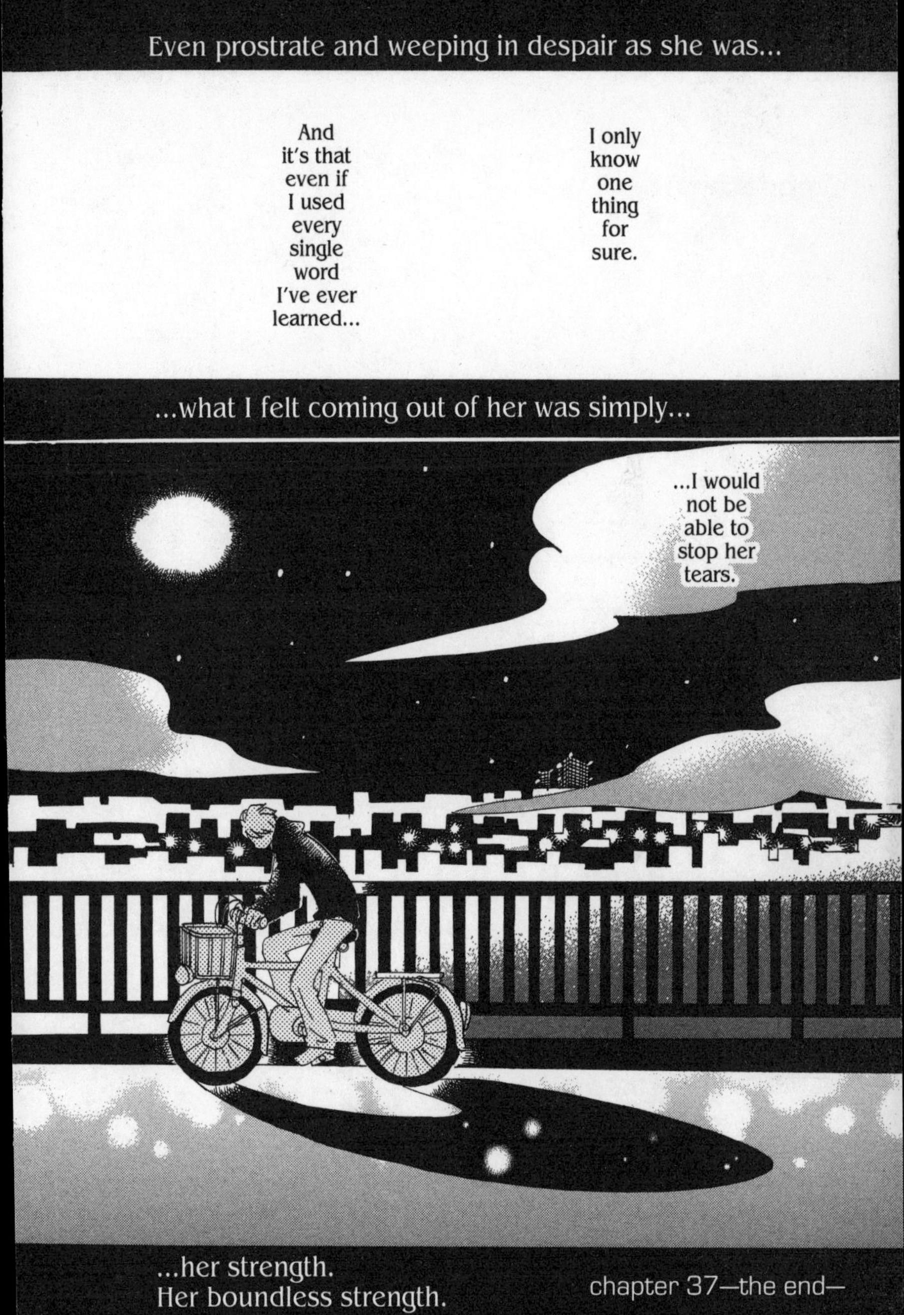
Even prostrate and weeping in despair as she was...
I only know one thing for sure.
And it's that even if I used every single word I've ever learned...
...what I felt coming out of her was simply...
...I would not be able to stop her tears.
...her strength. Her boundless strength.
chapter 37—the end—

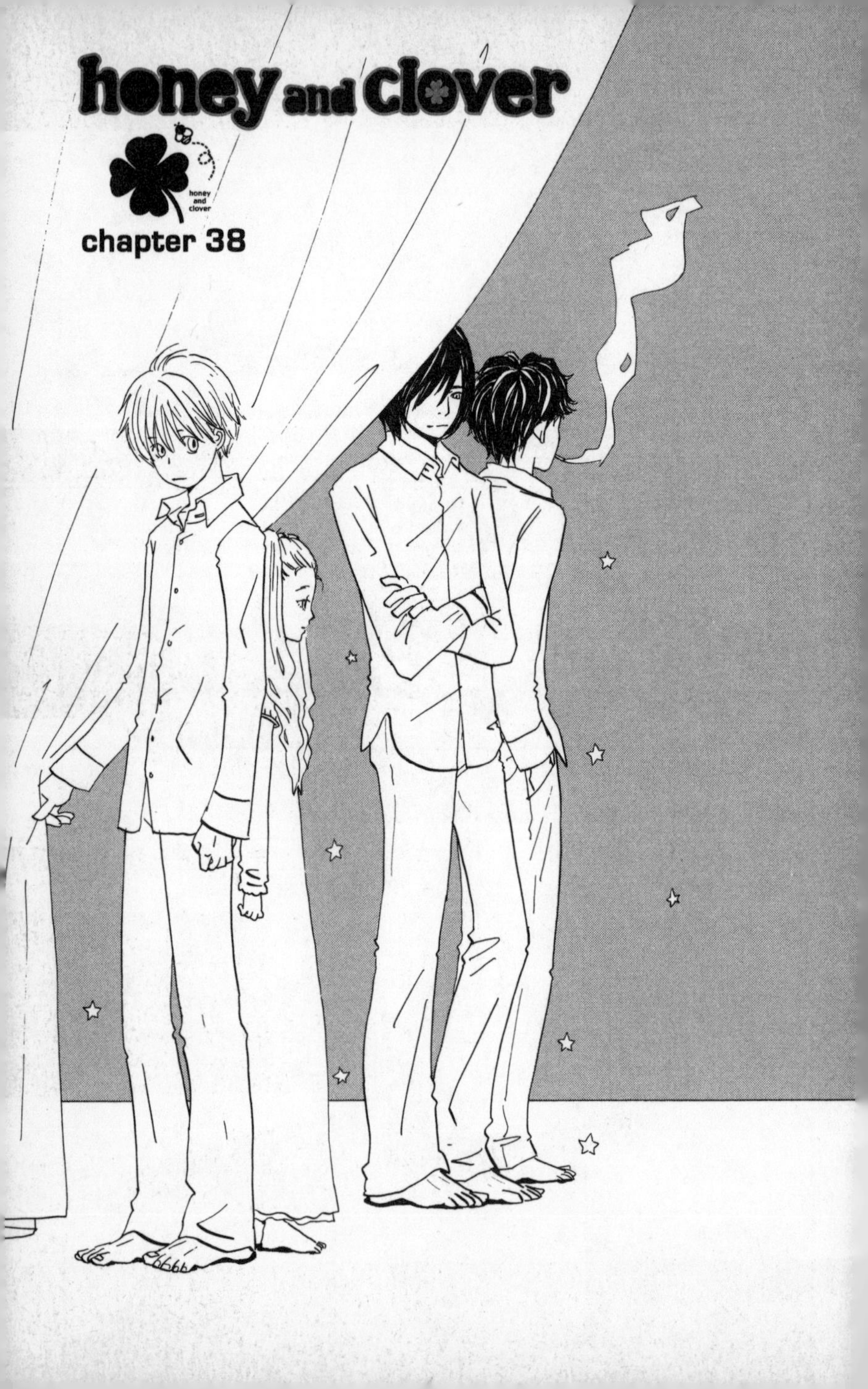
honey and clover
honey and clover
chapter 38

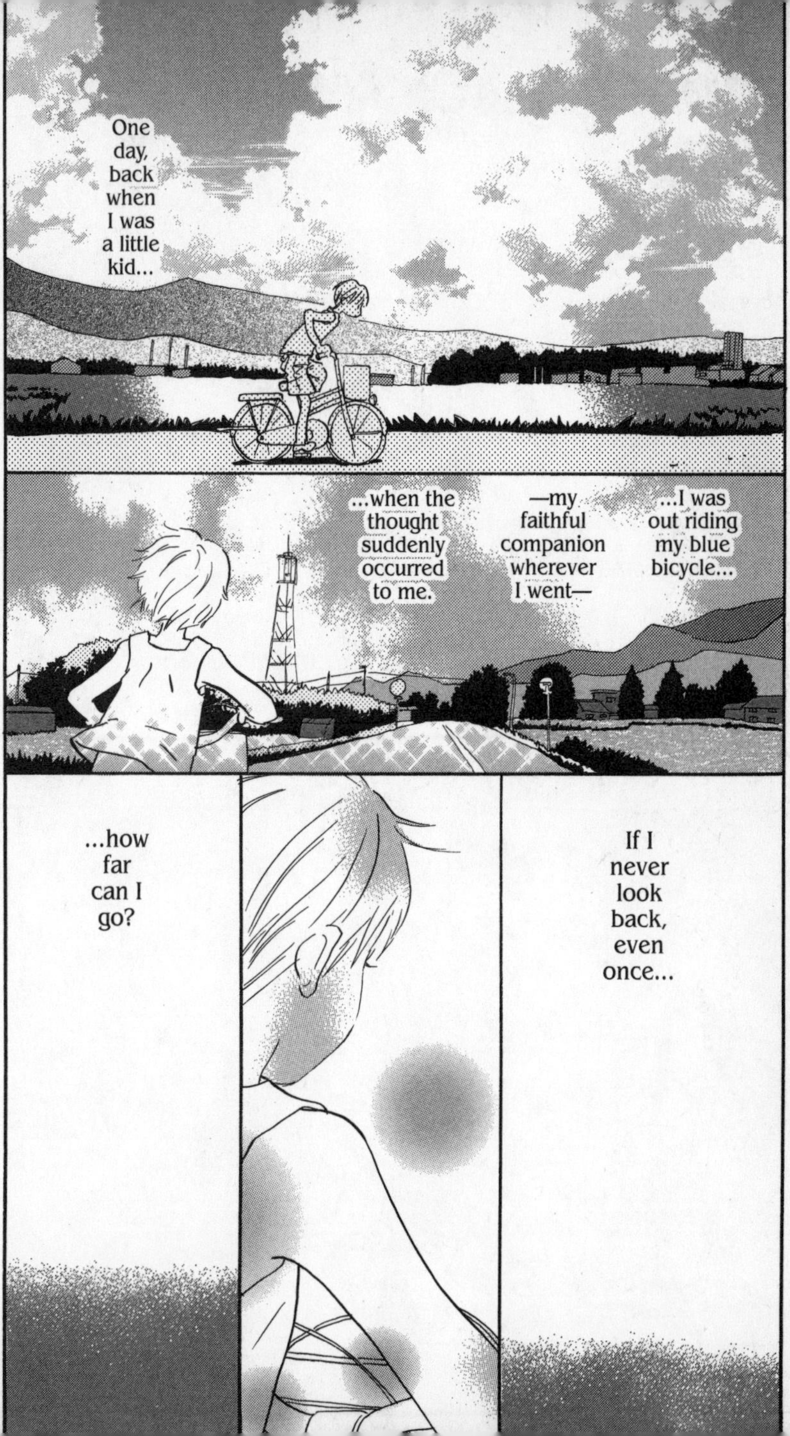
One day, back when I was a little kid...
...I was out riding my blue bicycle...
—my faithful companion wherever I went—
...when the thought suddenly occurred to me.
If I never look back, even once...
...how far can I go?

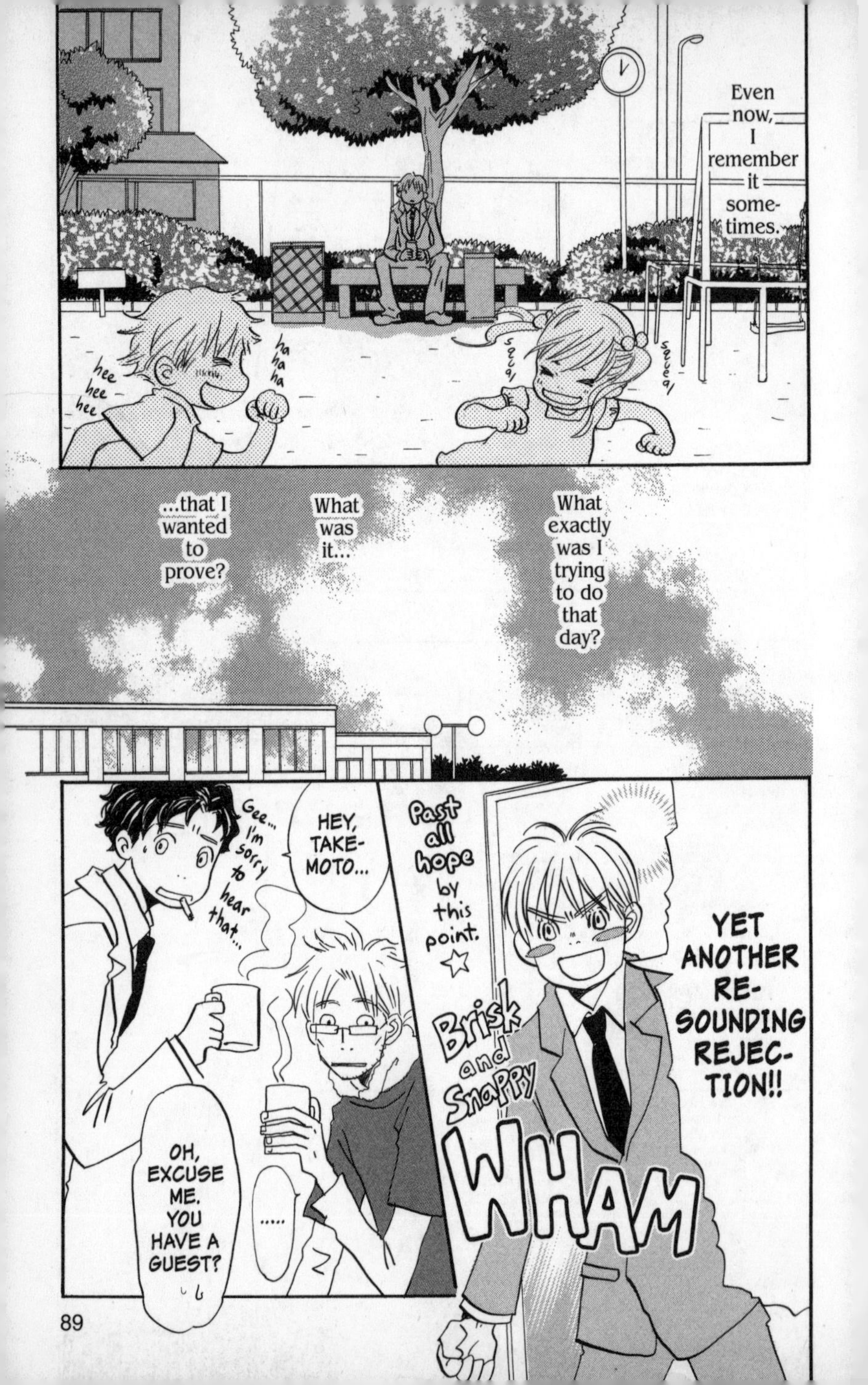
Even now, I remember it some-times.
squeal
squeal
ha ha ha
hee hee hee
What exactly was I trying to do that day?
What was it...
...that I wanted to prove?
YET ANOTHER RE-SOUNDING REJEC-TION!!
Brisk and Snappy
WHAM
Past all hope by this point. ☆
HEY, TAKE-MOTO...
Gee... I'm sorry to hear that...
.....
OH, EXCUSE ME. YOU HAVE A GUEST?

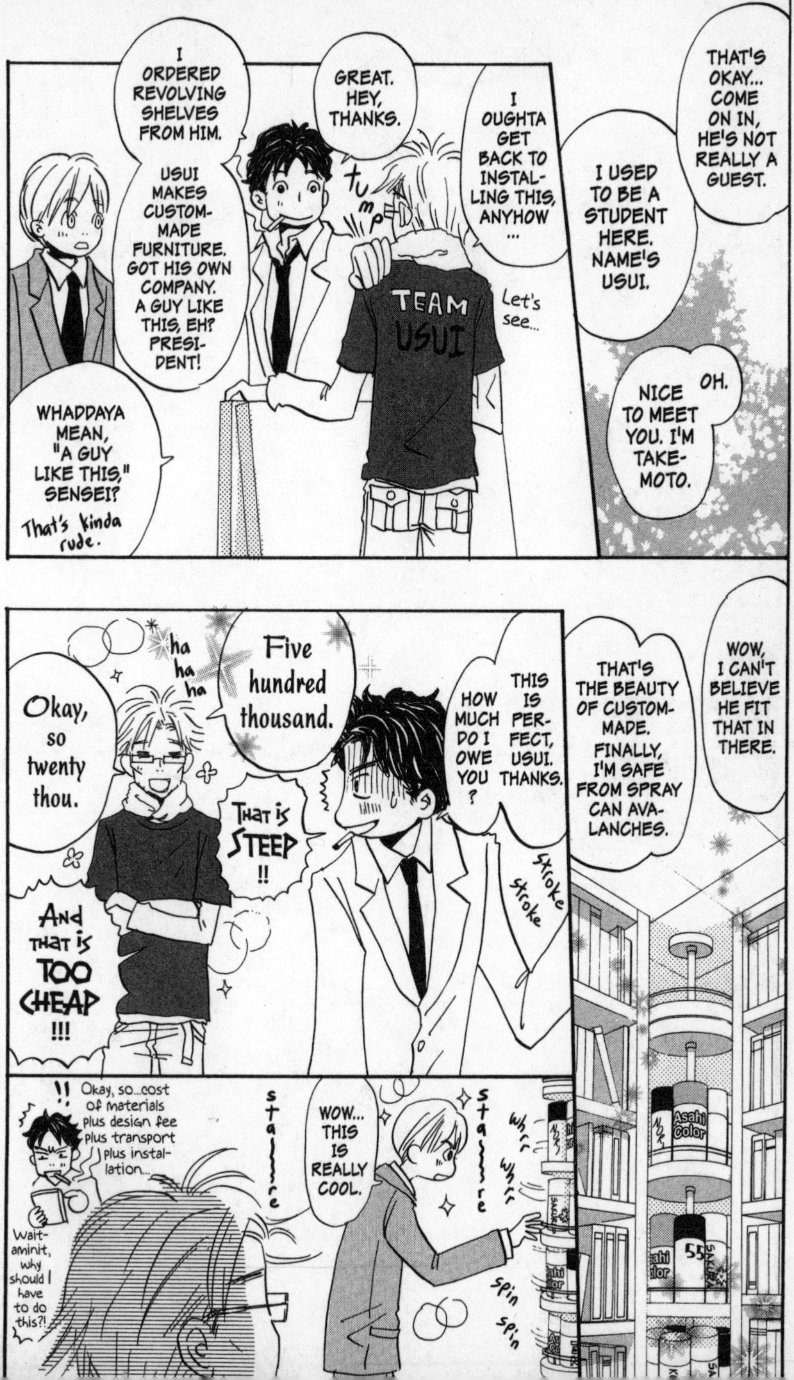
THAT'S OKAY... COME ON IN, HE'S NOT REALLY A GUEST.
OH.
NICE TO MEET YOU. I'M TAKE-MOTO.
I USED TO BE A STUDENT HERE. NAME'S USUI.
I OUGHTA GET BACK TO INSTALLING THIS, ANYHOW...
Let's see...
TEAM USUI
GREAT. HEY, THANKS.
tump
I ORDERED REVOLVING SHELVES FROM HIM.
USUI MAKES CUSTOM-MADE FURNITURE. GOT HIS OWN COMPANY. A GUY LIKE THIS, EH? PRESIDENT!
WHADDAYA MEAN, "A GUY LIKE THIS," SENSEI?
That's kinda rude.
WOW, I CAN'T BELIEVE HE FIT THAT IN THERE.
THAT'S THE BEAUTY OF CUSTOM-MADE. FINALLY, I'M SAFE FROM SPRAY CAN AVALANCHES.
THIS IS PERFECT, USUI. THANKS.
HOW MUCH DO I OWE YOU?
stroke stroke
Five hundred thousand.
ha ha ha
That is STEEP!!
Okay, so twenty thou.
And that is TOO CHEAP!!!
Asahi Color
whrr whrr
spin spin
stare
WOW... THIS IS REALLY COOL.
stare
!!
Okay, so...cost of materials plus design fee plus transport plus installation...
Wait-aminit, why should I have to do this?!

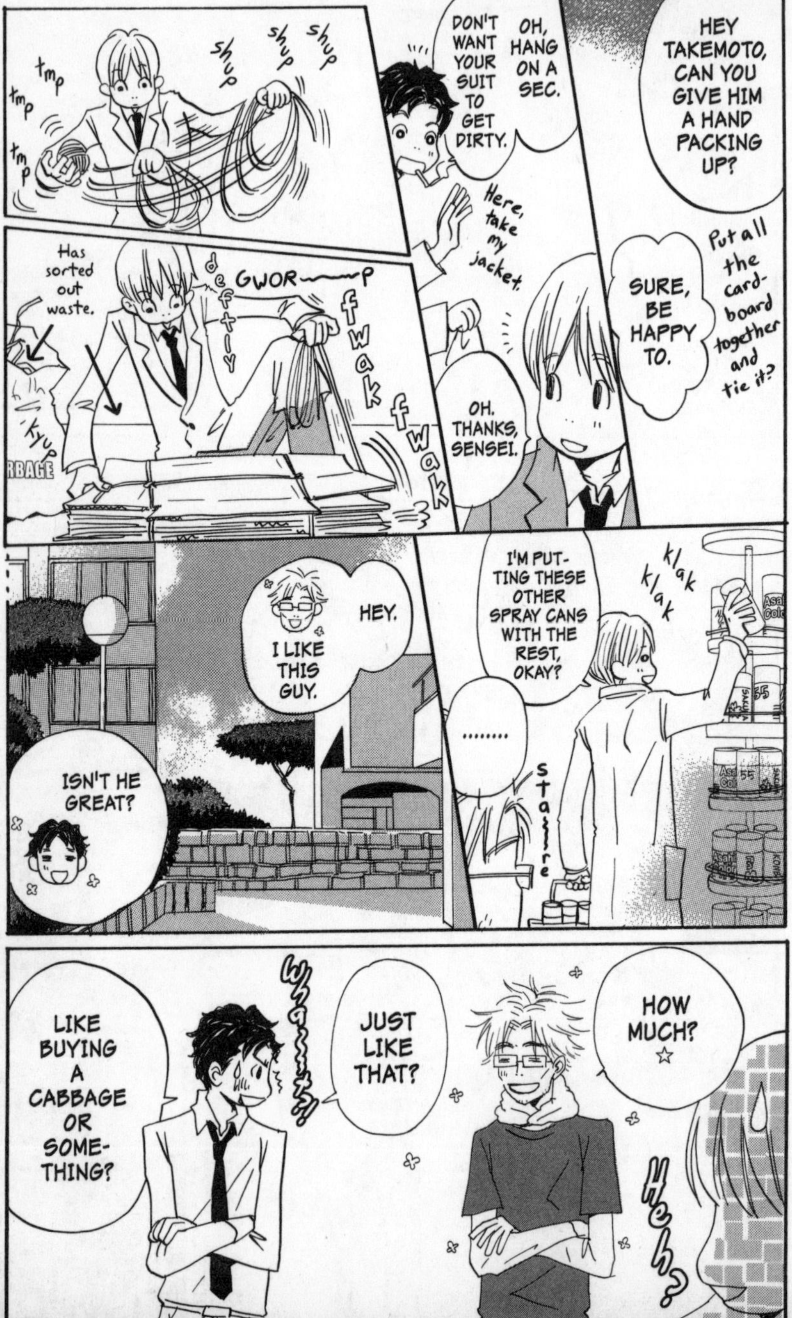
HEY TAKEMOTO, CAN YOU GIVE HIM A HAND PACKING UP?
Put all the cardboard together and tie it?
SURE, BE HAPPY TO.
OH, HANG ON A SEC.
DON'T WANT YOUR SUIT TO GET DIRTY.
Here, take my jacket.
OH. THANKS, SENSEI.
tmp tmp tmp
shup shup shup
Has sorted out waste.
deftly
GWOR~~~P
fwak fwak
kyup
RBAGE
klak klak
I'M PUTTING THESE OTHER SPRAY CANS WITH THE REST, OKAY?
....
stare
HEY.
I LIKE THIS GUY.
ISN'T HE GREAT?
HOW MUCH? ☆
Heh?
JUST LIKE THAT?
Wha~~t?!
LIKE BUYING A CABBAGE OR SOMETHING?

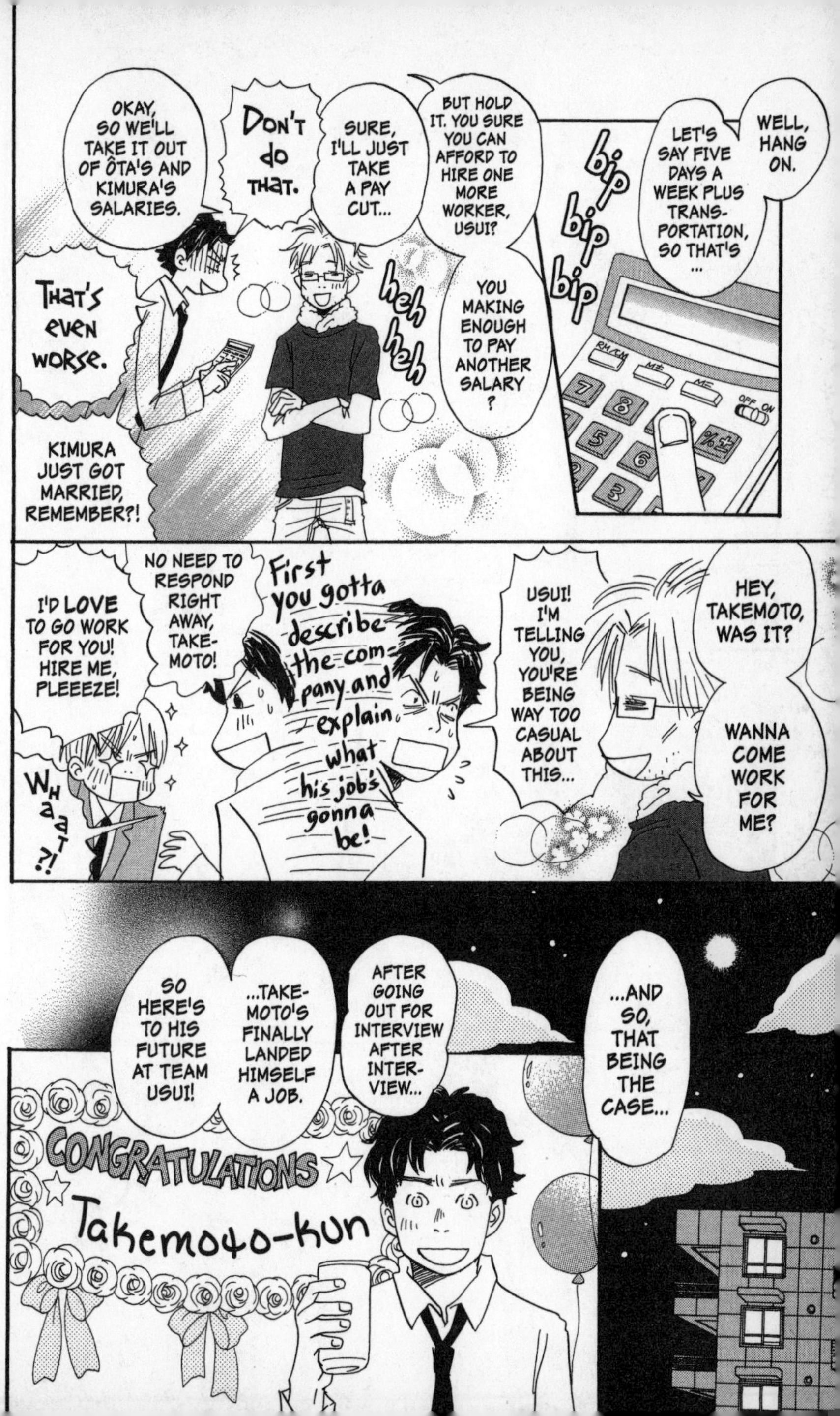
WELL, HANG ON.
LET'S SAY FIVE DAYS A WEEK PLUS TRANS-PORTATION, SO THAT'S ...
bip bip bip
BUT HOLD IT. YOU SURE YOU CAN AFFORD TO HIRE ONE MORE WORKER, USUI?
YOU MAKING ENOUGH TO PAY ANOTHER SALARY ?
heh heh
SURE, I'LL JUST TAKE A PAY CUT...
Don't do that.
OKAY, SO WE'LL TAKE IT OUT OF ÔTA'S AND KIMURA'S SALARIES.
That's even worse.
KIMURA JUST GOT MARRIED, REMEMBER?!
HEY, TAKEMOTO, WAS IT?
WANNA COME WORK FOR ME?
USUI! I'M TELLING YOU, YOU'RE BEING WAY TOO CASUAL ABOUT THIS...
First you gotta describe the company and explain what his job's gonna be!
NO NEED TO RESPOND RIGHT AWAY, TAKE-MOTO!
I'D LOVE TO GO WORK FOR YOU! HIRE ME, PLEEEZE!
WHaaT?!
...AND SO, THAT BEING THE CASE...
AFTER GOING OUT FOR INTERVIEW AFTER INTER-VIEW...
...TAKE-MOTO'S FINALLY LANDED HIMSELF A JOB.
SO HERE'S TO HIS FUTURE AT TEAM USUI!
CONGRATULATIONS ☆
Takemoto-kun

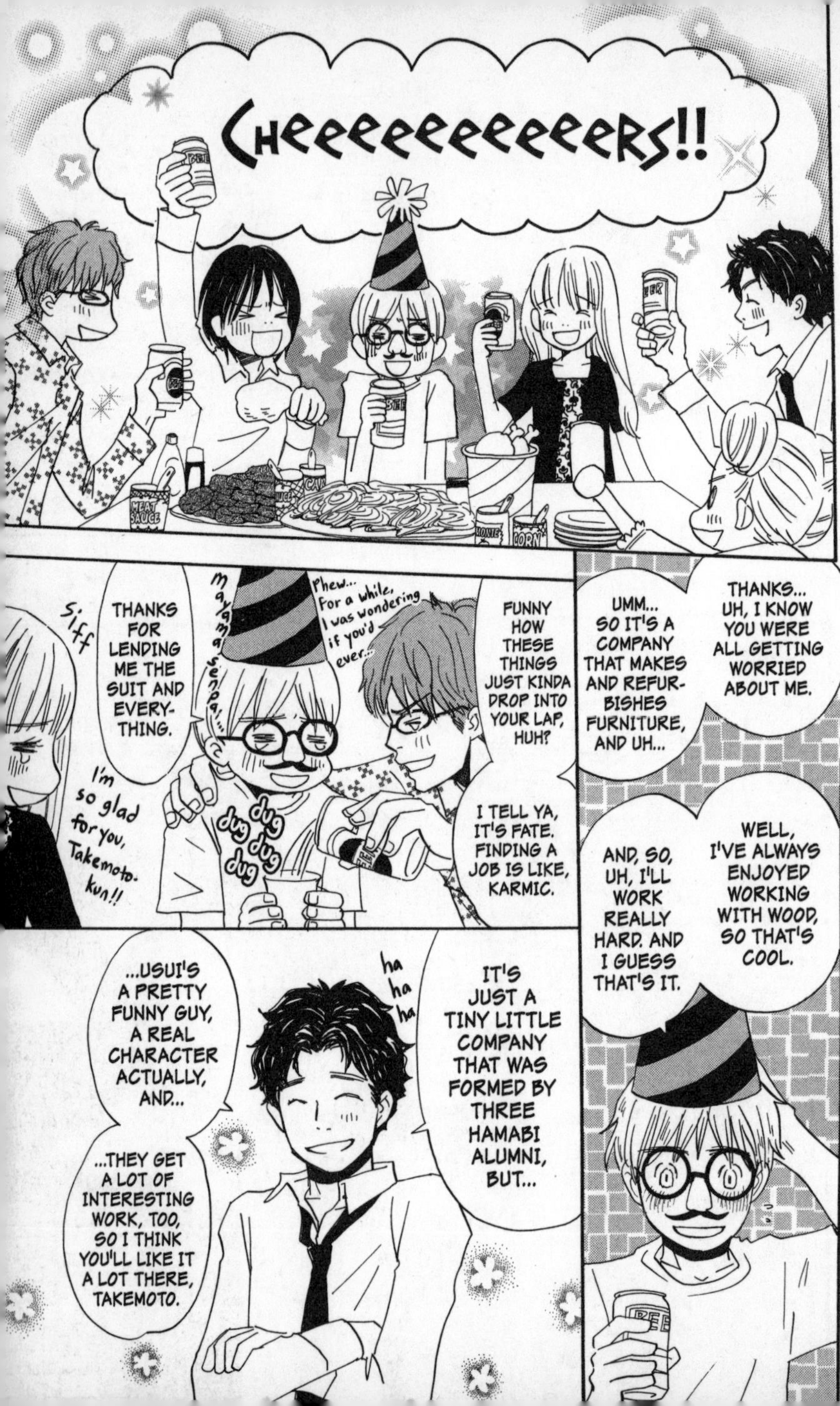
CHEEEEEEEEEERS!!
THANKS... UH, I KNOW YOU WERE ALL GETTING WORRIED ABOUT ME.
UMM... SO IT'S A COMPANY THAT MAKES AND REFURBISHES FURNITURE, AND UH...
WELL, I'VE ALWAYS ENJOYED WORKING WITH WOOD, SO THAT'S COOL.
AND, SO, UH, I'LL WORK REALLY HARD. AND I GUESS THAT'S IT.
FUNNY HOW THESE THINGS JUST KINDA DROP INTO YOUR LAP, HUH?
Phew... For a while, I was wondering if you'd ever...
THANKS FOR LENDING ME THE SUIT AND EVERYTHING.
Mayama-senpai...
I TELL YA, IT'S FATE. FINDING A JOB IS LIKE, KARMIC.
dug dug dug dug
siff
I'm so glad for you, Takemoto-kun!!
IT'S JUST A TINY LITTLE COMPANY THAT WAS FORMED BY THREE HAMABI ALUMNI, BUT...
ha ha ha
...USUI'S A PRETTY FUNNY GUY, A REAL CHARACTER ACTUALLY, AND...
...THEY GET A LOT OF INTERESTING WORK, TOO, SO I THINK YOU'LL LIKE IT A LOT THERE, TAKEMOTO.

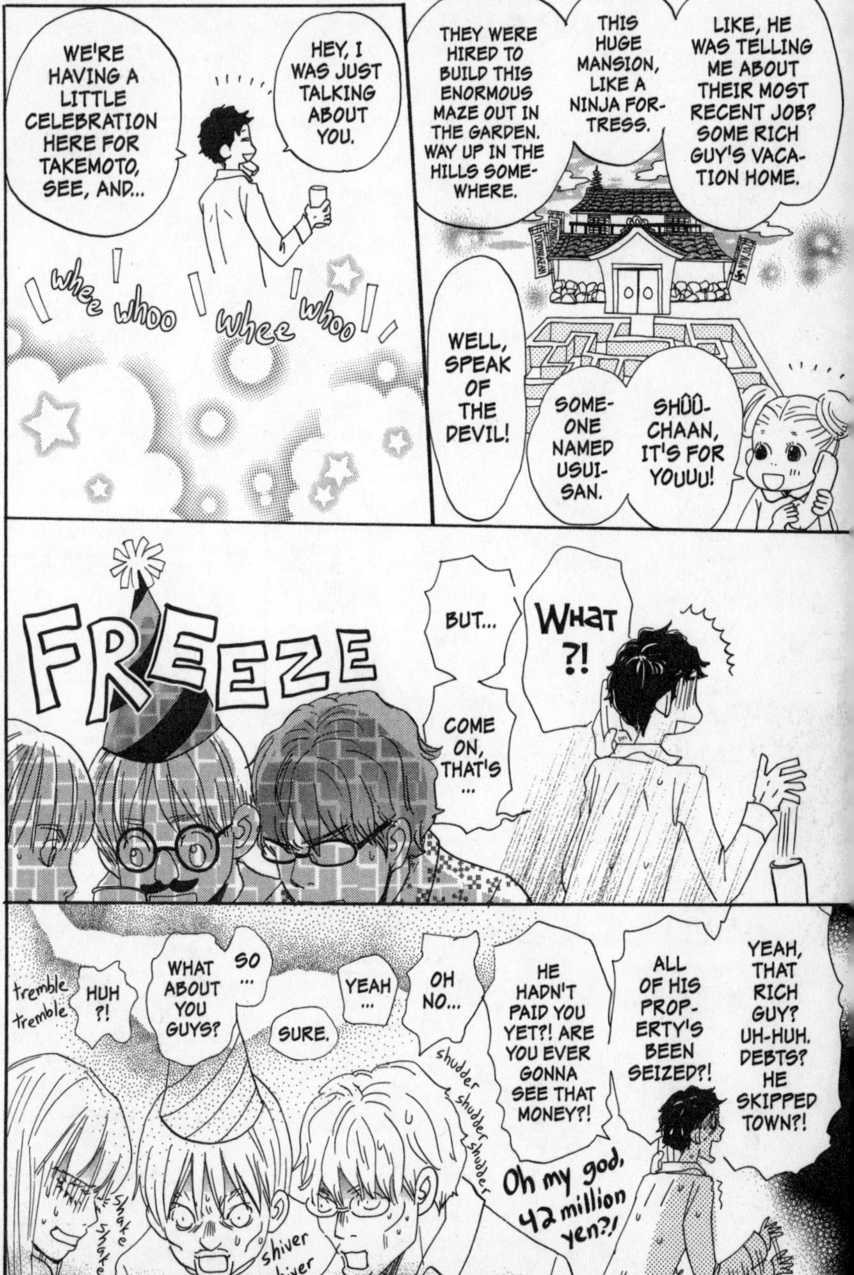
LIKE, HE WAS TELLING ME ABOUT THEIR MOST RECENT JOB? SOME RICH GUY'S VACATION HOME.
THIS HUGE MANSION, LIKE A NINJA FORTRESS.
THEY WERE HIRED TO BUILD THIS ENORMOUS MAZE OUT IN THE GARDEN. WAY UP IN THE HILLS SOMEWHERE.
SHÛÛ-CHAAN, IT'S FOR YOUUU!
SOMEONE NAMED USUI-SAN.
WELL, SPEAK OF THE DEVIL!
HEY, I WAS JUST TALKING ABOUT YOU.
WE'RE HAVING A LITTLE CELEBRATION HERE FOR TAKEMOTO, SEE, AND...
whee whoo whee whoo
WHAT ?!
BUT...
COME ON, THAT'S ...
FREEZE
YEAH, THAT RICH GUY? UH-HUH. DEBTS? HE SKIPPED TOWN?!
ALL OF HIS PROPERTY'S BEEN SEIZED?!
HE HADN'T PAID YOU YET?! ARE YOU EVER GONNA SEE THAT MONEY?!
Oh my god, 42 million yen?!
shudder shudder shudder
OH NO...
YEAH ...
SURE.
SO ...
WHAT ABOUT YOU GUYS?
shiver shiver
HUH ?!
tremble tremble
shake shake

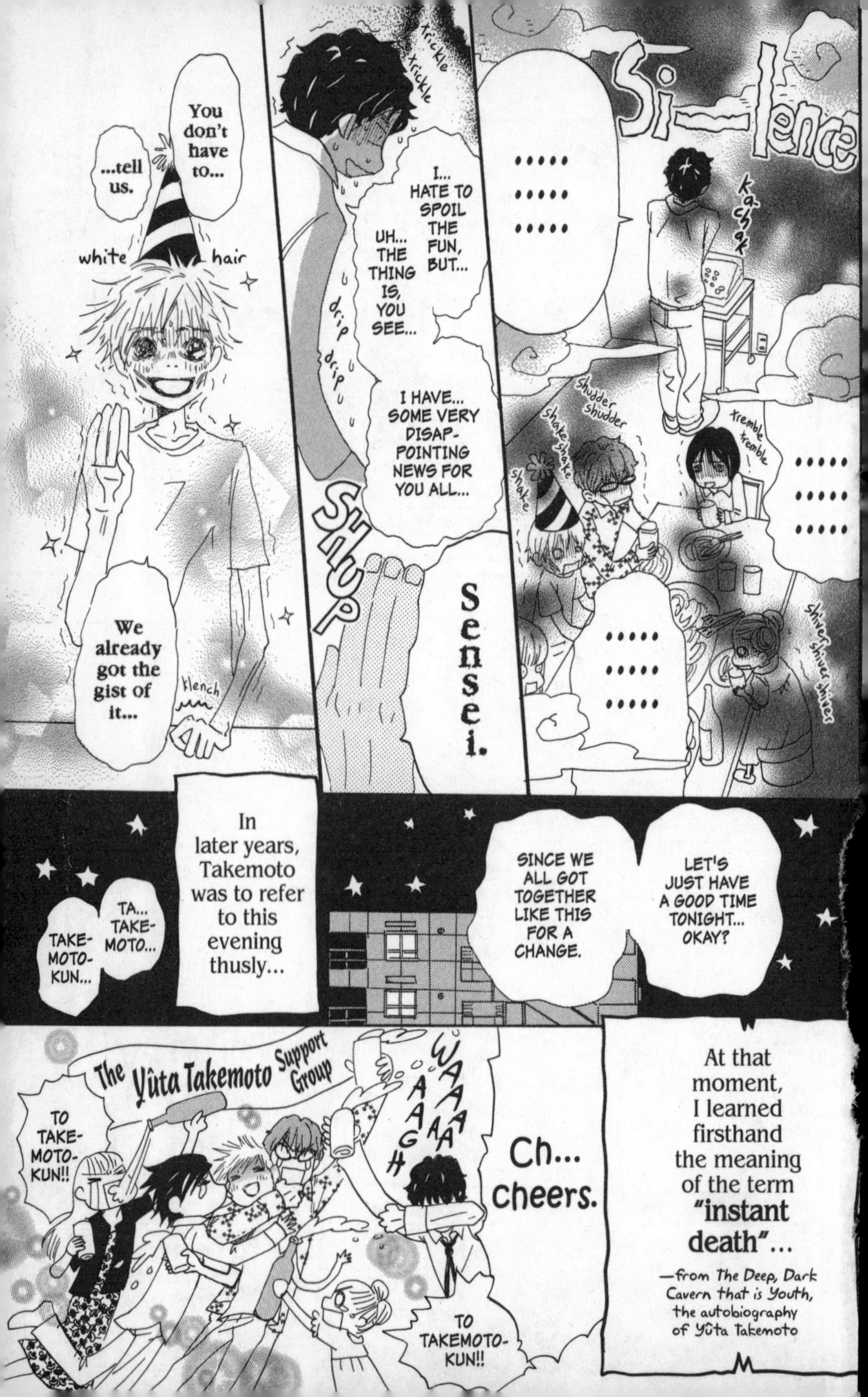
Si—lence
ka-chak
....
shudder shudder
shake shake shake
tremble tremble
....
shiver shiver shiver
....
trickle trickle
I... HATE TO SPOIL THE FUN, BUT...
UH... THE THING IS, YOU SEE...
drip drip
I HAVE... SOME VERY DISAPPOINTING NEWS FOR YOU ALL...
SHUP
Sensei.
You don't have to...
...tell us.
white hair
We already got the gist of it...
klench
LET'S JUST HAVE A GOOD TIME TONIGHT... OKAY?
SINCE WE ALL GOT TOGETHER LIKE THIS FOR A CHANGE.
In later years, Takemoto was to refer to this evening thusly...
TA... TAKE-MOTO...
TAKE-MOTO-KUN...
At that moment, I learned firsthand the meaning of the term "instant death"...
—from The Deep, Dark Cavern that is Youth, the autobiography of Yûta Takemoto
Ch... cheers.
WAAAAAAAAAGH
The Yûta Takemoto Support Group
TO TAKE-MOTO-KUN!!
TO TAKEMOTO-KUN!!

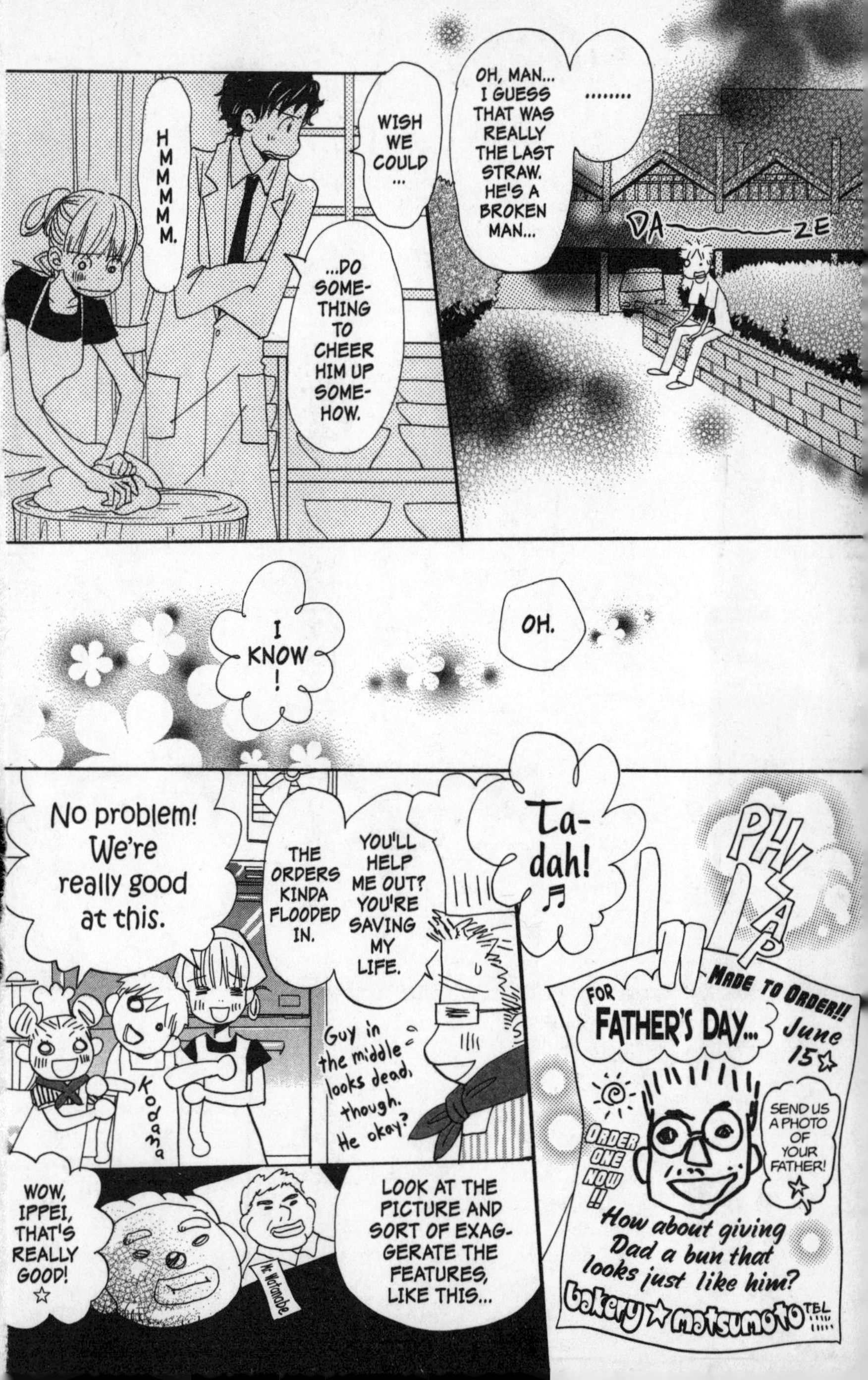
....
OH, MAN... I GUESS THAT WAS REALLY THE LAST STRAW. HE'S A BROKEN MAN...
DA——ZE
WISH WE COULD...
...DO SOMETHING TO CHEER HIM UP SOMEHOW.
HMMMMM.
OH.
I KNOW!
Ta-dah! ♫
PHLAP
MADE TO ORDER!!
FOR FATHER'S DAY... June 15☆
ORDER ONE NOW!!
SEND US A PHOTO OF YOUR FATHER! ☆
How about giving Dad a bun that looks just like him?
bakery☆matsumoto
YOU'LL HELP ME OUT? YOU'RE SAVING MY LIFE.
THE ORDERS KINDA FLOODED IN.
No problem! We're really good at this.
Guy in the middle looks dead though. He okay?
Kodama
LOOK AT THE PICTURE AND SORT OF EXAG-GERATE THE FEATURES, LIKE THIS...
WOW, IPPEI, THAT'S REALLY GOOD! ☆
Mr. Watanabe

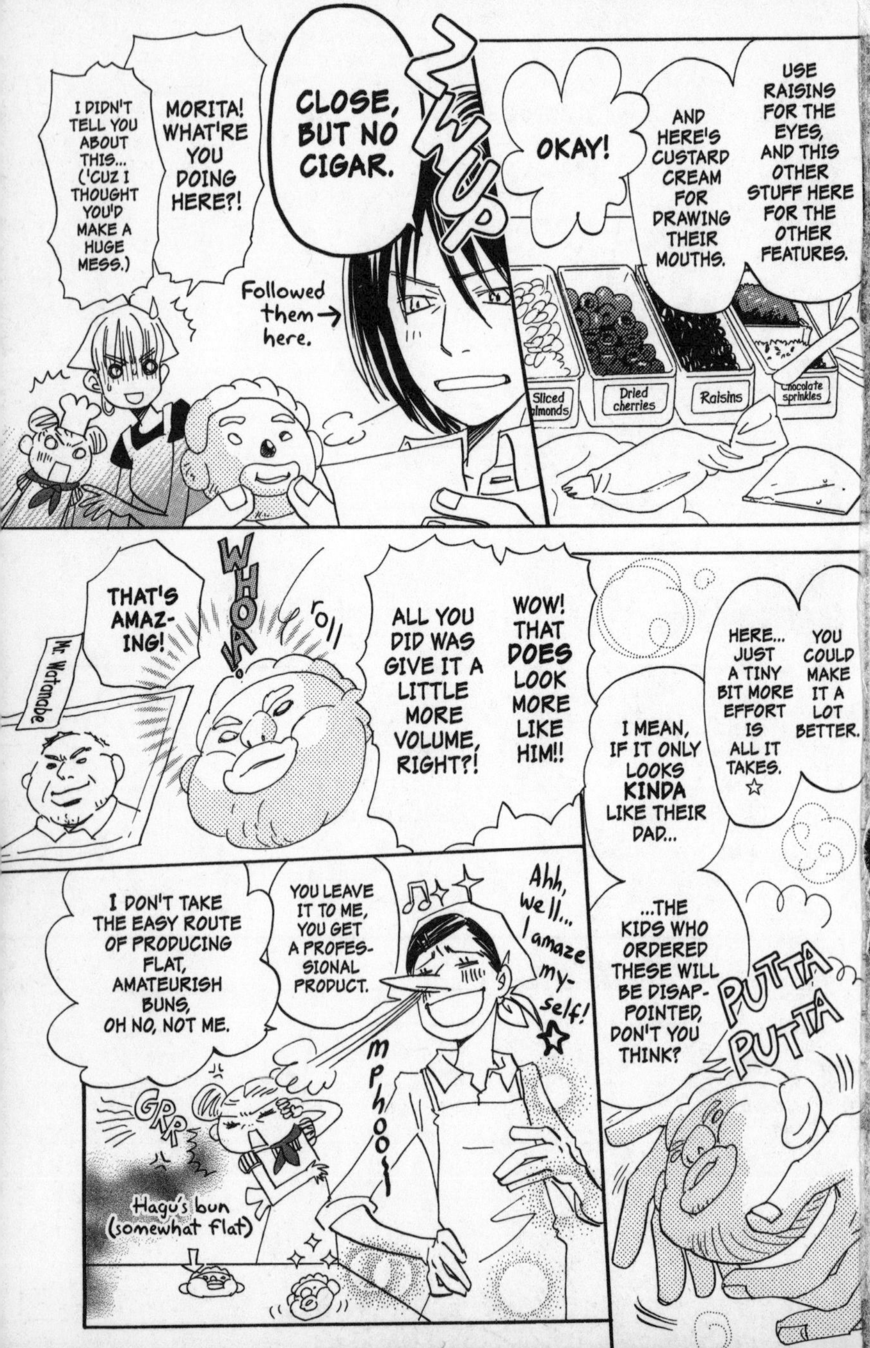
USE RAISINS FOR THE EYES, AND THIS OTHER STUFF HERE FOR THE OTHER FEATURES.
AND HERE'S CUSTARD CREAM FOR DRAWING THEIR MOUTHS.
OKAY!
Sliced almonds
Dried cherries
Raisins
Chocolate sprinkles
ZWUP
CLOSE, BUT NO CIGAR.
MORITA! WHAT'RE YOU DOING HERE?!
I DIDN'T TELL YOU ABOUT THIS... ('CUZ I THOUGHT YOU'D MAKE A HUGE MESS.)
Followed them here.
YOU COULD MAKE IT A LOT BETTER.
HERE... JUST A TINY BIT MORE EFFORT IS ALL IT TAKES. ☆
I MEAN, IF IT ONLY LOOKS KINDA LIKE THEIR DAD...
...THE KIDS WHO ORDERED THESE WILL BE DISAPPOINTED, DON'T YOU THINK?
PUTTA PUTTA
WOW! THAT DOES LOOK MORE LIKE HIM!!
ALL YOU DID WAS GIVE IT A LITTLE MORE VOLUME, RIGHT?!
roll
WHOA!
THAT'S AMAZING!
Mr. Watanabe
Ahh, well... I amaze myself!
YOU LEAVE IT TO ME, YOU GET A PROFESSIONAL PRODUCT.
I DON'T TAKE THE EASY ROUTE OF PRODUCING FLAT, AMATEURISH BUNS, OH NO, NOT ME.
mphooo
GRR
Hagu's bun (somewhat flat)

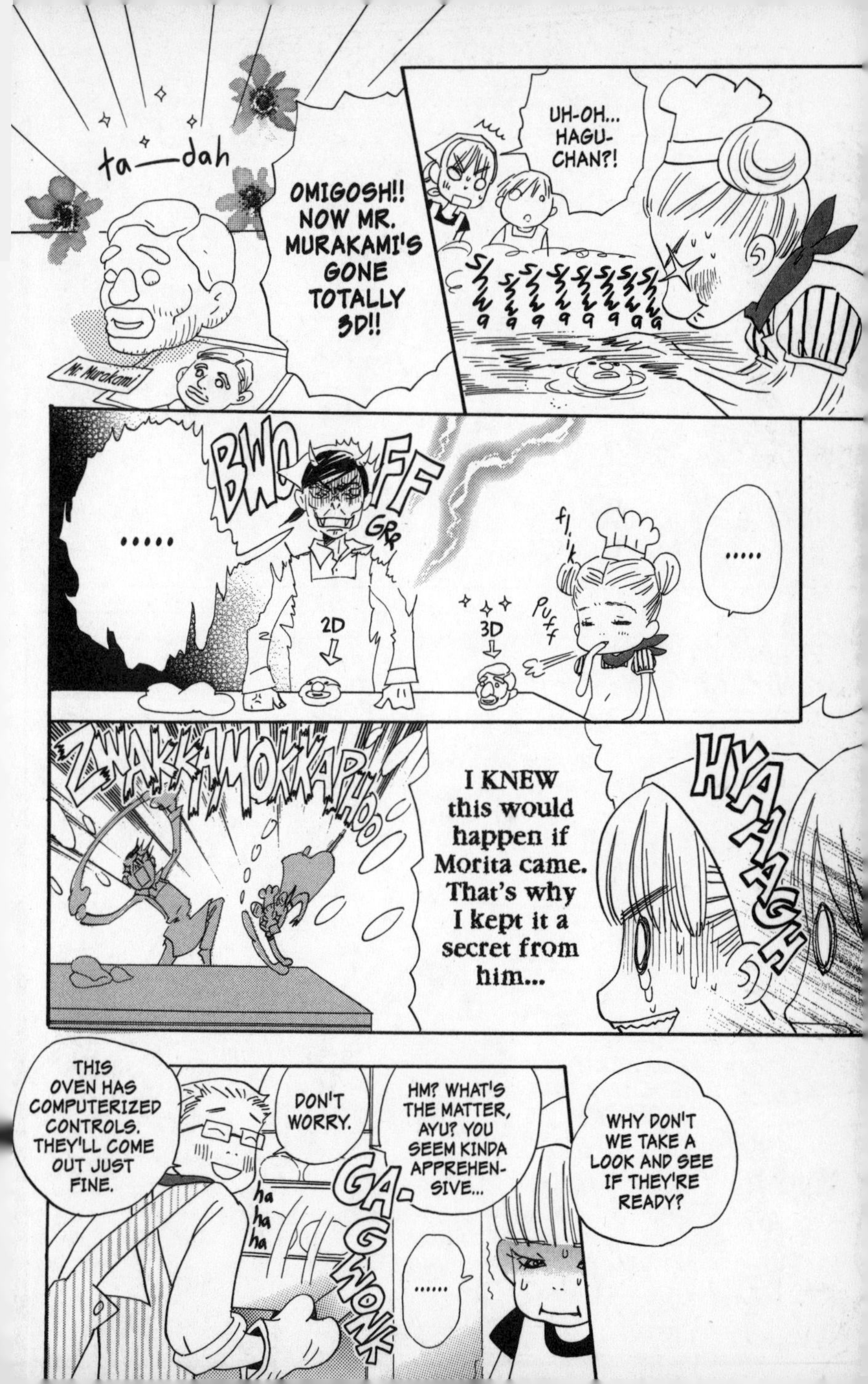

UH-OH... HAGU-CHAN?!
ta—dah
OMIGOSH!! NOW MR. MURAKAMI'S GONE TOTALLY 3D!!
Mr. Murakami
.....
PUFF
FLIK
3D
2D
GRR
BWOFF
.....
HYAAAGH
I KNEW this would happen if Morita came. That's why I kept it a secret from him...
ZWAKKAMOKKAPHOO
WHY DON'T WE TAKE A LOOK AND SEE IF THEY'RE READY?
HM? WHAT'S THE MATTER, AYU? YOU SEEM KINDA APPREHEN-SIVE...
......
GA-GWONK
DON'T WORRY.
ha ha ha
THIS OVEN HAS COMPUTERIZED CONTROLS. THEY'LL COME OUT JUST FINE.

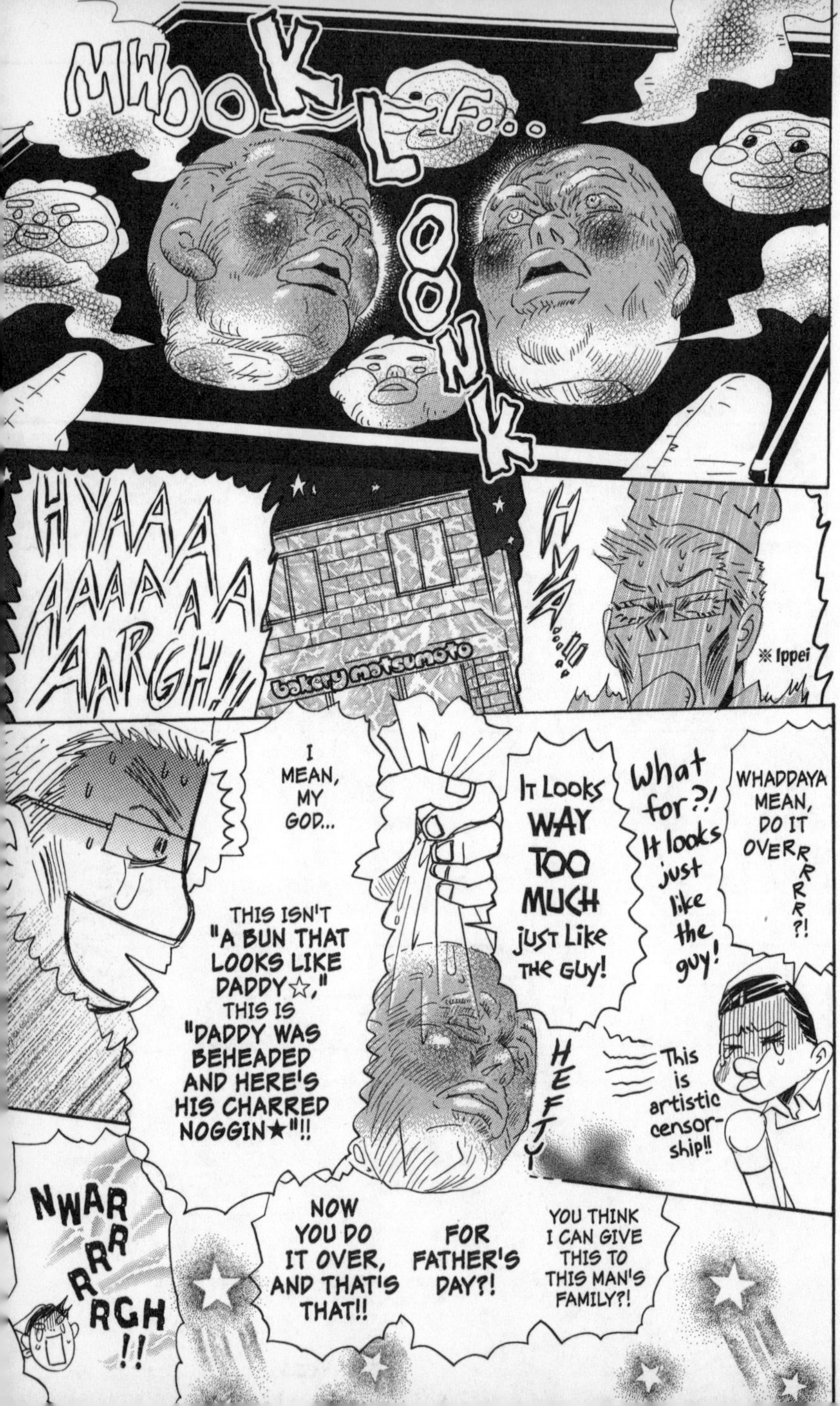
MWOOF...
KLOOONK
HYAA...!!
※ Ippei
HYAAAAAAAAARGH!!
bakery matsumoto
WHADDAYA MEAN, DO IT OVERRRRR?!
What for?! It looks just like the guy!
It Looks WAY TOO MUCH just Like the guy!
I MEAN, MY GOD...
THIS ISN'T "A BUN THAT LOOKS LIKE DADDY☆," THIS IS "DADDY WAS BEHEADED AND HERE'S HIS CHARRED NOGGIN★"!!
HEFTY
This is artistic censorship!!
YOU THINK I CAN GIVE THIS TO THIS MAN'S FAMILY?!
FOR FATHER'S DAY?!
NOW YOU DO IT OVER, AND THAT'S THAT!!
NWARRRRRRGH!!

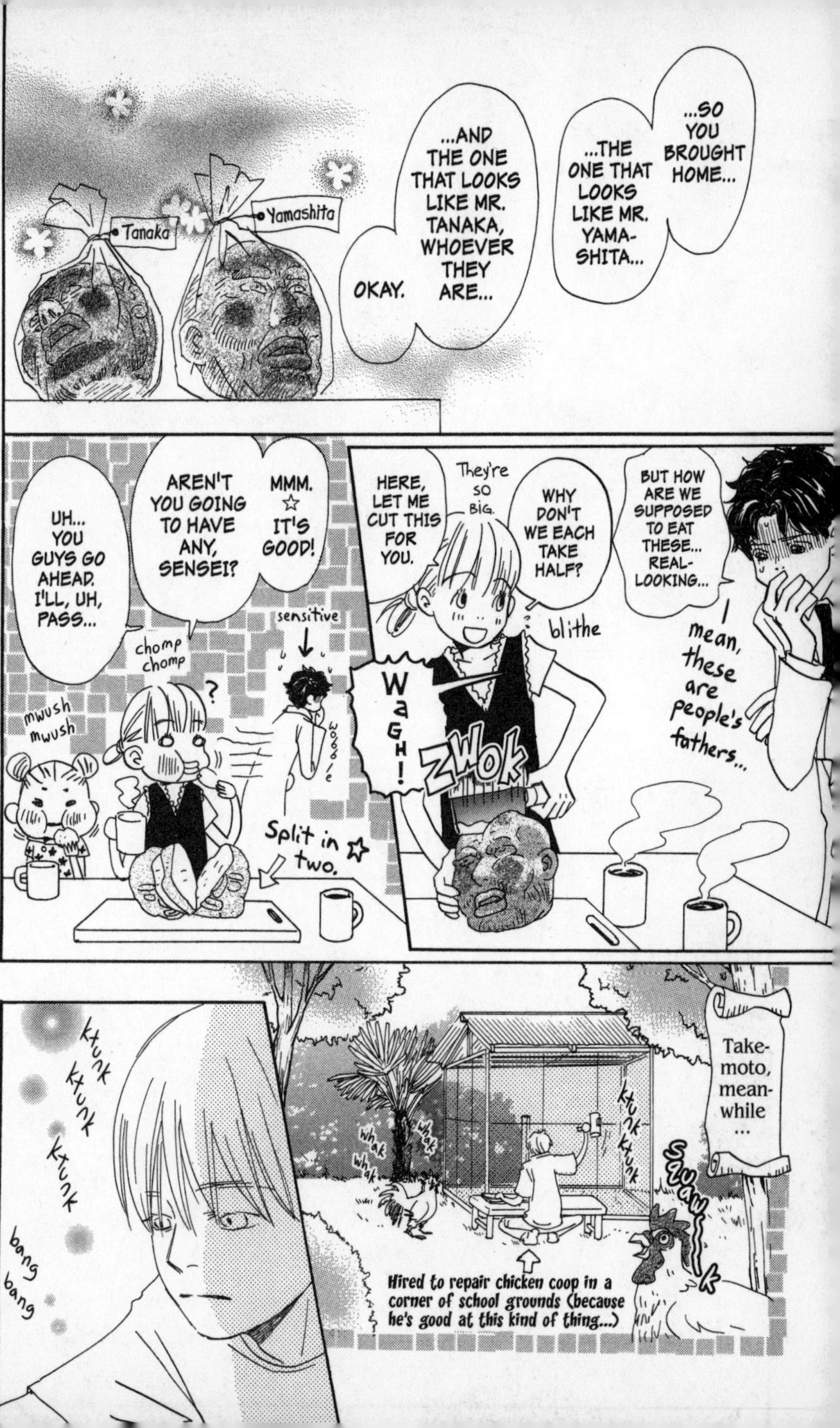
...SO YOU BROUGHT HOME...
...THE ONE THAT LOOKS LIKE MR. YAMASHITA...
...AND THE ONE THAT LOOKS LIKE MR. TANAKA, WHOEVER THEY ARE...
OKAY.
Yamashita
Tanaka
BUT HOW ARE WE SUPPOSED TO EAT THESE... REAL-LOOKING...
I mean, these are people's fathers...
WHY DON'T WE EACH TAKE HALF?
blithe
They're so big.
HERE, LET ME CUT THIS FOR YOU.
ZWOK
WAGH!
MMM. ☆ IT'S GOOD!
AREN'T YOU GOING TO HAVE ANY, SENSEI?
UH... YOU GUYS GO AHEAD. I'LL, UH, PASS...
sensitive
wobble
chomp chomp
?
mwush mwush
Split in two. ☆
Take-moto, mean-while...
SQUAWK
ktunk ktunk
whak whak whak
Hired to repair chicken coop in a corner of school grounds (because he's good at this kind of thing...)
ktunk ktunk ktunk
bang bang

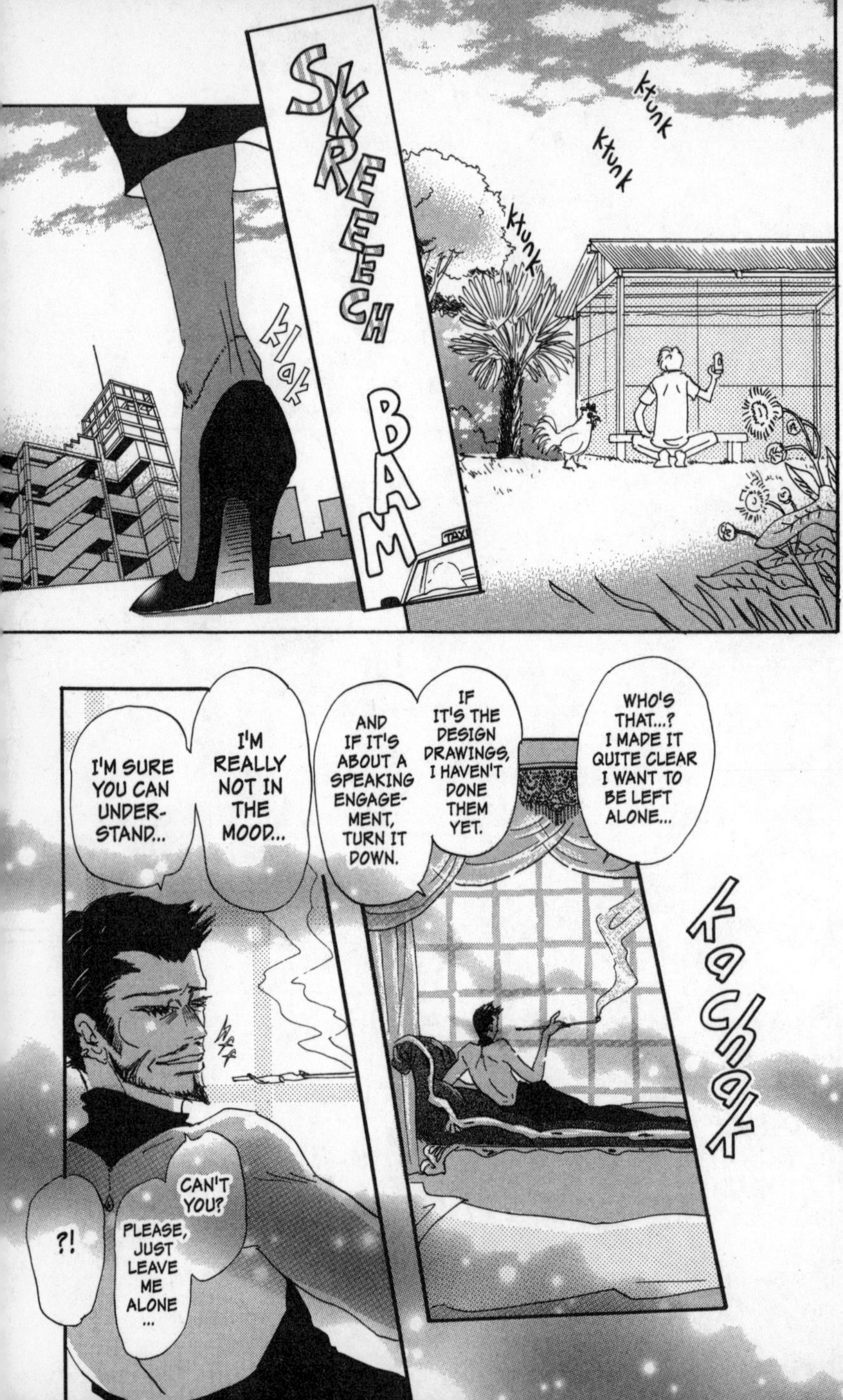
ktunk
ktunk
ktunk
SKREEECH
BAM
klak
TAXI
WHO'S THAT...? I MADE IT QUITE CLEAR I WANT TO BE LEFT ALONE...
IF IT'S THE DESIGN DRAWINGS, I HAVEN'T DONE THEM YET.
AND IF IT'S ABOUT A SPEAKING ENGAGEMENT, TURN IT DOWN.
kachak
I'M REALLY NOT IN THE MOOD...
I'M SURE YOU CAN UNDERSTAND...
CAN'T YOU?
PLEASE, JUST LEAVE ME ALONE...
?!

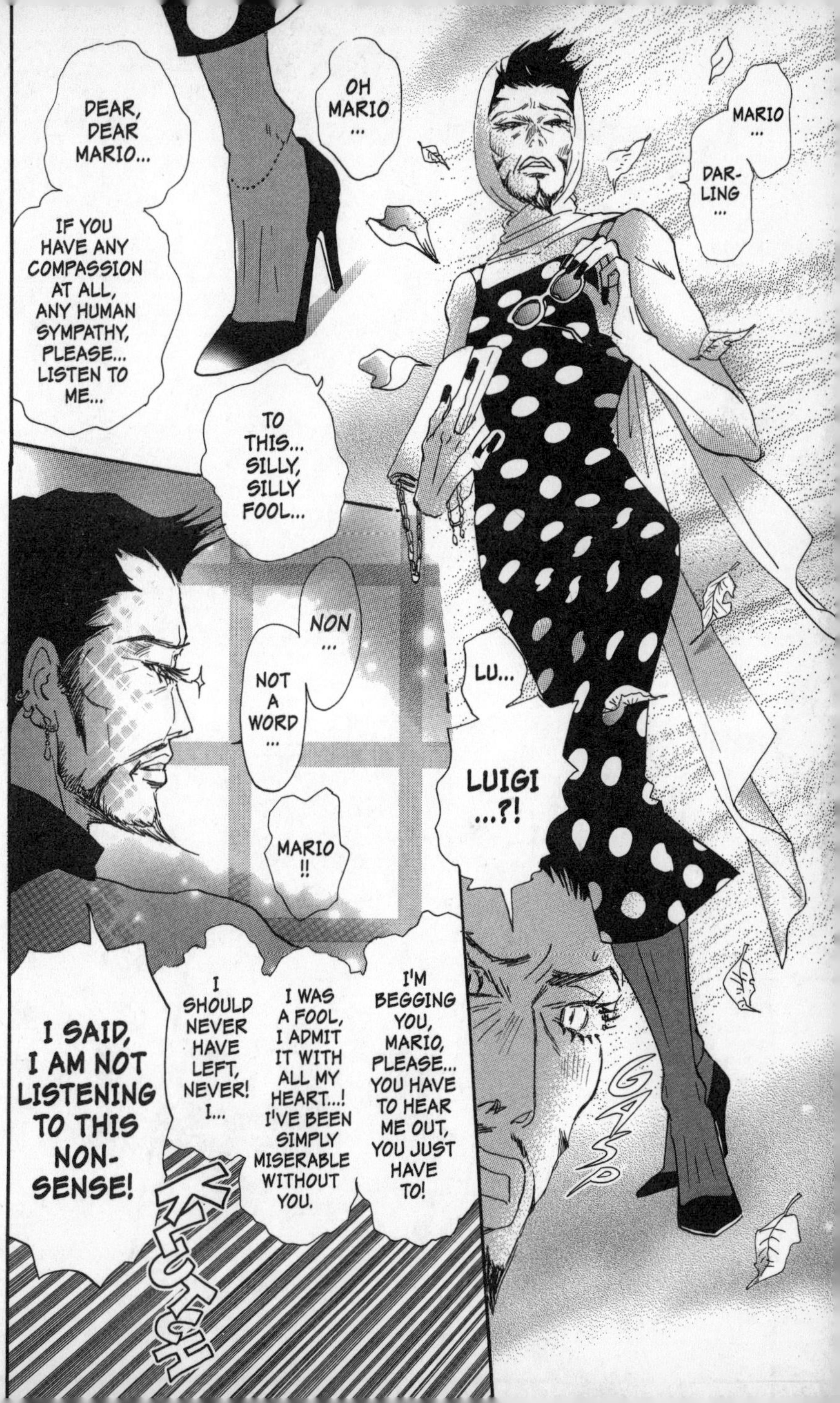
MARIO... DAR-LING...
OH MARIO...
DEAR, DEAR MARIO...
IF YOU HAVE ANY COMPASSION AT ALL, ANY HUMAN SYMPATHY, PLEASE... LISTEN TO ME...
TO THIS... SILLY, SILLY FOOL...
LU...
LUIGI...?!
NON... NOT A WORD...
MARIO!!
GASP
I'M BEGGING YOU, MARIO, PLEASE... YOU HAVE TO HEAR ME OUT, YOU JUST HAVE TO!
I WAS A FOOL, I ADMIT IT WITH ALL MY HEART...! I'VE BEEN SIMPLY MISERABLE WITHOUT YOU.
I SHOULD NEVER HAVE LEFT, NEVER! I...
I SAID, I AM NOT LISTENING TO THIS NON-SENSE!
KLUTCH

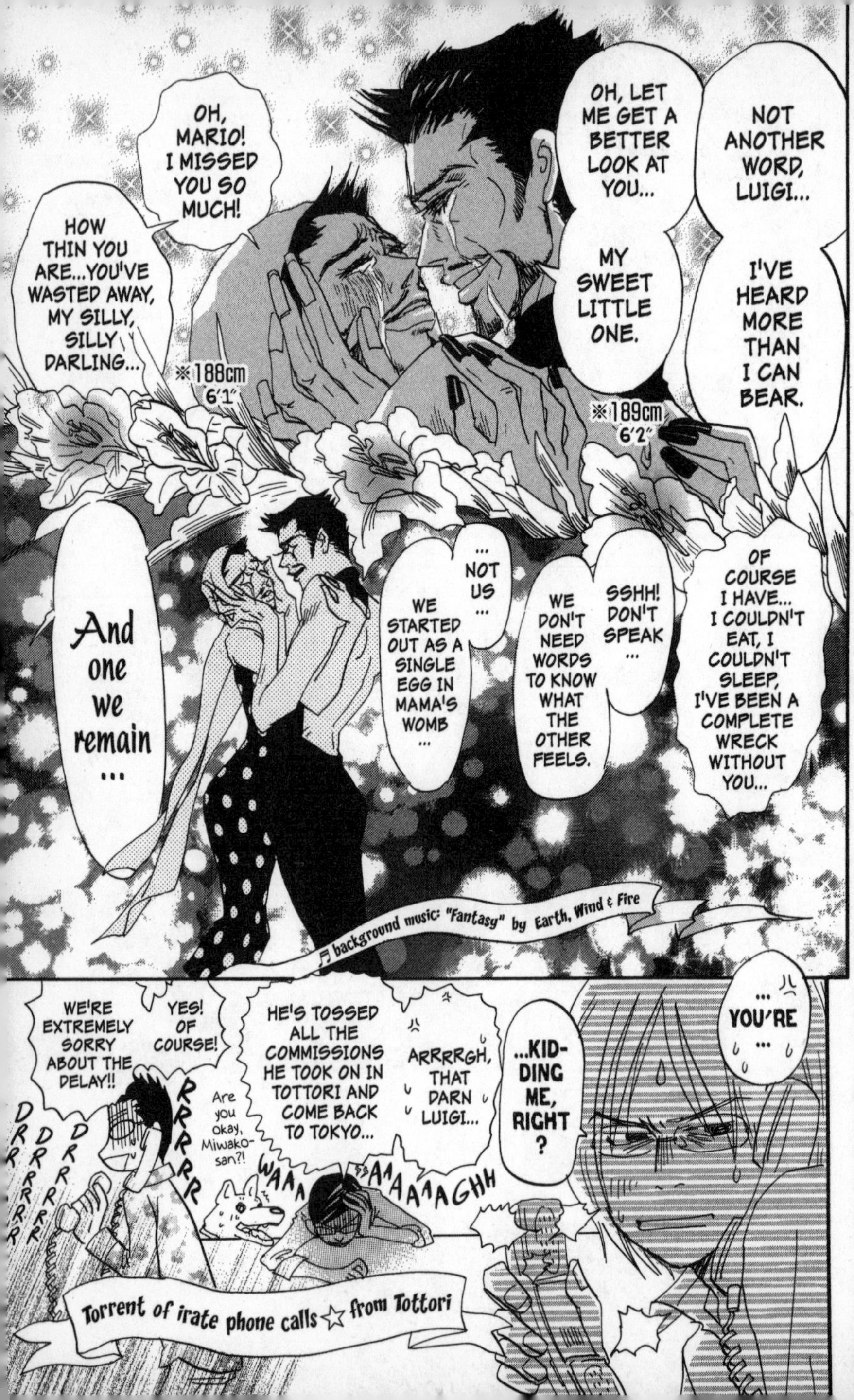
NOT ANOTHER WORD, LUIGI...
I'VE HEARD MORE THAN I CAN BEAR.
OH, LET ME GET A BETTER LOOK AT YOU...
MY SWEET LITTLE ONE.
※189cm 6'2"
OH, MARIO! I MISSED YOU SO MUCH!
HOW THIN YOU ARE...YOU'VE WASTED AWAY, MY SILLY, SILLY DARLING...
※188cm 6'1"
OF COURSE I HAVE... I COULDN'T EAT, I COULDN'T SLEEP, I'VE BEEN A COMPLETE WRECK WITHOUT YOU...
SSHH! DON'T SPEAK...
WE DON'T NEED WORDS TO KNOW WHAT THE OTHER FEELS.
...NOT US...
WE STARTED OUT AS A SINGLE EGG IN MAMA'S WOMB...
And one we remain...
♬ background music: "Fantasy" by Earth, Wind & Fire
...YOU'RE...
...KIDDING ME, RIGHT?
ARRRRGH, THAT DARN LUIGI...
HE'S TOSSED ALL THE COMMISSIONS HE TOOK ON IN TOTTORI AND COME BACK TO TOKYO...
AAAAAAAGHH
Are you okay, Miwako-san?!
WAAA
YES! OF COURSE!
WE'RE EXTREMELY SORRY ABOUT THE DELAY!!
RRRRRR
DRRRRRR
DRRRRRR
DRRRRRR
Torrent of irate phone calls☆from Tottori

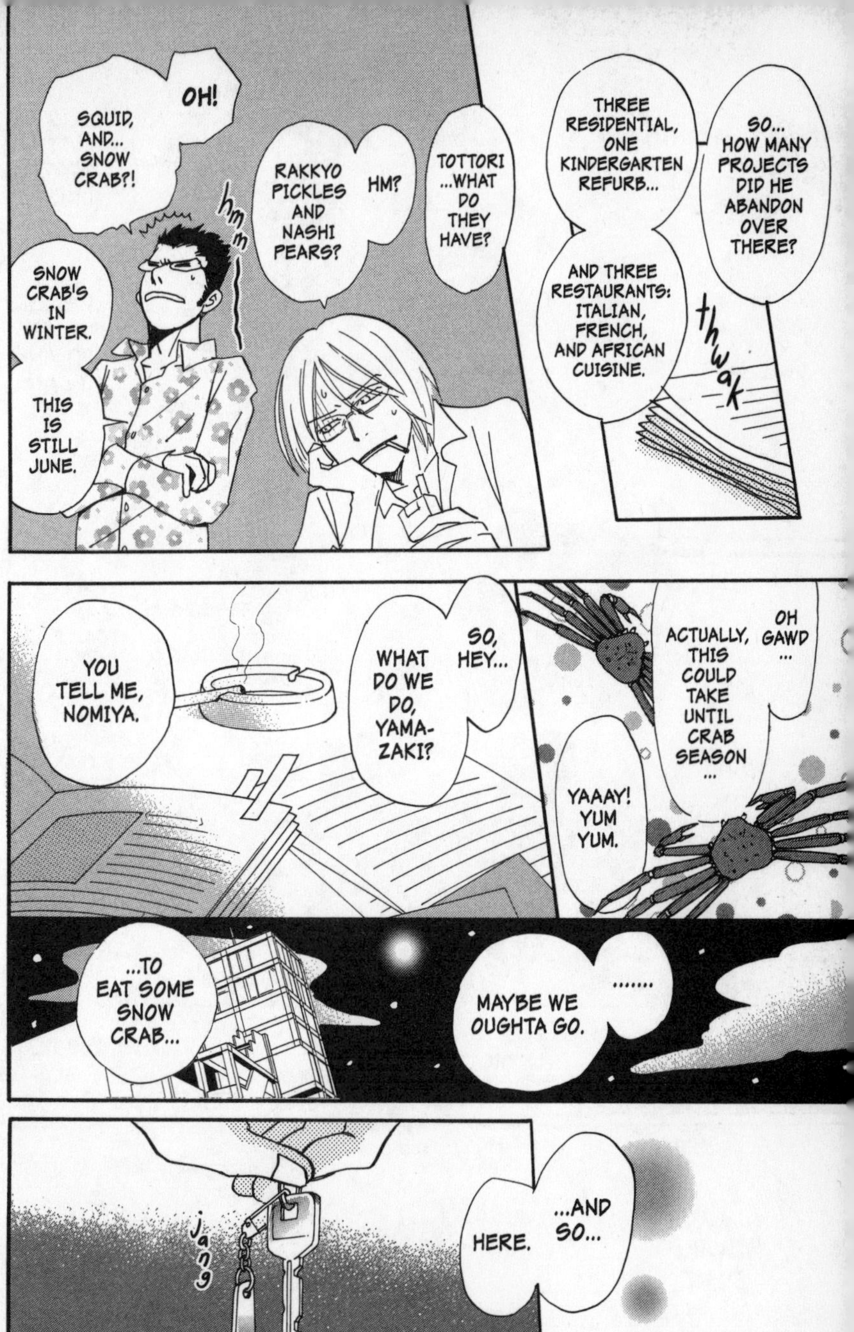
SO... HOW MANY PROJECTS DID HE ABANDON OVER THERE?
THREE RESIDENTIAL, ONE KINDERGARTEN REFURB...
AND THREE RESTAURANTS: ITALIAN, FRENCH, AND AFRICAN CUISINE.
thwak
TOTTORI ...WHAT DO THEY HAVE?
HM?
RAKKYO PICKLES AND NASHI PEARS?
OH!
SQUID, AND... SNOW CRAB?!
hmm
SNOW CRAB'S IN WINTER.
THIS IS STILL JUNE.
OH GAWD ...
ACTUALLY, THIS COULD TAKE UNTIL CRAB SEASON ...
YAAAY! YUM YUM.
SO, HEY...
WHAT DO WE DO, YAMA-ZAKI?
YOU TELL ME, NOMIYA.
....
MAYBE WE OUGHTA GO.
...TO EAT SOME SNOW CRAB...
...AND SO...
HERE.
jang

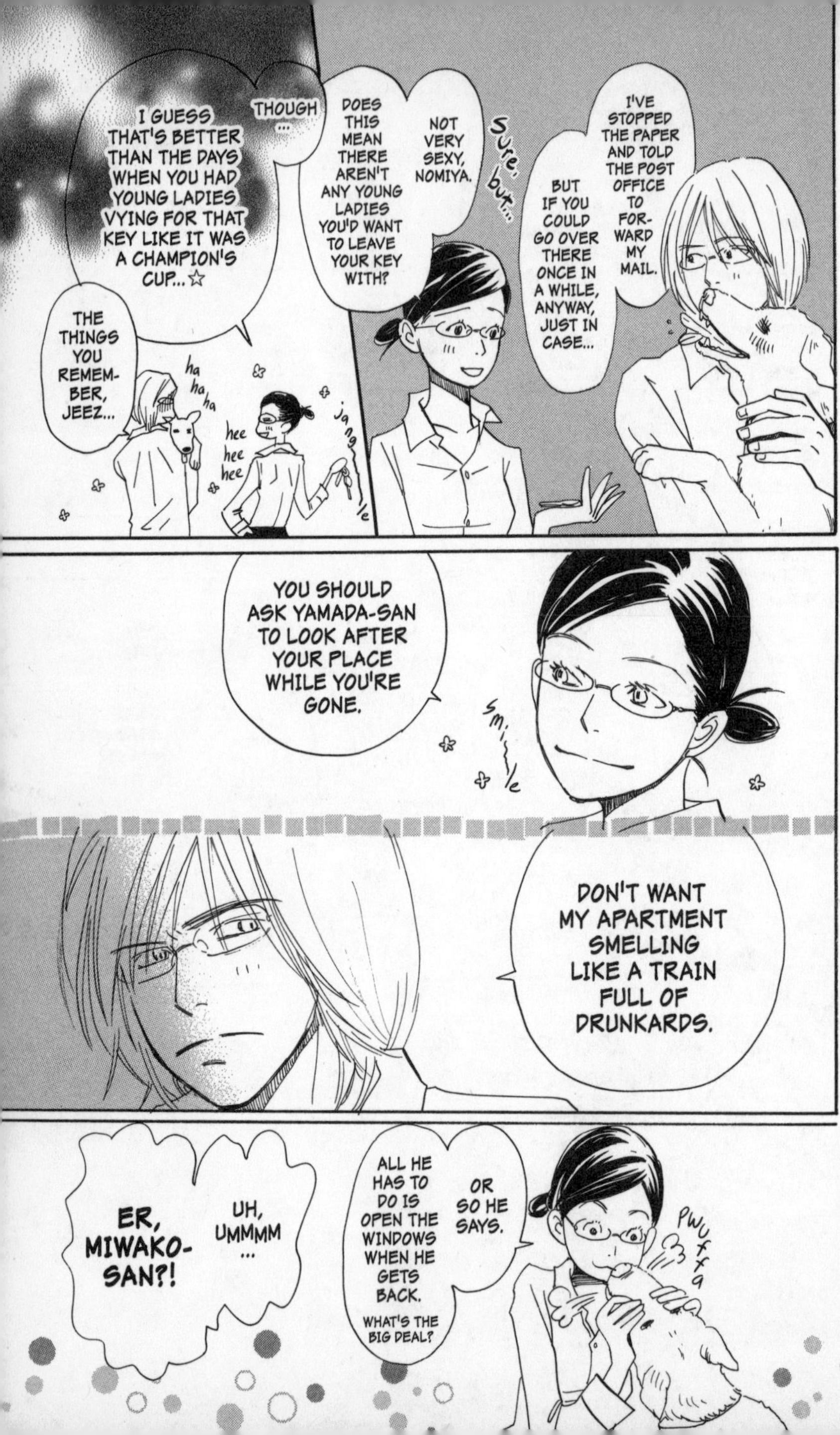
I'VE STOPPED THE PAPER AND TOLD THE POST OFFICE TO FORWARD MY MAIL.
BUT IF YOU COULD GO OVER THERE ONCE IN A WHILE, ANYWAY, JUST IN CASE...
Sure, but...
NOT VERY SEXY, NOMIYA.
DOES THIS MEAN THERE AREN'T ANY YOUNG LADIES YOU'D WANT TO LEAVE YOUR KEY WITH?
THOUGH...
I GUESS THAT'S BETTER THAN THE DAYS WHEN YOU HAD YOUNG LADIES VYING FOR THAT KEY LIKE IT WAS A CHAMPION'S CUP...☆
jangle
hee hee hee
ha ha ha
THE THINGS YOU REMEMBER, JEEZ...
YOU SHOULD ASK YAMADA-SAN TO LOOK AFTER YOUR PLACE WHILE YOU'RE GONE.
smile
DON'T WANT MY APARTMENT SMELLING LIKE A TRAIN FULL OF DRUNKARDS.
PWUffa
ALL HE HAS TO DO IS OPEN THE WINDOWS WHEN HE GETS BACK. OR SO HE SAYS.
WHAT'S THE BIG DEAL?
UH, UMMMM...
ER, MIWAKO-SAN?!

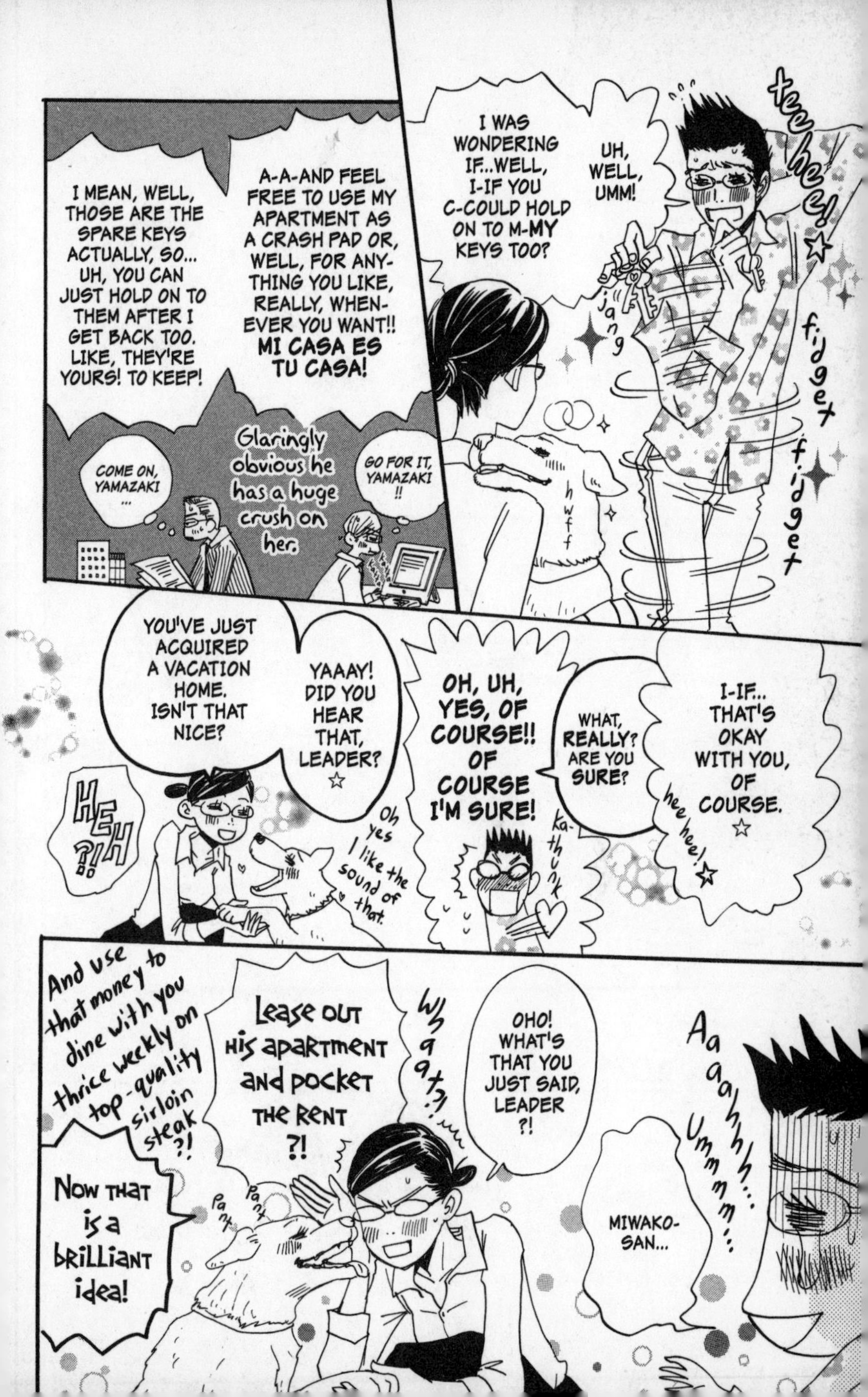
tee hee!☆
UH, WELL, UMM!
I WAS WONDERING IF...WELL, I-IF YOU C-COULD HOLD ON TO M-MY KEYS TOO?
jang
fidget fidget fidget
hwff
A-A-AND FEEL FREE TO USE MY APARTMENT AS A CRASH PAD OR, WELL, FOR ANYTHING YOU LIKE, REALLY, WHENEVER YOU WANT!! MI CASA ES TU CASA!
I MEAN, WELL, THOSE ARE THE SPARE KEYS ACTUALLY, SO... UH, YOU CAN JUST HOLD ON TO THEM AFTER I GET BACK TOO. LIKE, THEY'RE YOURS! TO KEEP!
GO FOR IT, YAMAZAKI!!
Glaringly obvious he has a huge crush on her.
COME ON, YAMAZAKI...
I-IF... THAT'S OKAY WITH YOU, OF COURSE.☆
hee hee!☆
WHAT, REALLY? ARE YOU SURE?
OH, UH, YES, OF COURSE!! OF COURSE I'M SURE!
ka-thunk
YAAAY! DID YOU HEAR THAT, LEADER?☆
YOU'VE JUST ACQUIRED A VACATION HOME. ISN'T THAT NICE?
Oh yes I like the sound of that.
HEH?!
Aaaahhh... Ummmm...
MIWAKO-SAN...
OHO! WHAT'S THAT YOU JUST SAID, LEADER?!
Whaat?!
Lease out his apartment and pocket the rent?!
And use that money to dine with you thrice weekly on top-quality sirloin steak?!
Now that is a brilliant idea!
Pant Pant

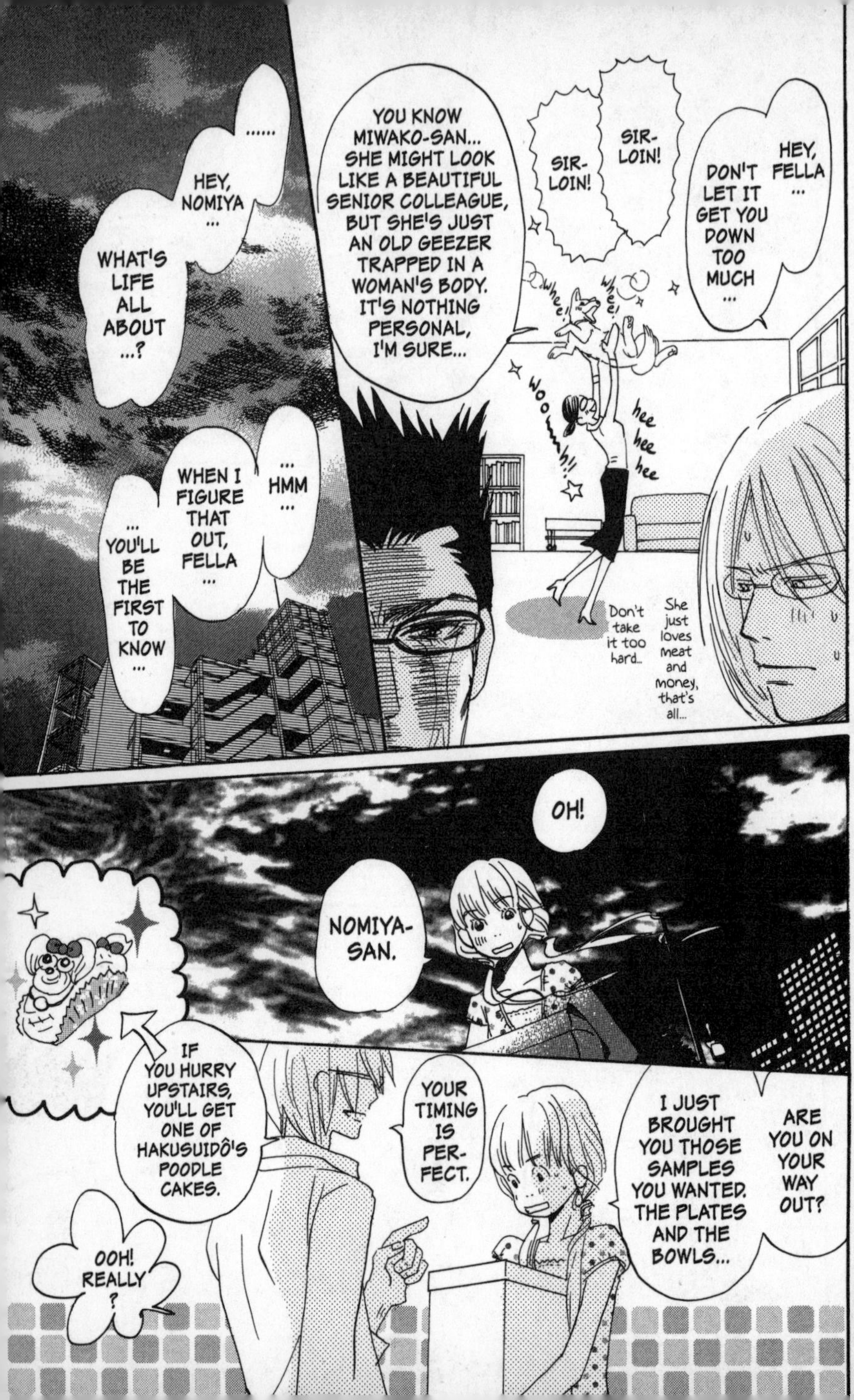
HEY, FELLA ...
DON'T LET IT GET YOU DOWN TOO MUCH ...
SIR-LOIN!
SIR-LOIN!
whee!
whee!
YOU KNOW MIWAKO-SAN... SHE MIGHT LOOK LIKE A BEAUTIFUL SENIOR COLLEAGUE, BUT SHE'S JUST AN OLD GEEZER TRAPPED IN A WOMAN'S BODY. IT'S NOTHING PERSONAL, I'M SURE...
woooh!!
hee hee hee
She just loves meat and money, that's all...
Don't take it too hard...
......
HEY, NOMIYA ...
WHAT'S LIFE ALL ABOUT ...?
... HMM ...
WHEN I FIGURE THAT OUT, FELLA ...
... YOU'LL BE THE FIRST TO KNOW ...
OH!
NOMIYA-SAN.
ARE YOU ON YOUR WAY OUT?
I JUST BROUGHT YOU THOSE SAMPLES YOU WANTED. THE PLATES AND THE BOWLS...
YOUR TIMING IS PER-FECT.
IF YOU HURRY UPSTAIRS, YOU'LL GET ONE OF HAKUSUIDÔ'S POODLE CAKES.
OOH! REALLY ?

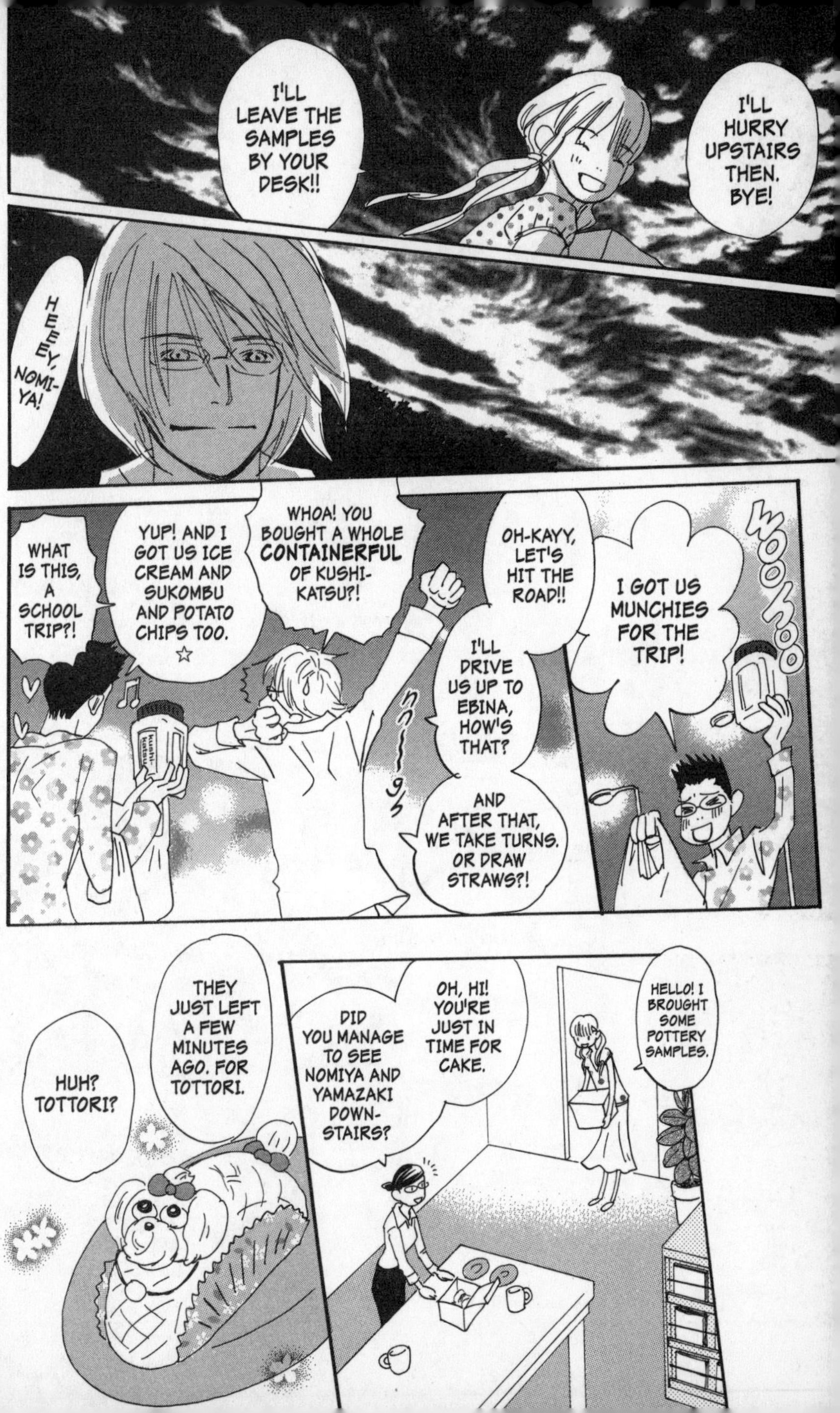
I'LL HURRY UPSTAIRS THEN. BYE!
I'LL LEAVE THE SAMPLES BY YOUR DESK!!
HEEEY, NOMIYA!
WOOHOO
I GOT US MUNCHIES FOR THE TRIP!
OH-KAYY, LET'S HIT THE ROAD!!
I'LL DRIVE US UP TO EBINA, HOW'S THAT?
AND AFTER THAT, WE TAKE TURNS. OR DRAW STRAWS?!
WHOA! YOU BOUGHT A WHOLE **CONTAINERFUL** OF KUSHI-KATSU?!
kushi-katsu
YUP! AND I GOT US ICE CREAM AND SUKOMBU AND POTATO CHIPS TOO. ☆
WHAT IS THIS, A SCHOOL TRIP?!
HELLO! I BROUGHT SOME POTTERY SAMPLES.
OH, HI! YOU'RE JUST IN TIME FOR CAKE.
DID YOU MANAGE TO SEE NOMIYA AND YAMAZAKI DOWN-STAIRS?
THEY JUST LEFT A FEW MINUTES AGO. FOR TOTTORI.
HUH? TOTTORI?

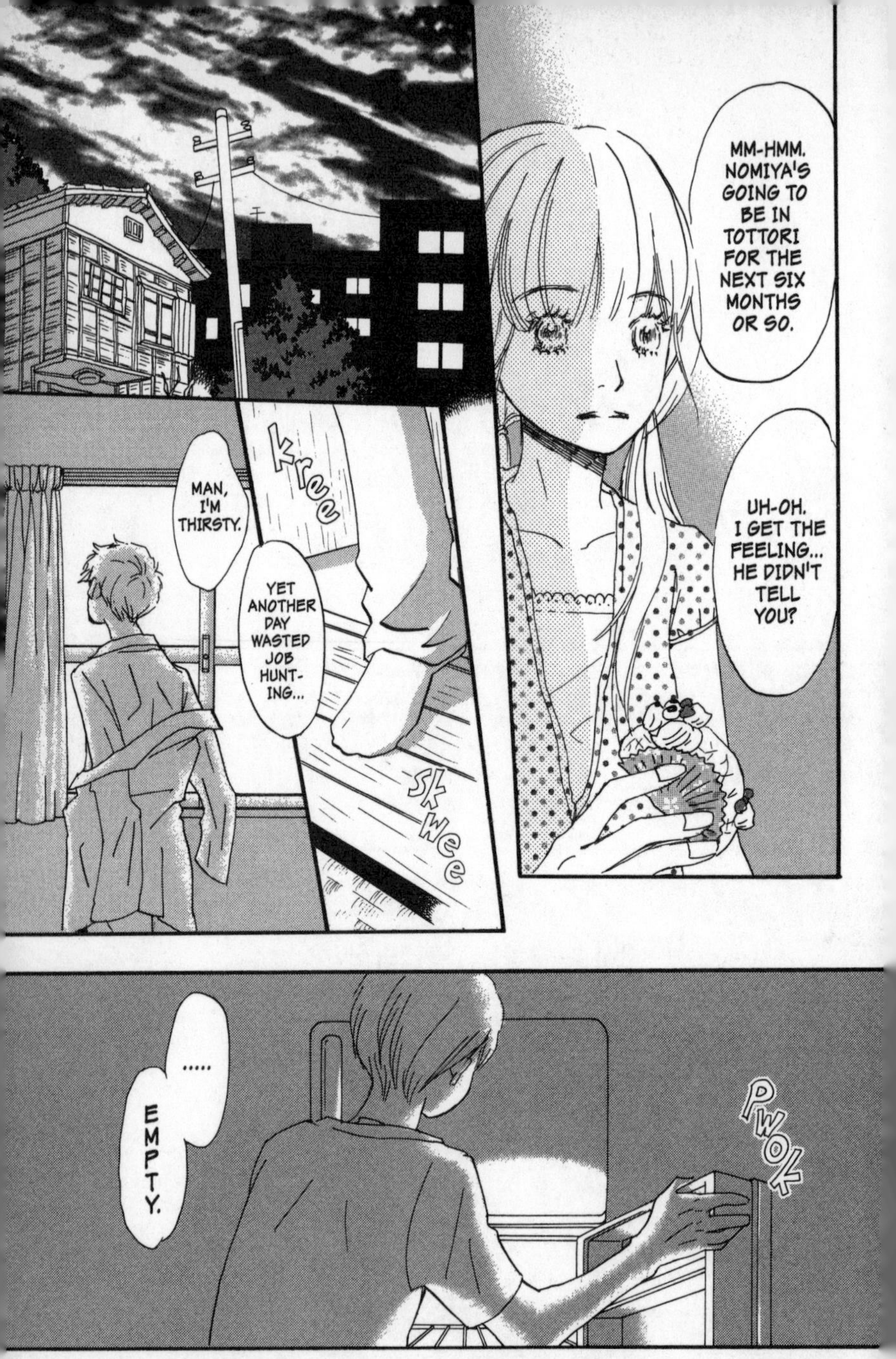
MM-HMM. NOMIYA'S GOING TO BE IN TOTTORI FOR THE NEXT SIX MONTHS OR SO.
UH-OH. I GET THE FEELING... HE DIDN'T TELL YOU?
kree
MAN, I'M THIRSTY.
YET ANOTHER DAY WASTED JOB HUNTING...
skwee
PWOK
......
EMPTY.

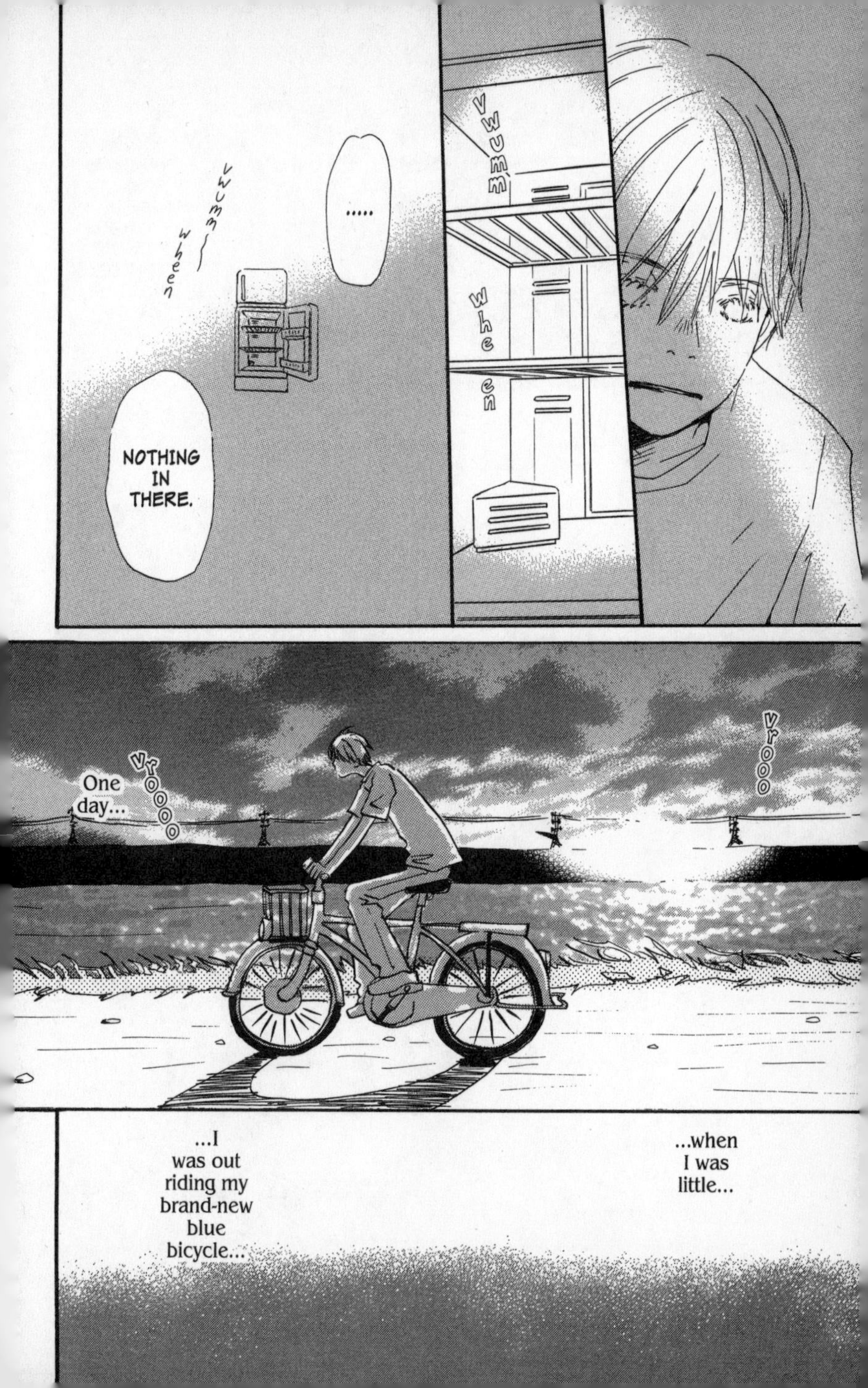
vwumm
wheen
.....
vwumm~
wheen
NOTHING IN THERE.
vrooo
One day...
vroooo
...when I was little...
...I was out riding my brand-new blue bicycle...

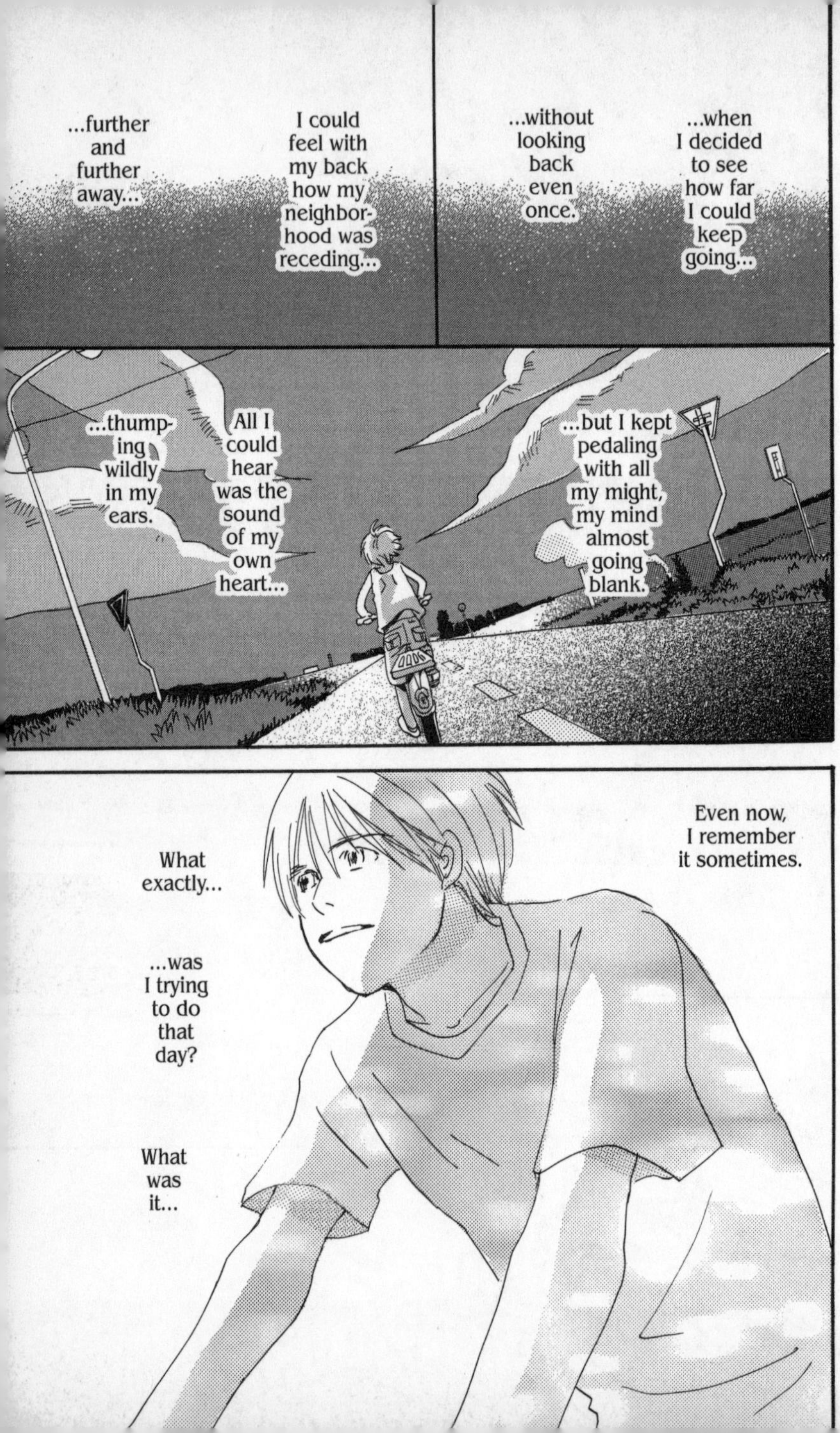
...when I decided to see how far I could keep going...
...without looking back even once.
I could feel with my back how my neighbor-hood was receding...
...further and further away...
...but I kept pedaling with all my might, my mind almost going blank.
All I could hear was the sound of my own heart...
...thump-ing wildly in my ears.
Even now, I remember it sometimes.
What exactly...
...was I trying to do that day?
What was it...

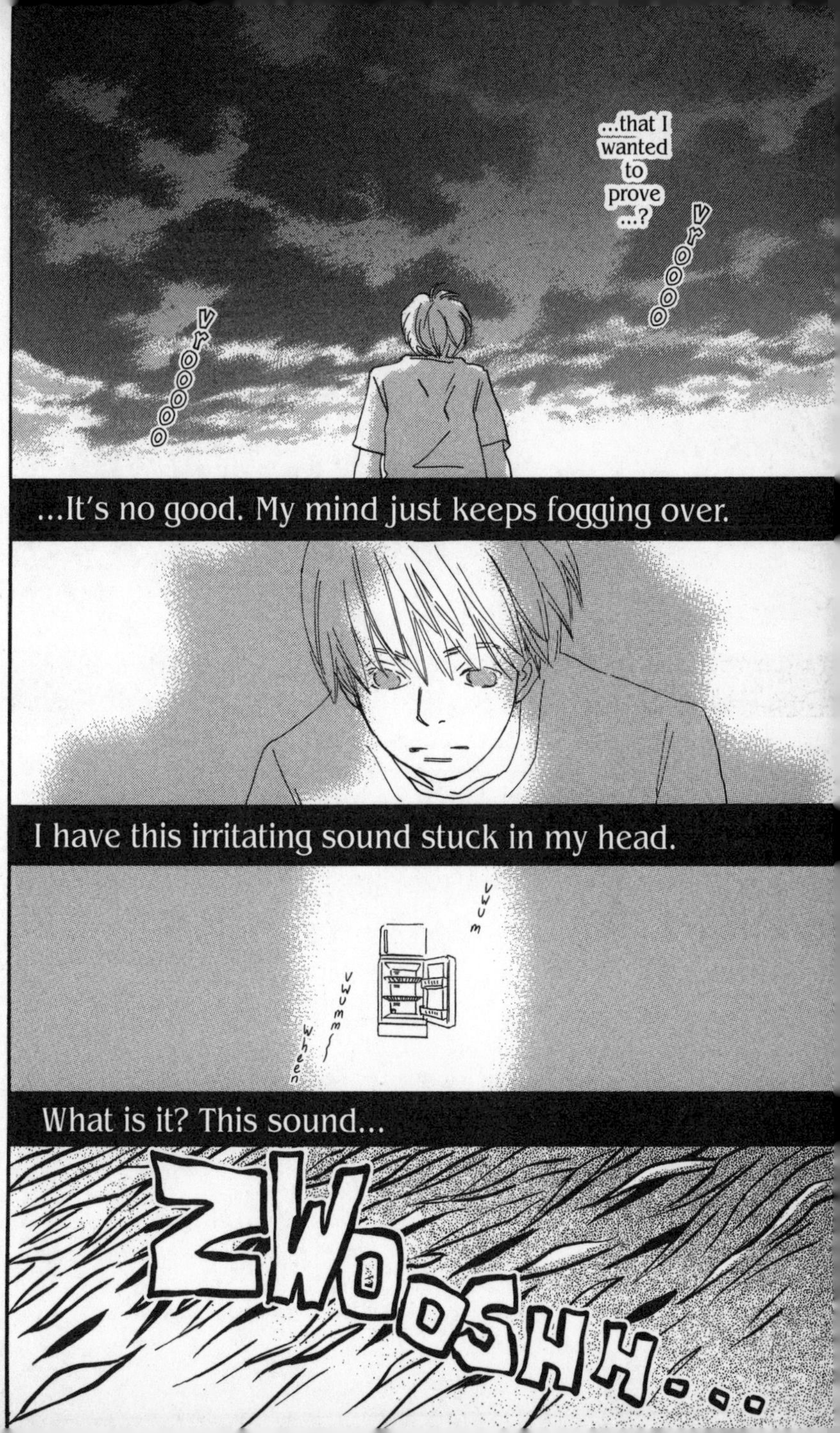
...that I wanted to prove ...?
Vroooooo
Vroooooo
...It's no good. My mind just keeps fogging over.
I have this irritating sound stuck in my head.
vwum
vwumm
wheen
What is it? This sound...
ZWOOSHH...

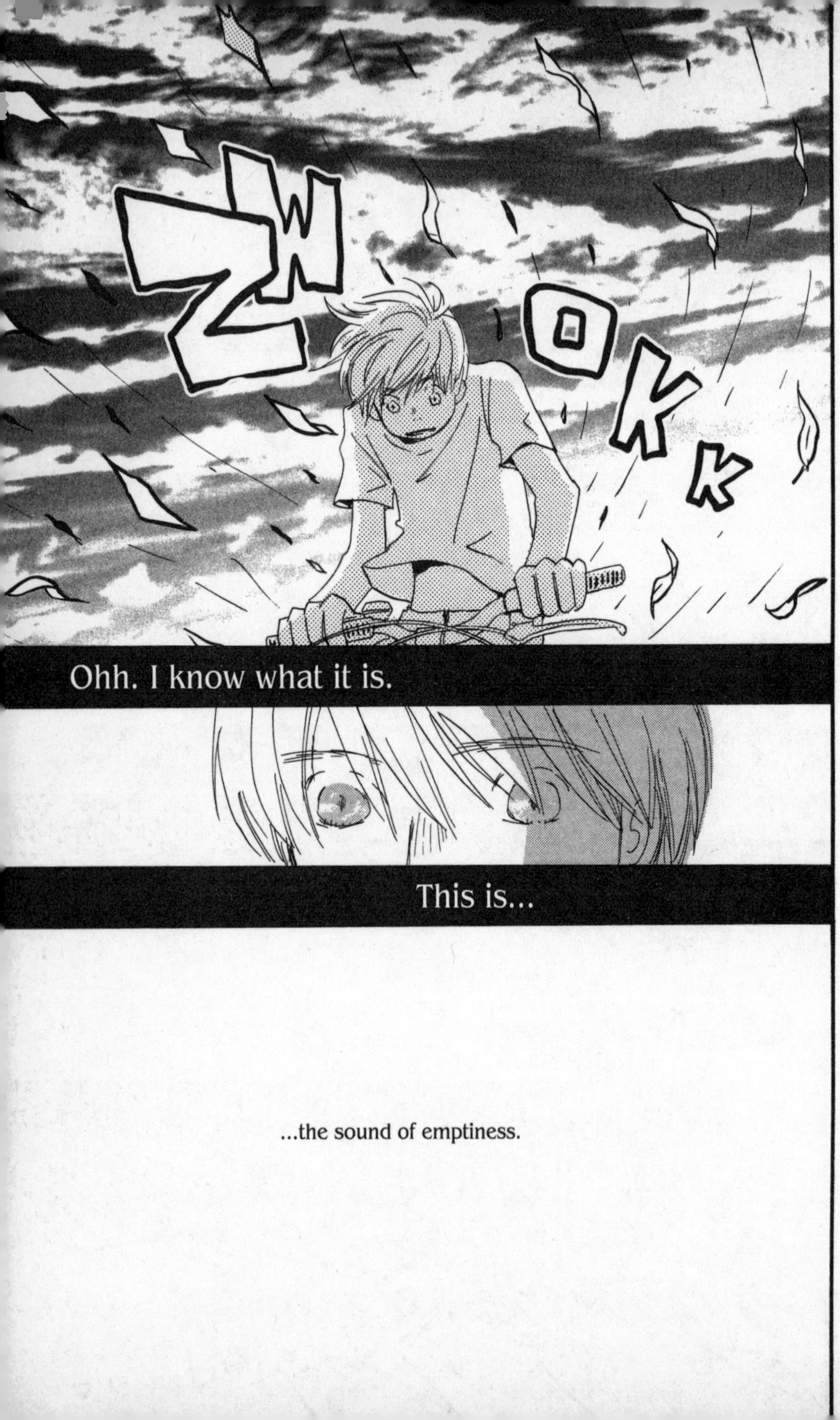
ZWOKK
Ohh. I know what it is.
This is...
...the sound of emptiness.

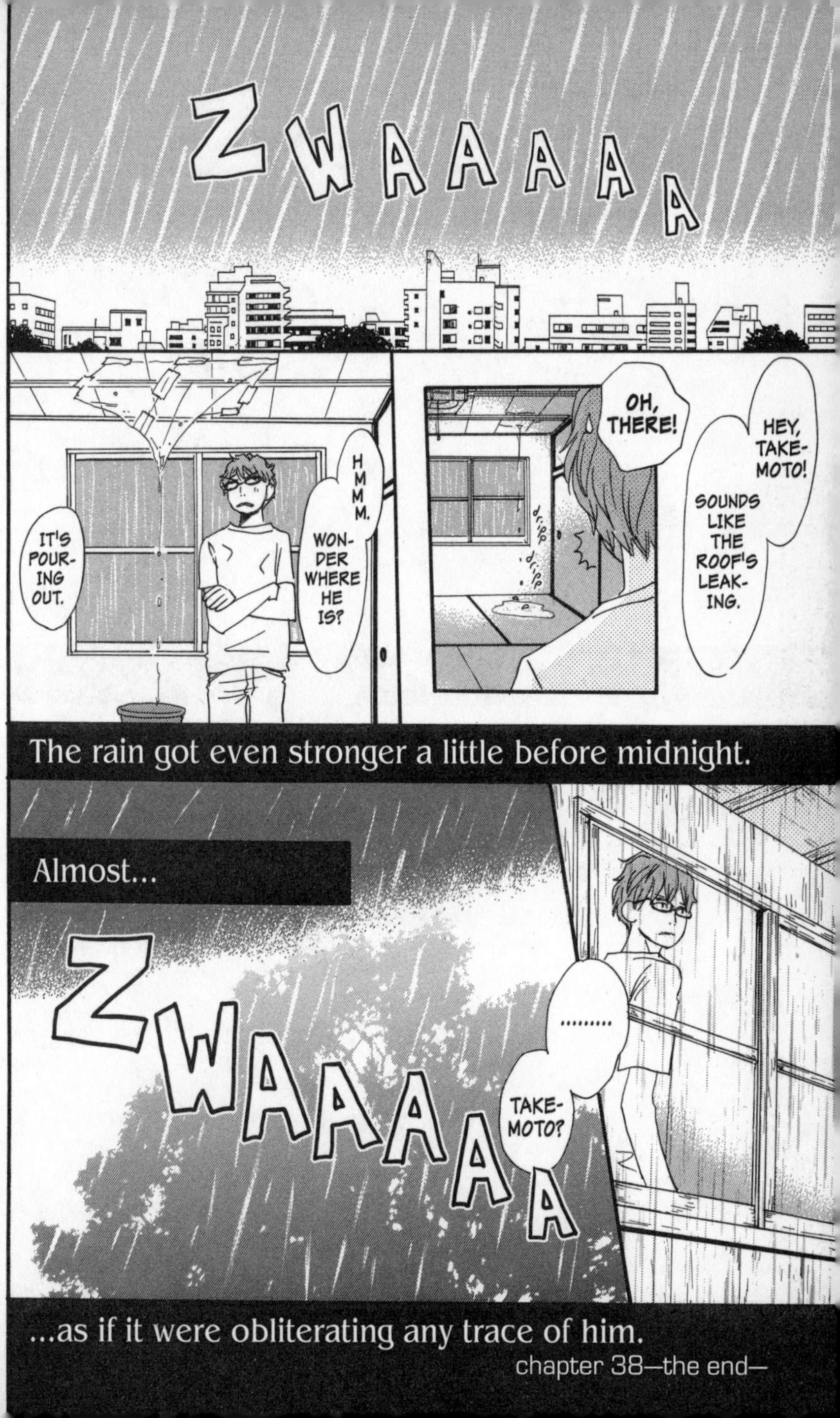
ZWAAAAAA
HEY, TAKEMOTO!
SOUNDS LIKE THE ROOF'S LEAKING.
OH, THERE!
drip drip
HMMM.
WONDER WHERE HE IS?
IT'S POURING OUT.
The rain got even stronger a little before midnight.
Almost...
....
TAKEMOTO?
ZWAAAAAA
...as if it were obliterating any trace of him.
chapter 38—the end—

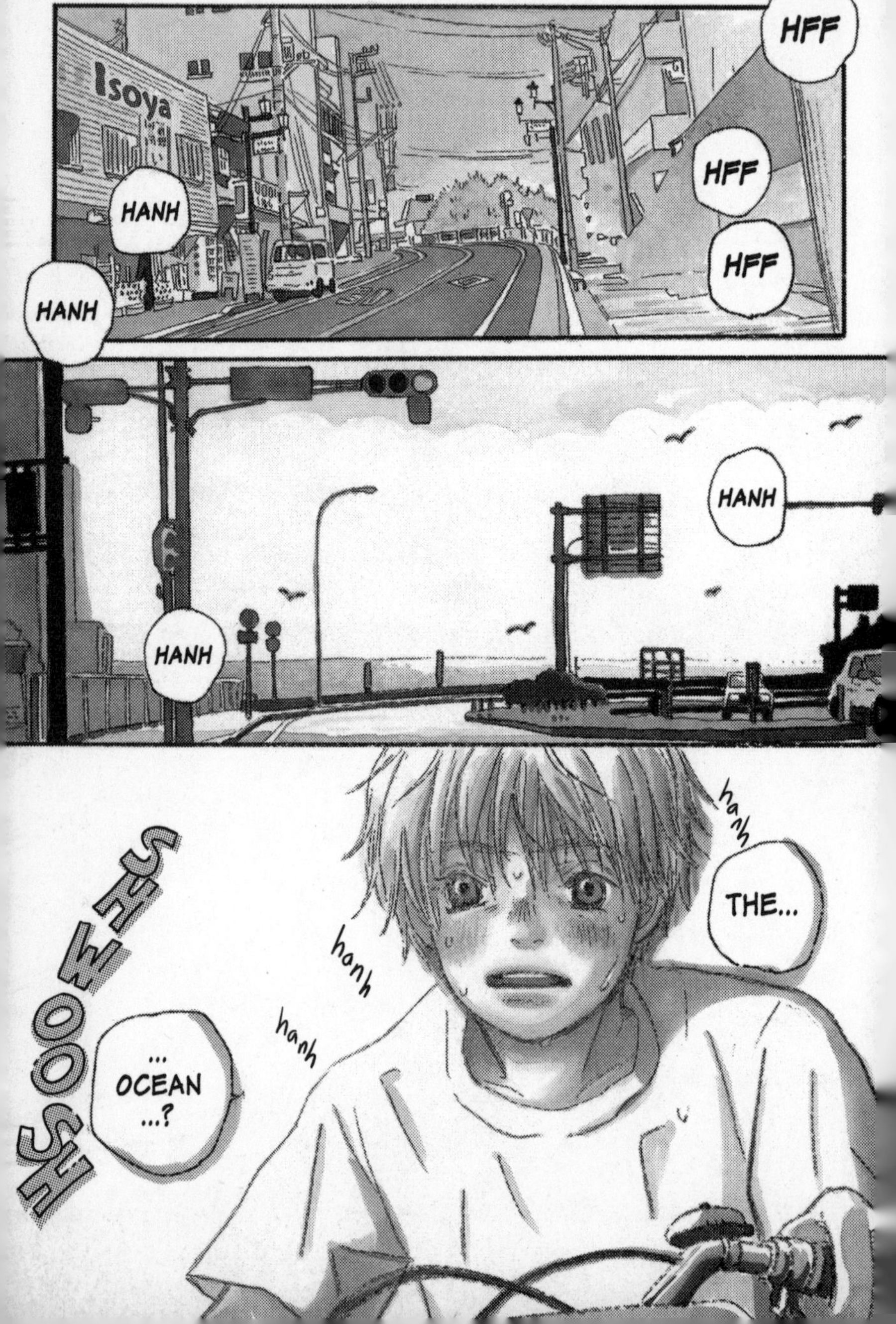
HFF
HFF
HFF
HANH
HANH
HANH
HANH
hanh
THE...
hanh
hanh
SHWOOSH
... OCEAN ...?

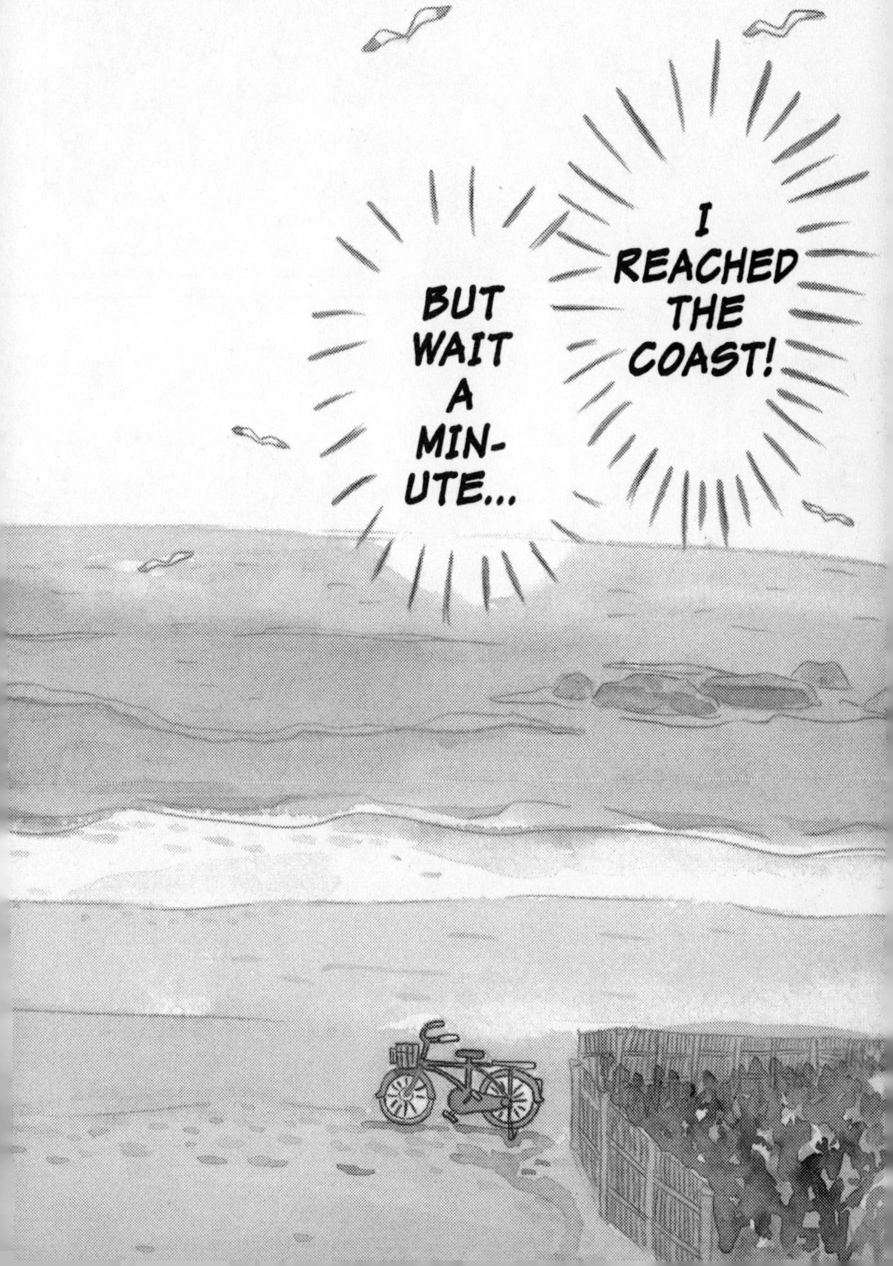
I REACHED THE COAST!
BUT WAIT A MIN-UTE...

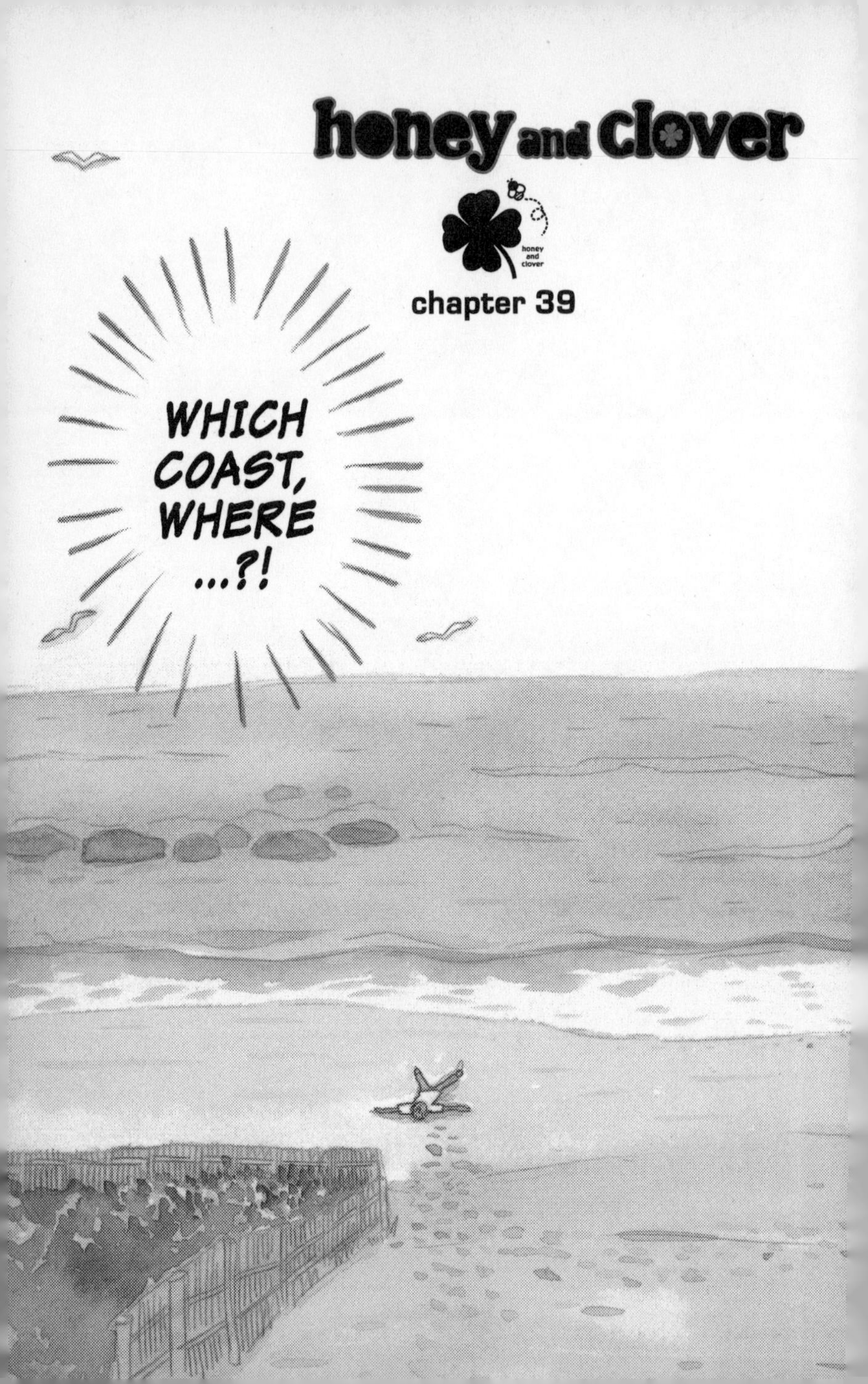
honey and clover
honey and clover
chapter 39
WHICH COAST, WHERE ...?!

Lindt vs. Jean-Paul Hévin Part 2

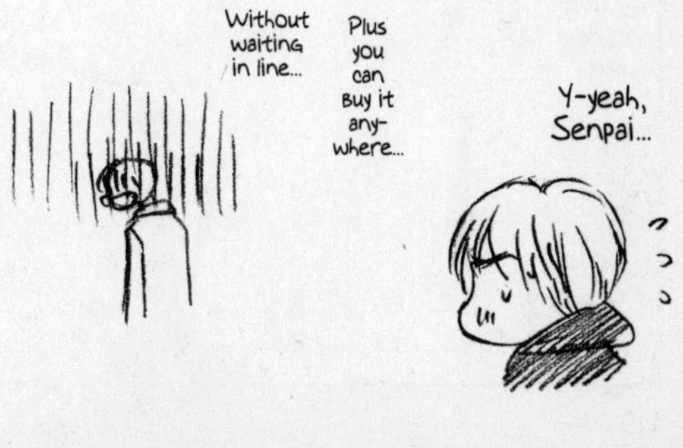
Without waiting in line...
Plus you can buy it anywhere...
Y-yeah, Senpai...

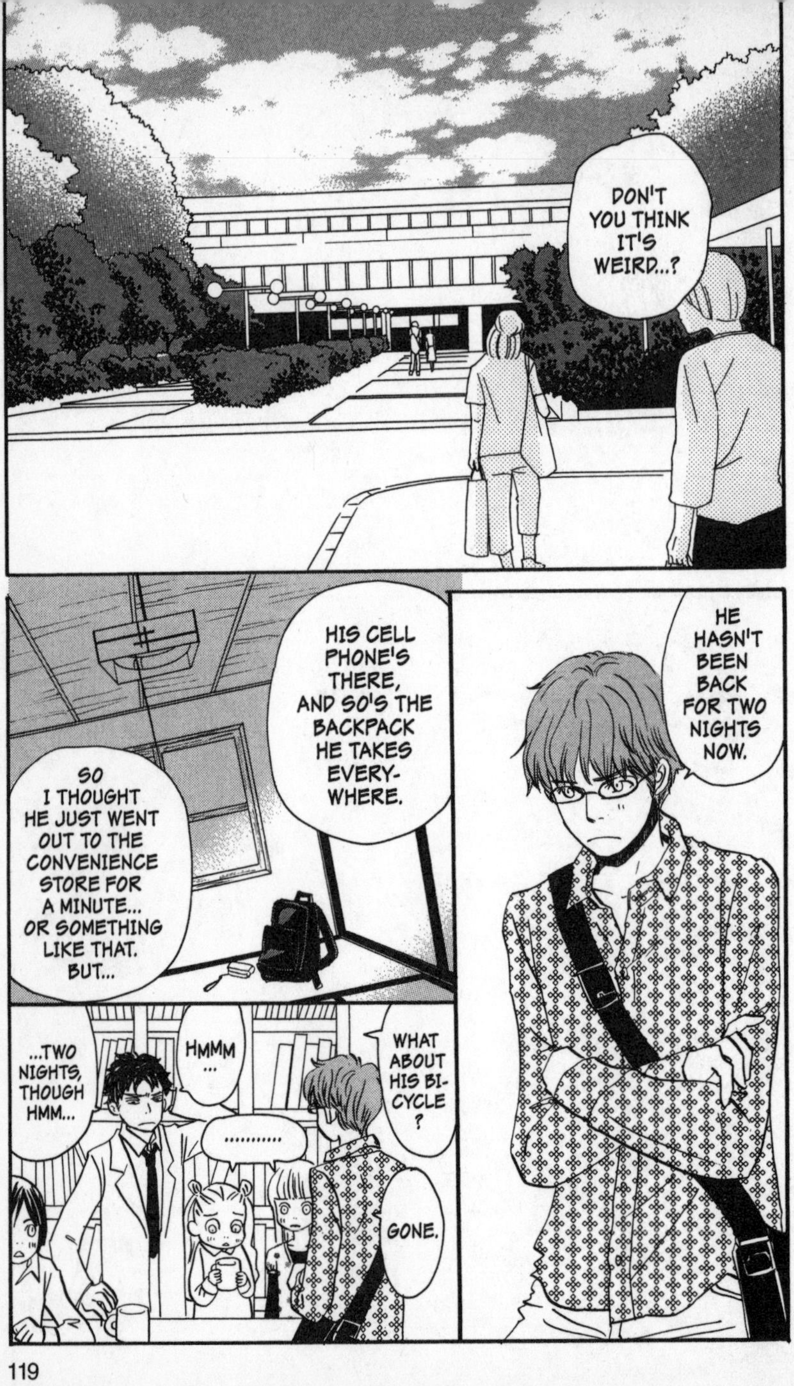
DON'T YOU THINK IT'S WEIRD...?
HE HASN'T BEEN BACK FOR TWO NIGHTS NOW.
HIS CELL PHONE'S THERE, AND SO'S THE BACKPACK HE TAKES EVERY-WHERE.
SO I THOUGHT HE JUST WENT OUT TO THE CONVENIENCE STORE FOR A MINUTE... OR SOMETHING LIKE THAT. BUT...
WHAT ABOUT HIS BI-CYCLE ?
HMMM ...
...TWO NIGHTS, THOUGH HMM...
....
GONE.

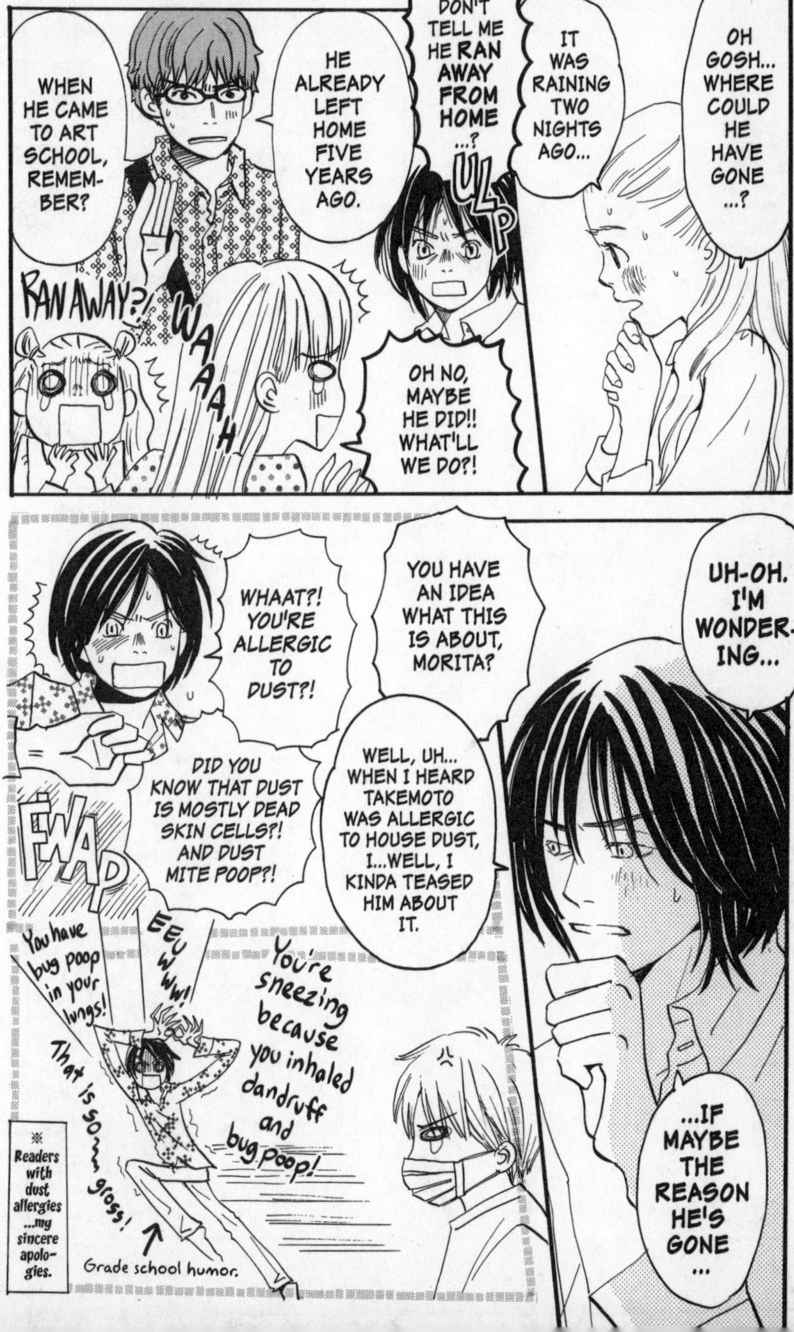
OH GOSH... WHERE COULD HE HAVE GONE ...?
IT WAS RAINING TWO NIGHTS AGO...
DON'T TELL ME HE RAN AWAY FROM HOME ...?
ULP
HE ALREADY LEFT HOME FIVE YEARS AGO.
WHEN HE CAME TO ART SCHOOL, REMEMBER?
OH NO, MAYBE HE DID!! WHAT'LL WE DO?!
WAAAAH
RAN AWAY?!
UH-OH. I'M WONDERING...
...IF MAYBE THE REASON HE'S GONE ...
YOU HAVE AN IDEA WHAT THIS IS ABOUT, MORITA?
WELL, UH... WHEN I HEARD TAKEMOTO WAS ALLERGIC TO HOUSE DUST, I...WELL, I KINDA TEASED HIM ABOUT IT.
WHAAT?! YOU'RE ALLERGIC TO DUST?!
DID YOU KNOW THAT DUST IS MOSTLY DEAD SKIN CELLS?! AND DUST MITE POOP?!
FWAP
You're sneezing because you inhaled dandruff and bug poop!
EEUWWW!
You have bug poop in your lungs!
That is so~~ gross!
Grade school humor.
※ Readers with dust allergies ...my sincere apologies.

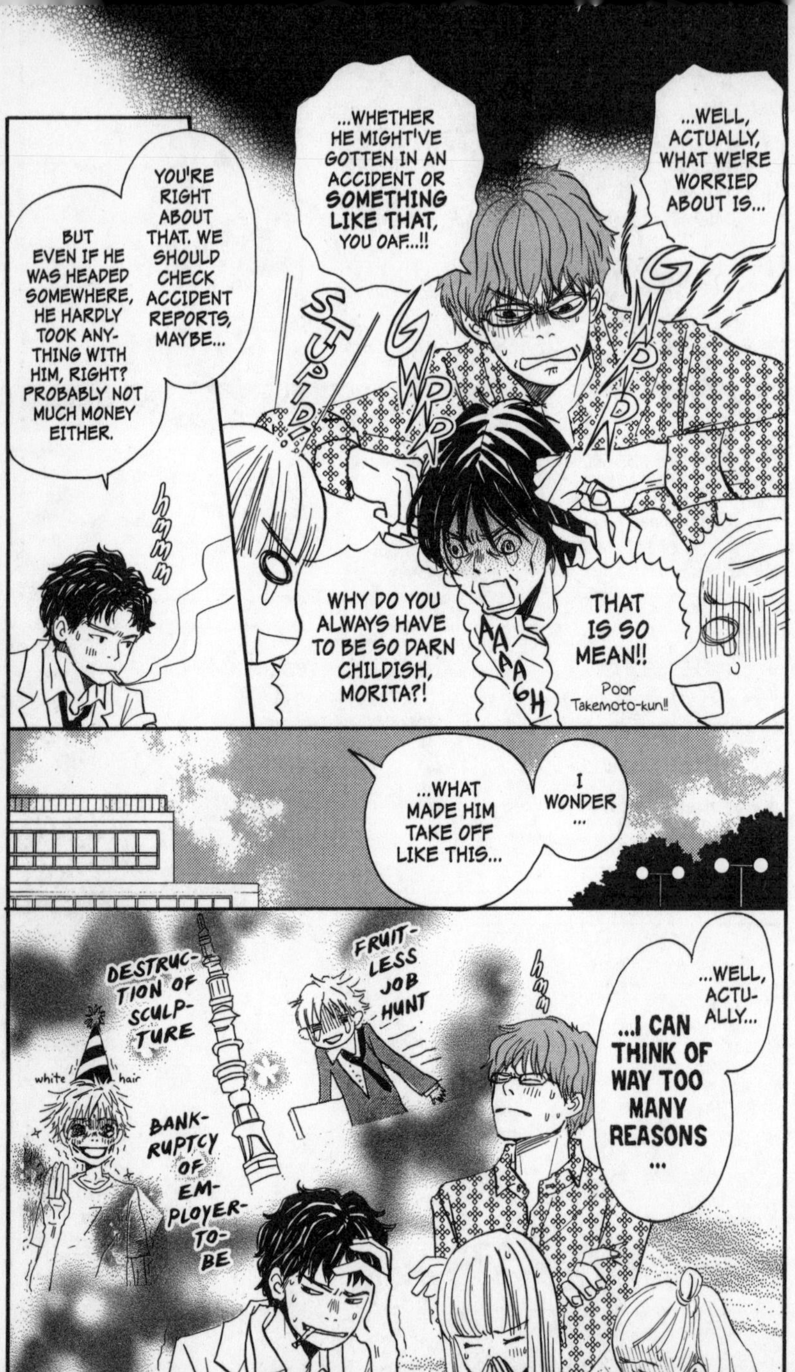
...WELL, ACTUALLY, WHAT WE'RE WORRIED ABOUT IS...
...WHETHER HE MIGHT'VE GOTTEN IN AN ACCIDENT OR SOMETHING LIKE THAT, YOU OAF...!!
GWRRR
GWRRR
STUPID!
THAT IS SO MEAN!!
Poor Takemoto-kun!!
AAAAAGH
WHY DO YOU ALWAYS HAVE TO BE SO DARN CHILDISH, MORITA?!
YOU'RE RIGHT ABOUT THAT. WE SHOULD CHECK ACCIDENT REPORTS, MAYBE...
BUT EVEN IF HE WAS HEADED SOMEWHERE, HE HARDLY TOOK ANYTHING WITH HIM, RIGHT? PROBABLY NOT MUCH MONEY EITHER.
hmmm
I WONDER...
...WHAT MADE HIM TAKE OFF LIKE THIS...
...WELL, ACTUALLY...
...I CAN THINK OF WAY TOO MANY REASONS...
hmm
FRUITLESS JOB HUNT
DESTRUCTION OF SCULPTURE
white hair
BANKRUPTCY OF EMPLOYER-TO-BE

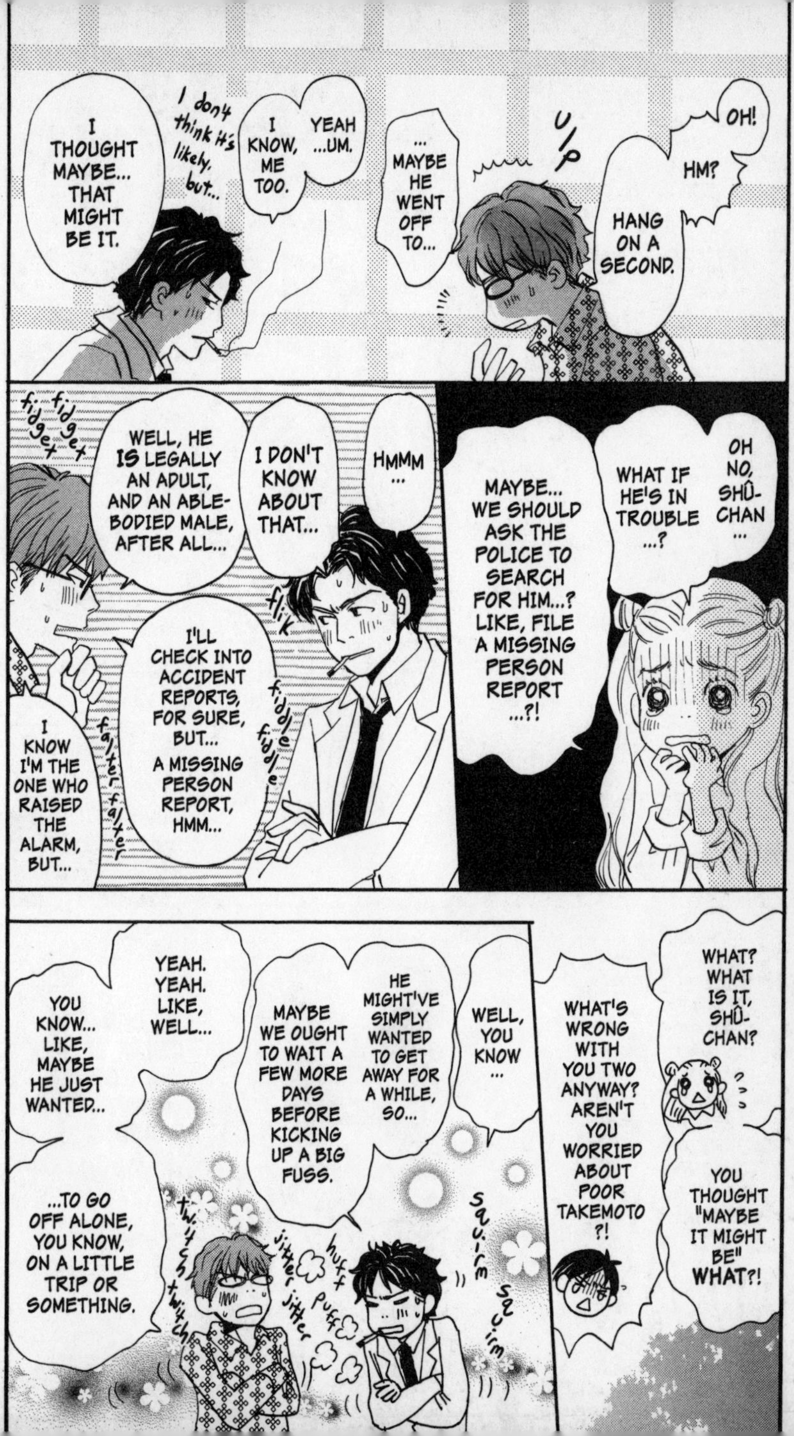
OH!
HM?
HANG ON A SECOND.
...MAYBE HE WENT OFF TO...
YEAH ...UM.
I KNOW, ME TOO.
I don't think it's likely, but...
I THOUGHT MAYBE... THAT MIGHT BE IT.
OH NO, SHÛ-CHAN...
WHAT IF HE'S IN TROUBLE...?
MAYBE... WE SHOULD ASK THE POLICE TO SEARCH FOR HIM...? LIKE, FILE A MISSING PERSON REPORT...?!
HMMM...
I DON'T KNOW ABOUT THAT...
WELL, HE IS LEGALLY AN ADULT, AND AN ABLE-BODIED MALE, AFTER ALL...
fidget fidget
flik
I'LL CHECK INTO ACCIDENT REPORTS, FOR SURE, BUT... A MISSING PERSON REPORT, HMM...
fiddle fiddle
falter falter
I KNOW I'M THE ONE WHO RAISED THE ALARM, BUT...
WHAT? WHAT IS IT, SHÛ-CHAN?
YOU THOUGHT "MAYBE IT MIGHT BE" WHAT?!
WHAT'S WRONG WITH YOU TWO ANYWAY? AREN'T YOU WORRIED ABOUT POOR TAKEMOTO?!
WELL, YOU KNOW...
HE MIGHT'VE SIMPLY WANTED TO GET AWAY FOR A WHILE, SO...
MAYBE WE OUGHT TO WAIT A FEW MORE DAYS BEFORE KICKING UP A BIG FUSS.
YEAH. YEAH. LIKE, WELL...
YOU KNOW... LIKE, MAYBE HE JUST WANTED...
...TO GO OFF ALONE, YOU KNOW, ON A LITTLE TRIP OR SOMETHING.
squirm squirm
huff puff
jitter jitter
twitch twitch

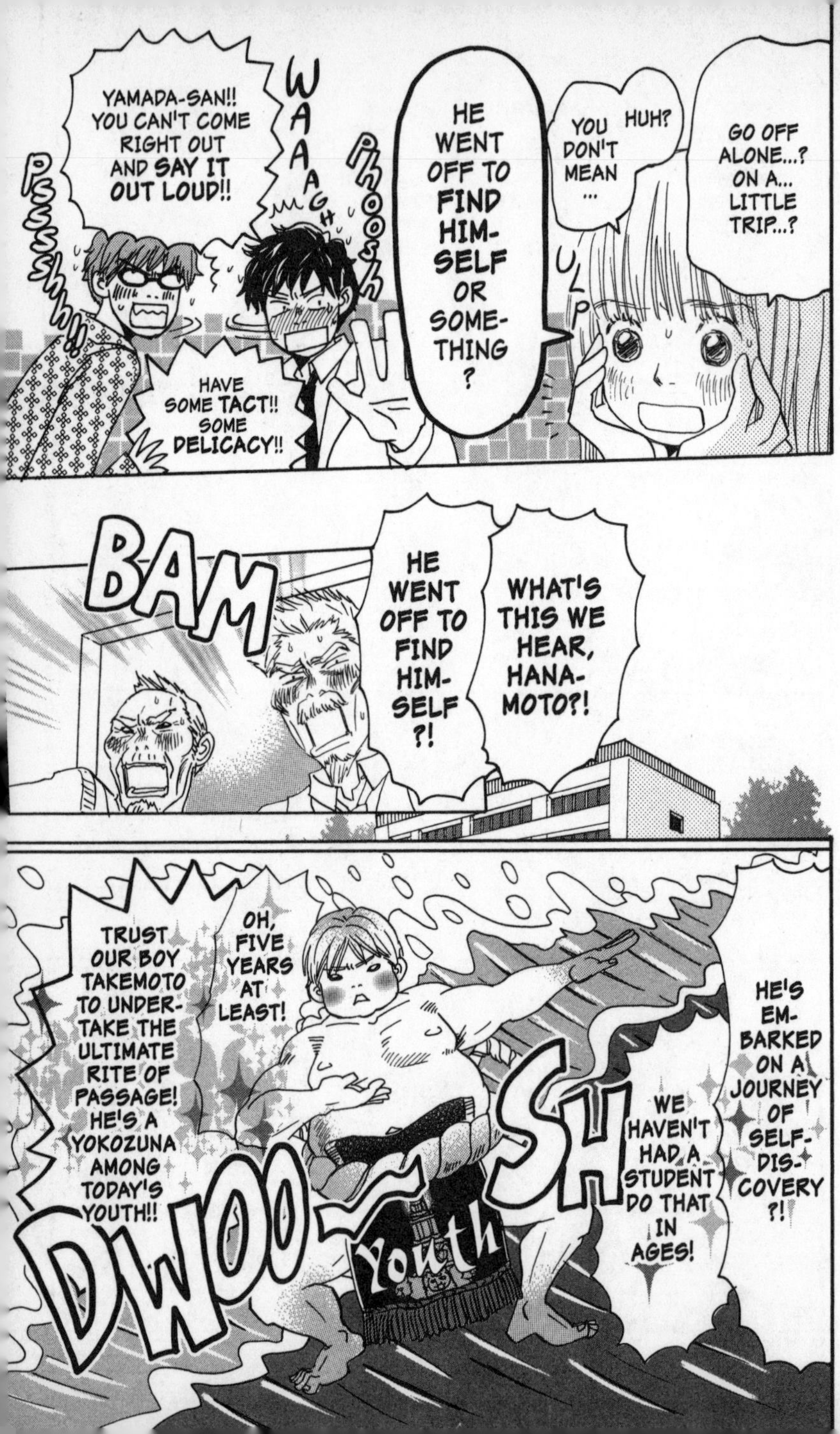
GO OFF ALONE...? ON A... LITTLE TRIP...?
HUH?
YOU DON'T MEAN ...
ULP
HE WENT OFF TO FIND HIMSELF OR SOMETHING?
PHOOOSH
WAAAAGH
YAMADA-SAN!! YOU CAN'T COME RIGHT OUT AND SAY IT OUT LOUD!!
HAVE SOME TACT!! SOME DELICACY!!
PSSSHH!!
WHAT'S THIS WE HEAR, HANAMOTO?!
HE WENT OFF TO FIND HIMSELF?!
BAM
HE'S EMBARKED ON A JOURNEY OF SELF-DISCOVERY?!
WE HAVEN'T HAD A STUDENT DO THAT IN AGES!
OH, FIVE YEARS AT LEAST!
TRUST OUR BOY TAKEMOTO TO UNDERTAKE THE ULTIMATE RITE OF PASSAGE! HE'S A YOKOZUNA AMONG TODAY'S YOUTH!!
DWOO~SH
youth

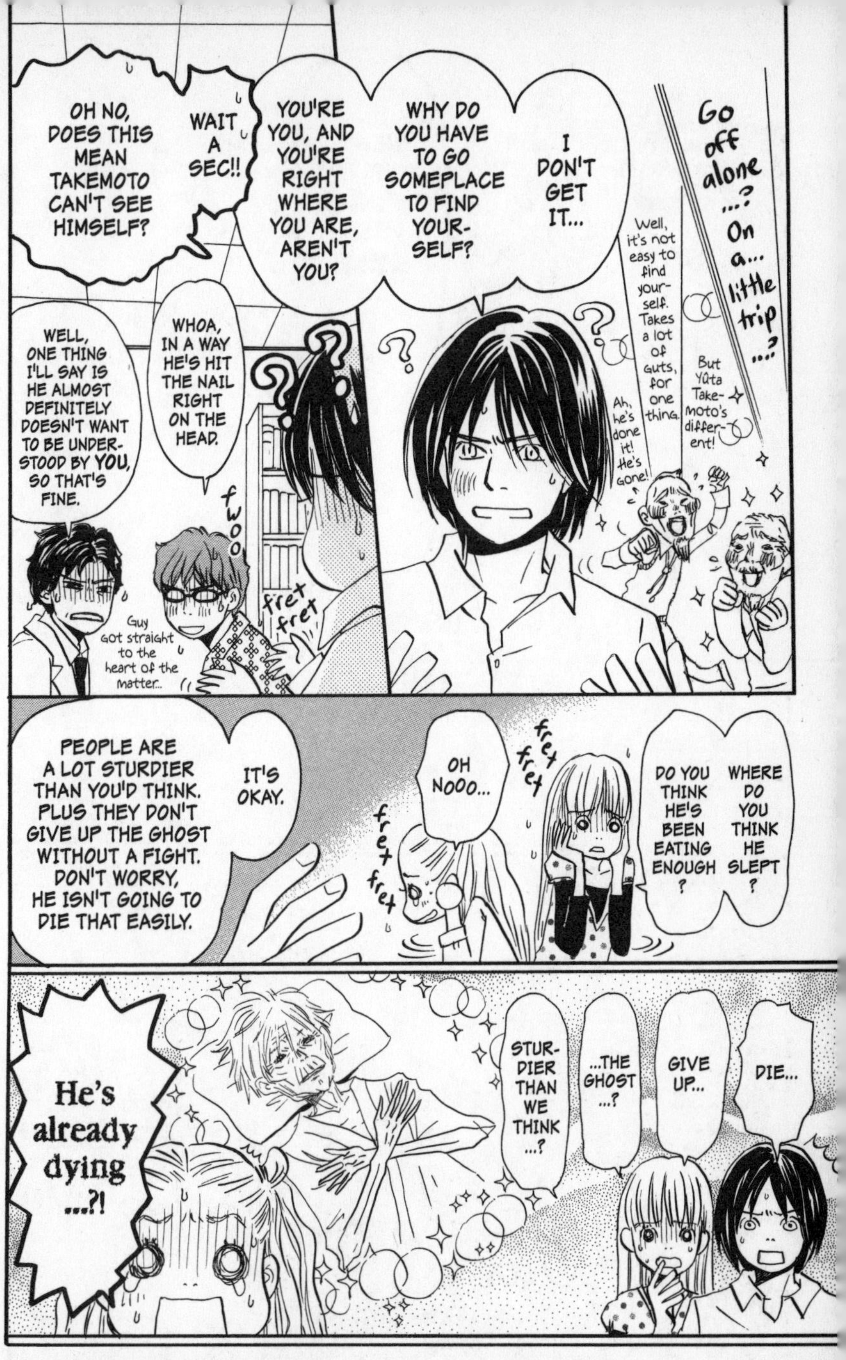
Go off alone ...? On a... little trip ...?
But Yūta Takemoto's different!
Well, it's not easy to find yourself. Takes a lot of guts, for one thing.
Ah, he's done it! He's gone!
I DON'T GET IT...
WHY DO YOU HAVE TO GO SOMEPLACE TO FIND YOURSELF?
YOU'RE YOU, AND YOU'RE RIGHT WHERE YOU ARE, AREN'T YOU?
WAIT A SEC!!
OH NO, DOES THIS MEAN TAKEMOTO CAN'T SEE HIMSELF?
fret fret
fwooo
WHOA, IN A WAY HE'S HIT THE NAIL RIGHT ON THE HEAD.
Guy got straight to the heart of the matter...
WELL, ONE THING I'LL SAY IS HE ALMOST DEFINITELY DOESN'T WANT TO BE UNDERSTOOD BY YOU, SO THAT'S FINE.
WHERE DO YOU THINK HE SLEPT?
DO YOU THINK HE'S BEEN EATING ENOUGH?
fret fret
OH NOOO...
fret fret
IT'S OKAY.
PEOPLE ARE A LOT STURDIER THAN YOU'D THINK. PLUS THEY DON'T GIVE UP THE GHOST WITHOUT A FIGHT. DON'T WORRY, HE ISN'T GOING TO DIE THAT EASILY.
DIE...
GIVE UP...
...THE GHOST ...?
STURDIER THAN WE THINK ...?
He's already dying ...?!

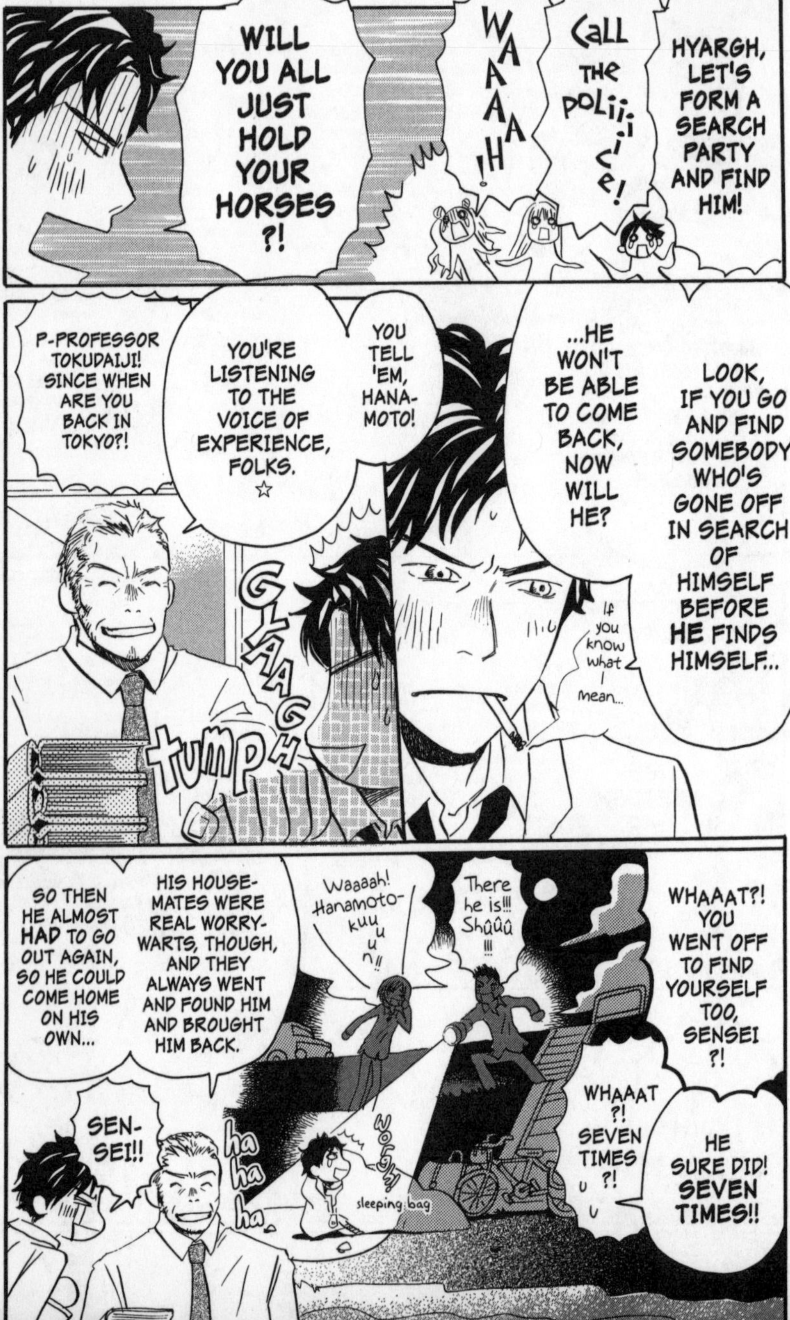
HYARGH, LET'S FORM A SEARCH PARTY AND FIND HIM!
Call the poliiiice!
WAAAAH!
WILL YOU ALL JUST HOLD YOUR HORSES?!
LOOK, IF YOU GO AND FIND SOMEBODY WHO'S GONE OFF IN SEARCH OF HIMSELF BEFORE **HE** FINDS HIMSELF...
...HE WON'T BE ABLE TO COME BACK, NOW WILL HE?
If you know what I mean...
YOU TELL 'EM, HANA-MOTO!
YOU'RE LISTENING TO THE VOICE OF EXPERIENCE, FOLKS. ☆
P-PROFESSOR TOKUDAIJI! SINCE WHEN ARE YOU BACK IN TOKYO?!
GYAAGH
tumph
WHAAAT?! YOU WENT OFF TO FIND YOURSELF TOO, SENSEI?!
There he is!!! Shûûû!!!
Waaaah! Hanamoto-kuuuun!!
HIS HOUSE-MATES WERE REAL WORRY-WARTS, THOUGH, AND THEY ALWAYS WENT AND FOUND HIM AND BROUGHT HIM BACK.
SO THEN HE ALMOST **HAD** TO GO OUT AGAIN, SO HE COULD COME HOME ON HIS OWN...
HE SURE DID! **SEVEN TIMES!!**
WHAAAT?! SEVEN TIMES?!
sleeping bag
ha ha ha ha
SEN-SEI!!

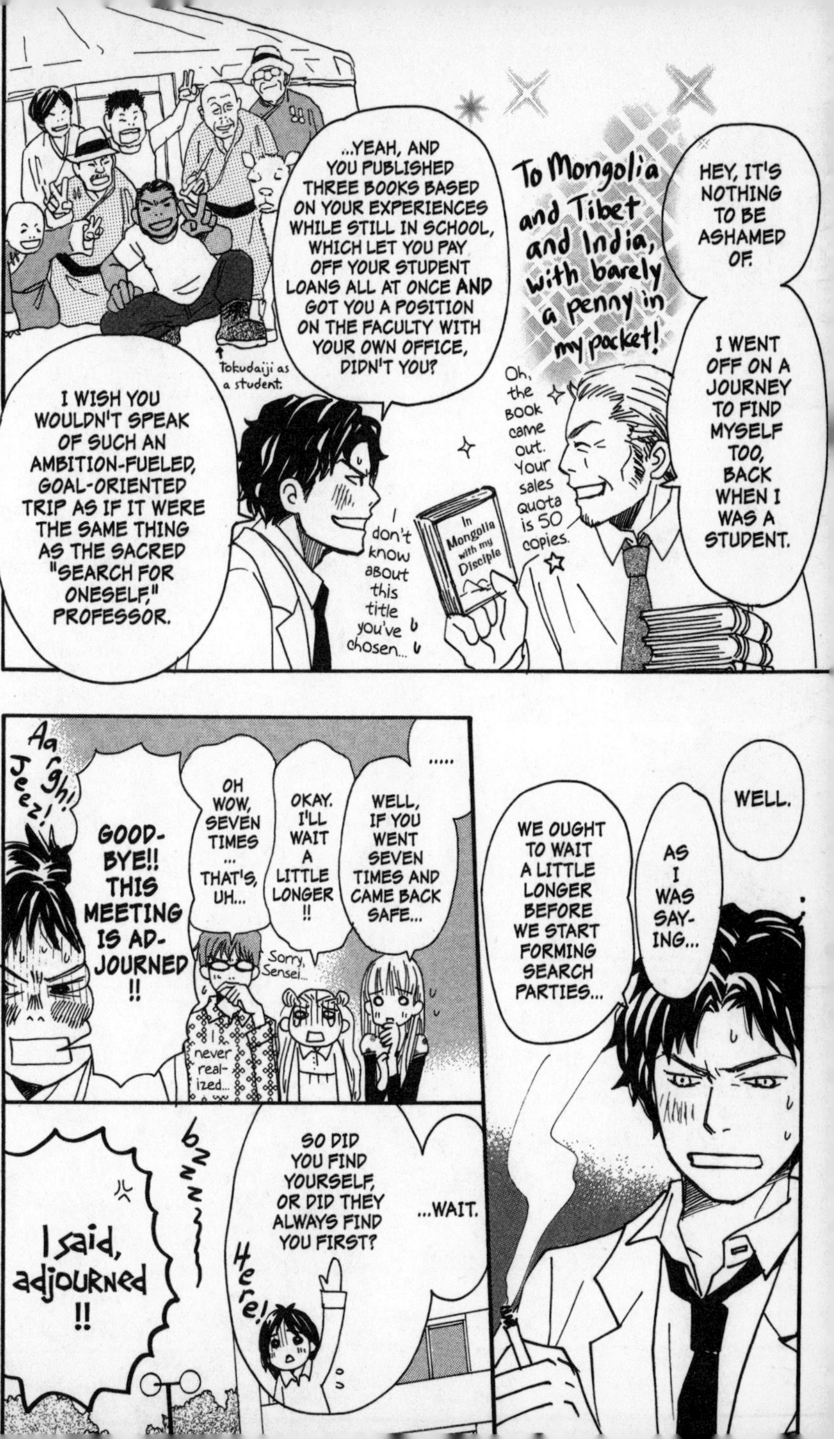
HEY, IT'S NOTHING TO BE ASHAMED OF.
I WENT OFF ON A JOURNEY TO FIND MYSELF TOO, BACK WHEN I WAS A STUDENT.
To Mongolia and Tibet and India, with barely a penny in my pocket!
Oh, the book came out. Your sales quota is 50 copies.
In Mongolia with my Disciple
...YEAH, AND YOU PUBLISHED THREE BOOKS BASED ON YOUR EXPERIENCES WHILE STILL IN SCHOOL, WHICH LET YOU PAY OFF YOUR STUDENT LOANS ALL AT ONCE AND GOT YOU A POSITION ON THE FACULTY WITH YOUR OWN OFFICE, DIDN'T YOU?
Tokudaiji as a student.
I don't know about this title you've chosen...
I WISH YOU WOULDN'T SPEAK OF SUCH AN AMBITION-FUELED, GOAL-ORIENTED TRIP AS IF IT WERE THE SAME THING AS THE SACRED "SEARCH FOR ONESELF," PROFESSOR.
WELL.
AS I WAS SAYING...
WE OUGHT TO WAIT A LITTLE LONGER BEFORE WE START FORMING SEARCH PARTIES...
.....
WELL, IF YOU WENT SEVEN TIMES AND CAME BACK SAFE...
OKAY. I'LL WAIT A LITTLE LONGER!!
OH WOW, SEVEN TIMES... THAT'S, UH...
Sorry, Sensei...
I never realized...
Aargh! Jeez!
GOOD-BYE!! THIS MEETING IS ADJOURNED!!
...WAIT.
SO DID YOU FIND YOURSELF, OR DID THEY ALWAYS FIND YOU FIRST?
Here!
bZZZ~
I said, adjourned!!

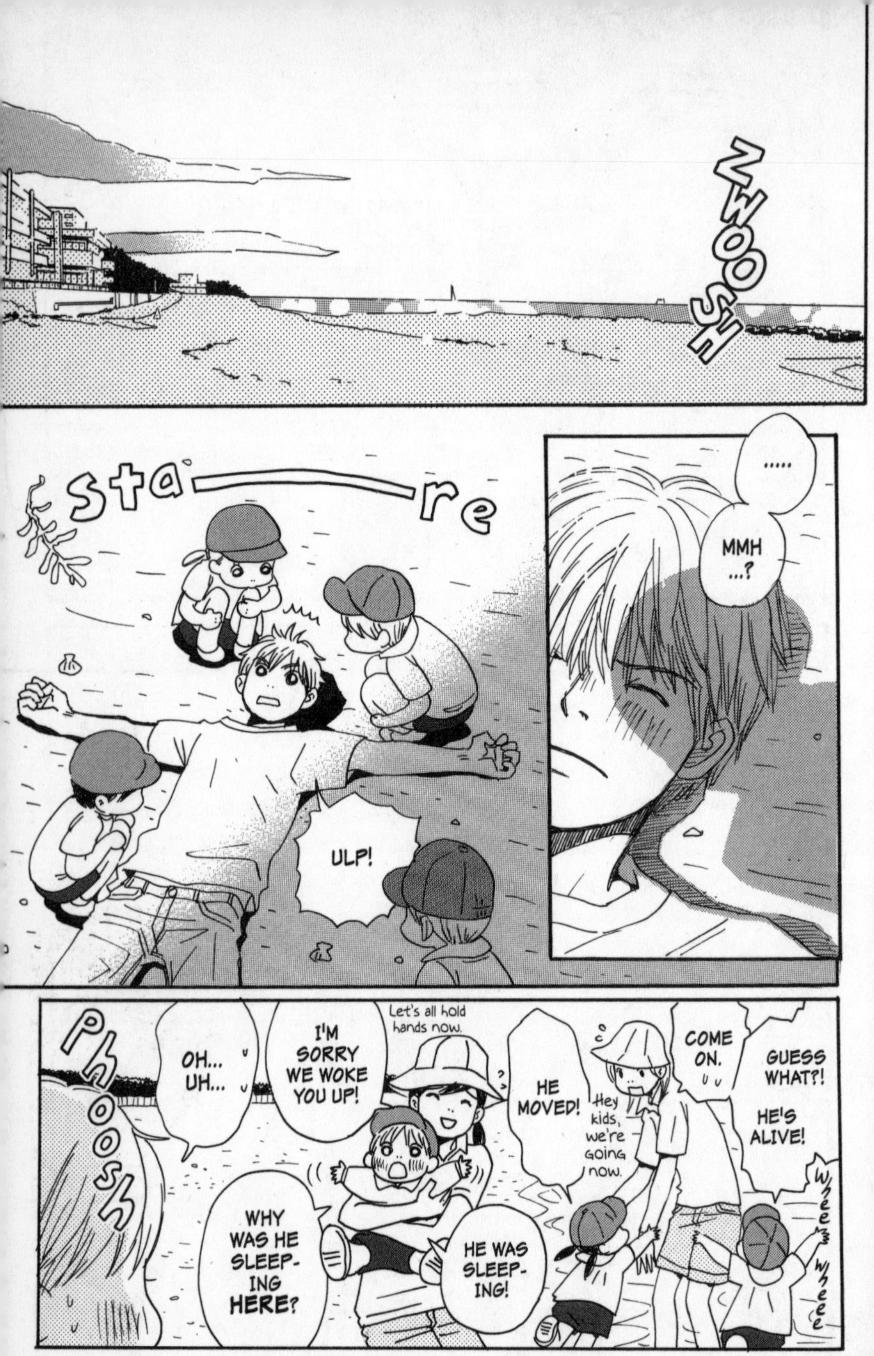
ZWOOSH
.....
MMH ...?
sta——re
ULP!
GUESS WHAT?!
HE'S ALIVE!
COME ON.
Wheee
Wheee
Hey kids, we're going now.
HE MOVED!
Let's all hold hands now.
I'M SORRY WE WOKE YOU UP!
OH... UH...
Phoosh
HE WAS SLEEPING!
WHY WAS HE SLEEPING HERE?

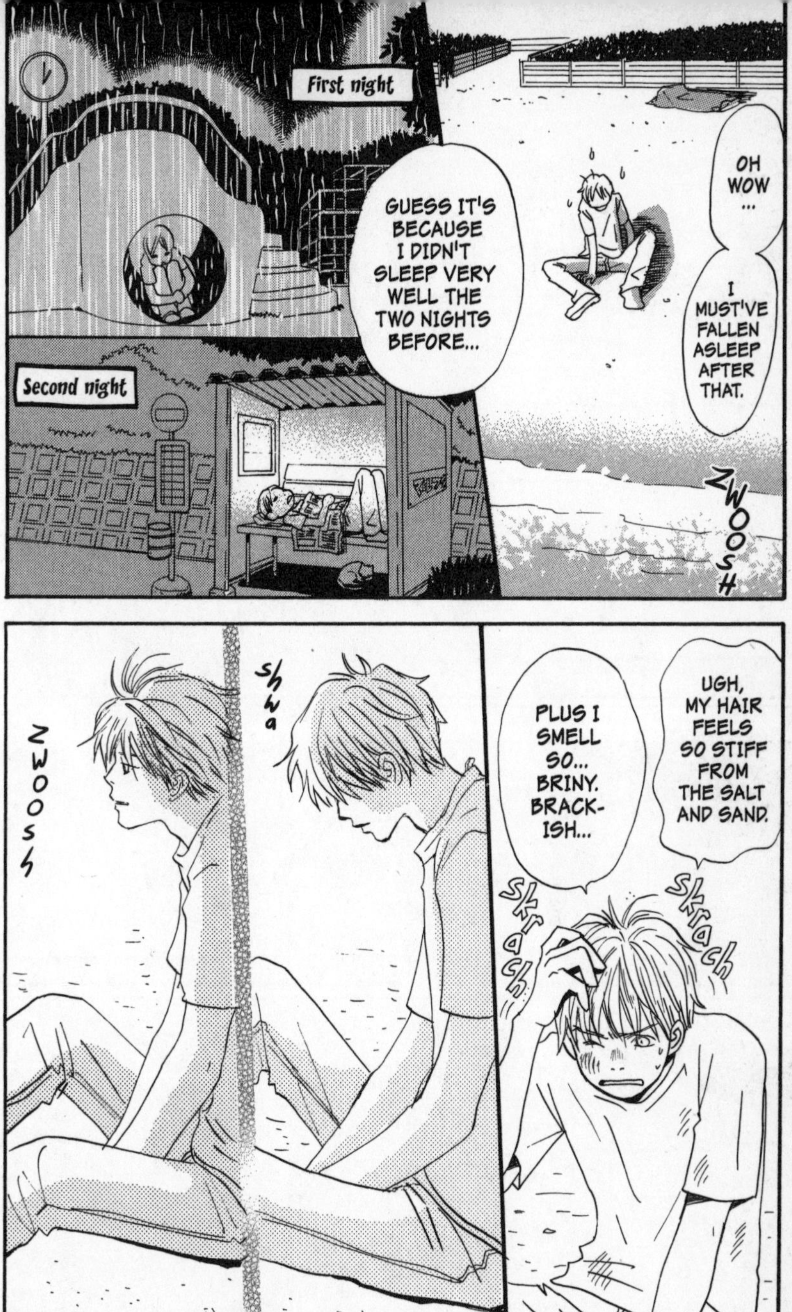

OH WOW...
I MUST'VE FALLEN ASLEEP AFTER THAT.
ZWOOSH
GUESS IT'S BECAUSE I DIDN'T SLEEP VERY WELL THE TWO NIGHTS BEFORE...
First night
Second night
UGH, MY HAIR FEELS SO STIFF FROM THE SALT AND SAND.
PLUS I SMELL SO... BRINY. BRACK-ISH...
Skrach
Skrach
shwa
ZWOOSSH

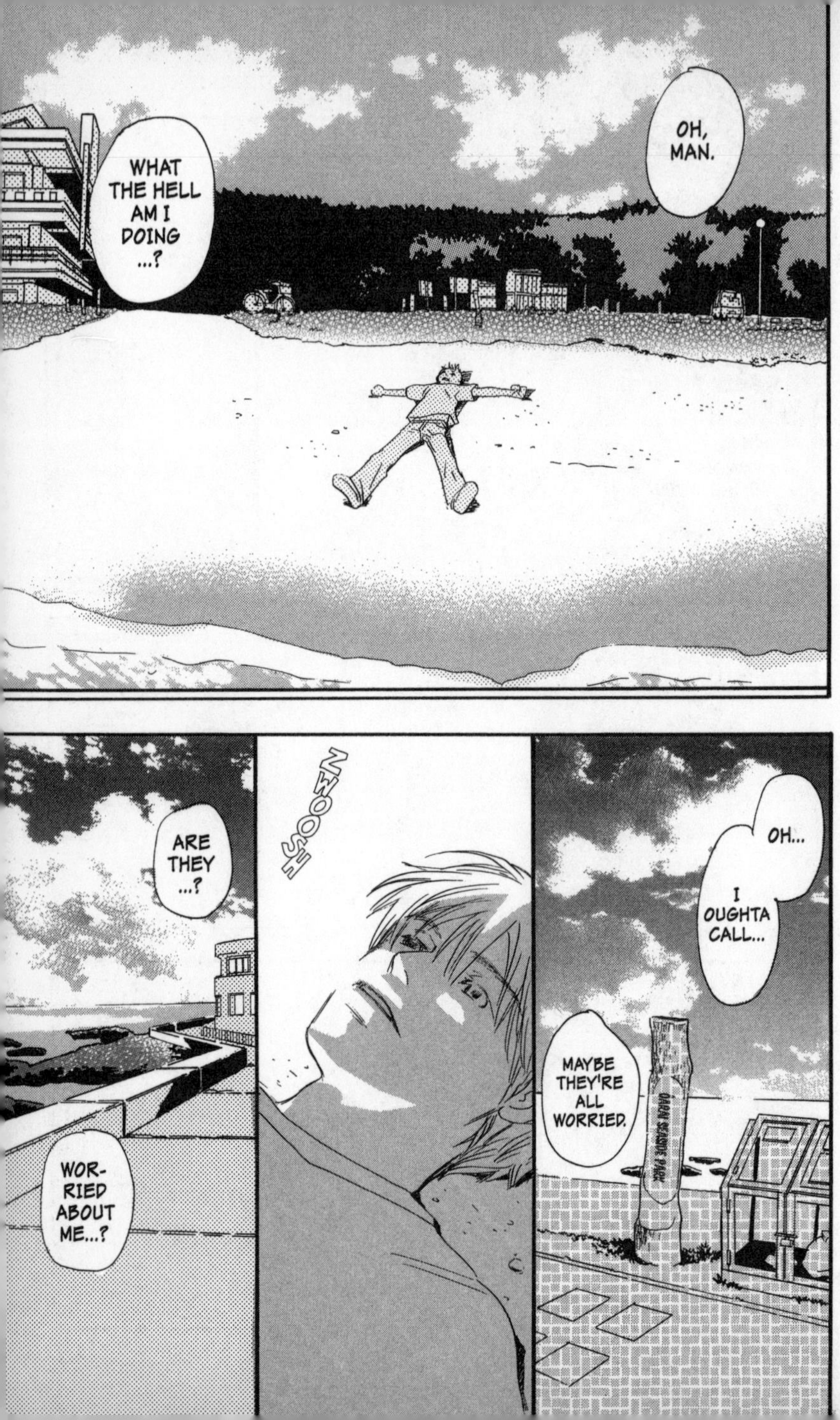
OH, MAN.
WHAT THE HELL AM I DOING ...?
OH...
I OUGHTA CALL...
MAYBE THEY'RE ALL WORRIED.
WHOOSH
ARE THEY ...?
WOR-RIED ABOUT ME...?

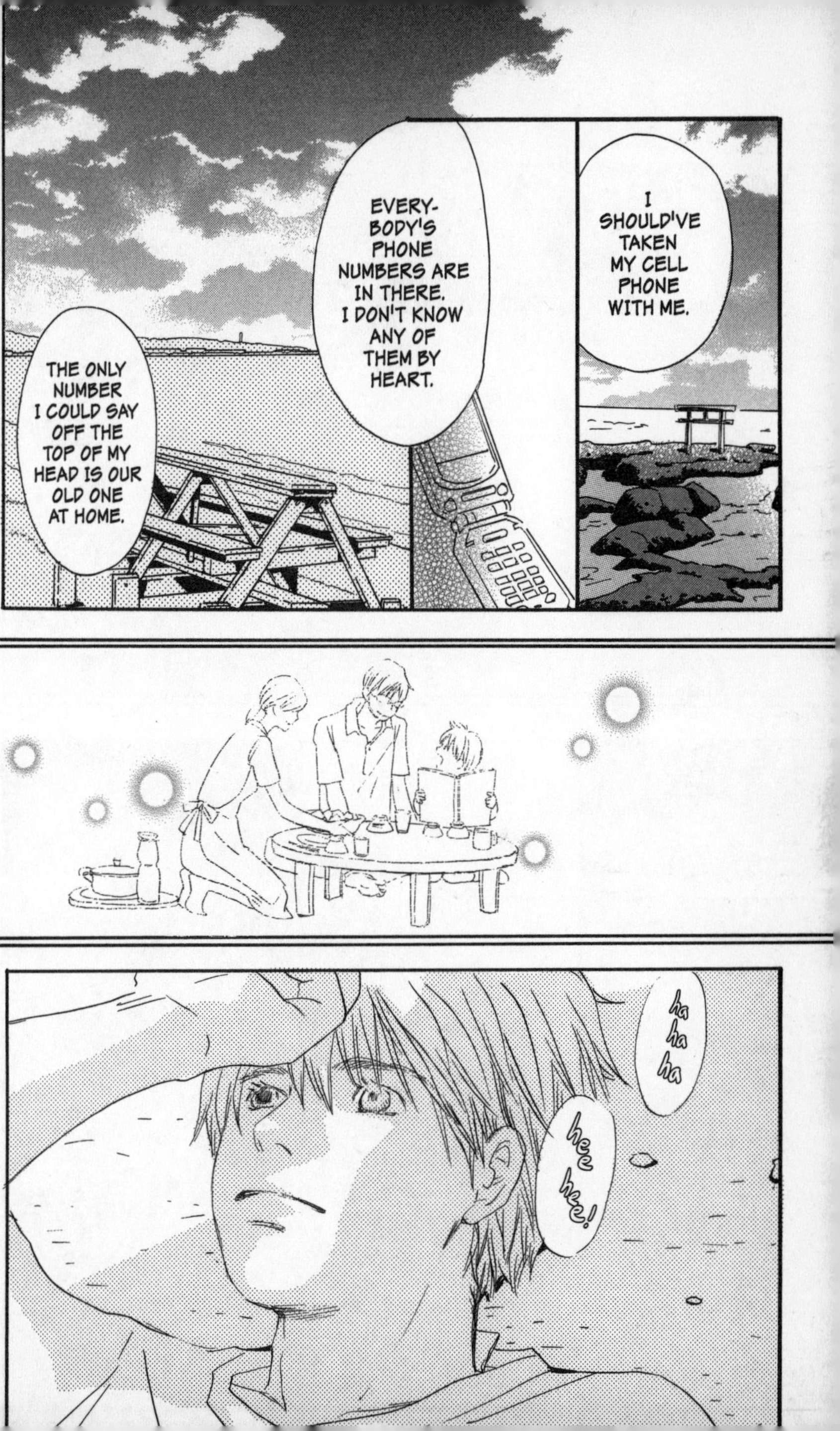
I SHOULD'VE TAKEN MY CELL PHONE WITH ME.
EVERY-BODY'S PHONE NUMBERS ARE IN THERE. I DON'T KNOW ANY OF THEM BY HEART.
THE ONLY NUMBER I COULD SAY OFF THE TOP OF MY HEAD IS OUR OLD ONE AT HOME.
ha ha ha
hee hee!

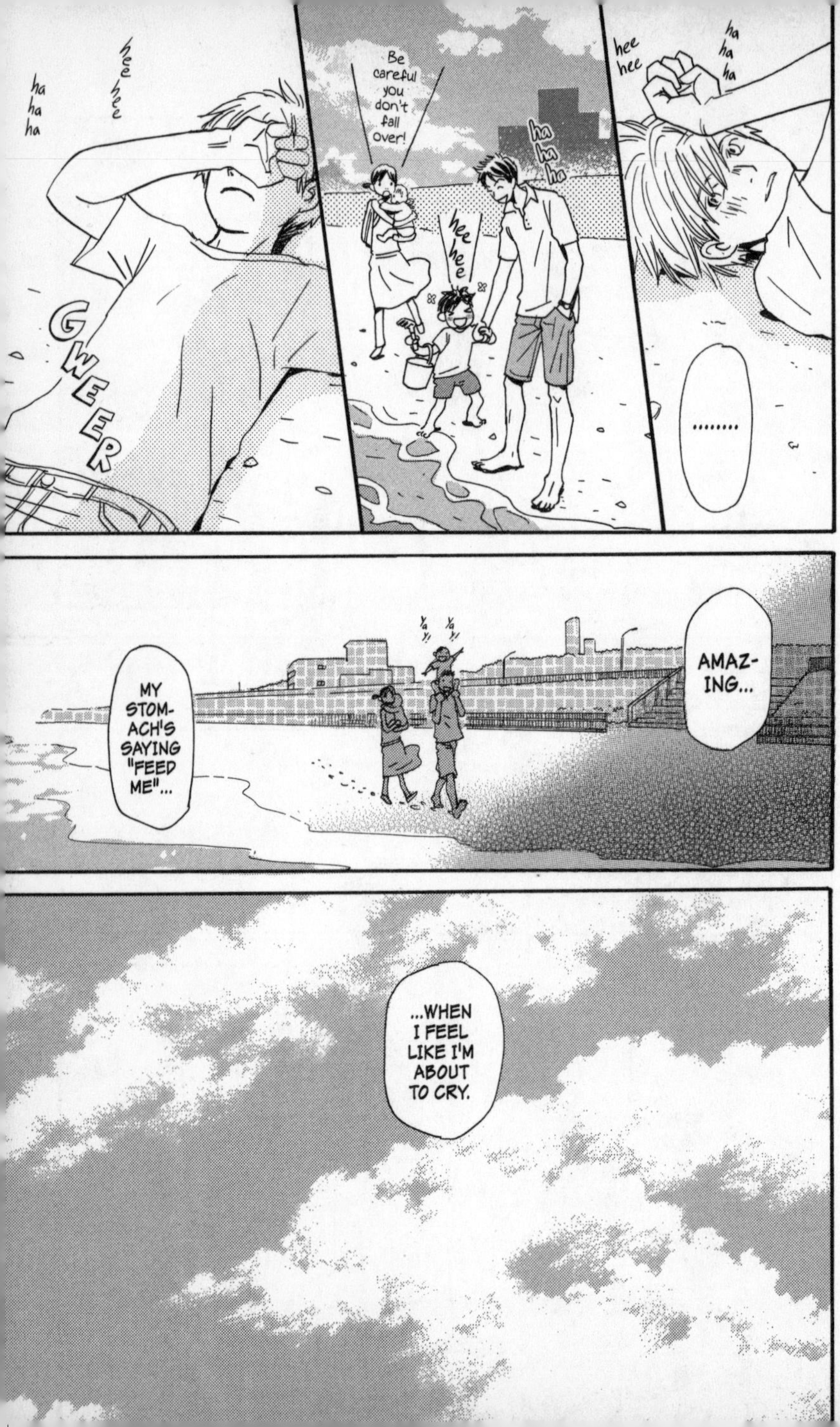
hee hee
ha ha ha
......
Be careful you don't fall over!
ha ha ha
hee hee
hee hee
ha ha ha
GWEER
AMAZ-ING...
Ya y!
Ya y!
MY STOM-ACH'S SAYING "FEED ME"...
...WHEN I FEEL LIKE I'M ABOUT TO CRY.

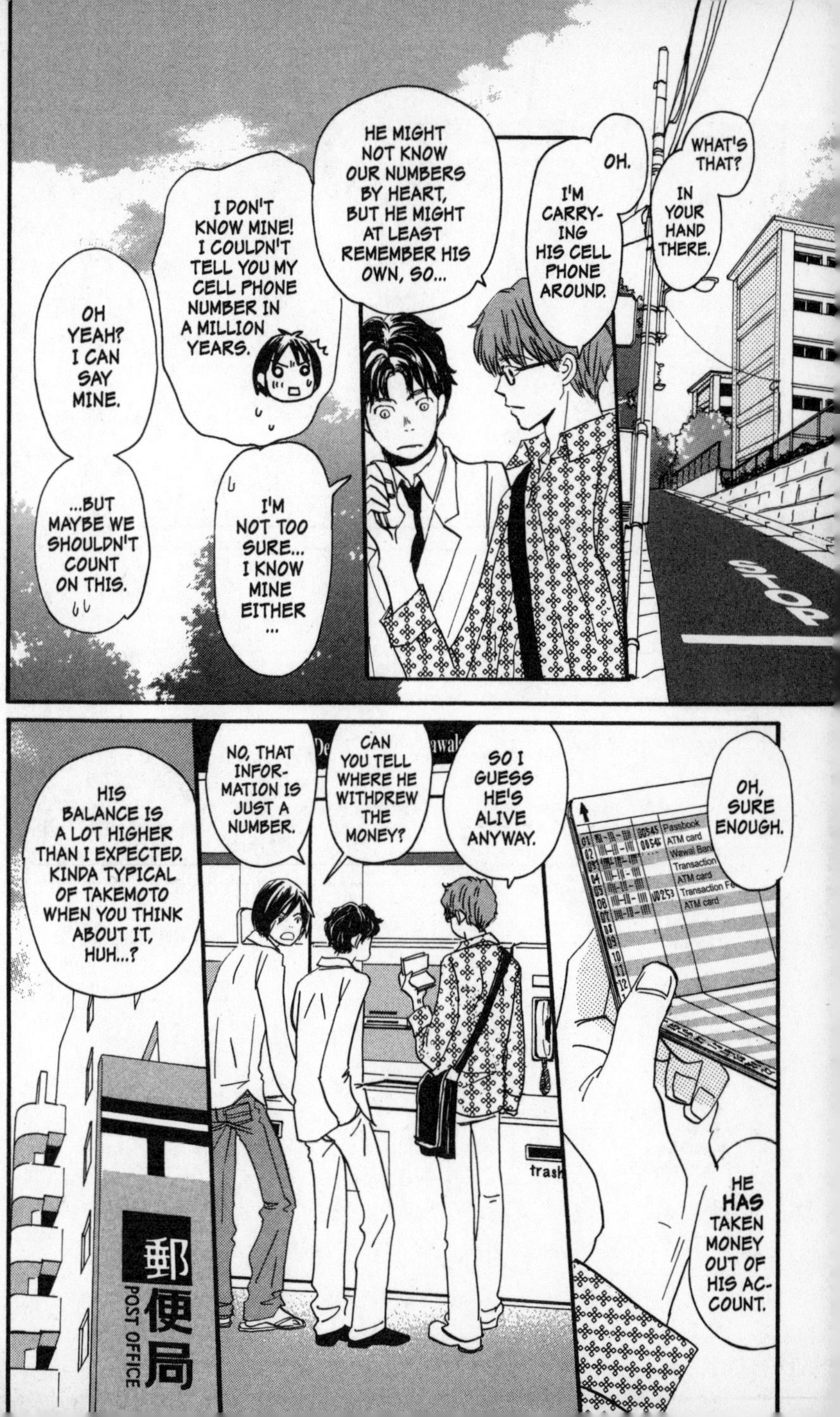
WHAT'S THAT? IN YOUR HAND THERE.
OH. I'M CARRYING HIS CELL PHONE AROUND.
HE MIGHT NOT KNOW OUR NUMBERS BY HEART, BUT HE MIGHT AT LEAST REMEMBER HIS OWN, SO...
I DON'T KNOW MINE! I COULDN'T TELL YOU MY CELL PHONE NUMBER IN A MILLION YEARS.
OH YEAH? I CAN SAY MINE.
I'M NOT TOO SURE... I KNOW MINE EITHER...
...BUT MAYBE WE SHOULDN'T COUNT ON THIS.
STOP
OH, SURE ENOUGH.
Passbook
ATM card
ATM card
ATM card
HE HAS TAKEN MONEY OUT OF HIS ACCOUNT.
SO I GUESS HE'S ALIVE ANYWAY.
CAN YOU TELL WHERE HE WITHDREW THE MONEY?
NO, THAT INFORMATION IS JUST A NUMBER.
HIS BALANCE IS A LOT HIGHER THAN I EXPECTED. KINDA TYPICAL OF TAKEMOTO WHEN YOU THINK ABOUT IT, HUH...?
trash
郵便局
POST OFFICE

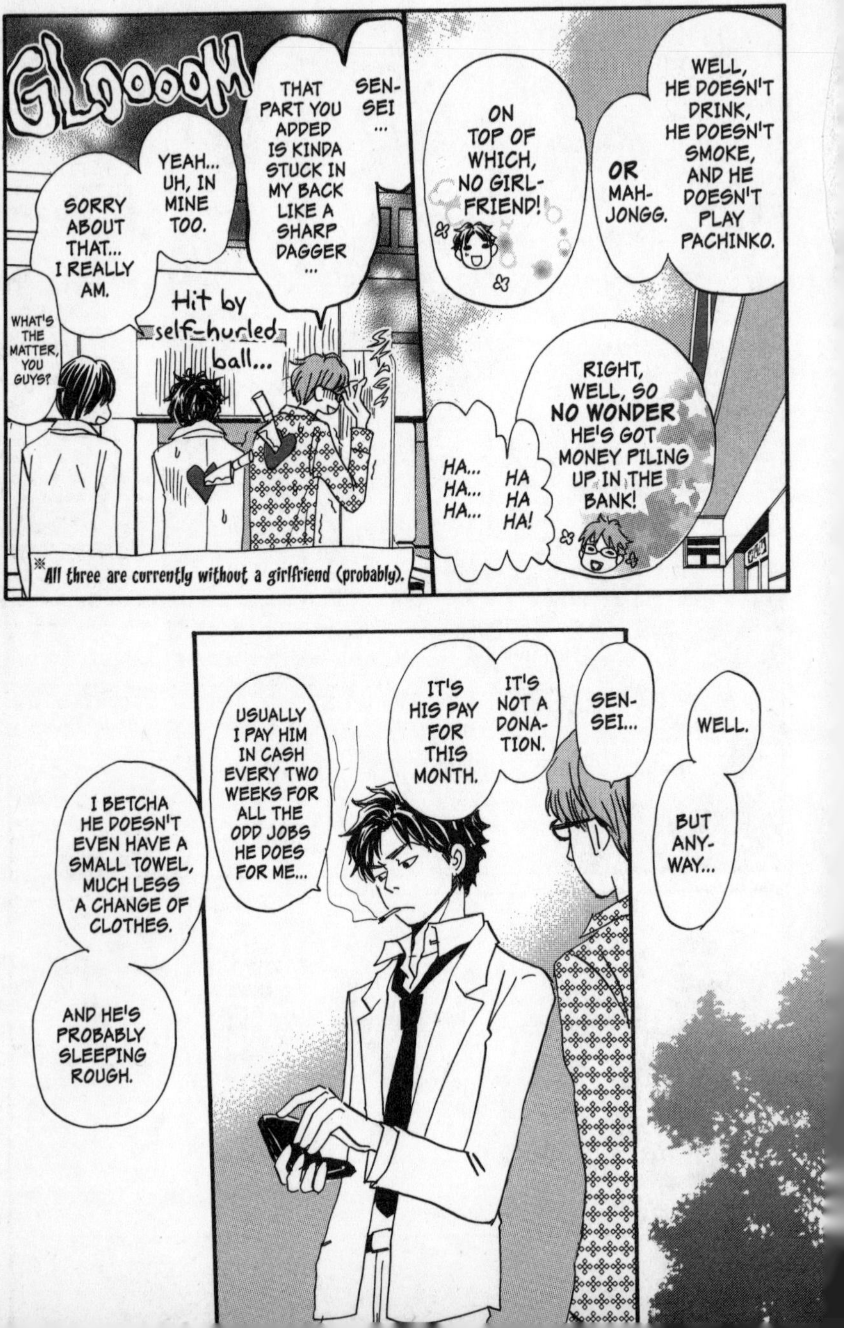
WELL, HE DOESN'T DRINK, HE DOESN'T SMOKE, AND HE DOESN'T PLAY PACHINKO.
OR MAH-JONGG.
ON TOP OF WHICH, NO GIRLFRIEND!
RIGHT, WELL, SO NO WONDER HE'S GOT MONEY PILING UP IN THE BANK!
HA HA HA!
HA... HA... HA...
SEN-SEI...
THAT PART YOU ADDED IS KINDA STUCK IN MY BACK LIKE A SHARP DAGGER...
YEAH... UH, IN MINE TOO.
GLOOOOM
SORRY ABOUT THAT... I REALLY AM.
WHAT'S THE MATTER, YOU GUYS?
Hit by self-hurled ball...
※All three are currently without a girlfriend (probably).
WELL.
BUT ANYWAY...
SEN-SEI...
IT'S NOT A DONATION.
IT'S HIS PAY FOR THIS MONTH.
USUALLY I PAY HIM IN CASH EVERY TWO WEEKS FOR ALL THE ODD JOBS HE DOES FOR ME...
I BETCHA HE DOESN'T EVEN HAVE A SMALL TOWEL, MUCH LESS A CHANGE OF CLOTHES.
AND HE'S PROBABLY SLEEPING ROUGH.

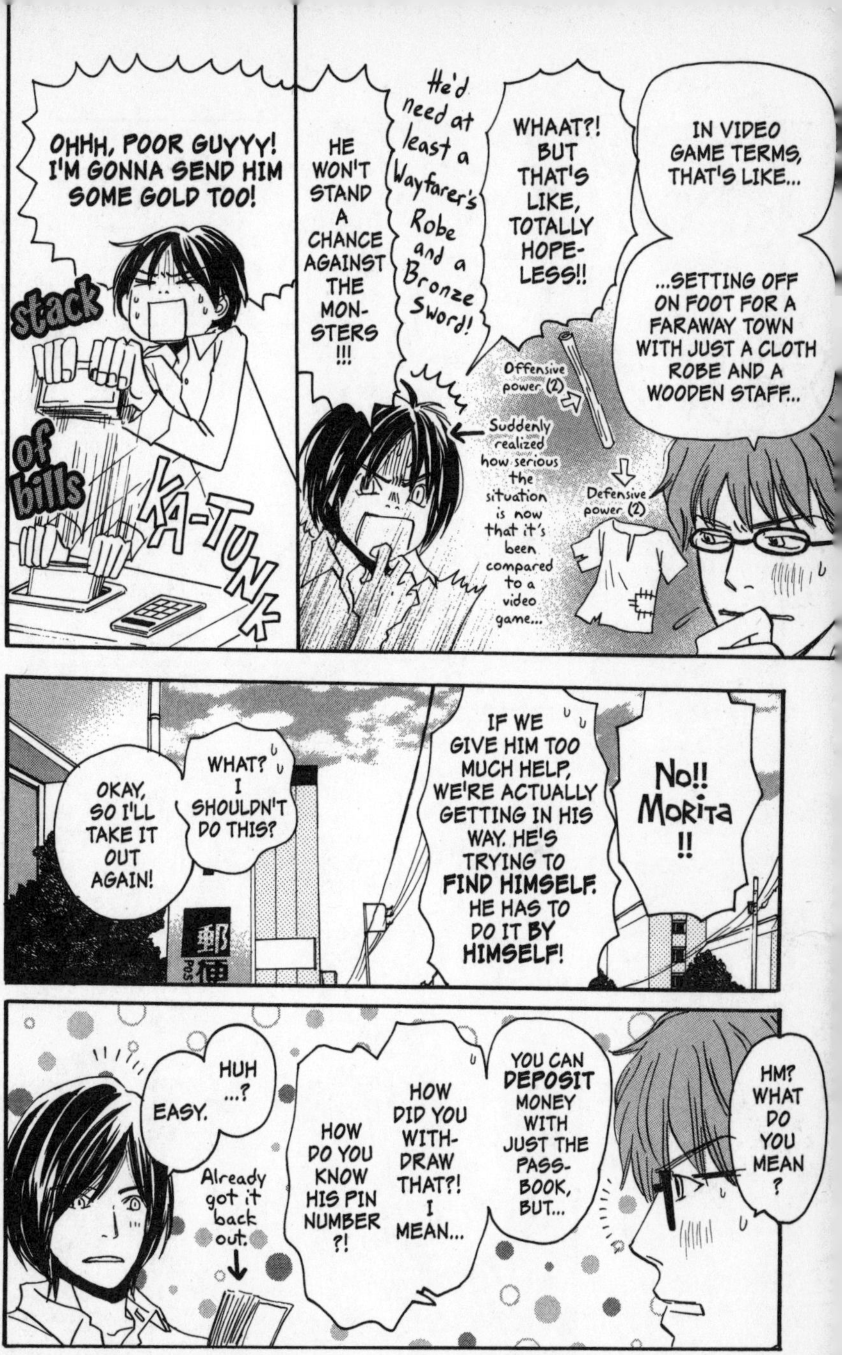
IN VIDEO GAME TERMS, THAT'S LIKE...
...SETTING OFF ON FOOT FOR A FARAWAY TOWN WITH JUST A CLOTH ROBE AND A WOODEN STAFF...
Offensive power (2)
Defensive power (2)
WHAAT?! BUT THAT'S LIKE, TOTALLY HOPE-LESS!!
Suddenly realized how serious the situation is now that it's been compared to a video game...
He'd need at least a Wayfarer's Robe and a Bronze Sword!
HE WON'T STAND A CHANCE AGAINST THE MON-STERS!!!
OHHH, POOR GUYYY! I'M GONNA SEND HIM SOME GOLD TOO!
stack of bills
KA-TUNK
No!! Morita!!
IF WE GIVE HIM TOO MUCH HELP, WE'RE ACTUALLY GETTING IN HIS WAY. HE'S TRYING TO FIND HIMSELF. HE HAS TO DO IT BY HIMSELF!
WHAT? I SHOULDN'T DO THIS?
OKAY, SO I'LL TAKE IT OUT AGAIN!
HM? WHAT DO YOU MEAN?
YOU CAN DEPOSIT MONEY WITH JUST THE PASS-BOOK, BUT...
HOW DID YOU WITH-DRAW THAT?! I MEAN...
HOW DO YOU KNOW HIS PIN NUMBER?!
HUH...? EASY.
Already got it back out.

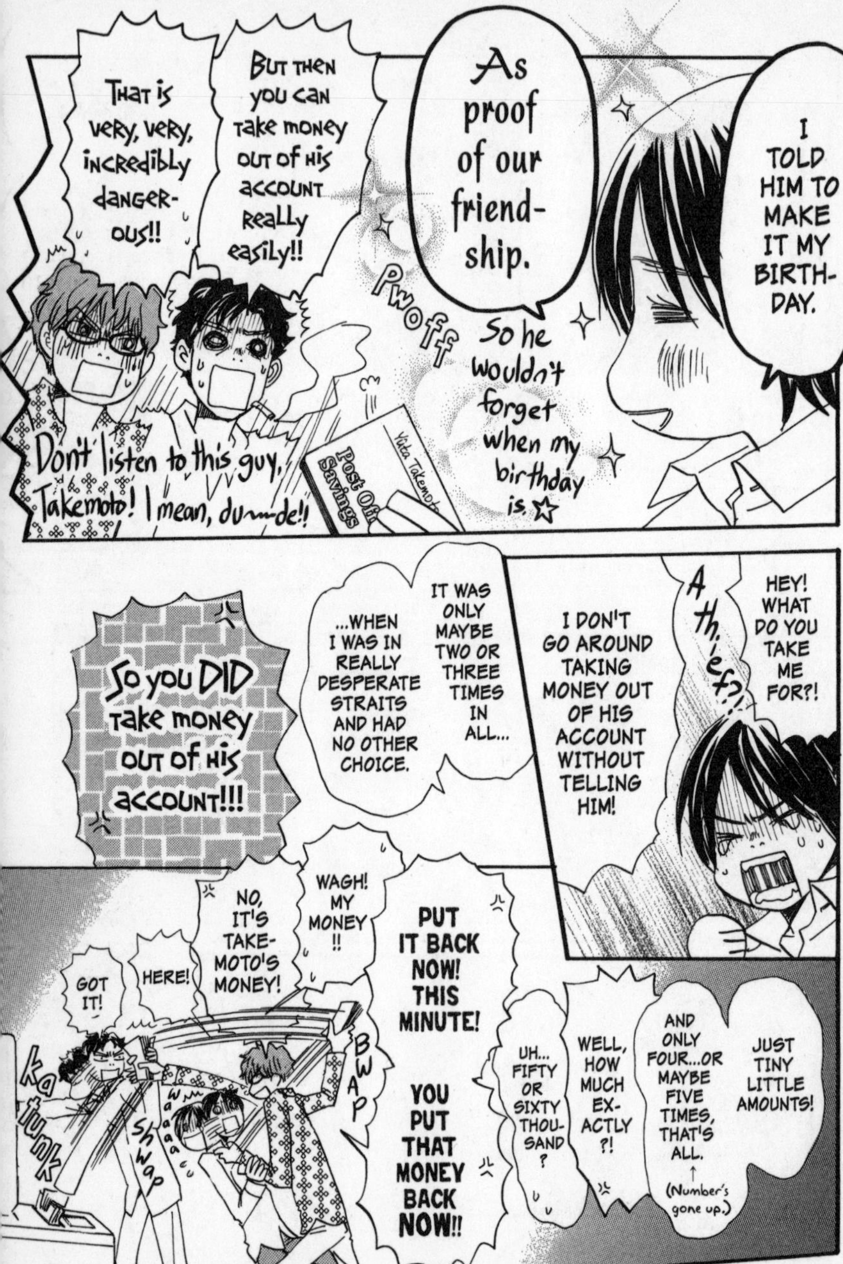
I TOLD HIM TO MAKE IT MY BIRTH-DAY.
As proof of our friend-ship.
So he wouldn't forget when my birthday is ☆
Pwoff
But then you can take money out of his account really easily!!
That is very, very, incredibly danger-ous!!
Don't listen to this guy, Takemoto! I mean, du—de!!
HEY! WHAT DO YOU TAKE ME FOR?!
A thief?!
I DON'T GO AROUND TAKING MONEY OUT OF HIS ACCOUNT WITHOUT TELLING HIM!
IT WAS ONLY MAYBE TWO OR THREE TIMES IN ALL...
...WHEN I WAS IN REALLY DESPERATE STRAITS AND HAD NO OTHER CHOICE.
So you DID take money out of his account!!!
JUST TINY LITTLE AMOUNTS!
AND ONLY FOUR...OR MAYBE FIVE TIMES, THAT'S ALL.
(Number's gone up.)
WELL, HOW MUCH EX-ACTLY?!
UH... FIFTY OR SIXTY THOU-SAND?
PUT IT BACK NOW! THIS MINUTE!
YOU PUT THAT MONEY BACK NOW!!
BWAP
WAGH! MY MONEY!!
NO, IT'S TAKE-MOTO'S MONEY!
HERE!
GOT IT!
Waaaaa
Shwap
ka tunk

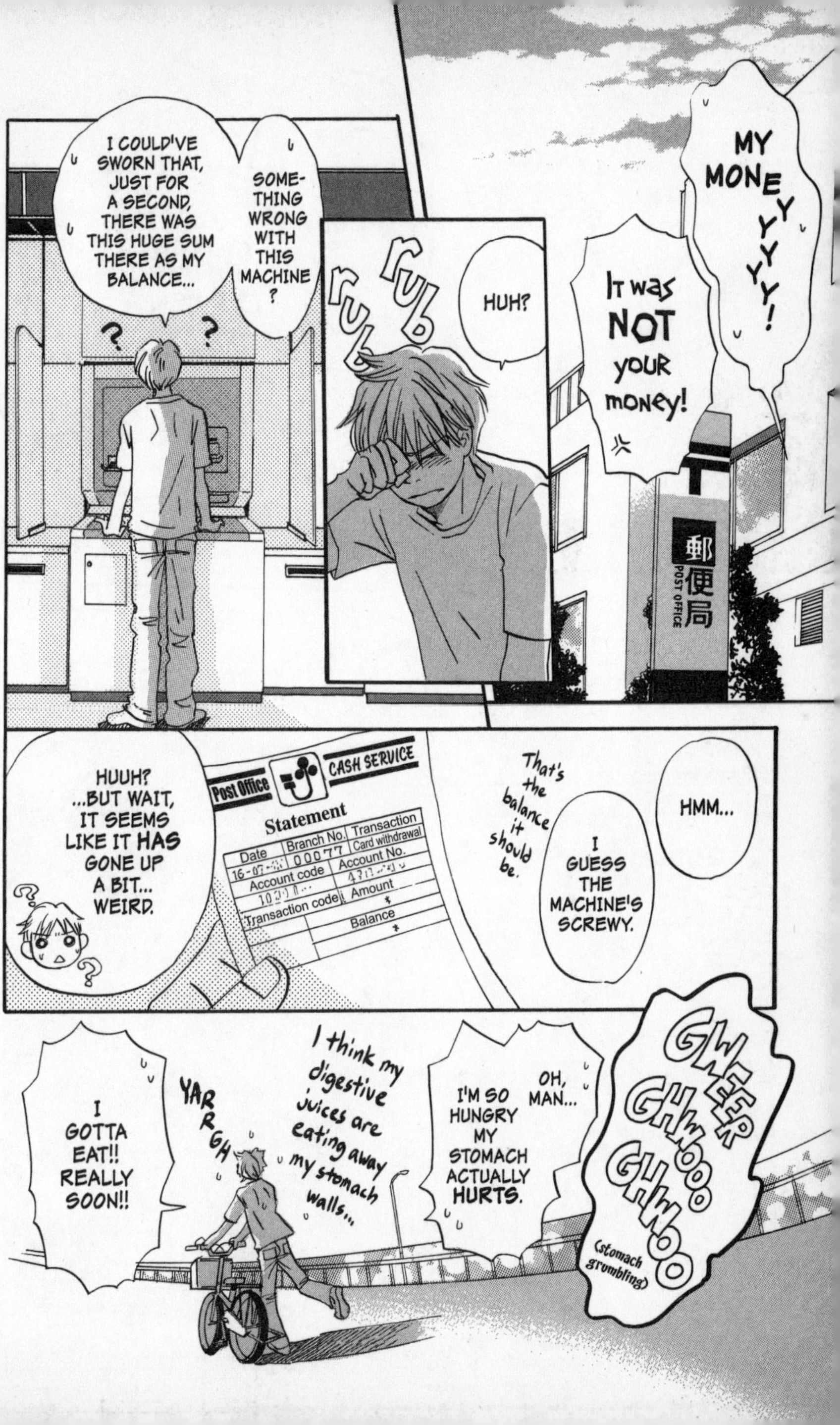

MY MONEYYYYY!
It was NOT your money!
rub rub
HUH?
SOME-THING WRONG WITH THIS MACHINE?
I COULD'VE SWORN THAT, JUST FOR A SECOND, THERE WAS THIS HUGE SUM THERE AS MY BALANCE...
郵便局
POST OFFICE
HMM...
I GUESS THE MACHINE'S SCREWY.
That's the balance it should be.
Post Office
CASH SERVICE
Statement
Date
Branch No.
Transaction
Card withdrawal
00077
Account code
Account No.
Amount
Transaction code
Balance
HUUH? ...BUT WAIT, IT SEEMS LIKE IT HAS GONE UP A BIT... WEIRD.
GWEER GHWOOO GHWOO
(stomach grumbling)
OH, MAN...
I'M SO HUNGRY MY STOMACH ACTUALLY HURTS.
I think my digestive juices are eating away my stomach walls...
YARRGH
I GOTTA EAT!! REALLY SOON!!

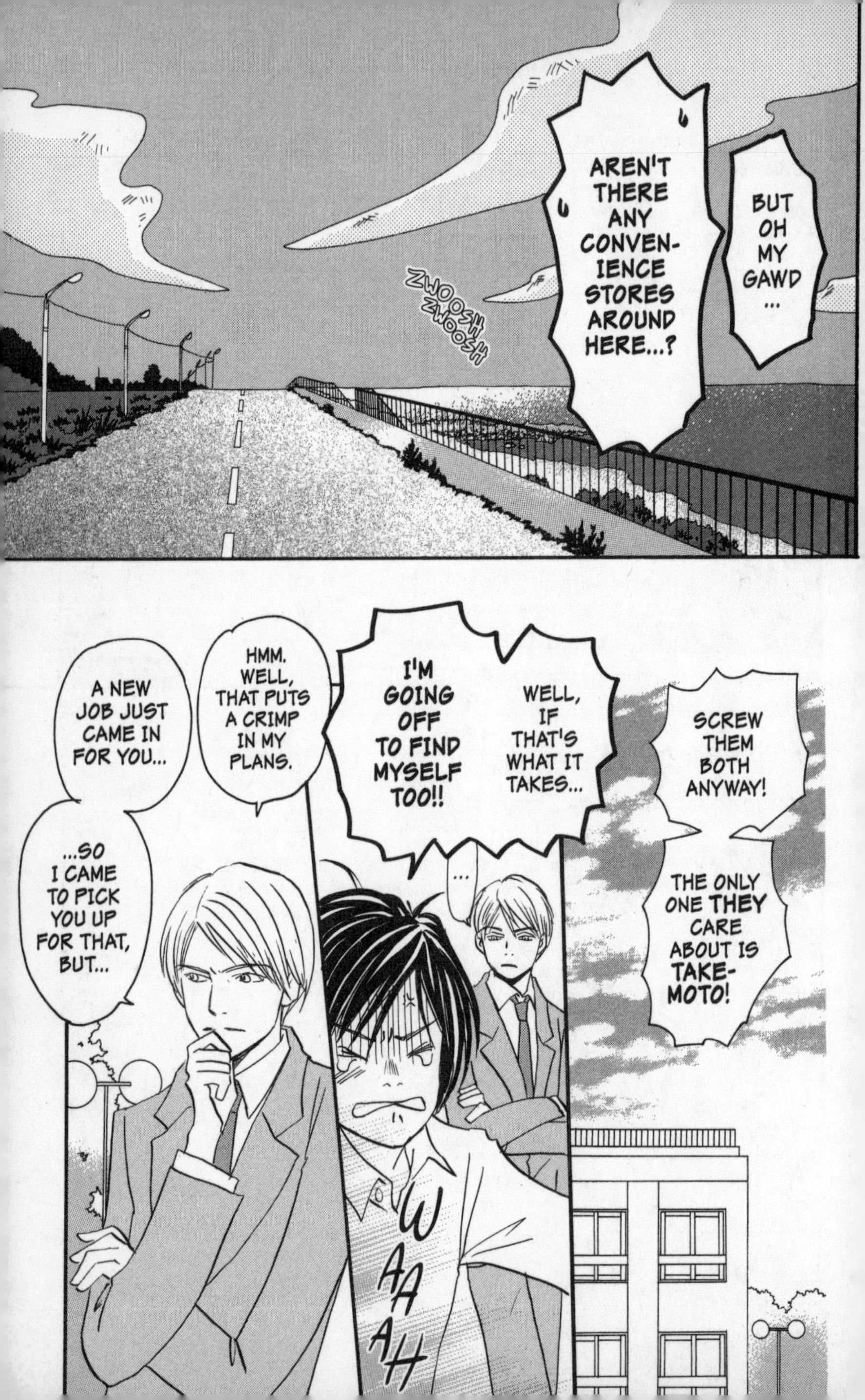
BUT OH MY GAWD...
AREN'T THERE ANY CONVEN-IENCE STORES AROUND HERE...?
ZWOOSH ZWOOSH
SCREW THEM BOTH ANYWAY!
THE ONLY ONE THEY CARE ABOUT IS TAKE-MOTO!
WELL, IF THAT'S WHAT IT TAKES...
I'M GOING OFF TO FIND MYSELF TOO!!
WAAAAH
...
HMM. WELL, THAT PUTS A CRIMP IN MY PLANS.
A NEW JOB JUST CAME IN FOR YOU...
...SO I CAME TO PICK YOU UP FOR THAT, BUT...

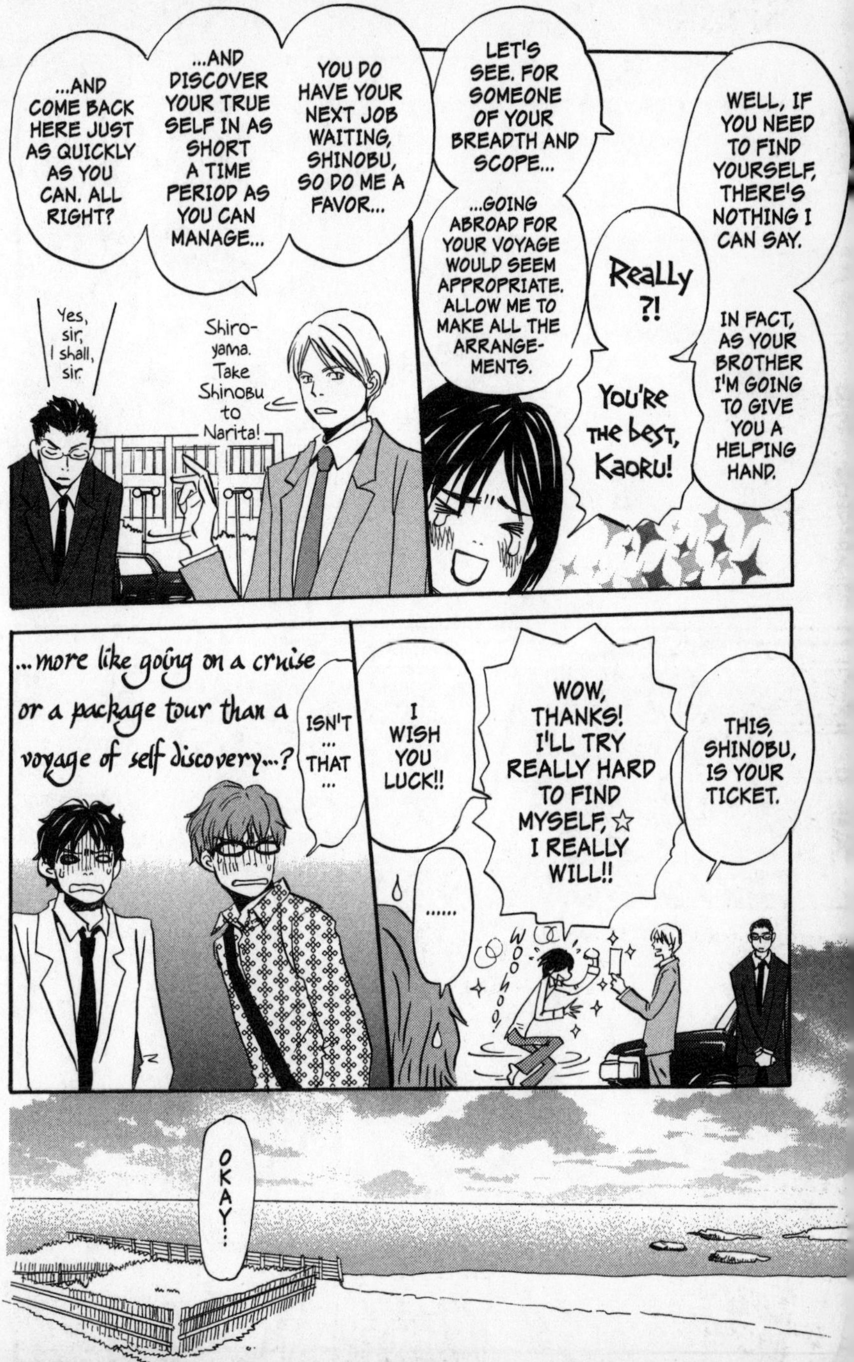
WELL, IF YOU NEED TO FIND YOURSELF, THERE'S NOTHING I CAN SAY.
IN FACT, AS YOUR BROTHER I'M GOING TO GIVE YOU A HELPING HAND.
Really ?!
You're the best, Kaoru!
LET'S SEE. FOR SOMEONE OF YOUR BREADTH AND SCOPE...
...GOING ABROAD FOR YOUR VOYAGE WOULD SEEM APPROPRIATE. ALLOW ME TO MAKE ALL THE ARRANGE-MENTS.
YOU DO HAVE YOUR NEXT JOB WAITING, SHINOBU, SO DO ME A FAVOR...
...AND DISCOVER YOUR TRUE SELF IN AS SHORT A TIME PERIOD AS YOU CAN MANAGE...
...AND COME BACK HERE JUST AS QUICKLY AS YOU CAN. ALL RIGHT?
Shiro-yama. Take Shinobu to Narita!
Yes, sir, I shall, sir.
THIS, SHINOBU, IS YOUR TICKET.
WOW, THANKS! I'LL TRY REALLY HARD TO FIND MYSELF, ☆ I REALLY WILL!!
Woohoo!
I WISH YOU LUCK!!
......
ISN'T ... THAT ...
...more like going on a cruise or a package tour than a voyage of self discovery...?
OKAY...

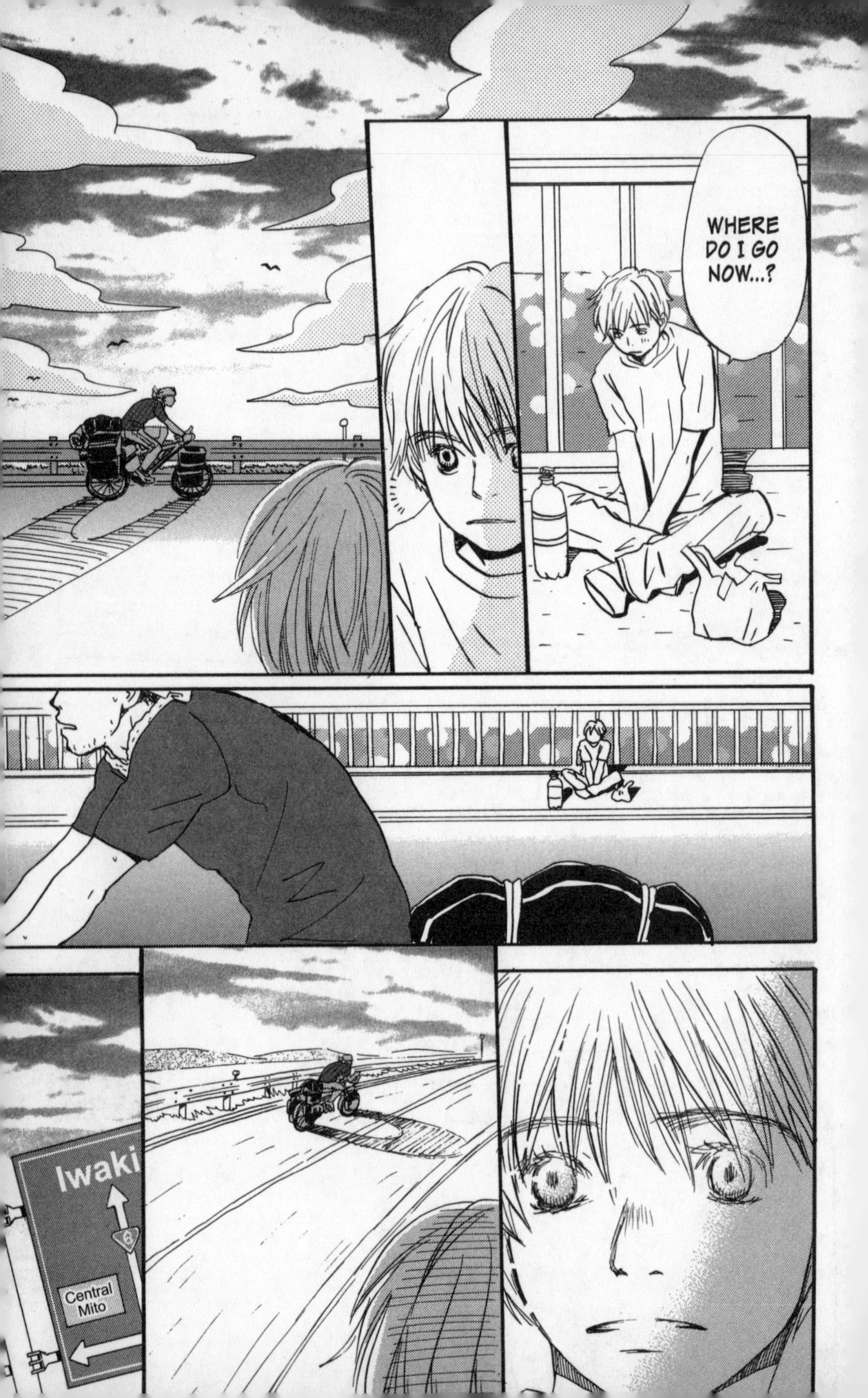
WHERE DO I GO NOW...?
Iwaki
6
Central Mito

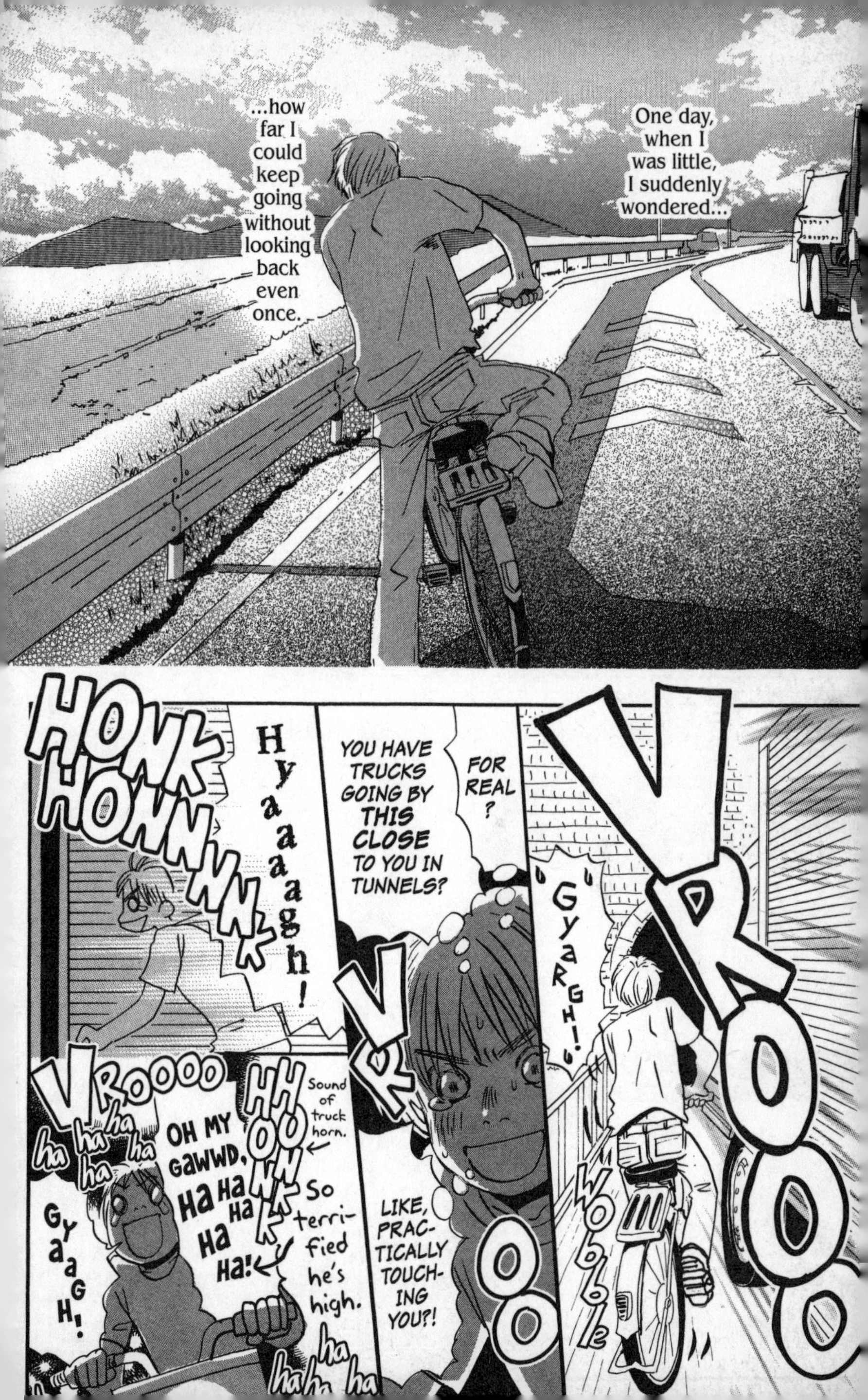
One day, when I was little, I suddenly wondered...
...how far I could keep going without looking back even once.
VROOOOO
Gyaragh!
Wobble
FOR REAL?
YOU HAVE TRUCKS GOING BY THIS CLOSE TO YOU IN TUNNELS?
LIKE, PRACTICALLY TOUCHING YOU?!
VROO
HONK HONNNNNNK
Hyaaaaagh!
VROOOO
HHOONNK
Sound of truck horn.
OH MY GAWWD, HA HA HA HA HA!
So terri-fied he's high.
ha ha ha
ha ha ha ha ha
Gyaagh!

When I started screaming, I finally figured it out.

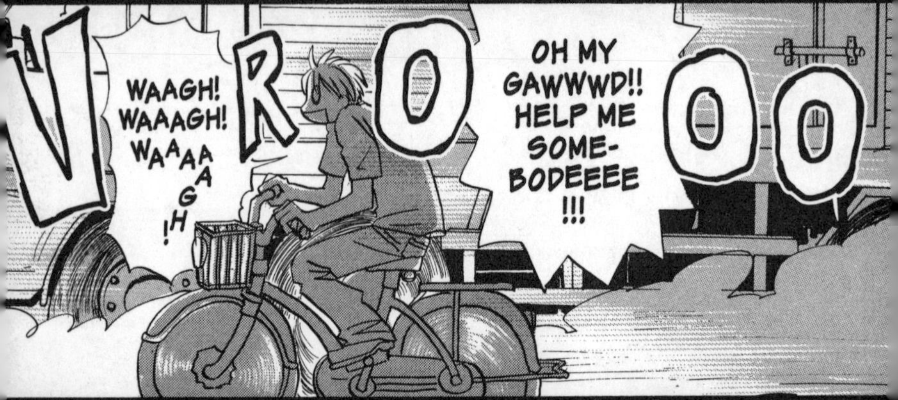
VROOO
OH MY GAWWWD!! HELP ME SOME-BODEEEE !!!
WAAGH! WAAAGH! WAAAAAGH!

I had always been afraid...

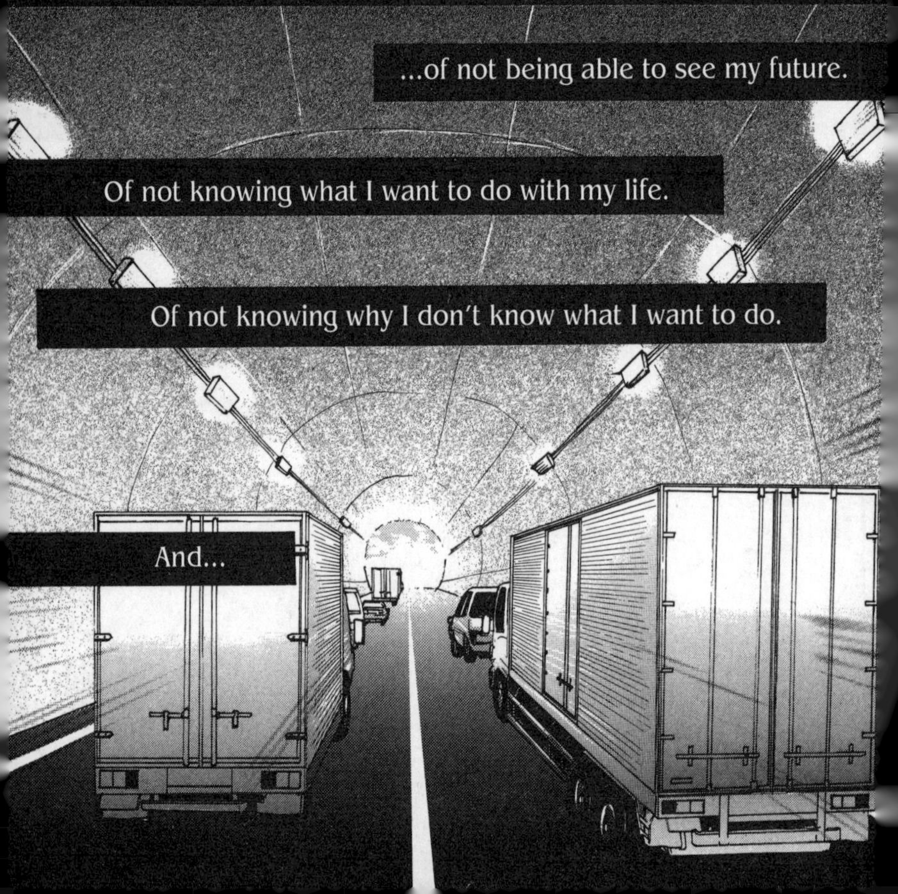
...of not being able to see my future.
Of not knowing what I want to do with my life.
Of not knowing why I don't know what I want to do.
And...

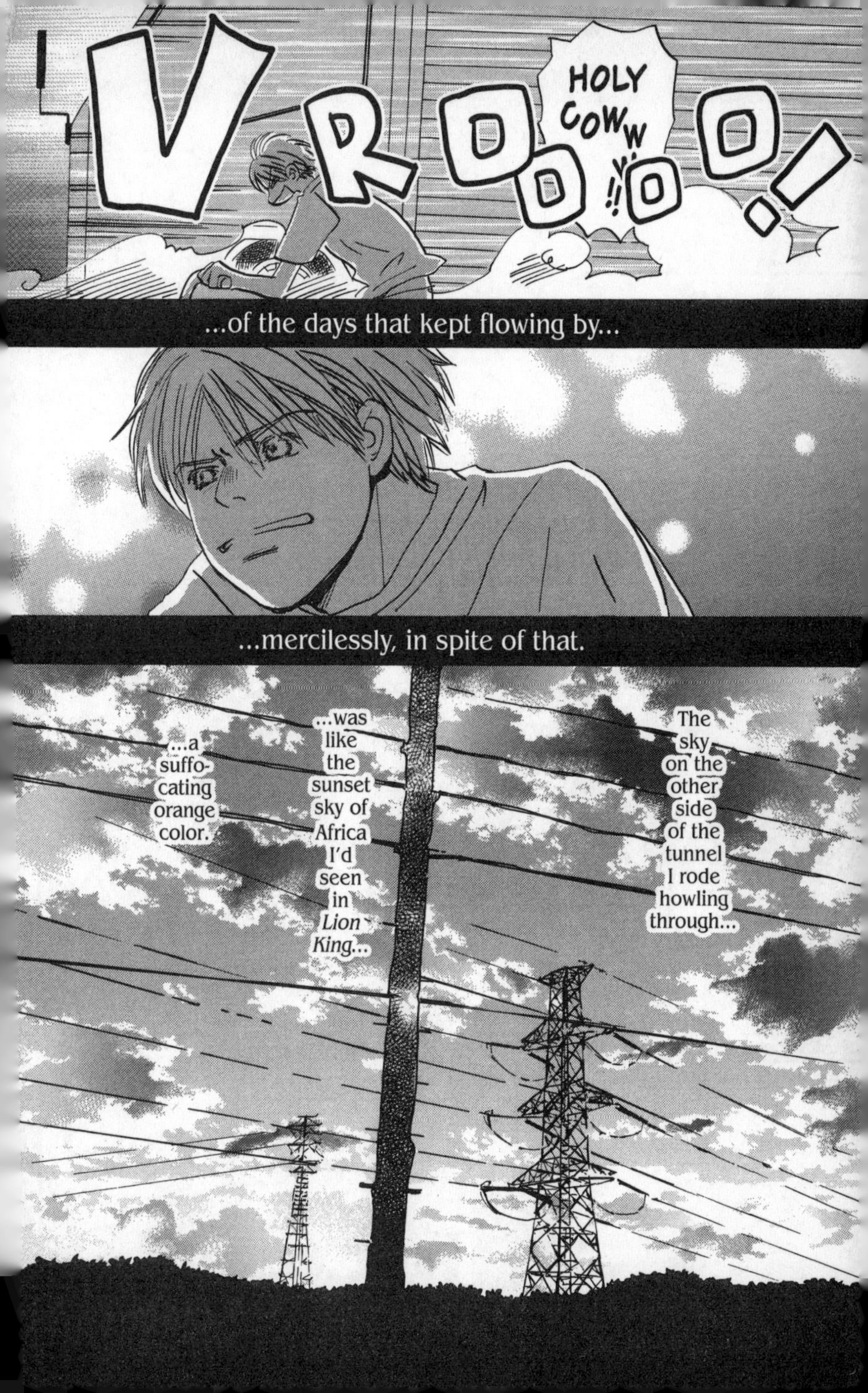
VROOOOO!
HOLY COWW!!
...of the days that kept flowing by...
...mercilessly, in spite of that.
The sky on the other side of the tunnel I rode howling through...
...was like the sunset sky of Africa I'd seen in *Lion King*...
...a suffocating orange color.

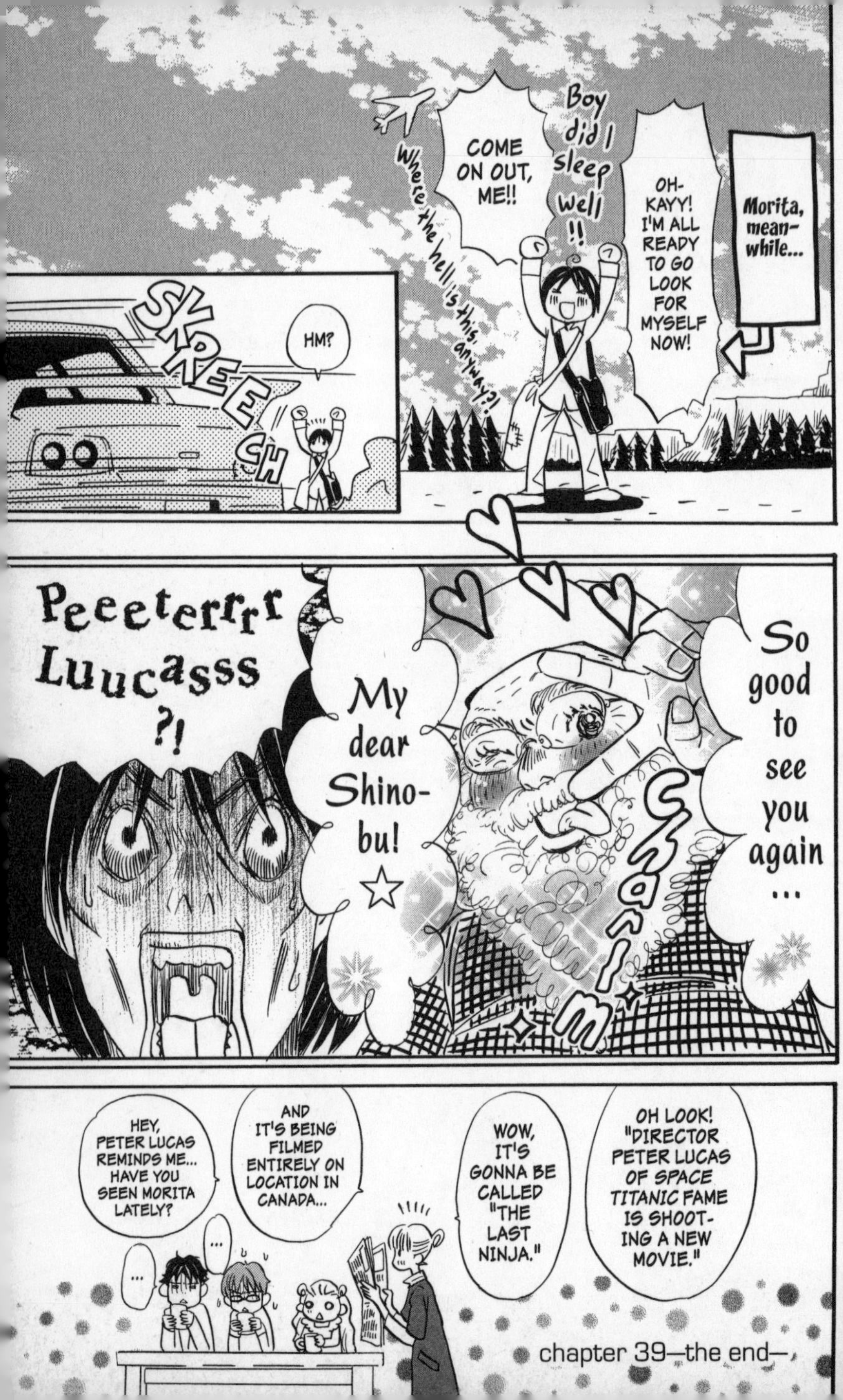
Morita, meanwhile...
OH-KAYY! I'M ALL READY TO GO LOOK FOR MYSELF NOW!
Boy did I sleep well!!
COME ON OUT, ME!!
Where the hell is this, anyway?!
SKREEECH
HM?
So good to see you again...
Sharim
My dear Shinobu! ☆
Peeeterrrr Luucasss ?!
OH LOOK! "DIRECTOR PETER LUCAS OF SPACE TITANIC FAME IS SHOOTING A NEW MOVIE."
WOW, IT'S GONNA BE CALLED "THE LAST NINJA."
AND IT'S BEING FILMED ENTIRELY ON LOCATION IN CANADA...
HEY, PETER LUCAS REMINDS ME... HAVE YOU SEEN MORITA LATELY?
...
...
chapter 39—the end—

Lindt vs. Jean-Paul Hévin Part 3

And above all, it's WAY CHEAPER.

He's right.

chomp chomp

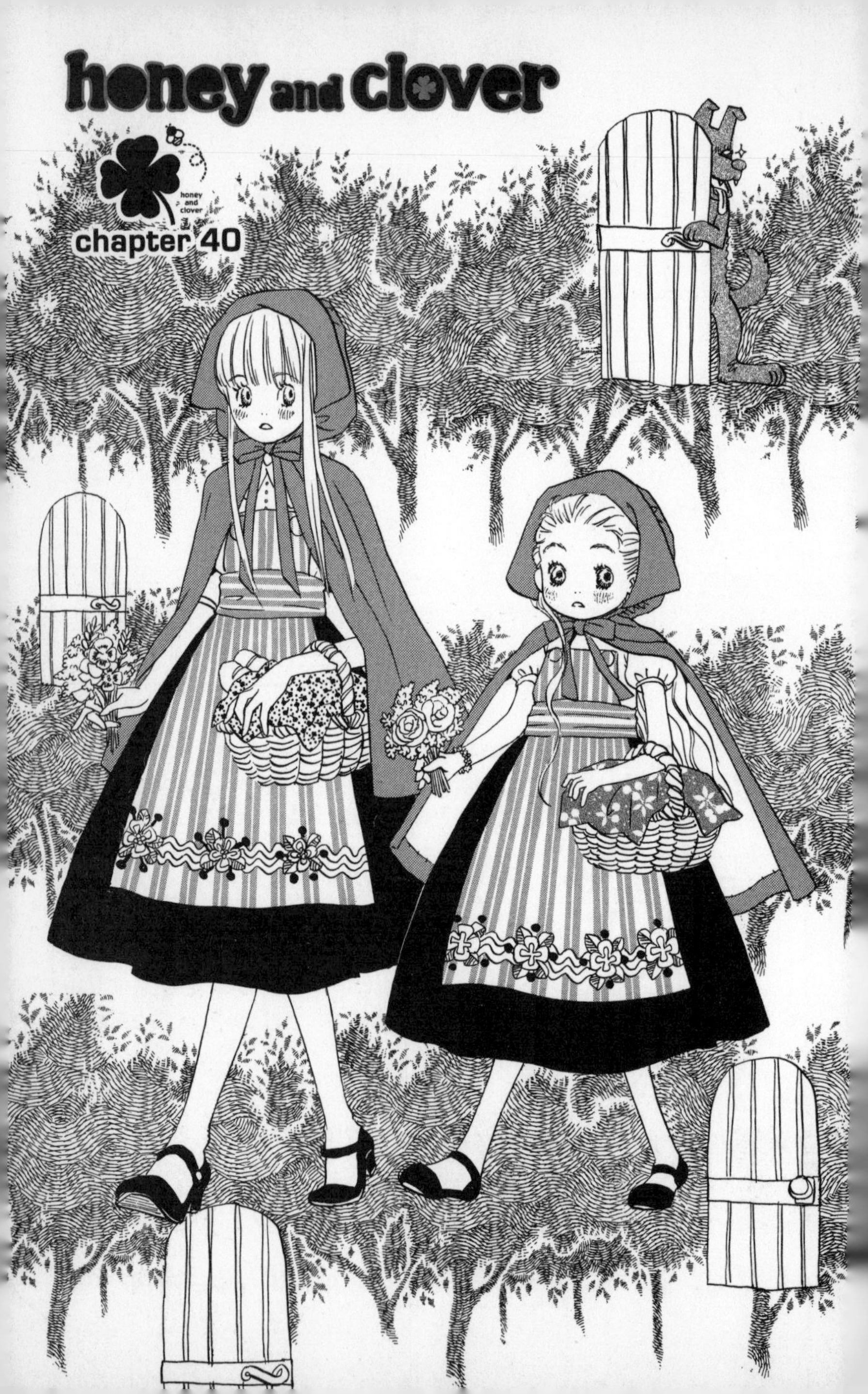
honey and clover
honey and clover
chapter 40

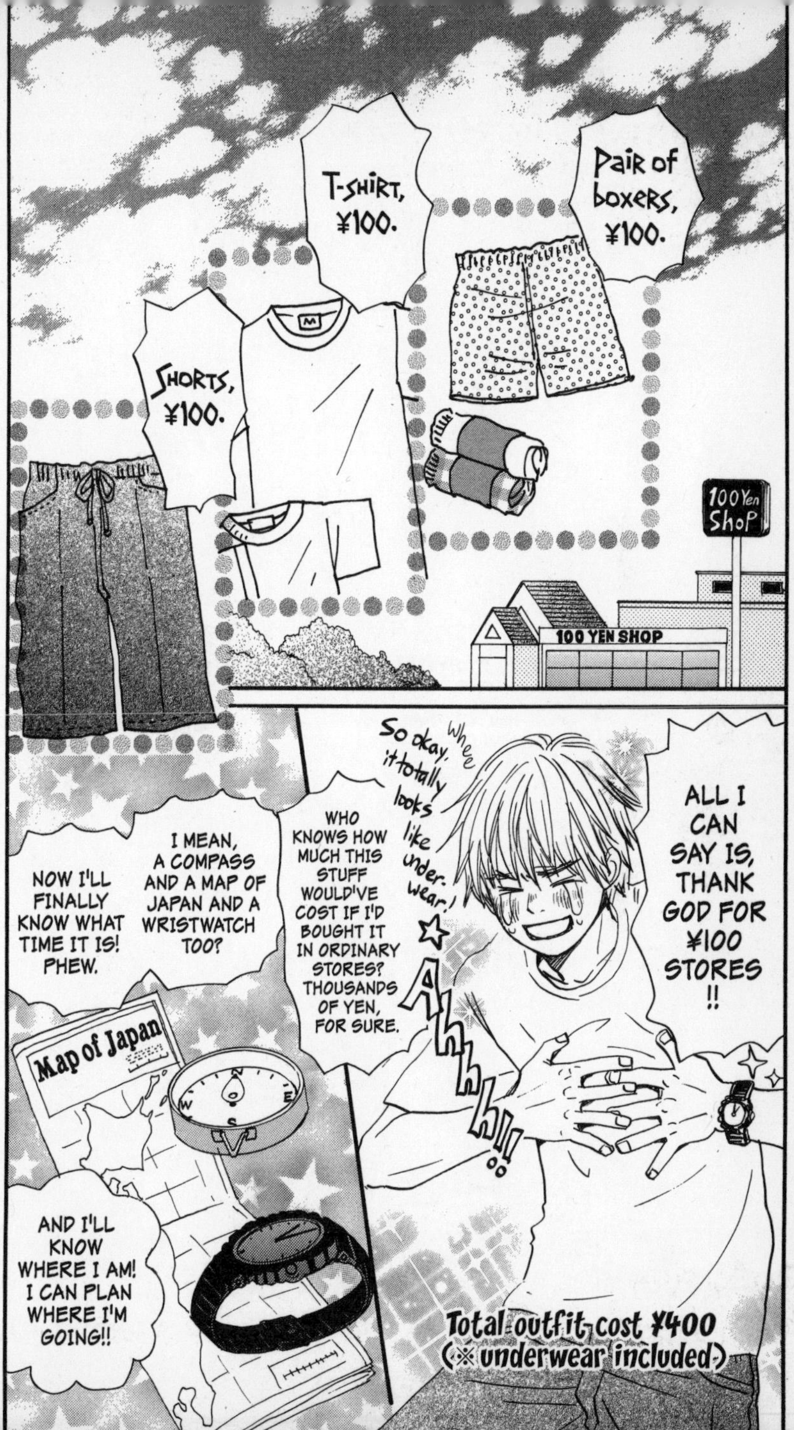
Pair of boxers, ¥100.
T-shirt, ¥100.
Shorts, ¥100.
100 Yen Shop
100 YEN SHOP
ALL I CAN SAY IS, THANK GOD FOR ¥100 STORES !!
So okay, it totally looks like under-wear!
whee
WHO KNOWS HOW MUCH THIS STUFF WOULD'VE COST IF I'D BOUGHT IT IN ORDINARY STORES? THOUSANDS OF YEN, FOR SURE.
Ahhh!!
Total outfit cost ¥400 (※ underwear included)
I MEAN, A COMPASS AND A MAP OF JAPAN AND A WRISTWATCH TOO?
NOW I'LL FINALLY KNOW WHAT TIME IT IS! PHEW.
Map of Japan
AND I'LL KNOW WHERE I AM! I CAN PLAN WHERE I'M GOING!!

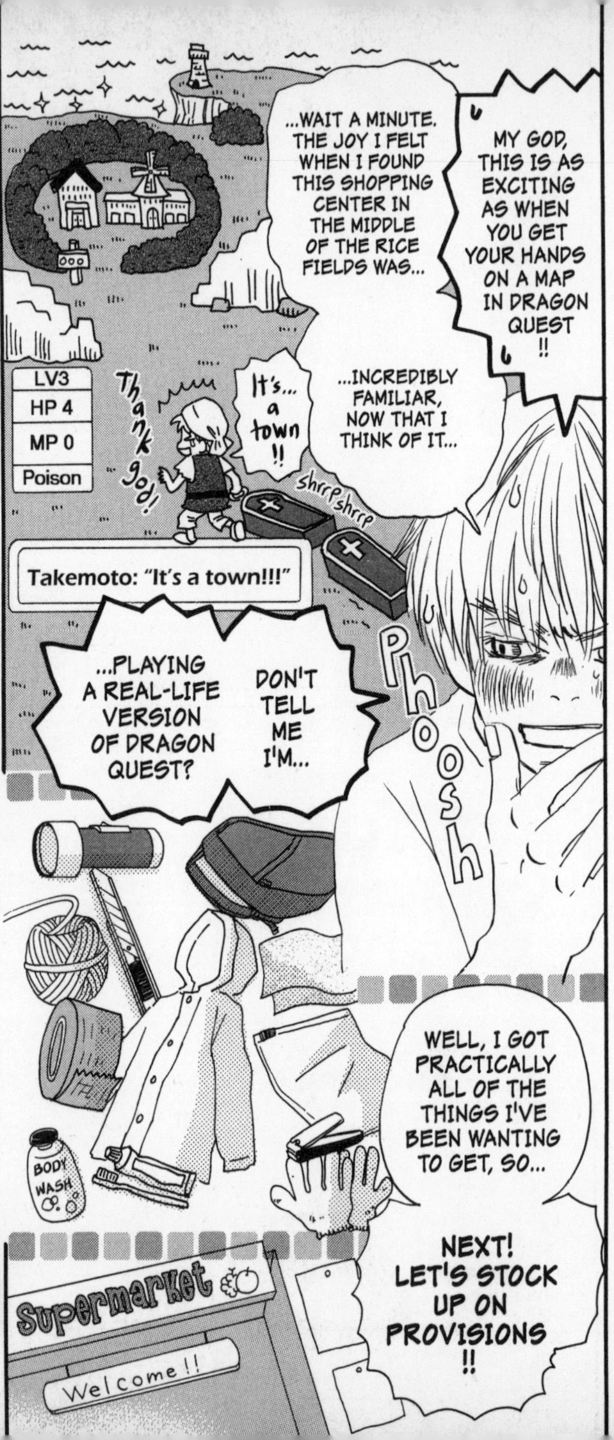
MY GOD, THIS IS AS EXCITING AS WHEN YOU GET YOUR HANDS ON A MAP IN DRAGON QUEST !!
...WAIT A MINUTE. THE JOY I FELT WHEN I FOUND THIS SHOPPING CENTER IN THE MIDDLE OF THE RICE FIELDS WAS...
...INCREDIBLY FAMILIAR, NOW THAT I THINK OF IT...
It's... a town !!
Thank god!
LV3
HP 4
MP 0
Poison
shrrp shrrp
Takemoto: "It's a town!!!"
DON'T TELL ME I'M...
...PLAYING A REAL-LIFE VERSION OF DRAGON QUEST?
Phoosh
WELL, I GOT PRACTICALLY ALL OF THE THINGS I'VE BEEN WANTING TO GET, SO...
BODY WASH
NEXT! LET'S STOCK UP ON PROVISIONS !!
Supermarket
Welcome !!

I love packed lunches!

* Rice-Balls
* Fish sausage
* Crunchy, sweet, yellow daikon pickle

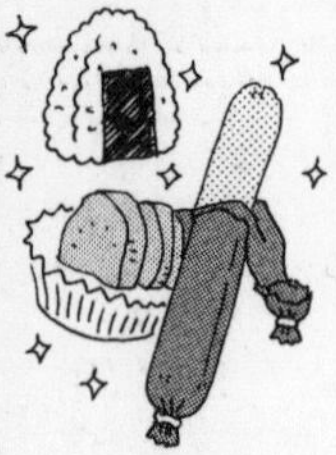

That's all I need to be perfectly happy. ☆

Chica Umino

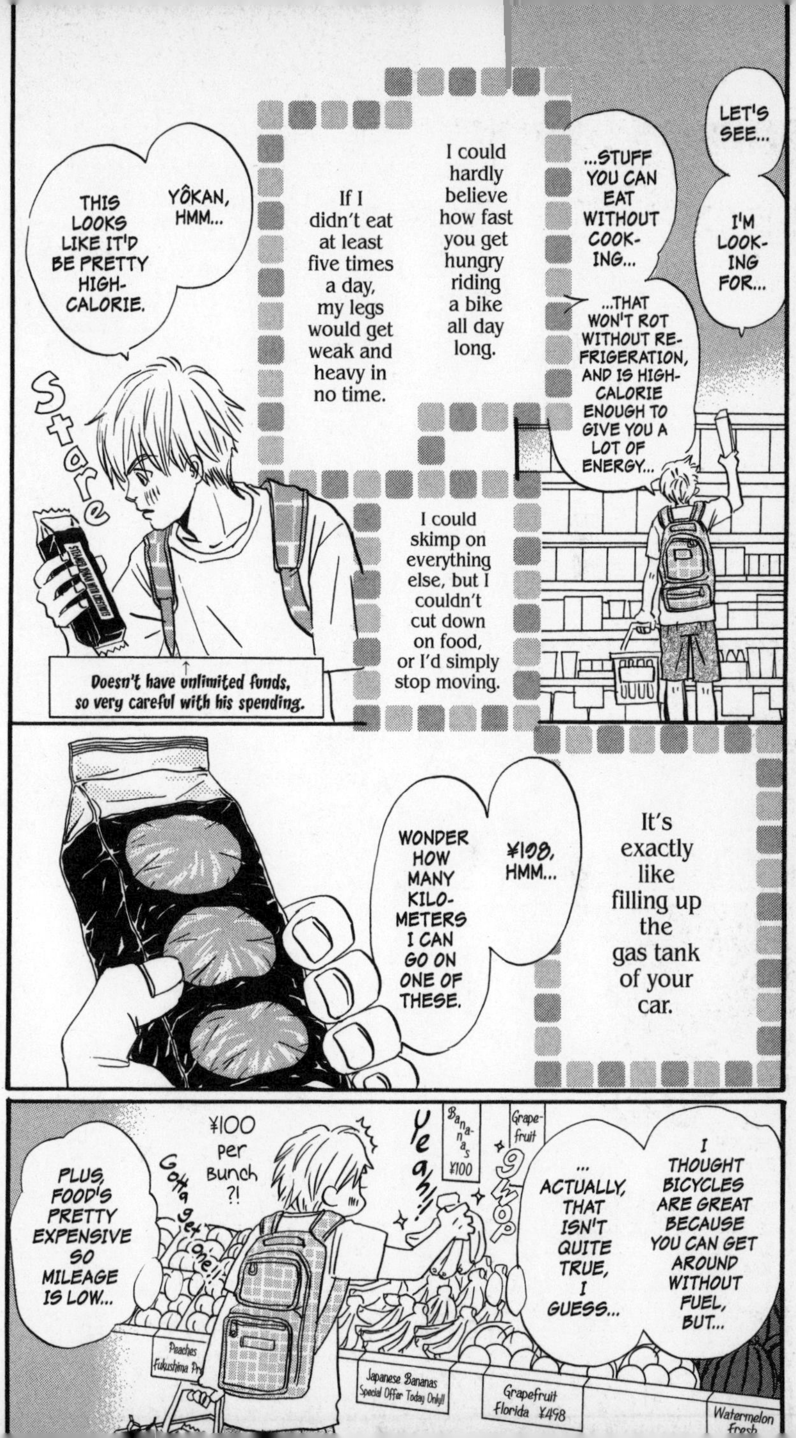
LET'S SEE...
I'M LOOKING FOR...
...STUFF YOU CAN EAT WITHOUT COOKING...
...THAT WON'T ROT WITHOUT REFRIGERATION, AND IS HIGH-CALORIE ENOUGH TO GIVE YOU A LOT OF ENERGY...
I could hardly believe how fast you get hungry riding a bike all day long.
If I didn't eat at least five times a day, my legs would get weak and heavy in no time.
YÔKAN, HMM...
THIS LOOKS LIKE IT'D BE PRETTY HIGH-CALORIE.
Stare
Doesn't have unlimited funds, so very careful with his spending.
I could skimp on everything else, but I couldn't cut down on food, or I'd simply stop moving.
It's exactly like filling up the gas tank of your car.
¥198, HMM...
WONDER HOW MANY KILOMETERS I CAN GO ON ONE OF THESE.
I THOUGHT BICYCLES ARE GREAT BECAUSE YOU CAN GET AROUND WITHOUT FUEL, BUT...
...ACTUALLY, THAT ISN'T QUITE TRUE, I GUESS...
Grapefruit
Bananas ¥100
Gwop
Yeah!!
¥100 per Bunch?!
Gotta get one!!
PLUS, FOOD'S PRETTY EXPENSIVE SO MILEAGE IS LOW...
Peaches
Japanese Bananas Special Offer Today Only!!
Grapefruit Florida ¥498
Watermelon

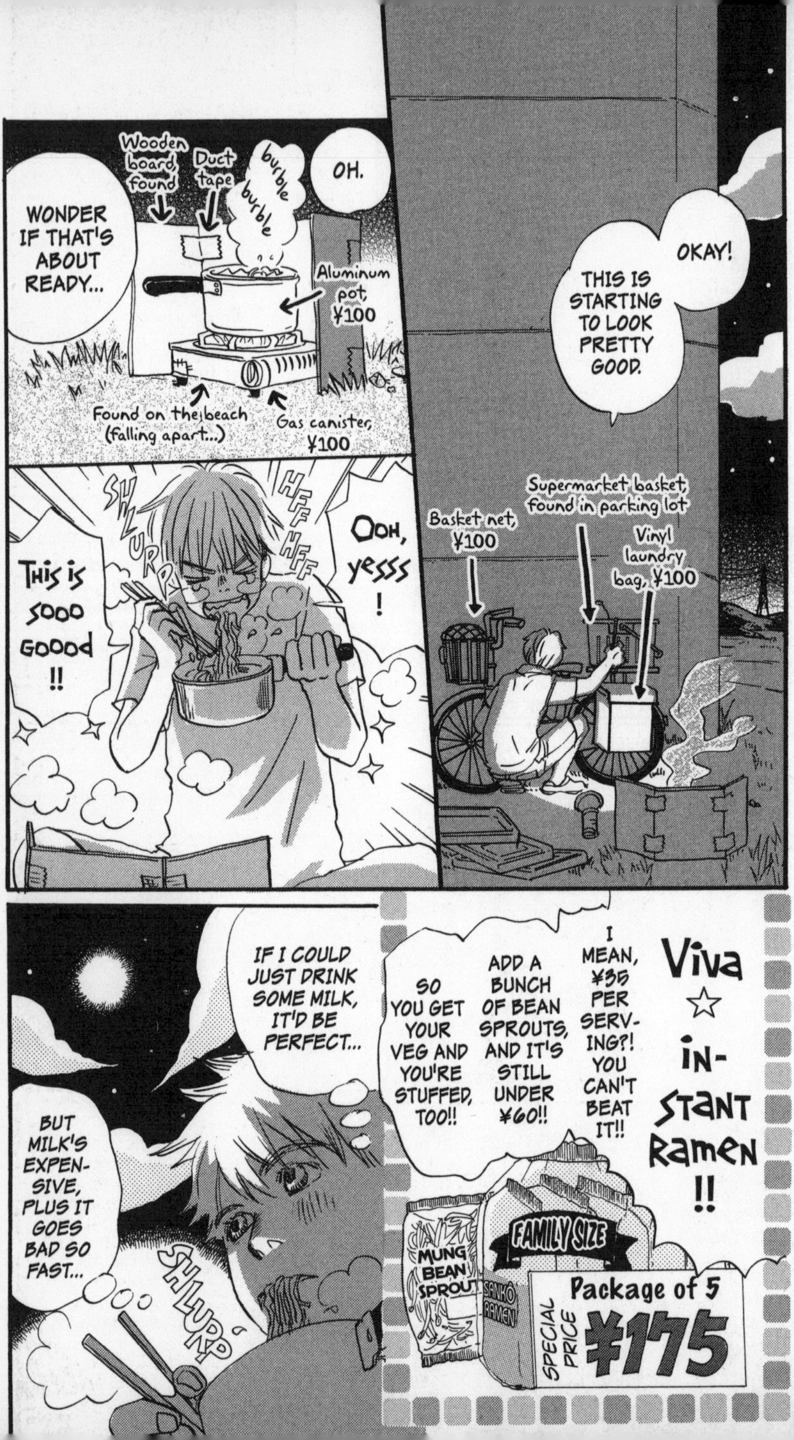
OKAY!
THIS IS STARTING TO LOOK PRETTY GOOD.
Supermarket basket, found in parking lot
Vinyl laundry bag, ¥100
Basket net, ¥100
OH.
burble burble
Aluminum pot, ¥100
Duct tape
Wooden board, found
WONDER IF THAT'S ABOUT READY...
Gas canister, ¥100
Found on the beach (falling apart...)
OOH, YESSS!
HFF HFF
SHLURP
THIS IS SOOO GOOOD!!
Viva ☆ INSTANT RAMEN!!
Package of 5
SPECIAL PRICE ¥175
FAMILY SIZE
SANKO RAMEN
MUNG BEAN SPROUT
I MEAN, ¥35 PER SERVING?! YOU CAN'T BEAT IT!!
ADD A BUNCH OF BEAN SPROUTS, AND IT'S STILL UNDER ¥60!!
SO YOU GET YOUR VEG AND YOU'RE STUFFED, TOO!!
IF I COULD JUST DRINK SOME MILK, IT'D BE PERFECT...
BUT MILK'S EXPENSIVE, PLUS IT GOES BAD SO FAST...
SHLURP

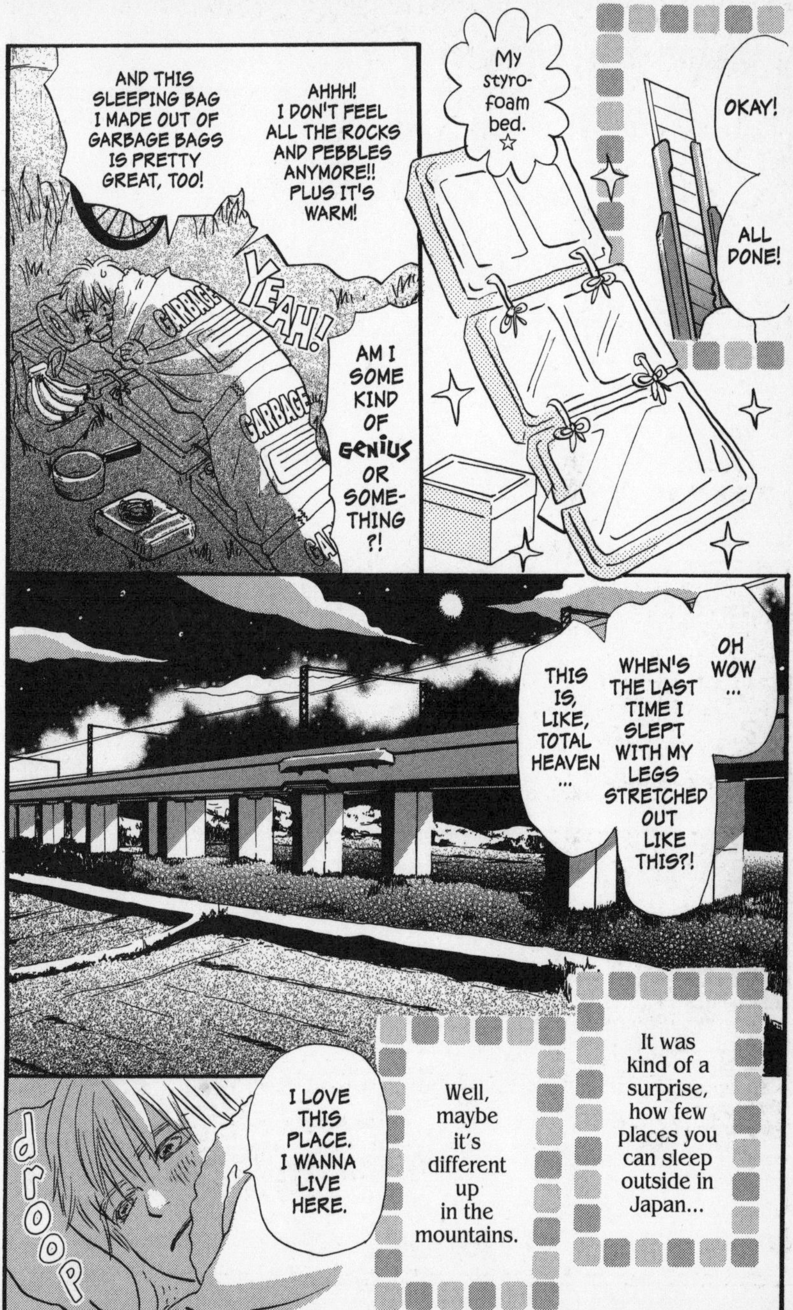
OKAY!
ALL DONE!
My styrofoam bed. ☆
AHHH! I DON'T FEEL ALL THE ROCKS AND PEBBLES ANYMORE!! PLUS IT'S WARM!
AND THIS SLEEPING BAG I MADE OUT OF GARBAGE BAGS IS PRETTY GREAT, TOO!
YEAH!
GARBAGE
GARBAGE
AM I SOME KIND OF GENIUS OR SOMETHING?!
OH WOW ...
WHEN'S THE LAST TIME I SLEPT WITH MY LEGS STRETCHED OUT LIKE THIS?!
THIS IS, LIKE, TOTAL HEAVEN ...
It was kind of a surprise, how few places you can sleep outside in Japan...
Well, maybe it's different up in the mountains.
I LOVE THIS PLACE. I WANNA LIVE HERE.
droop

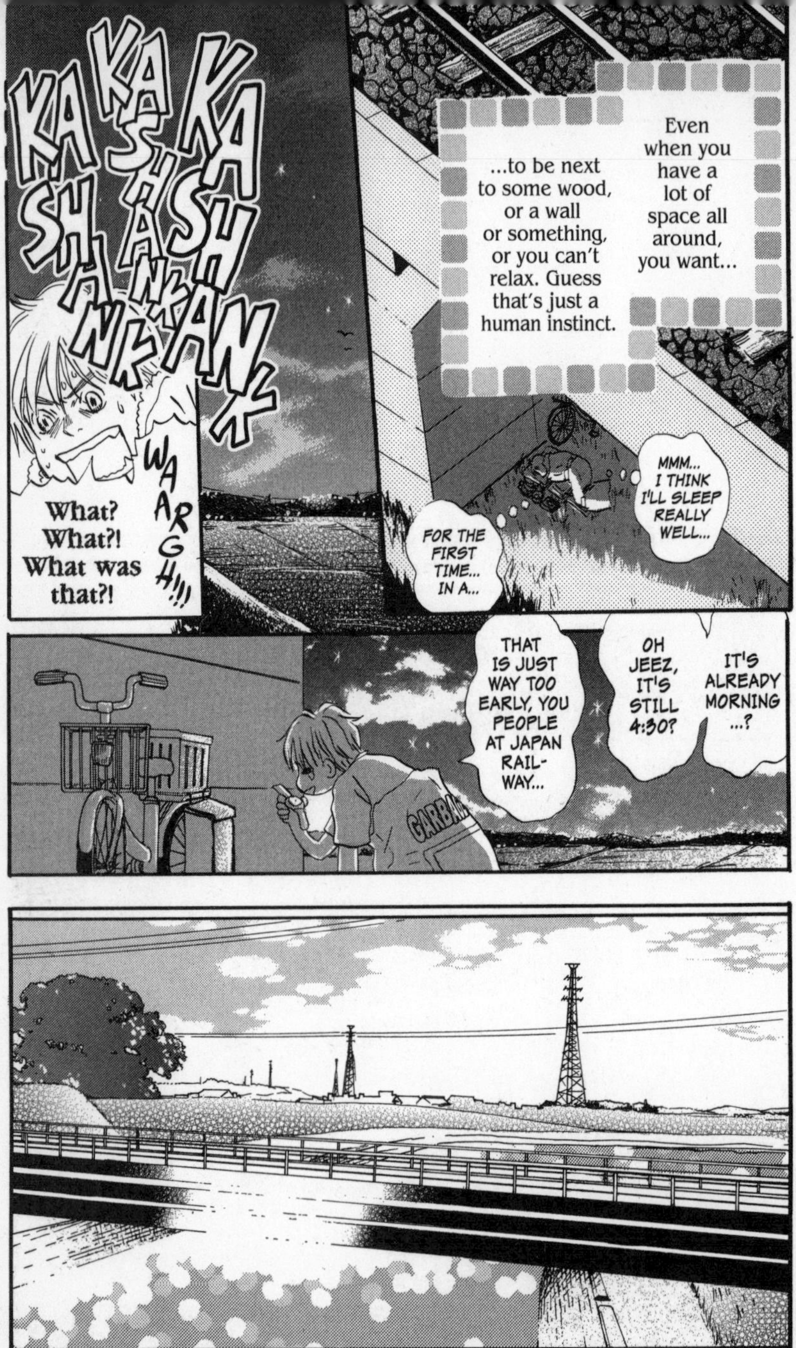
Even when you have a lot of space all around, you want...
...to be next to some wood, or a wall or something, or you can't relax. Guess that's just a human instinct.
MMM... I THINK I'LL SLEEP REALLY WELL...
FOR THE FIRST TIME... IN A...
KA KA KA
SHASHASHANKANKANK
WAARGH!!!
What? What?! What was that?!
IT'S ALREADY MORNING ...?
OH JEEZ, IT'S STILL 4:30?
THAT IS JUST WAY TOO EARLY, YOU PEOPLE AT JAPAN RAILWAY...

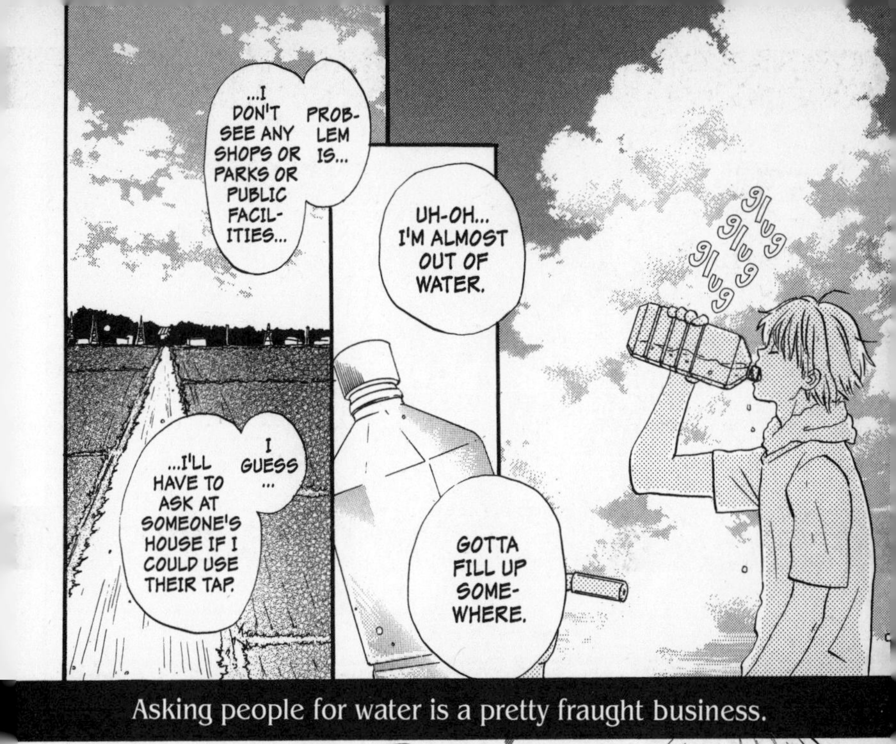
glug glug glug
UH-OH... I'M ALMOST OUT OF WATER.
GOTTA FILL UP SOMEWHERE.
PROBLEM IS...
...I DON'T SEE ANY SHOPS OR PARKS OR PUBLIC FACILITIES...
I GUESS...
...I'LL HAVE TO ASK AT SOMEONE'S HOUSE IF I COULD USE THEIR TAP.

Asking people for water is a pretty fraught business.

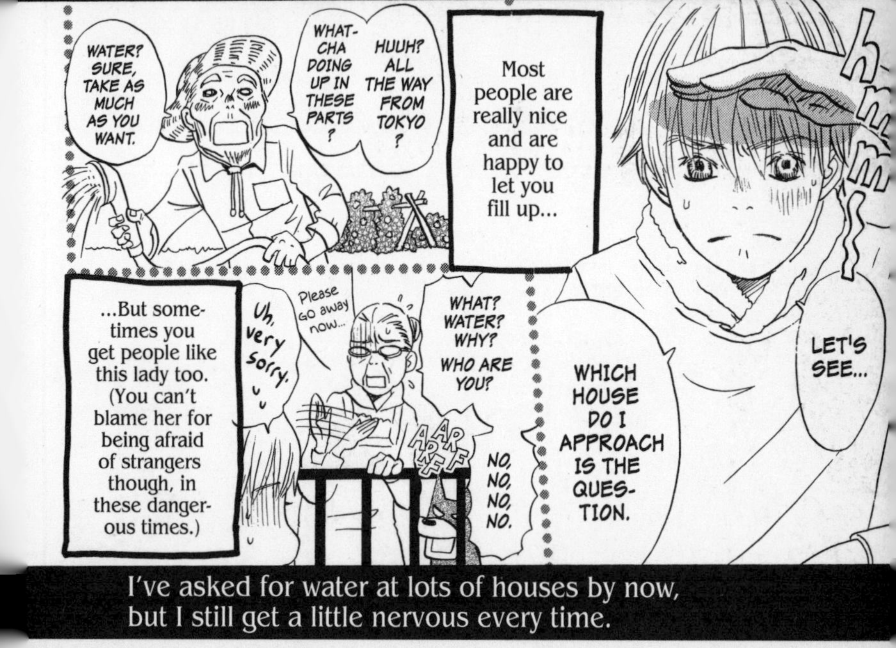
h-mm
LET'S SEE...
WHICH HOUSE DO I APPROACH IS THE QUESTION.
Most people are really nice and are happy to let you fill up...
HUUH? ALL THE WAY FROM TOKYO?
WHATCHA DOING UP IN THESE PARTS?
WATER? SURE, TAKE AS MUCH AS YOU WANT.
WHAT? WATER? WHY? WHO ARE YOU?
NO, NO, NO, NO.
ARF ARF
Please go away now...
Uh, very sorry.
...But sometimes you get people like this lady too. (You can't blame her for being afraid of strangers though, in these dangerous times.)

I've asked for water at lots of houses by now,
but I still get a little nervous every time.

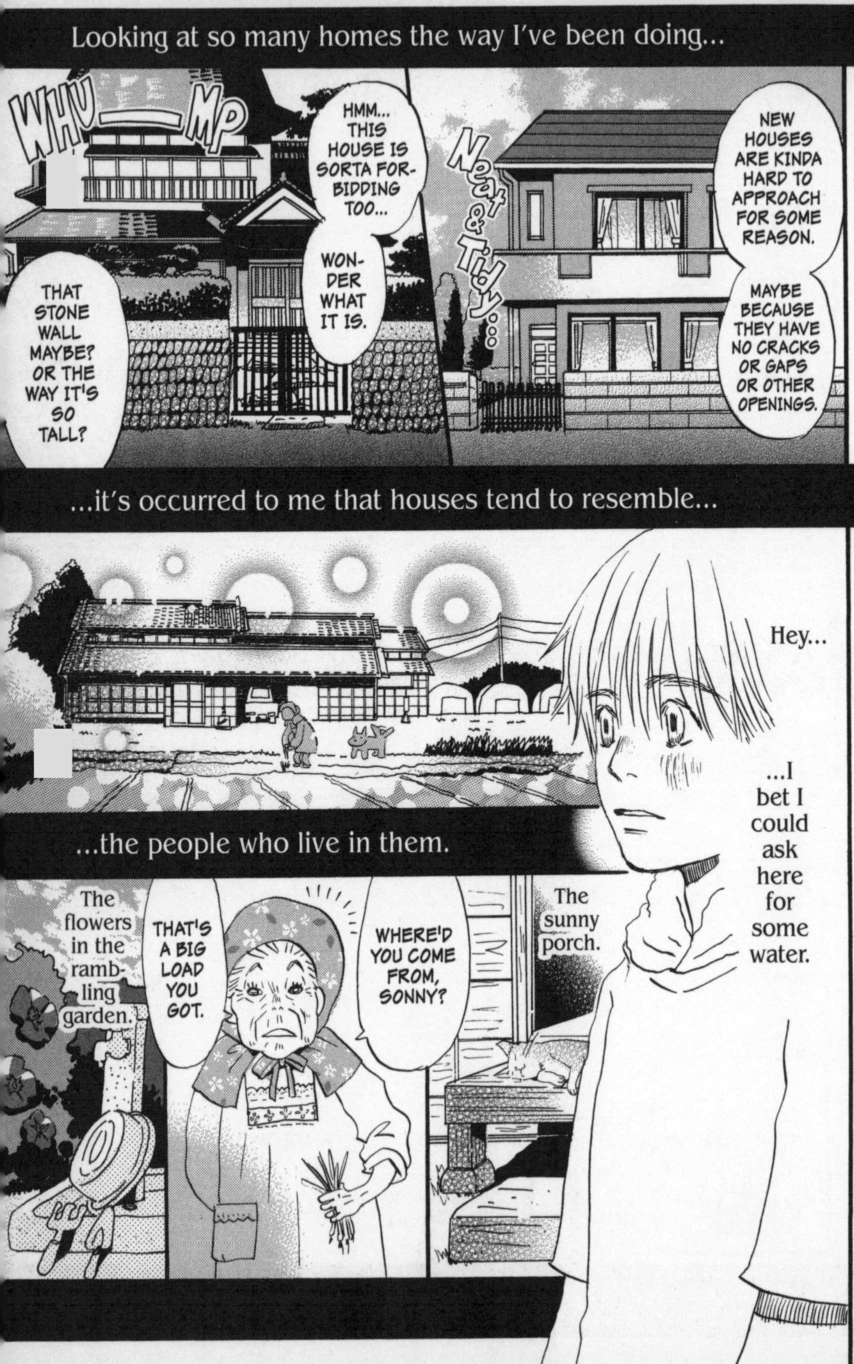
Looking at so many homes the way I've been doing...
NEW HOUSES ARE KINDA HARD TO APPROACH FOR SOME REASON.
MAYBE BECAUSE THEY HAVE NO CRACKS OR GAPS OR OTHER OPENINGS.
Neat & Tidy...
WHU—MP
HMM... THIS HOUSE IS SORTA FOR-BIDDING TOO...
WON-DER WHAT IT IS.
THAT STONE WALL MAYBE? OR THE WAY IT'S SO TALL?
...it's occurred to me that houses tend to resemble...
Hey...
...I bet I could ask here for some water.
...the people who live in them.
The sunny porch.
WHERE'D YOU COME FROM, SONNY?
THAT'S A BIG LOAD YOU GOT.
The flowers in the ramb-ling garden.

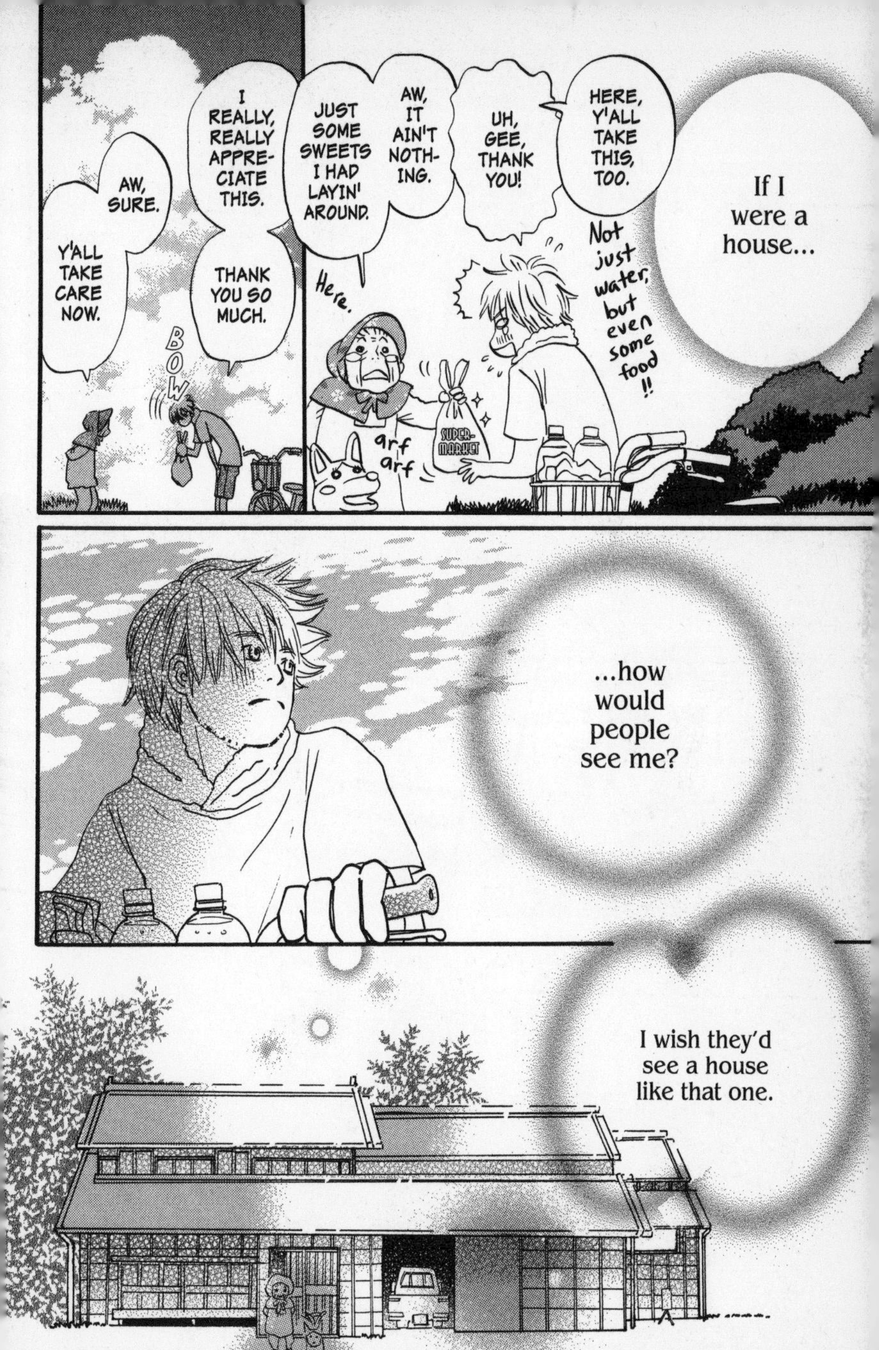
If I were a house...
HERE, Y'ALL TAKE THIS, TOO.
Not just water, but even some food!!
UH, GEE, THANK YOU!
AW, IT AIN'T NOTH-ING.
JUST SOME SWEETS I HAD LAYIN' AROUND.
Here.
SUPER-MARKET
arf arf
I REALLY, REALLY APPRECIATE THIS.
AW, SURE.
THANK YOU SO MUCH.
BOW
Y'ALL TAKE CARE NOW.
...how would people see me?
I wish they'd see a house like that one.

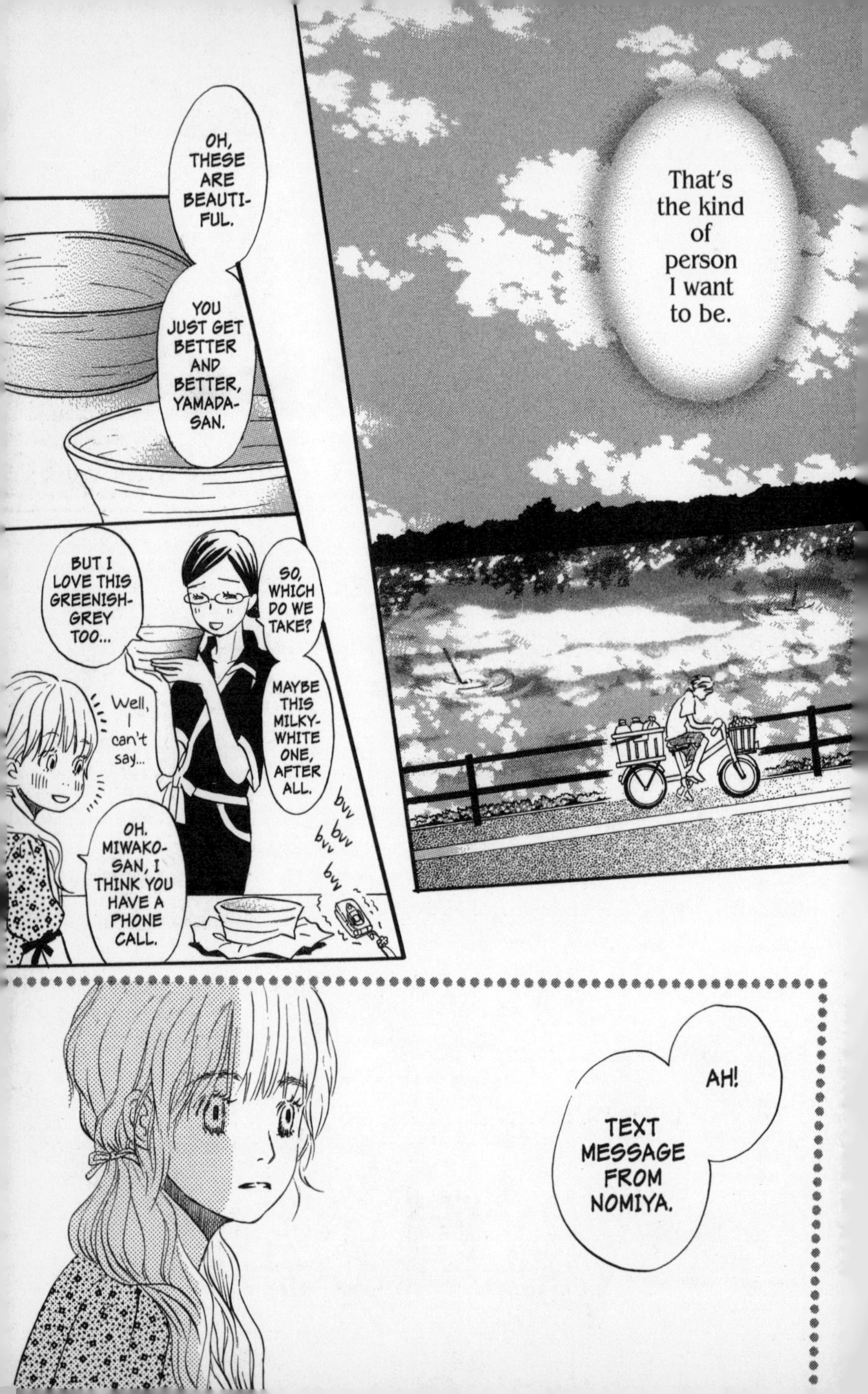
That's the kind of person I want to be.
OH, THESE ARE BEAUTI-FUL.
YOU JUST GET BETTER AND BETTER, YAMADA-SAN.
SO, WHICH DO WE TAKE?
MAYBE THIS MILKY-WHITE ONE, AFTER ALL.
BUT I LOVE THIS GREENISH-GREY TOO...
bvv bvv bvv bvv
Well, I can't say...
OH. MIWAKO-SAN, I THINK YOU HAVE A PHONE CALL.
AH!
TEXT MESSAGE FROM NOMIYA.

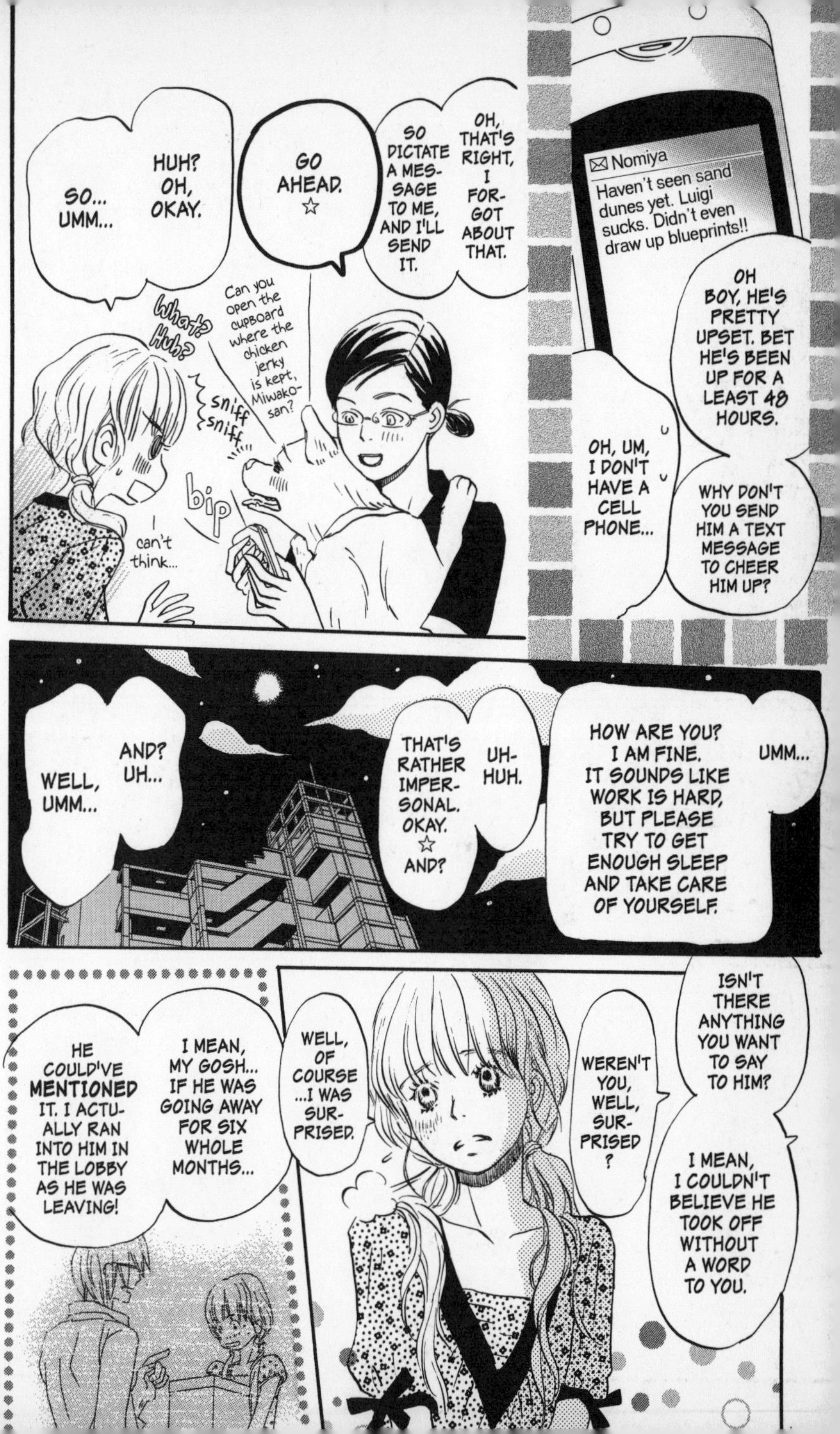
Nomiya
Haven't seen sand dunes yet. Luigi sucks. Didn't even draw up blueprints!!
OH BOY, HE'S PRETTY UPSET. BET HE'S BEEN UP FOR A LEAST 48 HOURS.
WHY DON'T YOU SEND HIM A TEXT MESSAGE TO CHEER HIM UP?
OH, UM, I DON'T HAVE A CELL PHONE...
OH, THAT'S RIGHT, I FORGOT ABOUT THAT.
SO DICTATE A MESSAGE TO ME, AND I'LL SEND IT.
GO AHEAD. ☆
HUH? OH, OKAY.
SO... UMM...
Can you open the cupboard where the chicken jerky is kept, Miwako-san?
What? Huh?
sniff sniff
bip
I can't think...
UMM...
HOW ARE YOU? I AM FINE. IT SOUNDS LIKE WORK IS HARD, BUT PLEASE TRY TO GET ENOUGH SLEEP AND TAKE CARE OF YOURSELF.
UH-HUH.
THAT'S RATHER IMPERSONAL. OKAY. ☆ AND?
AND? UH...
WELL, UMM...
ISN'T THERE ANYTHING YOU WANT TO SAY TO HIM?
I MEAN, I COULDN'T BELIEVE HE TOOK OFF WITHOUT A WORD TO YOU.
WEREN'T YOU, WELL, SURPRISED?
WELL, OF COURSE ...I WAS SURPRISED.
I MEAN, MY GOSH... IF HE WAS GOING AWAY FOR SIX WHOLE MONTHS...
HE COULD'VE MENTIONED IT. I ACTUALLY RAN INTO HIM IN THE LOBBY AS HE WAS LEAVING!

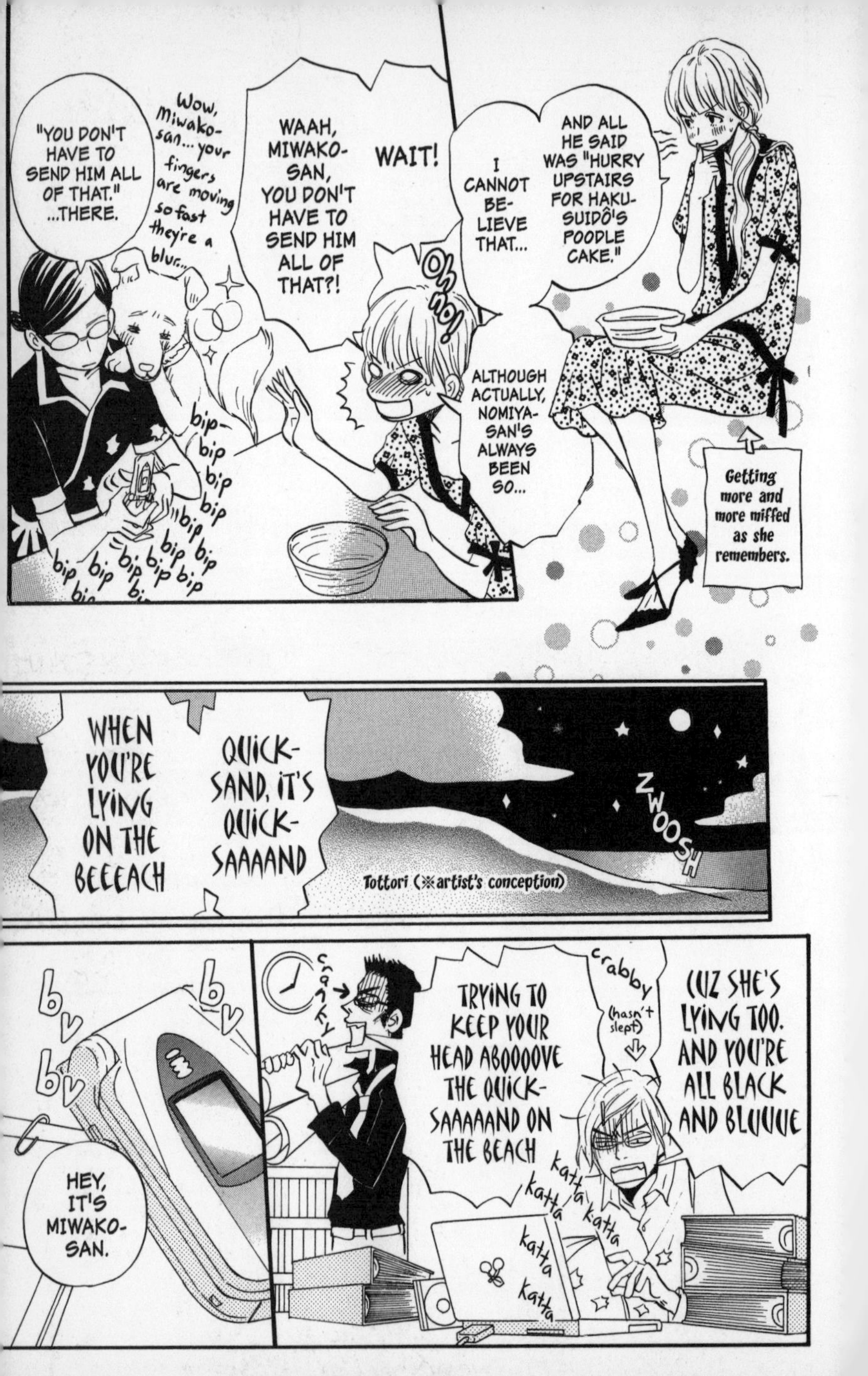
I CANNOT BE-LIEVE THAT...
AND ALL HE SAID WAS "HURRY UPSTAIRS FOR HAKU-SUIDÔ'S POODLE CAKE."
Getting more and more miffed as she remembers.
WAIT!
WAAH, MIWAKO-SAN, YOU DON'T HAVE TO SEND HIM ALL OF THAT?!
Oh no!
ALTHOUGH ACTUALLY, NOMIYA-SAN'S ALWAYS BEEN SO...
Wow, miwako-san... your fingers are moving so fast they're a blur...
"YOU DON'T HAVE TO SEND HIM ALL OF THAT." ...THERE.
bip-bip bip bip bip bip bip bip bip bip bip
QUICK-SAND, IT'S QUICK-SAAAAND
WHEN YOU'RE LYING ON THE BEEEACH
ZWOOSH
Tottori (※artist's conception)
CUZ SHE'S LYING TOO. AND YOU'RE ALL BLACK AND BLUUUE
crabby
(hasn't slept)
TRYING TO KEEP YOUR HEAD ABOOOOVE THE QUICK-SAAAAAND ON THE BEACH
cranky
katta katta katta katta katta katta
bv bv bv
HEY, IT'S MIWAKO-SAN.

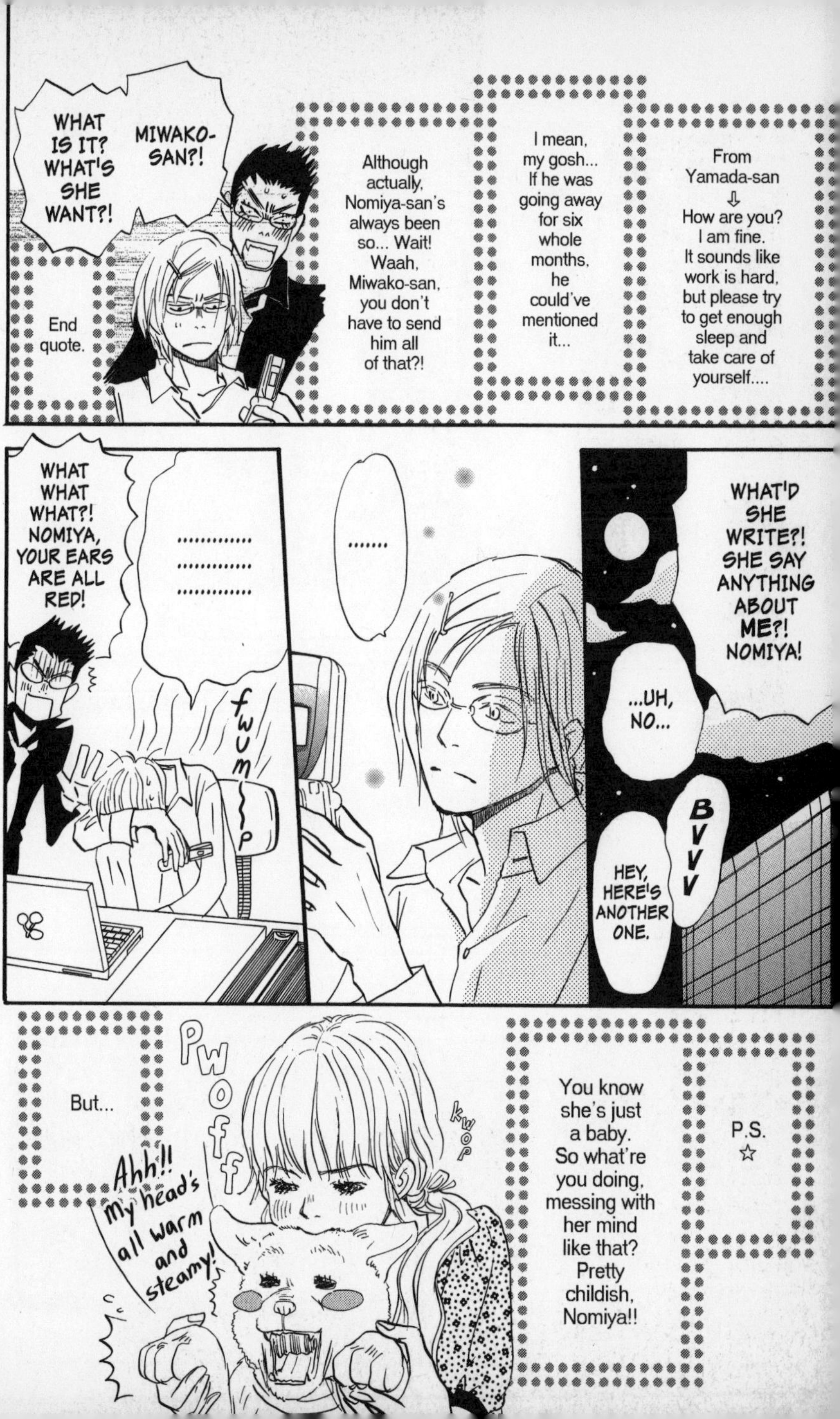

From Yamada-san ⇩ How are you? I am fine. It sounds like work is hard, but please try to get enough sleep and take care of yourself....
I mean, my gosh... If he was going away for six whole months, he could've mentioned it...
Although actually, Nomiya-san's always been so... Wait! Waah, Miwako-san, you don't have to send him all of that?!
MIWAKO-SAN?!
WHAT IS IT? WHAT'S SHE WANT?!
End quote.
WHAT'D SHE WRITE?! SHE SAY ANYTHING ABOUT ME?! NOMIYA!
...UH, NO...
BVVV
HEY, HERE'S ANOTHER ONE.
....
....
WHAT WHAT WHAT?! NOMIYA, YOUR EARS ARE ALL RED!
fwump
P.S. ☆
You know she's just a baby. So what're you doing, messing with her mind like that? Pretty childish, Nomiya!!
But...
KWOP
Pwoff
Ahh!! my head's all warm and steamy!

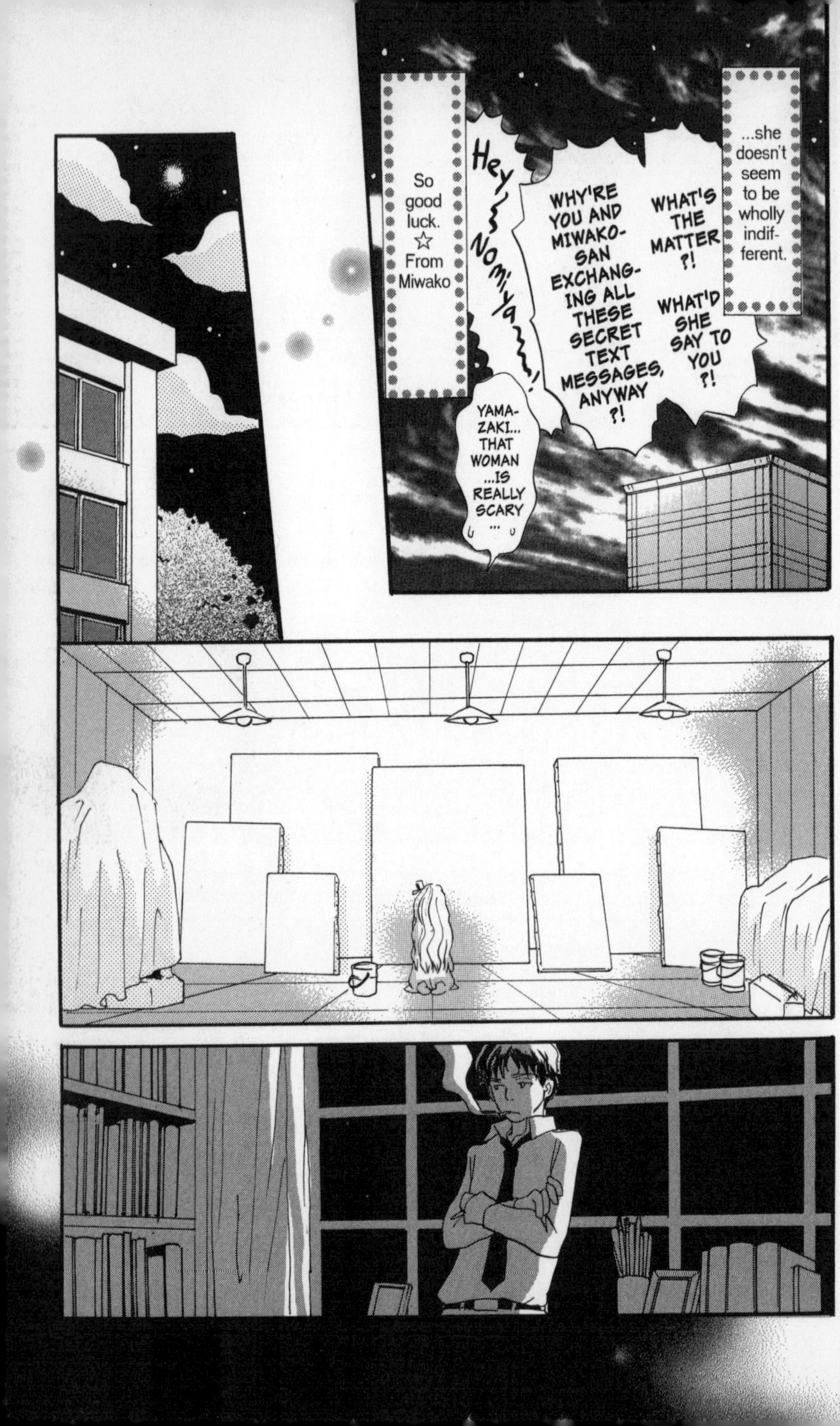
...she doesn't seem to be wholly indif-ferent.
WHAT'S THE MATTER ?!
WHAT'D SHE SAY TO YOU ?!
WHY'RE YOU AND MIWAKO-SAN EXCHANG-ING ALL THESE SECRET TEXT MESSAGES, ANYWAY ?!
Hey~ Nomiya~!
So good luck. ☆ From Miwako
YAMA-ZAKI... THAT WOMAN ...IS REALLY SCARY ...

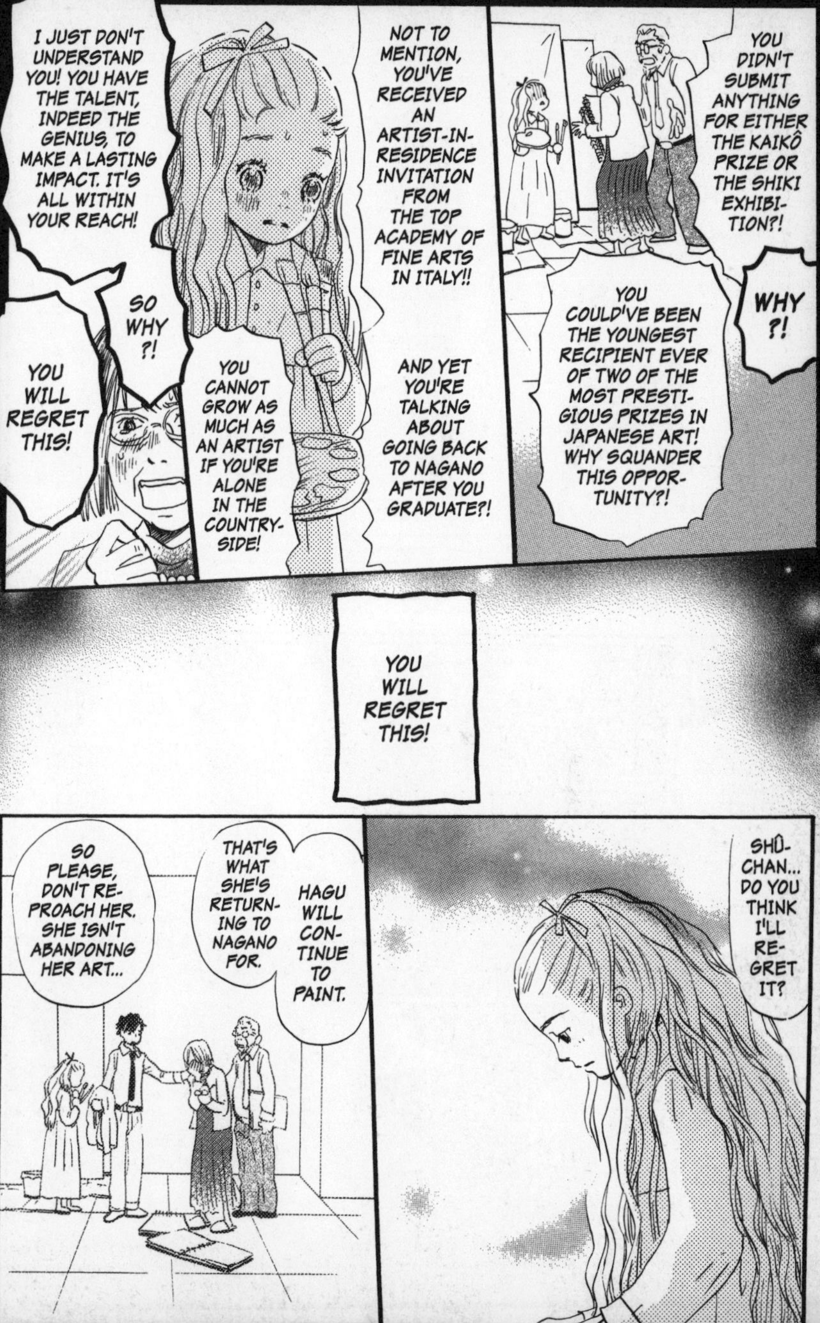
YOU DIDN'T SUBMIT ANYTHING FOR EITHER THE KAIKÔ PRIZE OR THE SHIKI EXHIBITION?!
WHY ?!
YOU COULD'VE BEEN THE YOUNGEST RECIPIENT EVER OF TWO OF THE MOST PRESTIGIOUS PRIZES IN JAPANESE ART! WHY SQUANDER THIS OPPORTUNITY?!
NOT TO MENTION, YOU'VE RECEIVED AN ARTIST-IN-RESIDENCE INVITATION FROM THE TOP ACADEMY OF FINE ARTS IN ITALY!!
AND YET YOU'RE TALKING ABOUT GOING BACK TO NAGANO AFTER YOU GRADUATE?!
YOU CANNOT GROW AS MUCH AS AN ARTIST IF YOU'RE ALONE IN THE COUNTRYSIDE!
I JUST DON'T UNDERSTAND YOU! YOU HAVE THE TALENT, INDEED THE GENIUS, TO MAKE A LASTING IMPACT. IT'S ALL WITHIN YOUR REACH!
SO WHY ?!
YOU WILL REGRET THIS!
YOU WILL REGRET THIS!
SHÛ-CHAN... DO YOU THINK I'LL REGRET IT?
HAGU WILL CONTINUE TO PAINT.
THAT'S WHAT SHE'S RETURNING TO NAGANO FOR.
SO PLEASE, DON'T REPROACH HER. SHE ISN'T ABANDONING HER ART...

SHE SPENT YEARS IN PARIS, STUDYING AND TRYING TO MAKE A NAME FOR HER-SELF AS A PAINTER. SHE KEPT AT IT UNTIL SHE FINALLY COLLAPSED.

PRO-FESSOR KÔDA, YOU SEE... HAS GONE THROUGH A LOT.

...THEIR POINT IS THAT ONE WAY OF MEASURING THAT...

BUT...

YOU SIMPLY WANT TO SEE FOR YOURSELF HOW FAR YOU'VE PRO-GRESSED AS AN ARTIST.

SO I GUESS SHE SEES HERSELF IN YOU, HAGU.

SHE CAN'T HELP PROJECTING HER OWN DREAMS ONTO YOU.

...IS TO SEND YOUR WORK OUT INTO THE WORLD AND SEE WHAT KIND OF REACTIONS YOU GET.

I'LL TELL YOU WHAT I THINK, HAGU.

NEITHER CHOICE IS BETTER THAN THE OTHER. THEY'RE BOTH RIGHT.

THE IMPORTANT THING IS, NO MATTER WHICH PATH YOU CHOOSE...

...YOU DON'T USE IT AS A JUSTIFI-CATION FOR ANYTHING LATER.

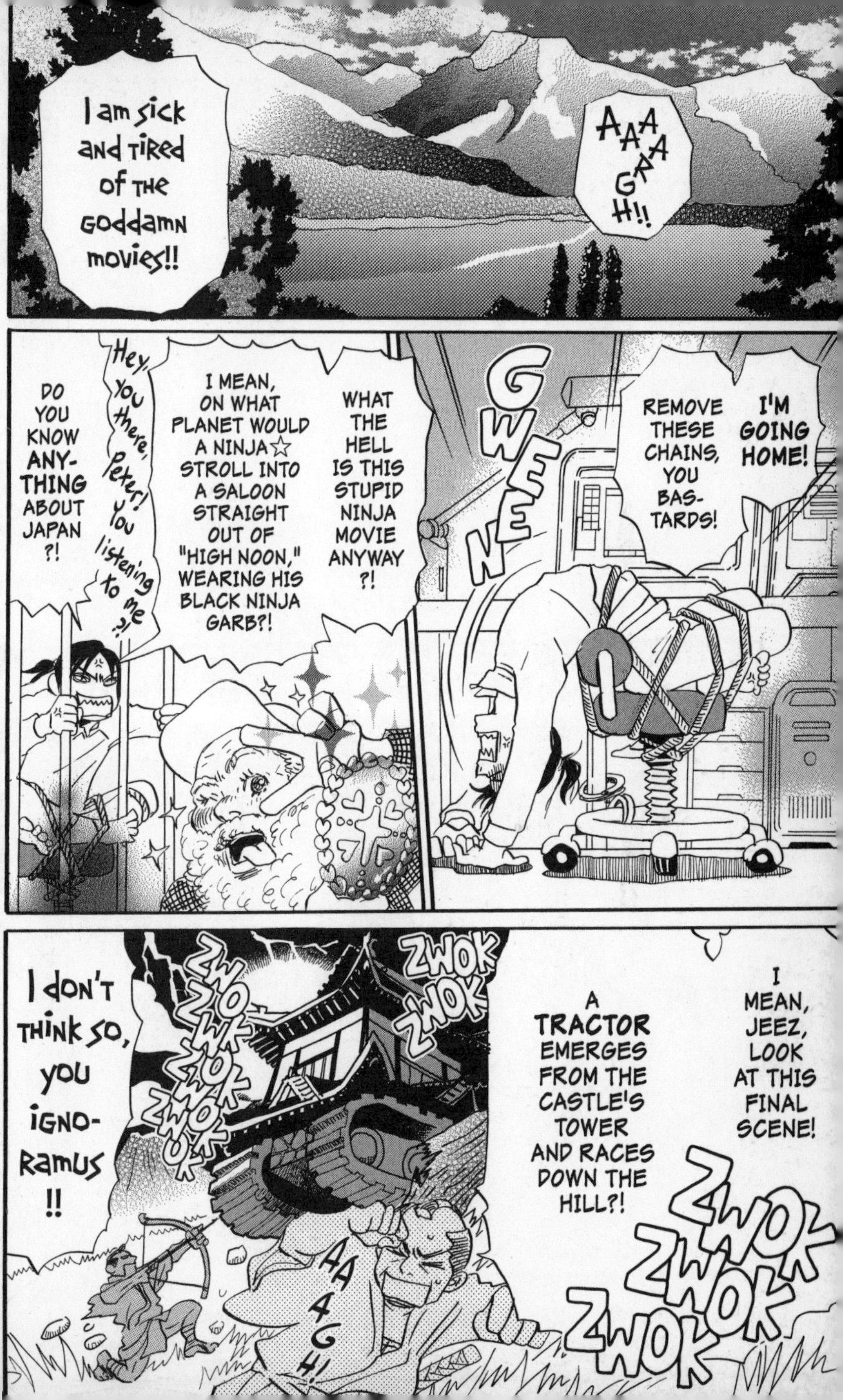
AAAARGH!!
I am sick and tired of the goddamn movies!!
GWEEN
I'M GOING HOME!
REMOVE THESE CHAINS, YOU BASTARDS!
WHAT THE HELL IS THIS STUPID NINJA MOVIE ANYWAY?!
I MEAN, ON WHAT PLANET WOULD A NINJA☆ STROLL INTO A SALOON STRAIGHT OUT OF "HIGH NOON," WEARING HIS BLACK NINJA GARB?!
Hey, you there, Peter! You listening to me?!
DO YOU KNOW ANYTHING ABOUT JAPAN?!
I MEAN, JEEZ, LOOK AT THIS FINAL SCENE!
A TRACTOR EMERGES FROM THE CASTLE'S TOWER AND RACES DOWN THE HILL?!
ZWOK ZWOK
ZWOK ZWOK ZWOK ZWOK
I don't think so, you ignoramus!!
AAAGH!
ZWOK ZWOK ZWOK

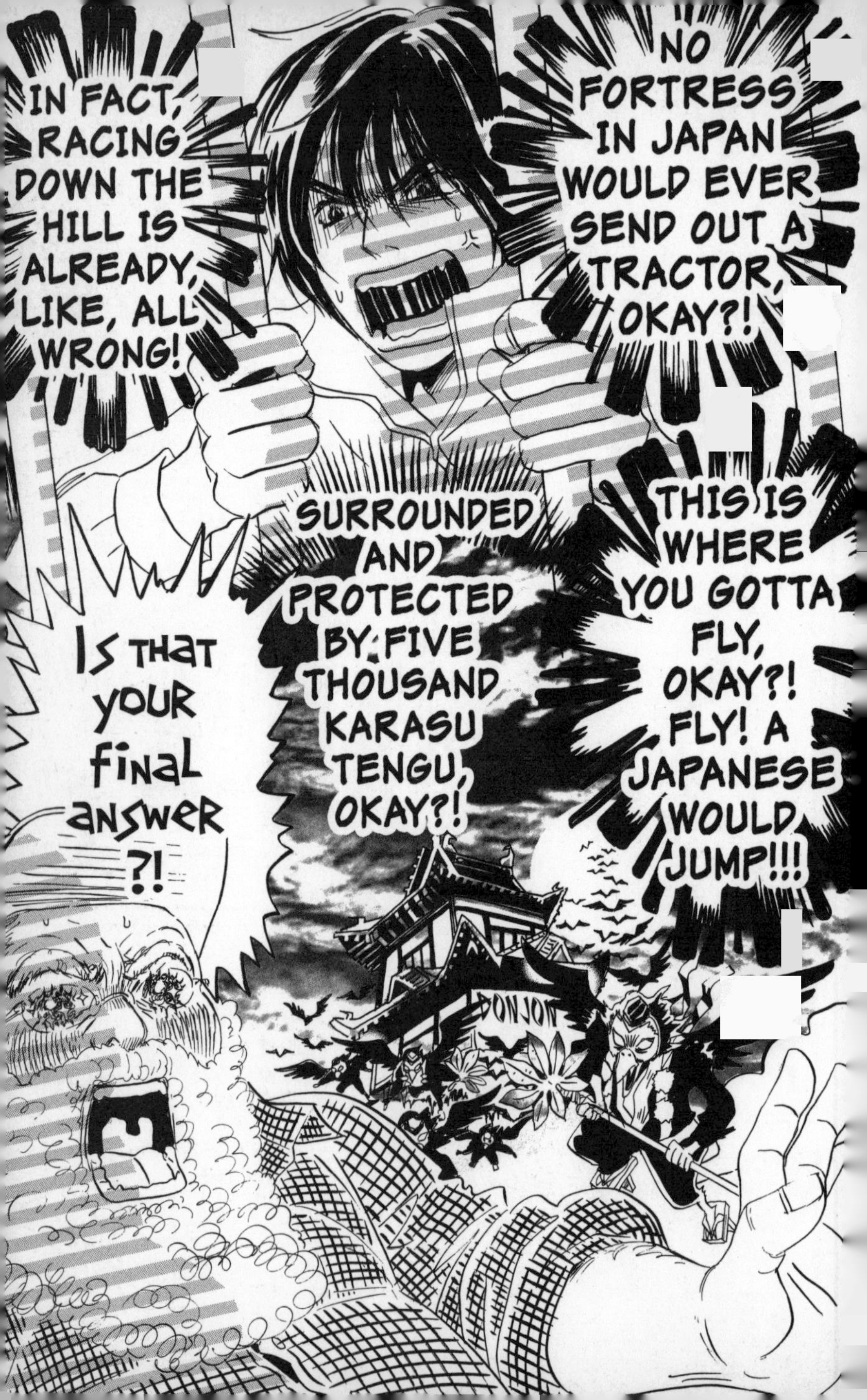
NO FORTRESS IN JAPAN WOULD EVER SEND OUT A TRACTOR, OKAY?!
IN FACT, RACING DOWN THE HILL IS ALREADY, LIKE, ALL WRONG!
THIS IS WHERE YOU GOTTA FLY, OKAY?! FLY! A JAPANESE WOULD JUMP!!!
SURROUNDED AND PROTECTED BY FIVE THOUSAND KARASU TENGU, OKAY?!
DONJON
IS THAT YOUR FINAL ANSWER?!

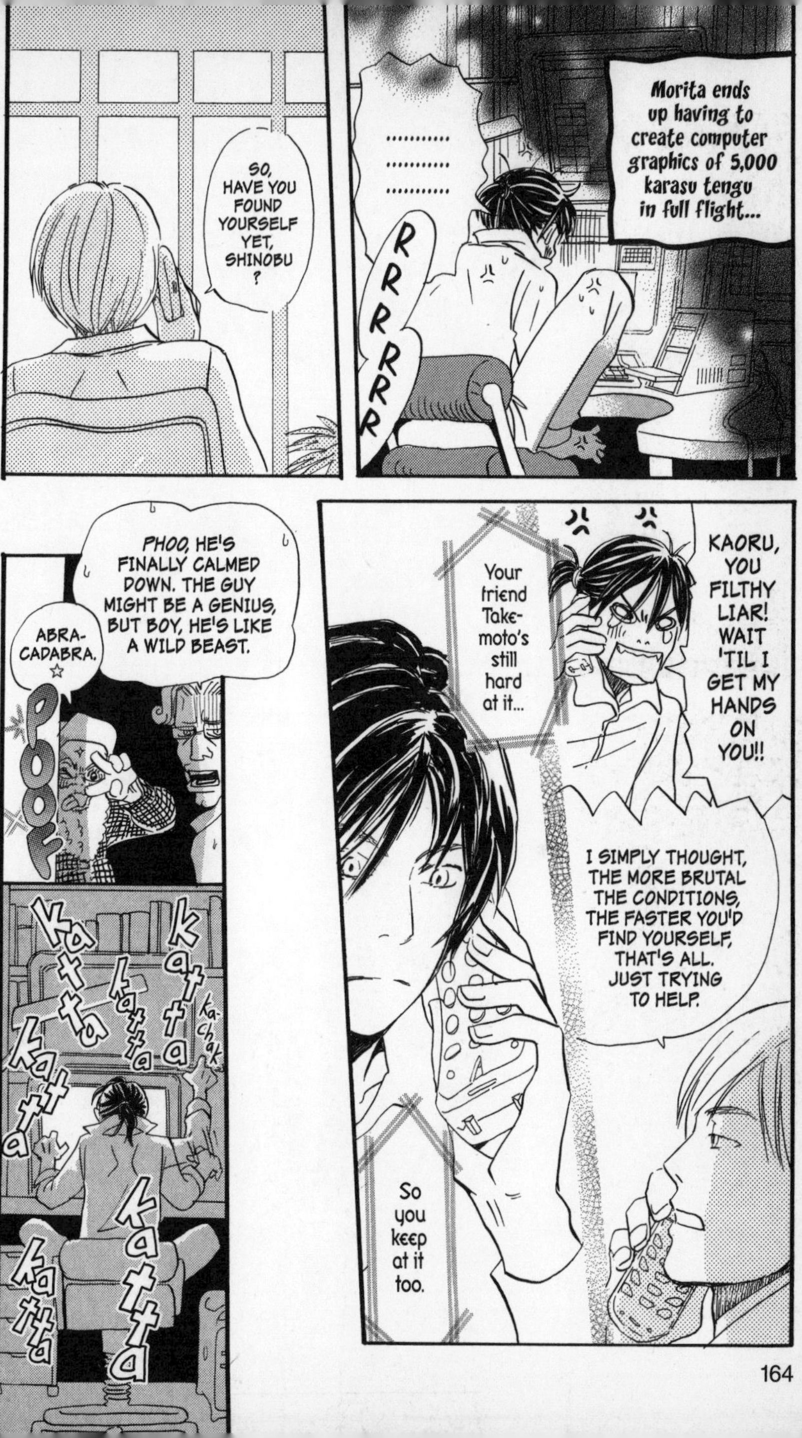
Morita ends up having to create computer graphics of 5,000 karasu tengu in full flight...
....
....
....
RRRRRRR
SO, HAVE YOU FOUND YOURSELF YET, SHINOBU?
KAORU, YOU FILTHY LIAR! WAIT 'TIL I GET MY HANDS ON YOU!!
Your friend Take-moto's still hard at it...
I SIMPLY THOUGHT, THE MORE BRUTAL THE CONDITIONS, THE FASTER YOU'D FIND YOURSELF, THAT'S ALL. JUST TRYING TO HELP.
So you keep at it too.
PHOO, HE'S FINALLY CALMED DOWN. THE GUY MIGHT BE A GENIUS, BUT BOY, HE'S LIKE A WILD BEAST.
ABRA-CADABRA. ☆
POOF
katta
katta
ka-chak
katta
katta
katta
katta

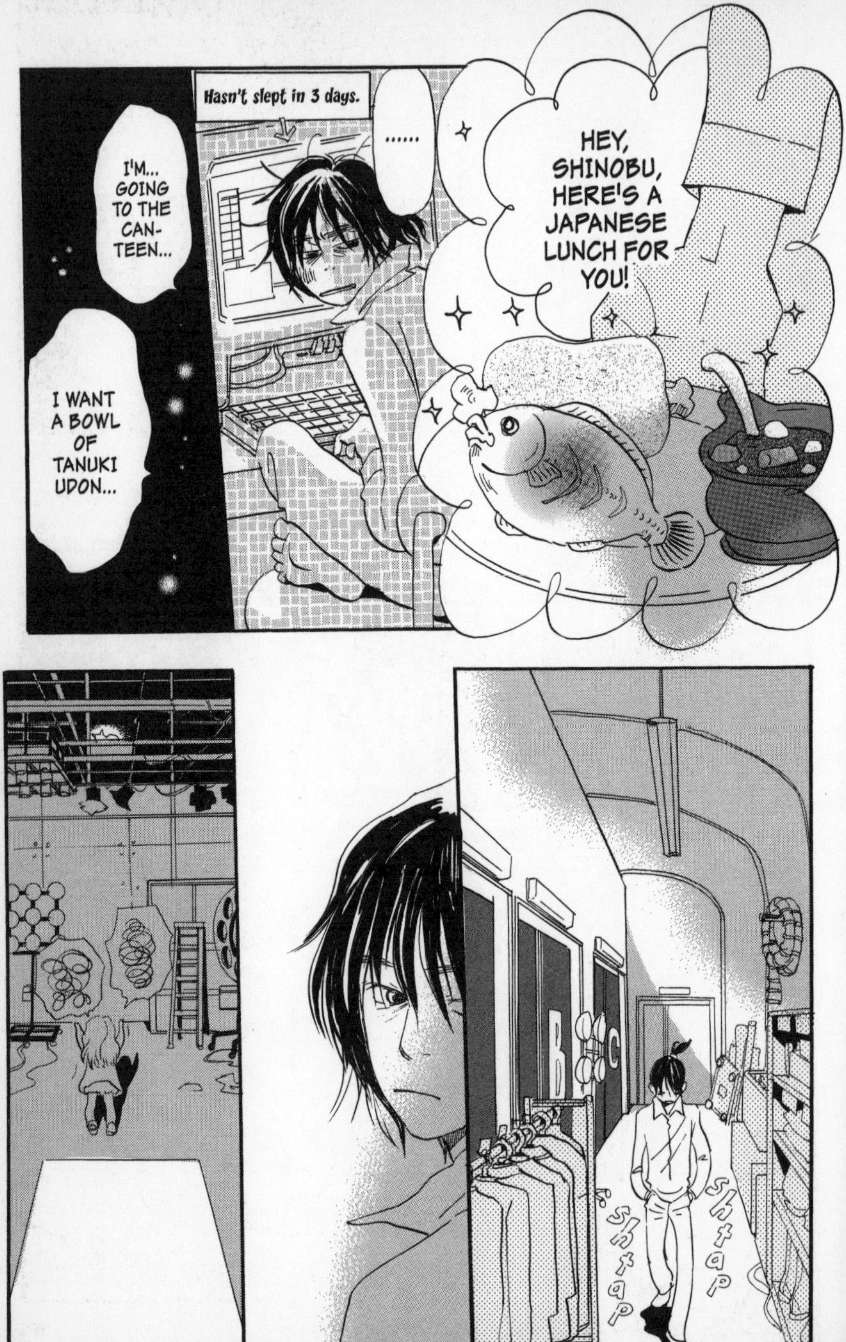
HEY, SHINOBU, HERE'S A JAPANESE LUNCH FOR YOU!
Hasn't slept in 3 days.
......
I'M... GOING TO THE CAN-TEEN...
I WANT A BOWL OF TANUKI UDON...
Shtap
Shtap

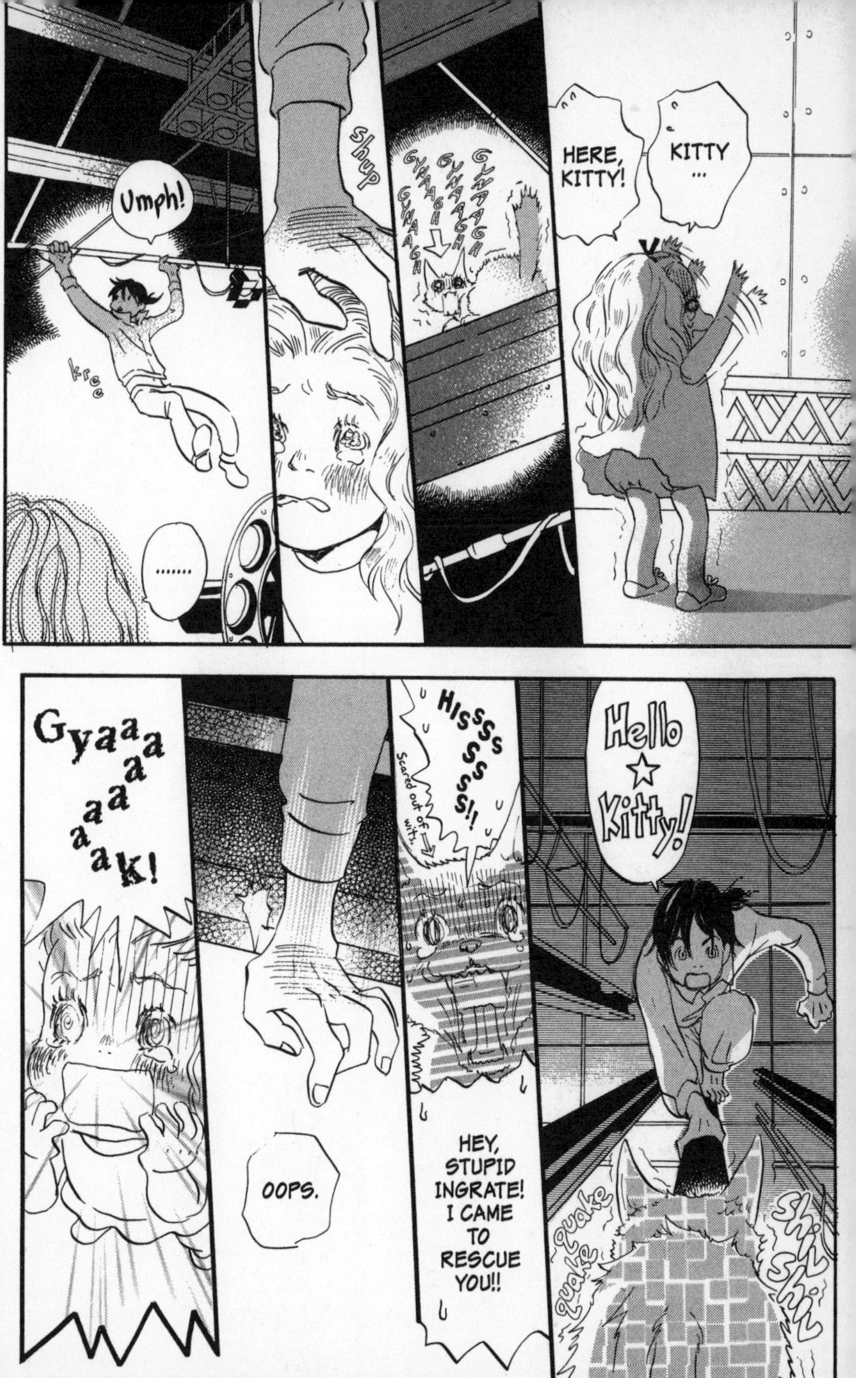
KITTY ...
HERE, KITTY!
GYNAAGH GYNAAGH GYNAAGH GYNAAGH
Shup
Umph!
kree
....
Hello ☆ Kitty!
Shin Shin
quake quake
HISSSSSSSSS!!
Scared out of wits.
HEY, STUPID INGRATE! I CAME TO RESCUE YOU!!
OOPS.
Gyaaaaaaaaak!

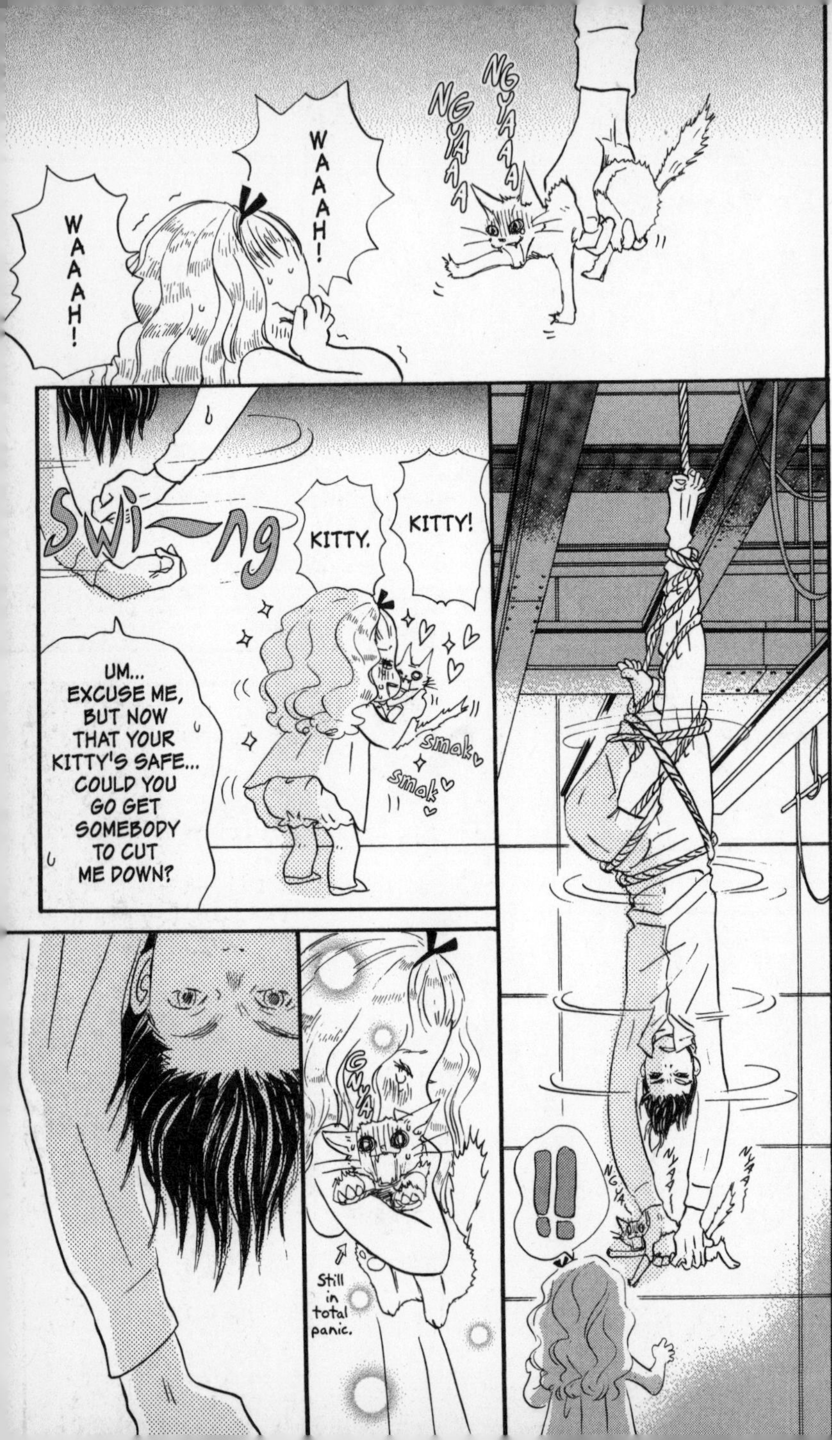
NGYAAAA
NGYAAAA
WAAAAH!
WAAAAH!
NYAAA
NYAAA
NGYA
!!
KITTY!
KITTY.
SWI-NG
smak
smak
UM... EXCUSE ME, BUT NOW THAT YOUR KITTY'S SAFE... COULD YOU GO GET SOMEBODY TO CUT ME DOWN?
GNYA
Still in total panic.

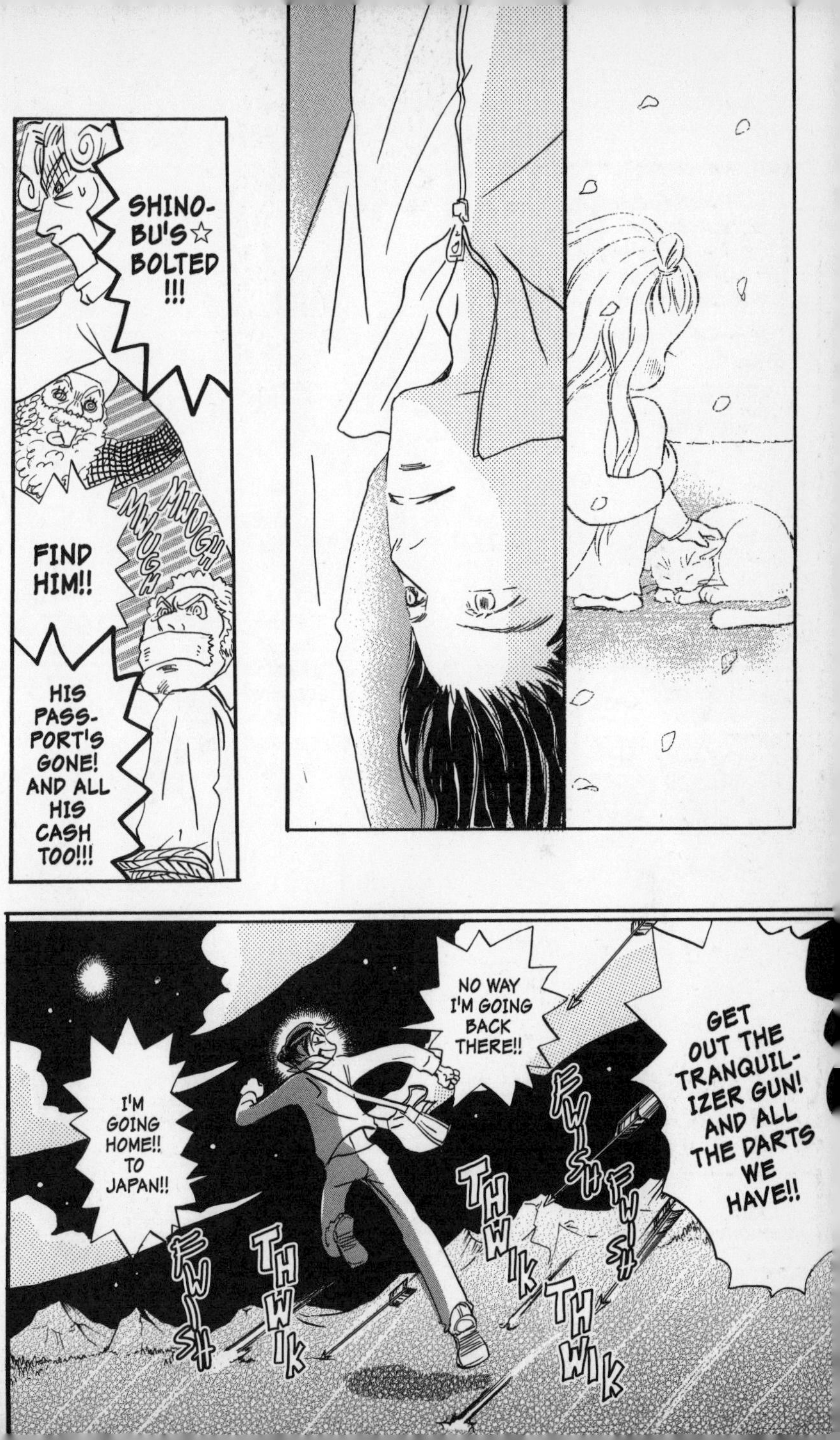
SHINO-BU'S☆ BOLTED!!!
MWUGH MWUGH
FIND HIM!!
HIS PASS-PORT'S GONE! AND ALL HIS CASH TOO!!!
GET OUT THE TRANQUIL-IZER GUN! AND ALL THE DARTS WE HAVE!!
NO WAY I'M GOING BACK THERE!!
I'M GOING HOME!! TO JAPAN!!
FWISH FWISH
THWIK THWIK
FWISH
THWIK THWIK

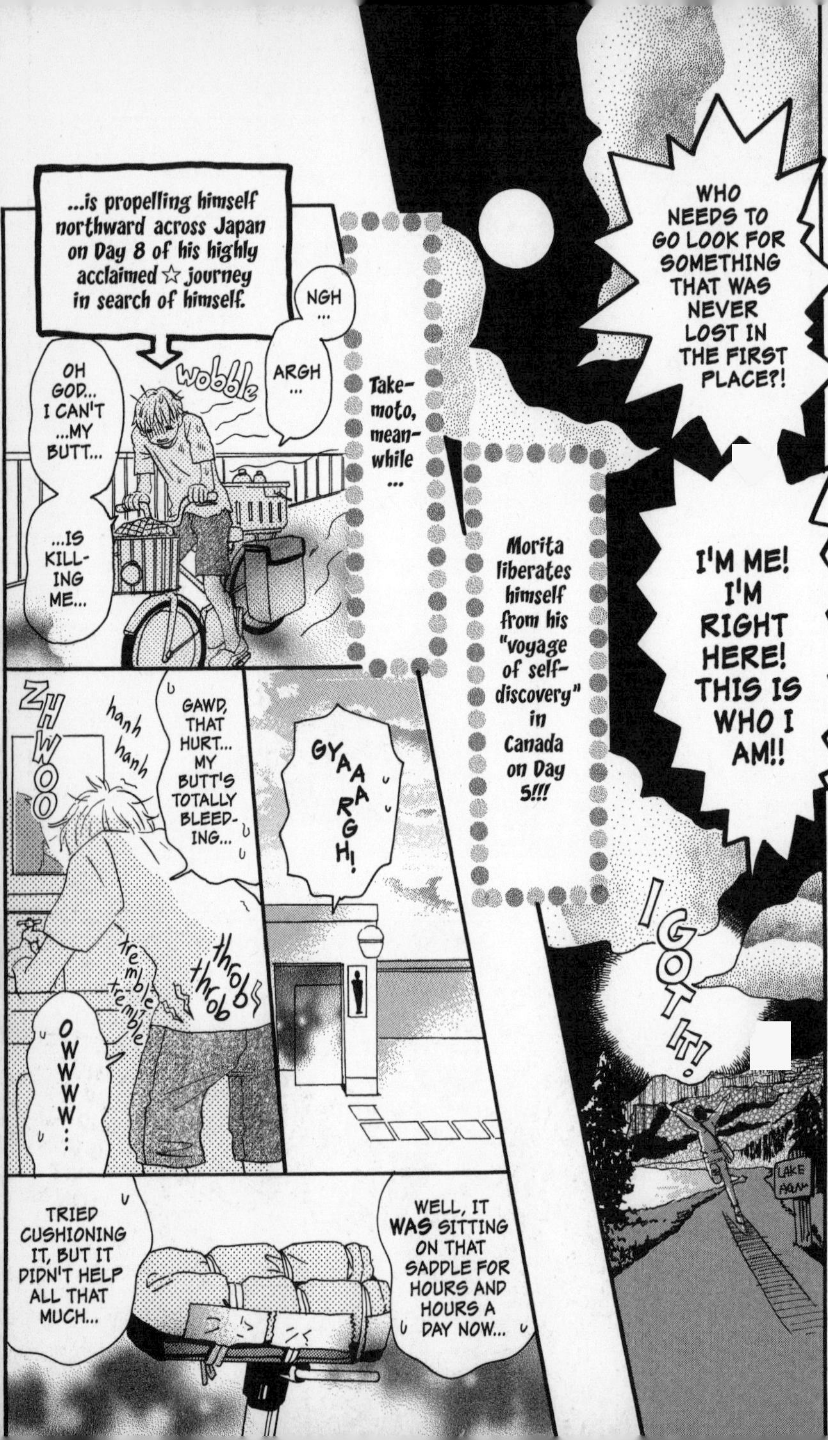
WHO NEEDS TO GO LOOK FOR SOMETHING THAT WAS NEVER LOST IN THE FIRST PLACE?!
I'M ME! I'M RIGHT HERE! THIS IS WHO I AM!!
Morita liberates himself from his "voyage of self-discovery" in Canada on Day 5!!!
I GOT IT!
LAKE AAN
Take-moto, mean-while...
...is propelling himself northward across Japan on Day 8 of his highly acclaimed ☆ journey in search of himself.
NGH...
ARGH...
wobble
OH GOD... I CAN'T ...MY BUTT...
...IS KILL-ING ME...
GYAAAARGH!
GAWD, THAT HURT... MY BUTT'S TOTALLY BLEED-ING...
hanh hanh
ZHWOO
throb throb
tremble tremble
OWWWW...
WELL, IT WAS SITTING ON THAT SADDLE FOR HOURS AND HOURS A DAY NOW...
TRIED CUSHIONING IT, BUT IT DIDN'T HELP ALL THAT MUCH...

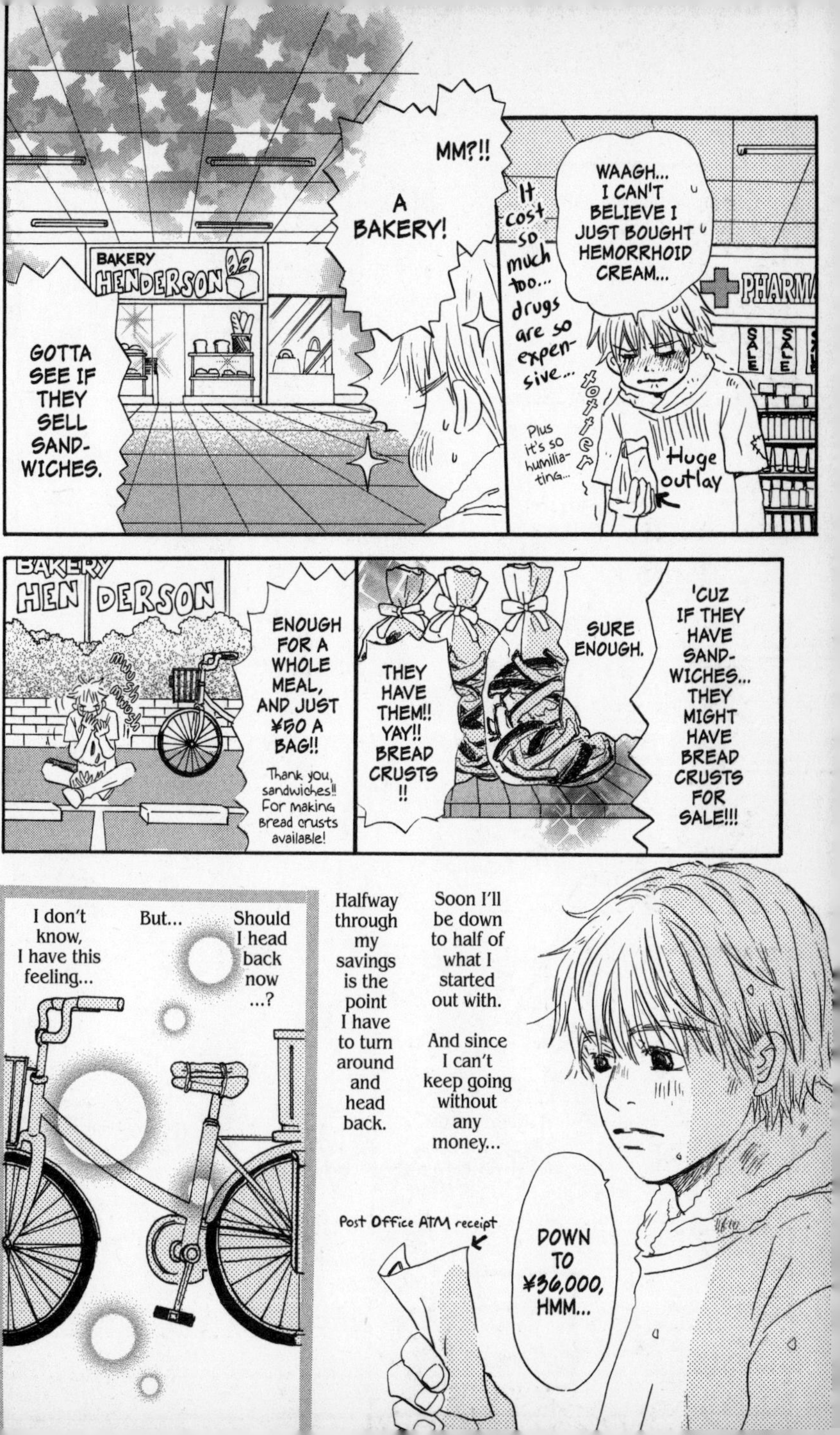
PHARMA
SALE
WAAGH... I CAN'T BELIEVE I JUST BOUGHT HEMORRHOID CREAM...
It cost so much too... drugs are so expensive...
totter
Plus it's so humiliating...
Huge outlay
MM?!!
A BAKERY!
BAKERY HENDERSON
GOTTA SEE IF THEY SELL SANDWICHES.
'CUZ IF THEY HAVE SANDWICHES... THEY MIGHT HAVE BREAD CRUSTS FOR SALE!!!
SURE ENOUGH.
THEY HAVE THEM!! YAY!! BREAD CRUSTS!!
BAKERY HENDERSON
ENOUGH FOR A WHOLE MEAL, AND JUST ¥50 A BAG!!
Thank you, sandwiches!! For making bread crusts available!
mwush mwush
DOWN TO ¥36,000, HMM...
Post Office ATM receipt
Soon I'll be down to half of what I started out with.
And since I can't keep going without any money...
Halfway through my savings is the point I have to turn around and head back.
Should I head back now ...?
But...
I don't know, I have this feeling...

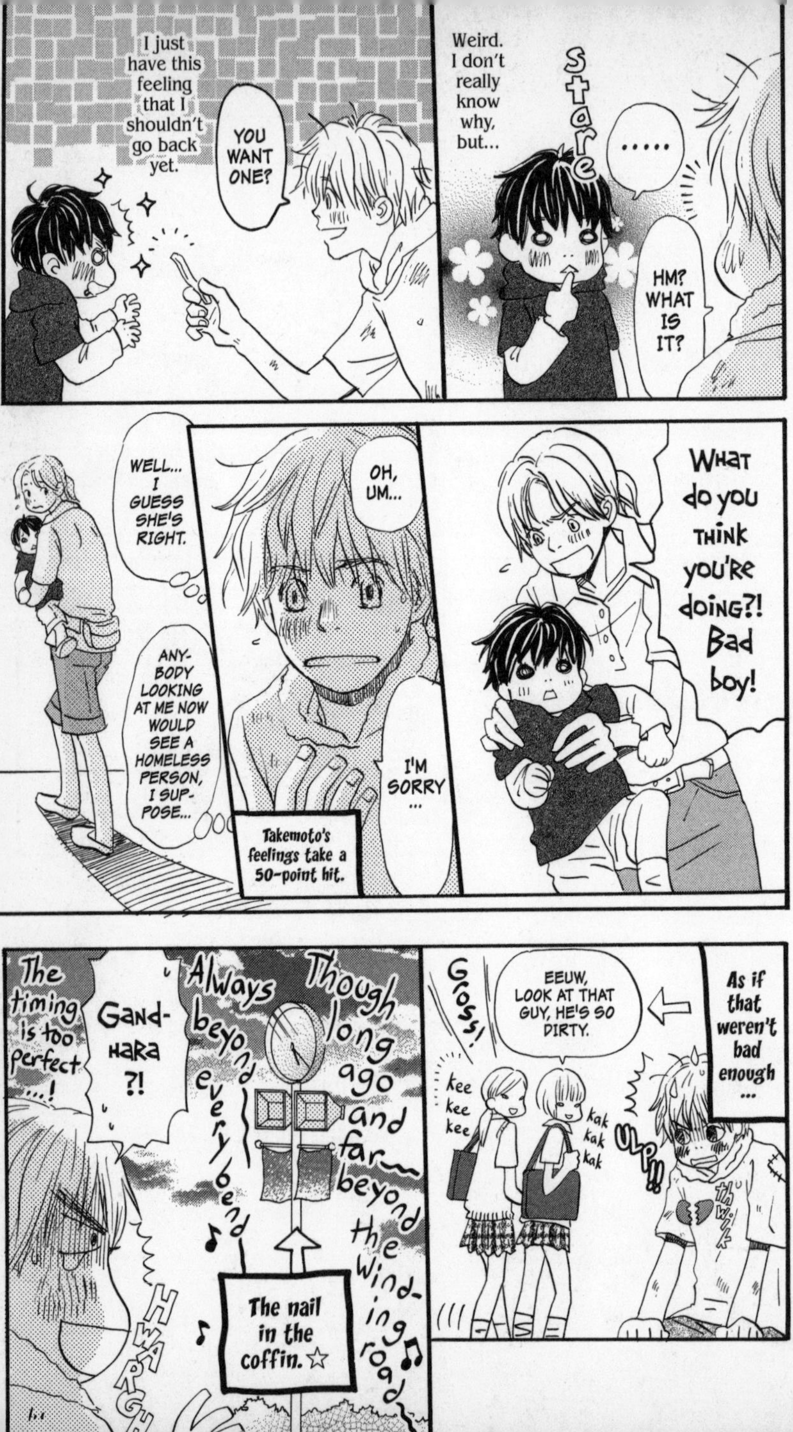

Weird. I don't really know why, but...
Stare
.....
HM? WHAT IS IT?
I just have this feeling that I shouldn't go back yet.
YOU WANT ONE?
What do you think you're doing?! Bad boy!
OH, UM...
I'M SORRY...
Takemoto's feelings take a 50-point hit.
WELL... I GUESS SHE'S RIGHT.
ANY-BODY LOOKING AT ME NOW WOULD SEE A HOMELESS PERSON, I SUP-POSE...
As if that weren't bad enough...
EEUW, LOOK AT THAT GUY, HE'S SO DIRTY.
Gross!
kee kee kee
kak kak kak
ULP!!
thwik
Though long ago and far~ beyond the wind-ing road~
Always beyond~ every bend~
Gand-hara ?!
The timing is too perfect...!
HWARGH
The nail in the coffin.☆

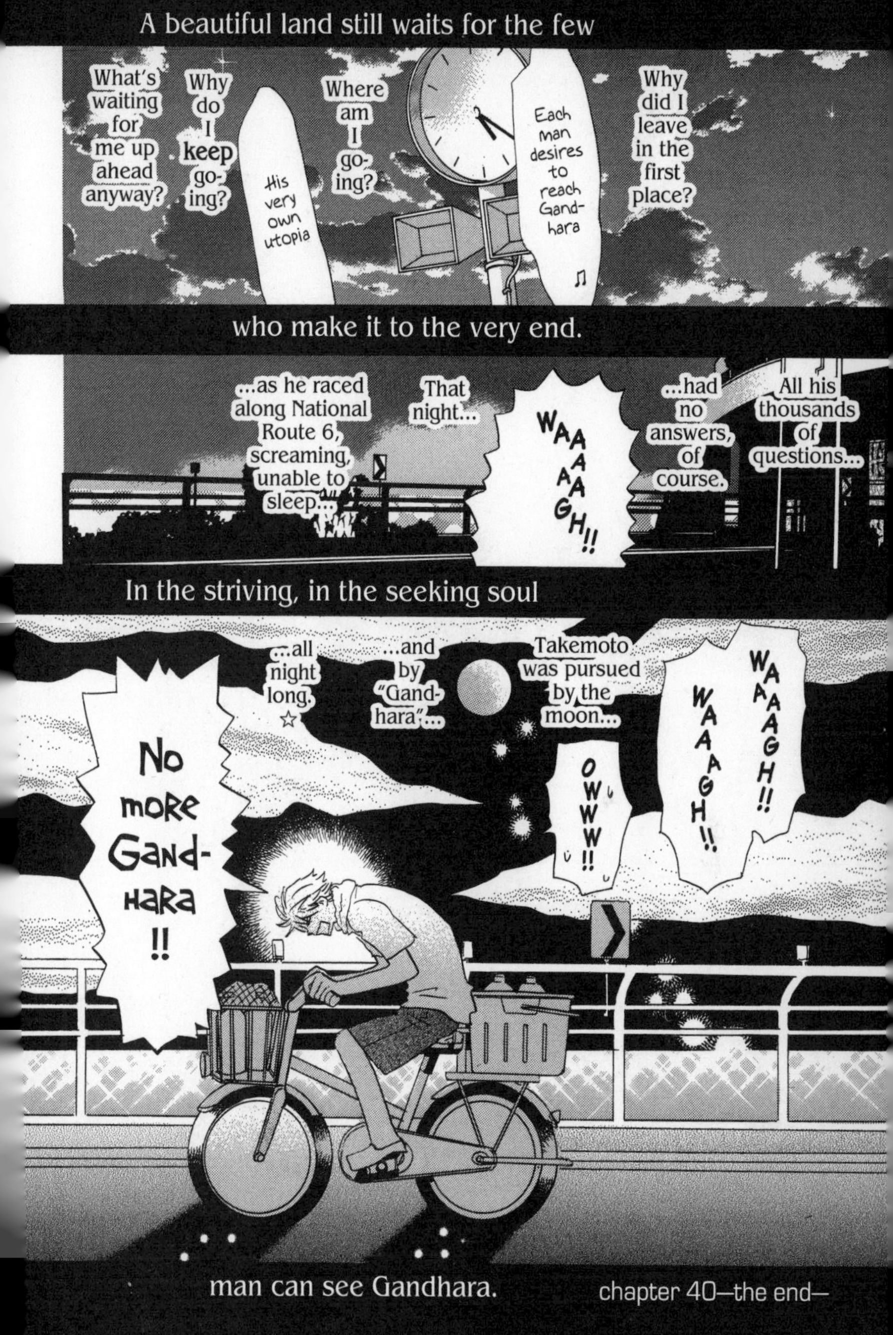
A beautiful land still waits for the few
Why did I leave in the first place?
Each man desires to reach Gandhara ♫
Where am I going?
His very own utopia
Why do I keep going?
What's waiting for me up ahead anyway?
who make it to the very end.
All his thousands of questions...
...had no answers, of course.
WAAAAAGH!!
That night...
...as he raced along National Route 6, screaming, unable to sleep...
In the striving, in the seeking soul
WAAAAGH!!
WAAAAGH!!
Takemoto was pursued by the moon...
OWWWW!!
...and by "Gandhara"...
...all night long. ☆
No more Gandhara!!
man can see Gandhara.
chapter 40—the end—

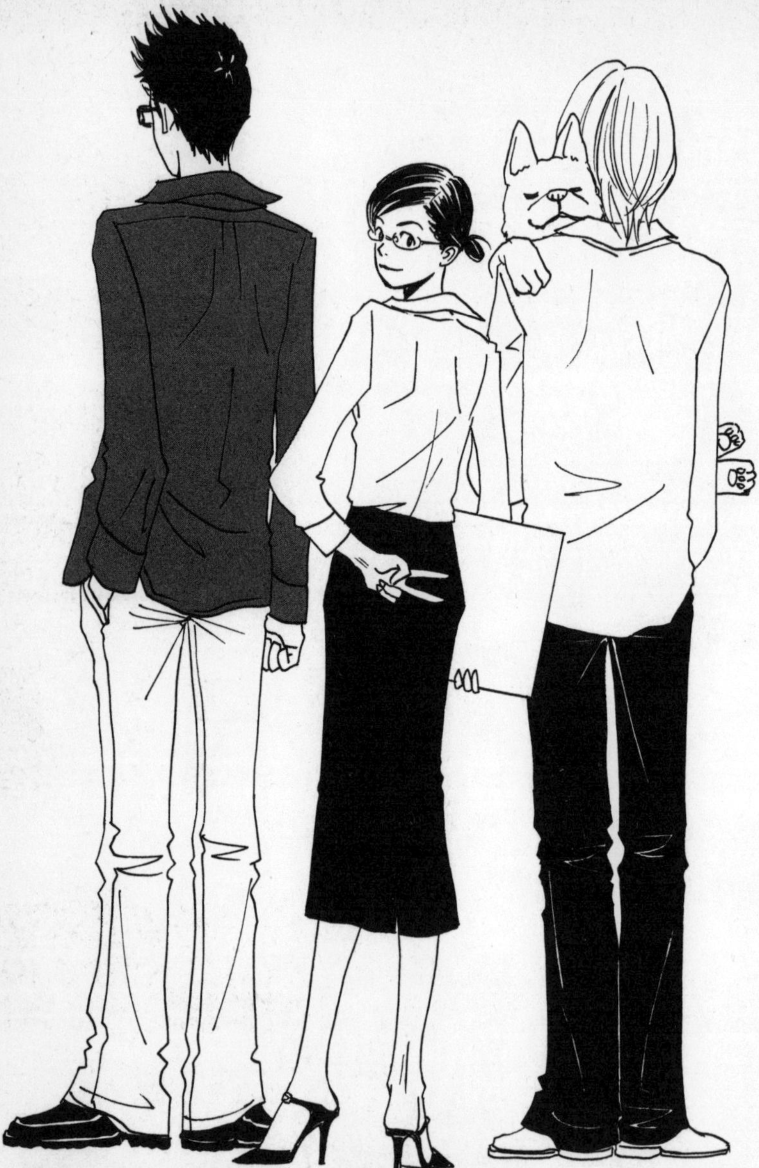

honey and clover

Bonus Chapter

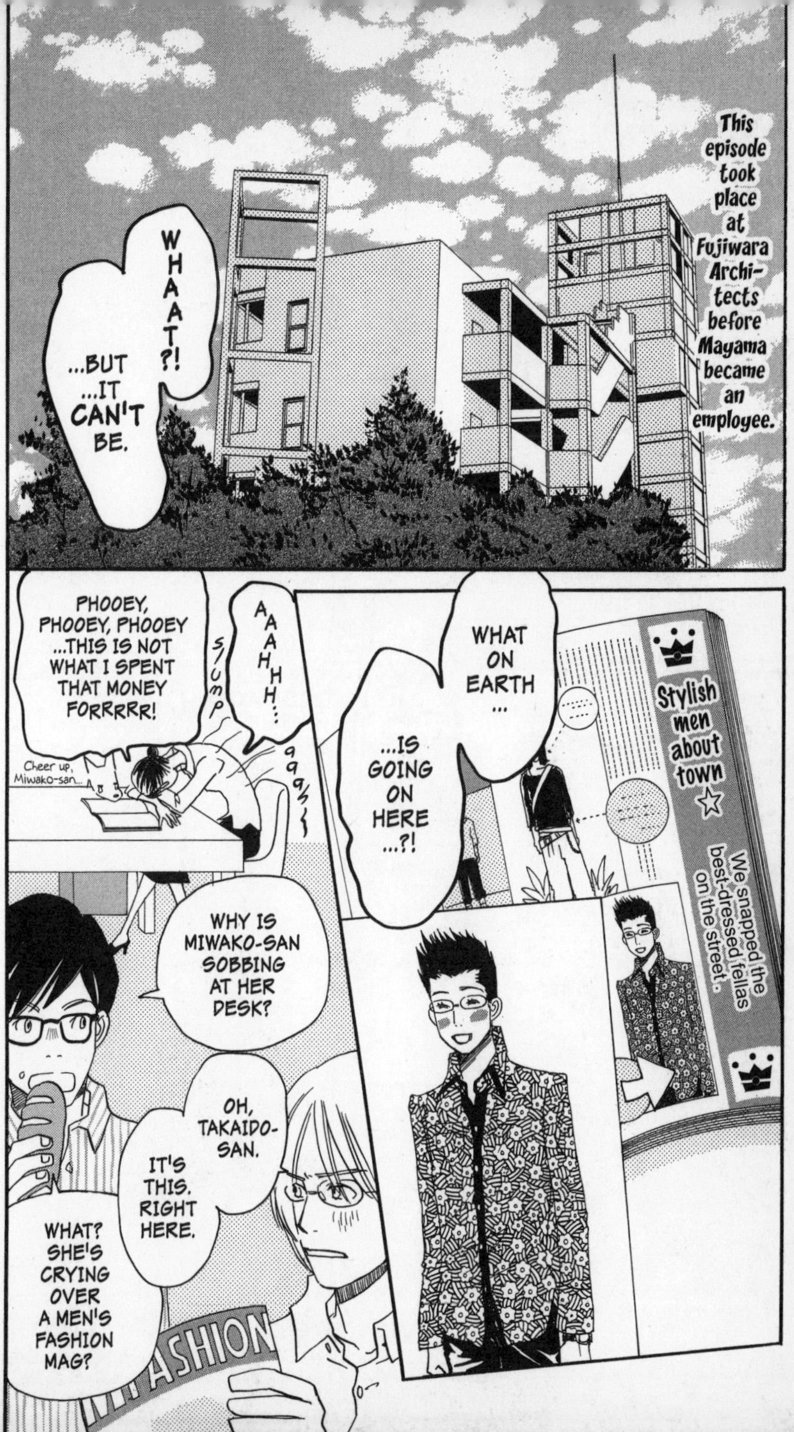
This episode took place at Fujiwara Architects before Mayama became an employee.
WHAAAT?!
...BUT ...IT CAN'T BE.
WHAT ON EARTH ...
...IS GOING ON HERE ...?!
Stylish men about town ☆
We snapped the best-dressed fellas on the street.
AAAHHH...
SLUMP
PHOOEY, PHOOEY, PHOOEY ...THIS IS NOT WHAT I SPENT THAT MONEY FORRRRR!
Cheer up, Miwako-san...
WHY IS MIWAKO-SAN SOBBING AT HER DESK?
OH, TAKAIDO-SAN.
IT'S THIS. RIGHT HERE.
WHAT? SHE'S CRYING OVER A MEN'S FASHION MAG?
FASHION

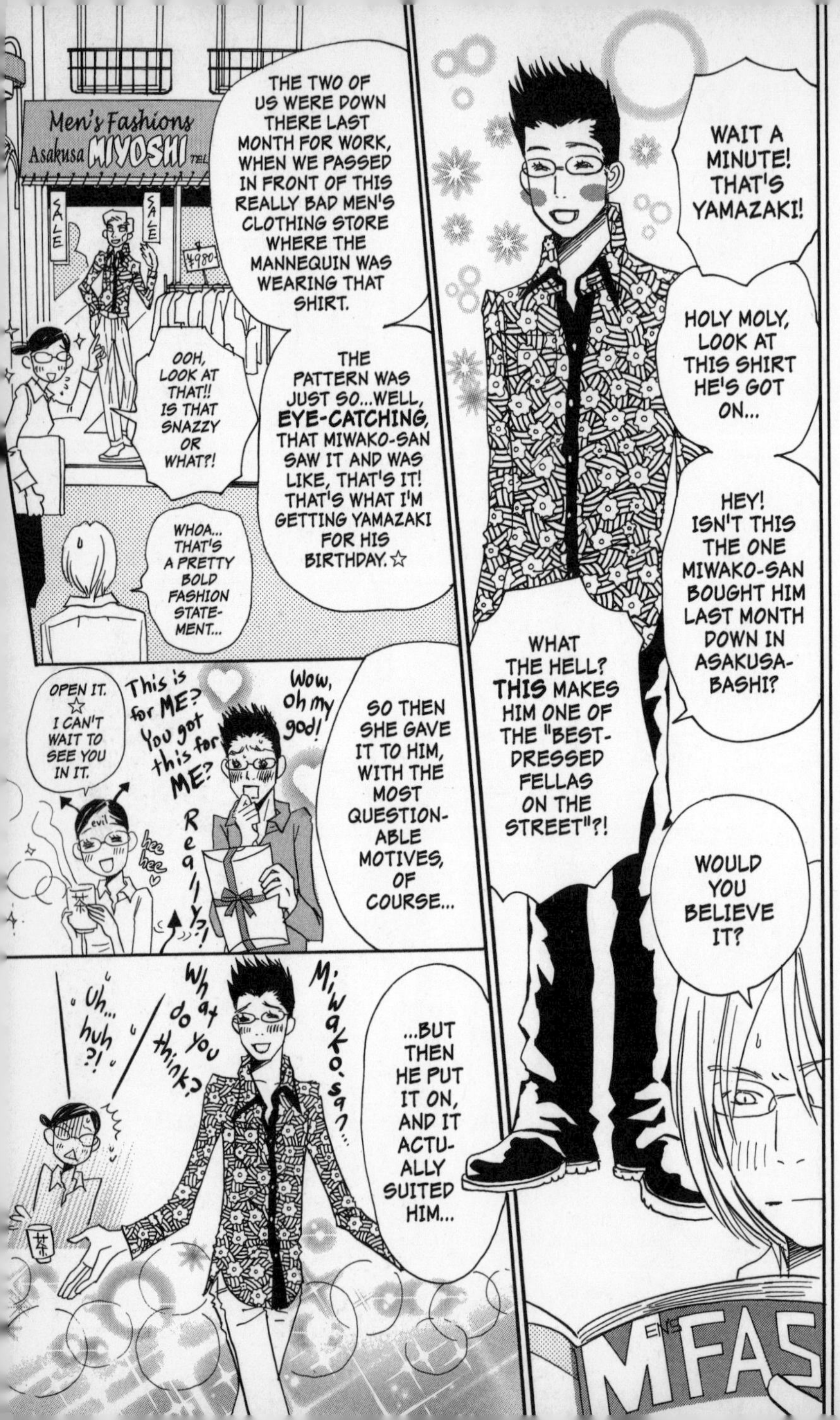
WAIT A MINUTE! THAT'S YAMAZAKI!
HOLY MOLY, LOOK AT THIS SHIRT HE'S GOT ON...
HEY! ISN'T THIS THE ONE MIWAKO-SAN BOUGHT HIM LAST MONTH DOWN IN ASAKUSA-BASHI?
WHAT THE HELL? THIS MAKES HIM ONE OF THE "BEST-DRESSED FELLAS ON THE STREET"?!
WOULD YOU BELIEVE IT?
THE TWO OF US WERE DOWN THERE LAST MONTH FOR WORK, WHEN WE PASSED IN FRONT OF THIS REALLY BAD MEN'S CLOTHING STORE WHERE THE MANNEQUIN WAS WEARING THAT SHIRT.
THE PATTERN WAS JUST SO...WELL, EYE-CATCHING, THAT MIWAKO-SAN SAW IT AND WAS LIKE, THAT'S IT! THAT'S WHAT I'M GETTING YAMAZAKI FOR HIS BIRTHDAY.☆
Men's Fashions
Asakusa MIYOSHI TEL
SALE
SALE
¥980
OOH, LOOK AT THAT!! IS THAT SNAZZY OR WHAT?!
WHOA... THAT'S A PRETTY BOLD FASHION STATEMENT...
SO THEN SHE GAVE IT TO HIM, WITH THE MOST QUESTIONABLE MOTIVES, OF COURSE...
Wow, oh my god!
This is for ME? You got this for ME?
Really?!
OPEN IT. ☆ I CAN'T WAIT TO SEE YOU IN IT.
evil
hee hee ♥
...BUT THEN HE PUT IT ON, AND IT ACTUALLY SUITED HIM...
Miwako-san...
What do you think?
Uh... huh?!

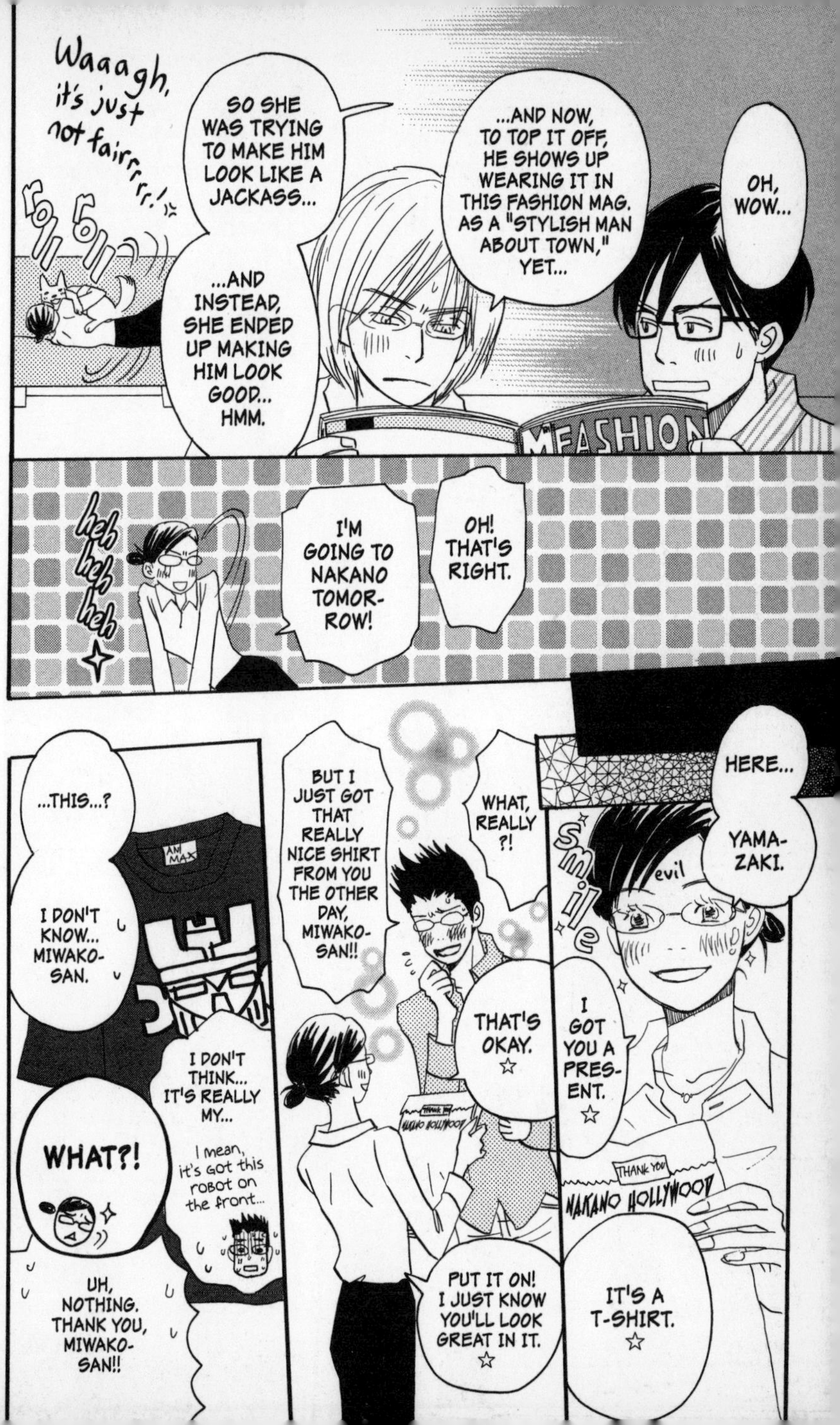
OH, WOW...
...AND NOW, TO TOP IT OFF, HE SHOWS UP WEARING IT IN THIS FASHION MAG. AS A "STYLISH MAN ABOUT TOWN," YET...
SO SHE WAS TRYING TO MAKE HIM LOOK LIKE A JACKASS...
...AND INSTEAD, SHE ENDED UP MAKING HIM LOOK GOOD... HMM.
Waaaagh, it's just not fairrrrr!
roll roll
OH! THAT'S RIGHT.
I'M GOING TO NAKANO TOMOR-ROW!
heh heh heh
HERE...
YAMA-ZAKI.
smile
evil
I GOT YOU A PRES-ENT. ☆
THANK YOU
NAKANO HOLLYWOOD
IT'S A T-SHIRT. ☆
WHAT, REALLY ?!
BUT I JUST GOT THAT REALLY NICE SHIRT FROM YOU THE OTHER DAY, MIWAKO-SAN!!
THAT'S OKAY. ☆
PUT IT ON! I JUST KNOW YOU'LL LOOK GREAT IN IT. ☆
...THIS...?
ANI MAX
I DON'T KNOW... MIWAKO-SAN.
I DON'T THINK... IT'S REALLY MY...
I mean, it's got this robot on the front...
WHAT?!
UH, NOTHING. THANK YOU, MIWAKO-SAN!!

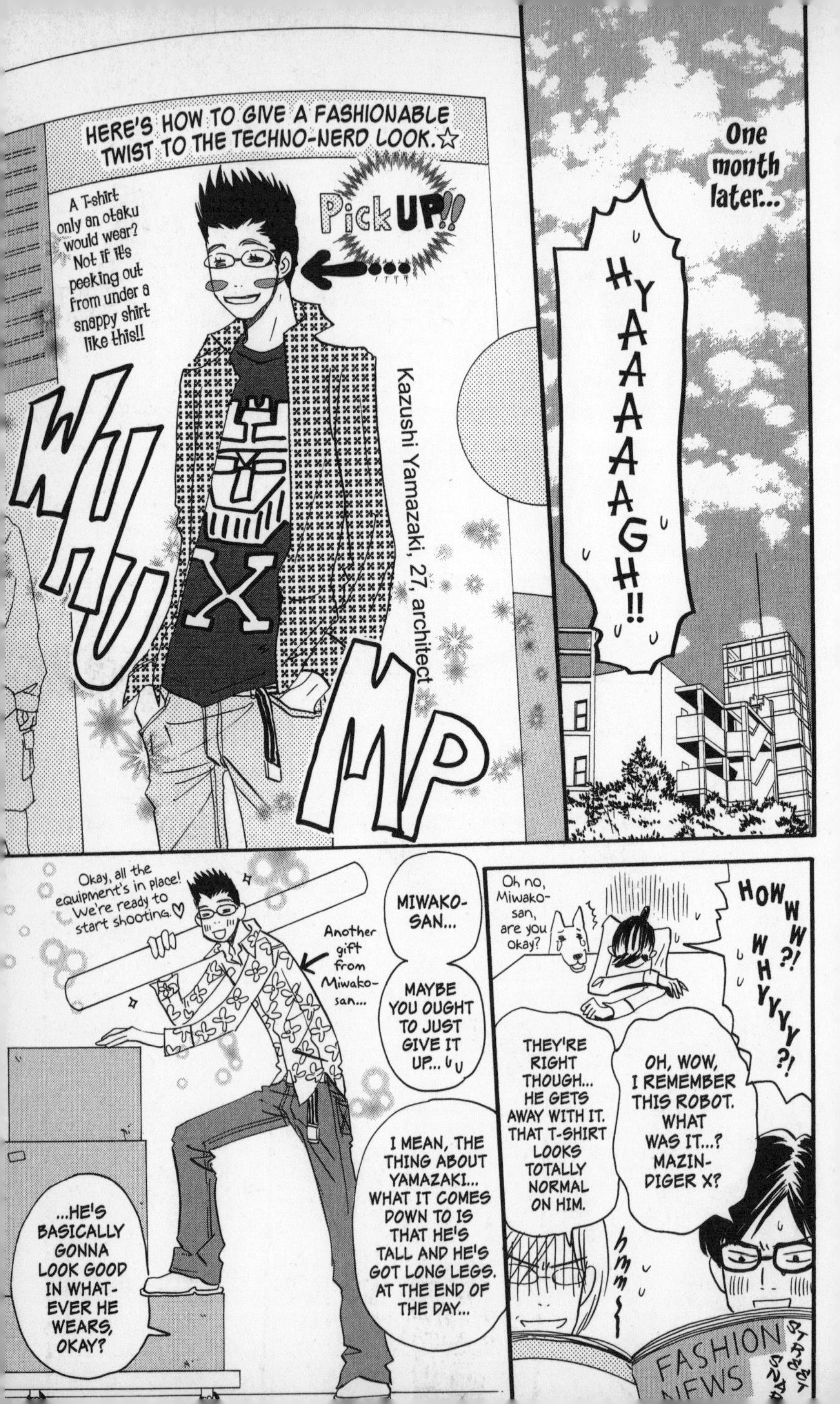
One month later...
HYAAAAAAGH!!
HERE'S HOW TO GIVE A FASHIONABLE TWIST TO THE TECHNO-NERD LOOK.☆
Pick UP!!
Kazushi Yamazaki, 27, architect
A T-shirt only an otaku would wear? Not if it's peeking out from under a snappy shirt like this!!
WHUMP
HOWWW?! WHYYYYY?!
Oh no, Miwako-san, are you okay?
OH, WOW, I REMEMBER THIS ROBOT. WHAT WAS IT...? MAZIN-DIGER X?
THEY'RE RIGHT THOUGH... HE GETS AWAY WITH IT. THAT T-SHIRT LOOKS TOTALLY NORMAL ON HIM.
hmm~
STREET SNAP
FASHION NEWS
MIWAKO-SAN...
MAYBE YOU OUGHT TO JUST GIVE IT UP...
Another gift from Miwako-san...
Okay, all the equipment's in place! We're ready to start shooting.♡
I MEAN, THE THING ABOUT YAMAZAKI... WHAT IT COMES DOWN TO IS THAT HE'S TALL AND HE'S GOT LONG LEGS. AT THE END OF THE DAY...
...HE'S BASICALLY GONNA LOOK GOOD IN WHATEVER HE WEARS, OKAY?

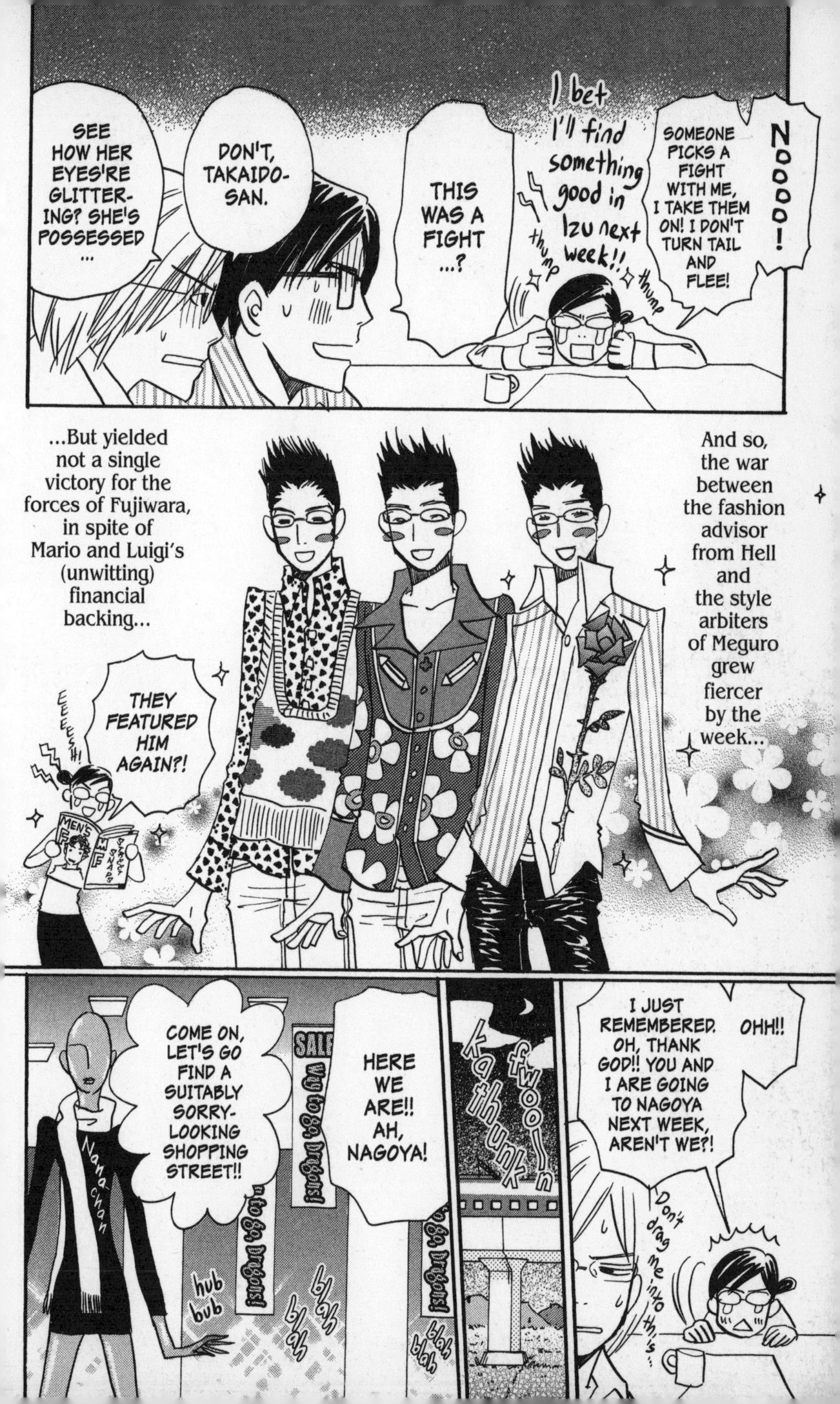
NOOOO!
SOMEONE PICKS A FIGHT WITH ME, I TAKE THEM ON! I DON'T TURN TAIL AND FLEE!
I bet I'll find something good in Izu next week!!
thump
thump
THIS WAS A FIGHT ...?
DON'T, TAKAIDO-SAN.
SEE HOW HER EYES'RE GLITTER-ING? SHE'S POSSESSED ...
And so, the war between the fashion advisor from Hell and the style arbiters of Meguro grew fiercer by the week...
...But yielded not a single victory for the forces of Fujiwara, in spite of Mario and Luigi's (unwitting) financial backing...
THEY FEATURED HIM AGAIN?!
EEEESH!
MEN'S
OHH!!
I JUST REMEMBERED. OH, THANK GOD!! YOU AND I ARE GOING TO NAGOYA NEXT WEEK, AREN'T WE?!
Don't drag me into this...
fwoo-n
ka thunk
HERE WE ARE!! AH, NAGOYA!
SALE
COME ON, LET'S GO FIND A SUITABLY SORRY-LOOKING SHOPPING STREET!!
Nana-chan
hub bub
blah blah
blah blah

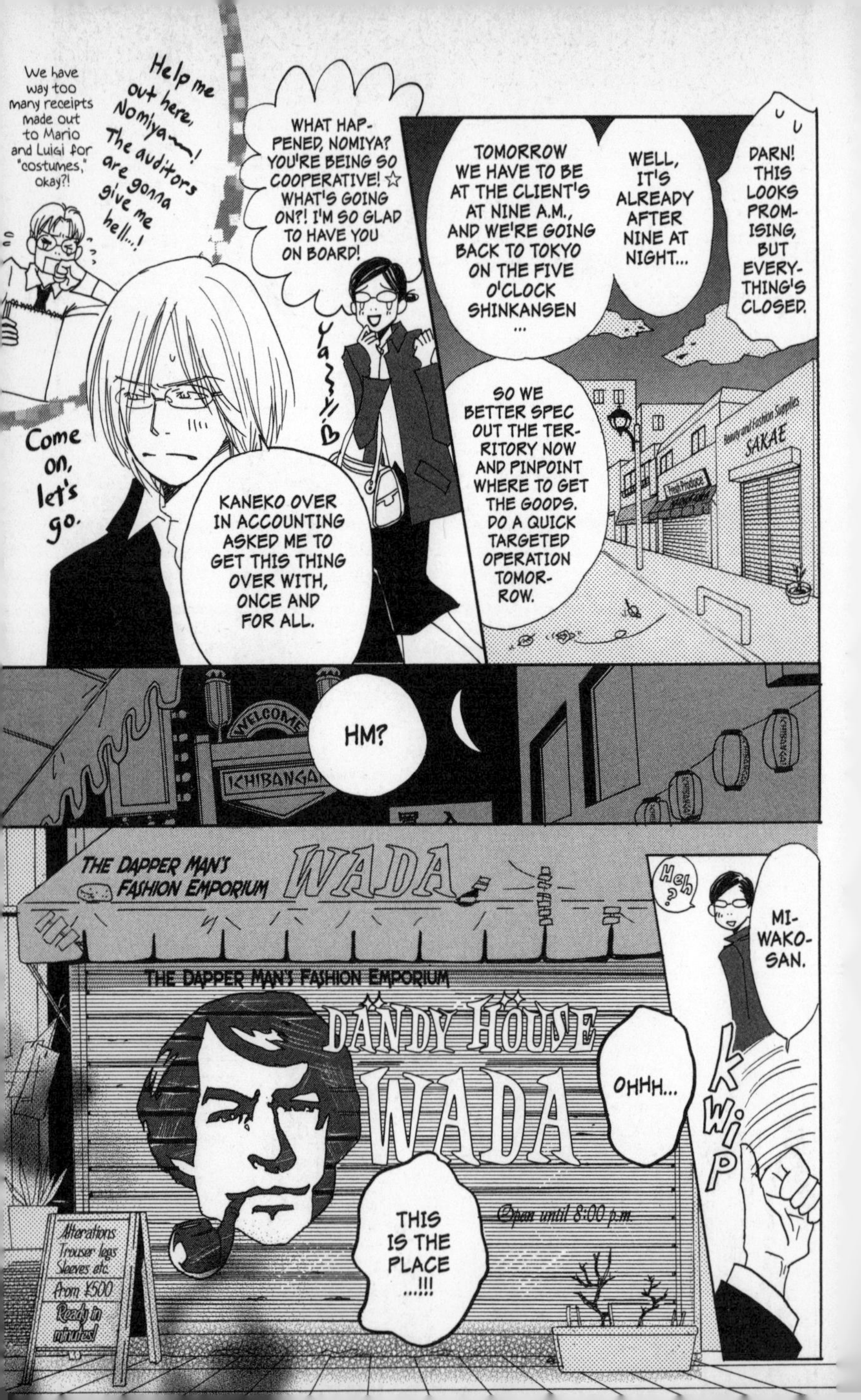
DARN! THIS LOOKS PROMISING, BUT EVERYTHING'S CLOSED.
WELL, IT'S ALREADY AFTER NINE AT NIGHT...
TOMORROW WE HAVE TO BE AT THE CLIENT'S AT NINE A.M., AND WE'RE GOING BACK TO TOKYO ON THE FIVE O'CLOCK SHINKANSEN ...
SO WE BETTER SPEC OUT THE TERRITORY NOW AND PINPOINT WHERE TO GET THE GOODS. DO A QUICK TARGETED OPERATION TOMORROW.
Beauty and Fashion Supplies
SAKAE
Fresh Produce
WHAT HAPPENED, NOMIYA? YOU'RE BEING SO COOPERATIVE! ☆ WHAT'S GOING ON?! I'M SO GLAD TO HAVE YOU ON BOARD!
Yaaay!! ♡
Help me out here, Nomiyaaa! The auditors are gonna give me hell...!
We have way too many receipts made out to Mario and Luigi for "costumes," okay?!
KANEKO OVER IN ACCOUNTING ASKED ME TO GET THIS THING OVER WITH, ONCE AND FOR ALL.
Come on, let's go.
HM?
WELCOME
ICHIBANGA
MI-WAKO-SAN.
Heh?
KWIP
THE DAPPER MAN'S FASHION EMPORIUM
WADA
THE DAPPER MAN'S FASHION EMPORIUM
DANDY HOUSE
WADA
Open until 8:00 p.m.
OHHH...
THIS IS THE PLACE ...!!!
Alterations
Trouser legs
Sleeves etc.
from ¥500
Ready in minutes!

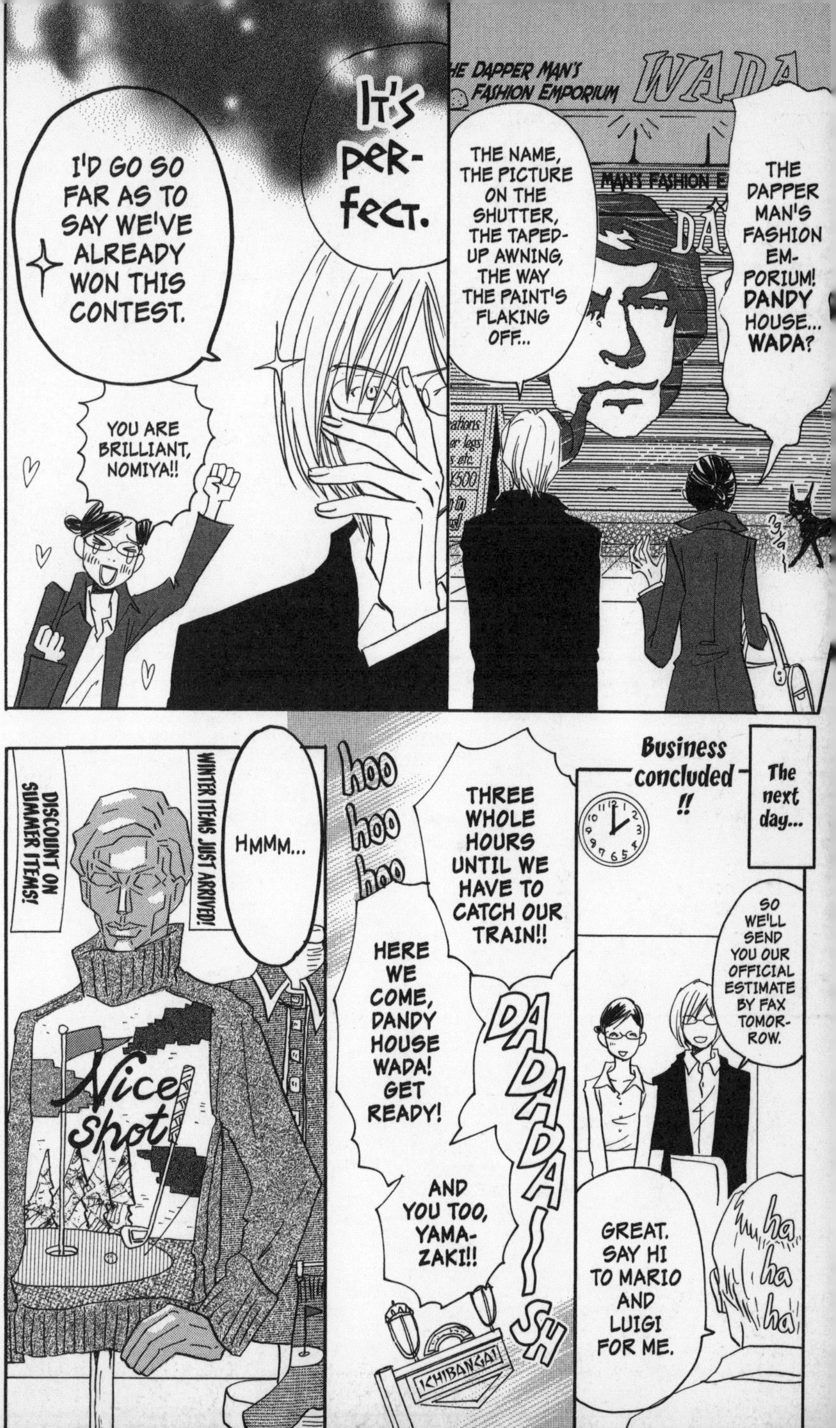
THE DAPPER MAN'S FASHION EMPORIUM
WADA
MAN'S FASHION E
DA
THE DAPPER MAN'S FASHION EM-PORIUM! DANDY HOUSE... WADA?
THE NAME, THE PICTURE ON THE SHUTTER, THE TAPED-UP AWNING, THE WAY THE PAINT'S FLAKING OFF...
ngya
It's per-fect.
I'D GO SO FAR AS TO SAY WE'VE ALREADY WON THIS CONTEST.
YOU ARE BRILLIANT, NOMIYA!!
Business concluded!!
The next day...
SO WE'LL SEND YOU OUR OFFICIAL ESTIMATE BY FAX TOMOR-ROW.
GREAT. SAY HI TO MARIO AND LUIGI FOR ME.
ha ha ha
hoo hoo hoo
THREE WHOLE HOURS UNTIL WE HAVE TO CATCH OUR TRAIN!!
HERE WE COME, DANDY HOUSE WADA! GET READY!
AND YOU TOO, YAMA-ZAKI!!
DADADADA-SH
ICHIBANGAI
HMMM...
WINTER ITEMS JUST ARRIVED!
DISCOUNT ON SUMMER ITEMS!
Nice shot

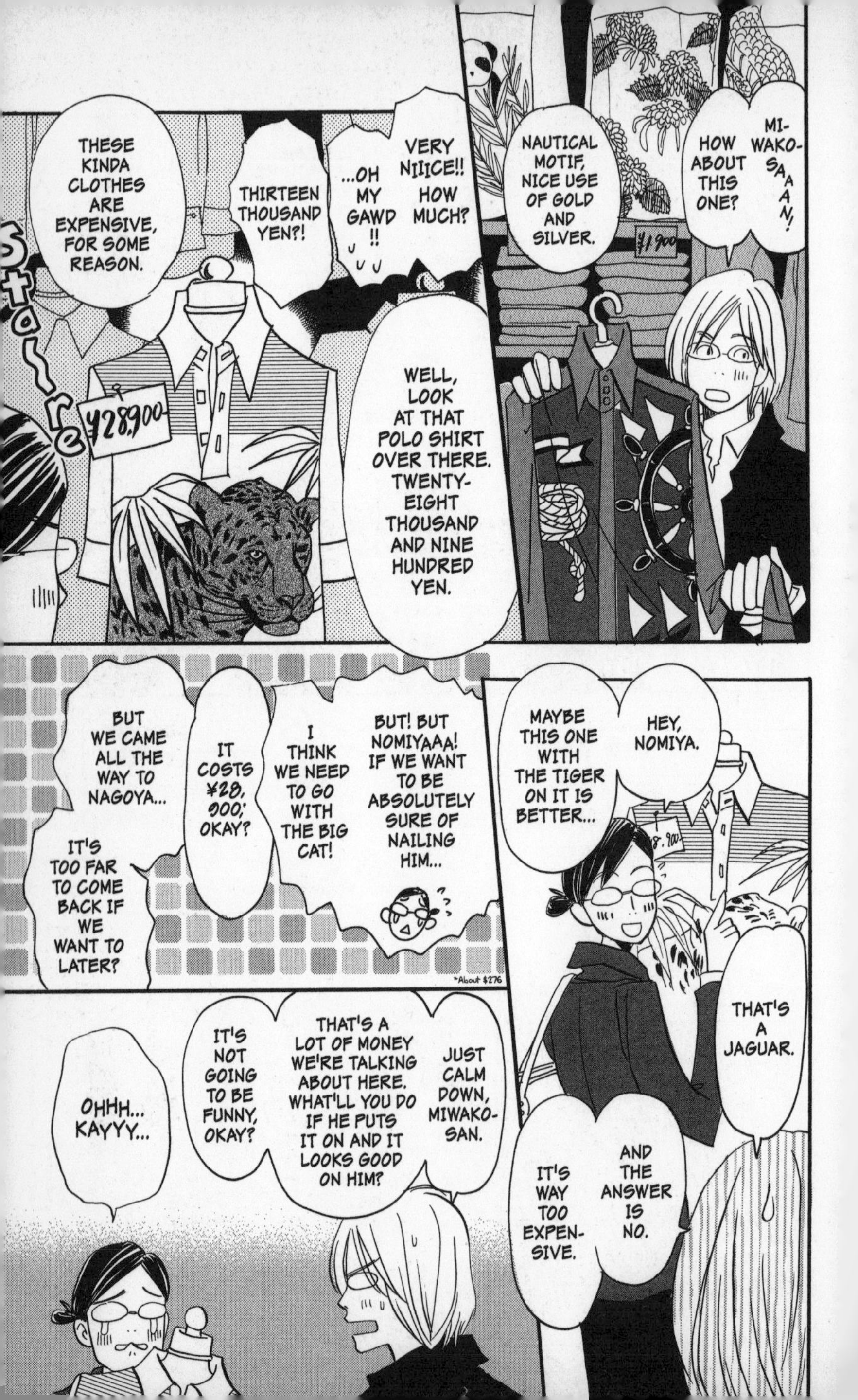
MI-WAKO-SAAAN!
HOW ABOUT THIS ONE?
NAUTICAL MOTIF, NICE USE OF GOLD AND SILVER.
¥1,900
VERY NIIICE!! HOW MUCH?
...OH MY GAWD!!
THIRTEEN THOUSAND YEN?!
THESE KINDA CLOTHES ARE EXPENSIVE, FOR SOME REASON.
WELL, LOOK AT THAT POLO SHIRT OVER THERE. TWENTY-EIGHT THOUSAND AND NINE HUNDRED YEN.
¥28,900-
sta~re
HEY, NOMIYA.
MAYBE THIS ONE WITH THE TIGER ON IT IS BETTER...
THAT'S A JAGUAR.
BUT! BUT NOMIYAAA! IF WE WANT TO BE ABSOLUTELY SURE OF NAILING HIM...
I THINK WE NEED TO GO WITH THE BIG CAT!
IT COSTS ¥28,900,* OKAY?
BUT WE CAME ALL THE WAY TO NAGOYA...
IT'S TOO FAR TO COME BACK IF WE WANT TO LATER?
*About $276
AND THE ANSWER IS NO.
IT'S WAY TOO EXPENSIVE.
JUST CALM DOWN, MIWAKO-SAN.
THAT'S A LOT OF MONEY WE'RE TALKING ABOUT HERE. WHAT'LL YOU DO IF HE PUTS IT ON AND IT LOOKS GOOD ON HIM?
IT'S NOT GOING TO BE FUNNY, OKAY?
OHHH... KAYYY...

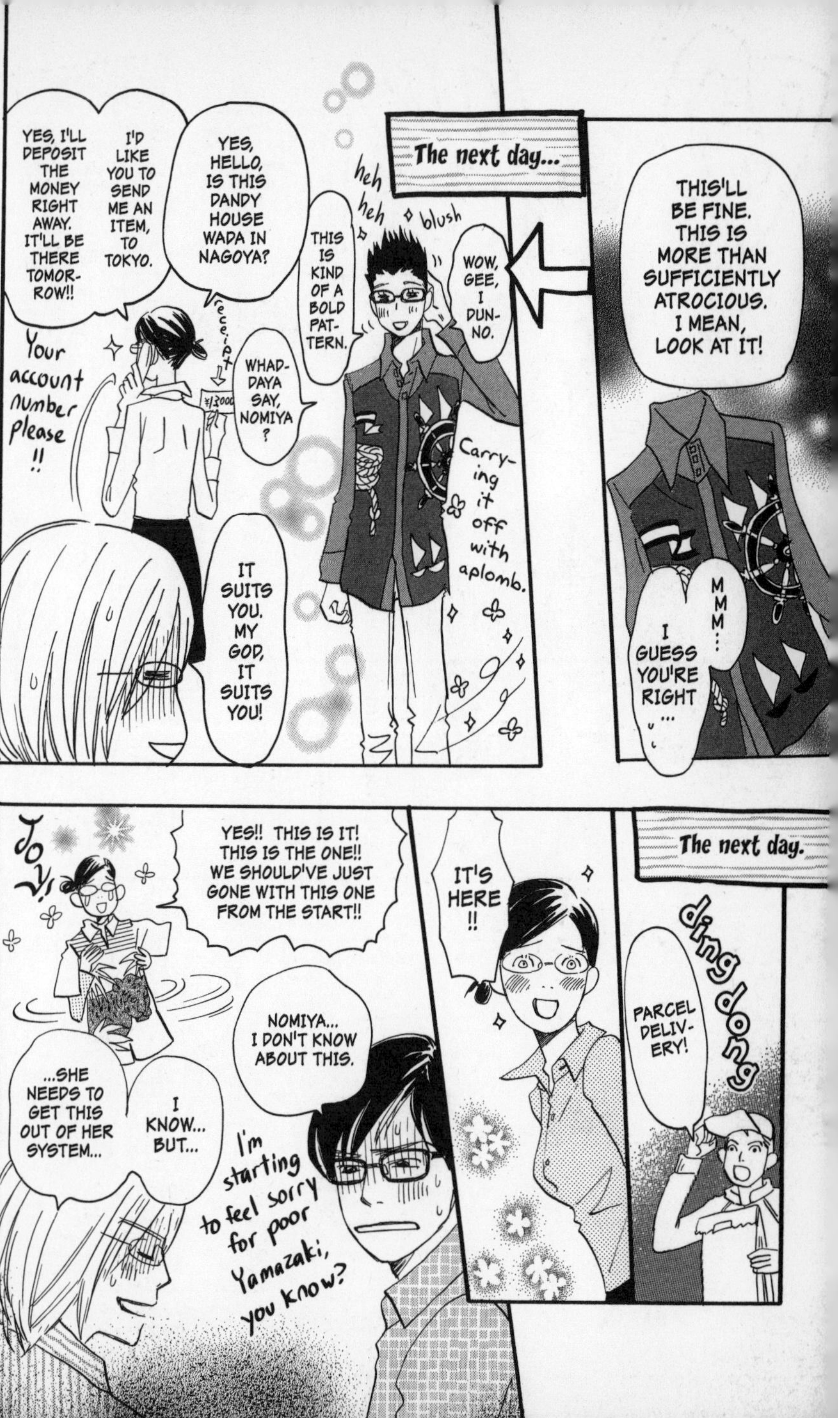
The next day...
THIS'LL BE FINE. THIS IS MORE THAN SUFFICIENTLY ATROCIOUS. I MEAN, LOOK AT IT!
MMM... I GUESS YOU'RE RIGHT...
WOW, GEE, I DUNNO.
blush
heh heh
THIS IS KIND OF A BOLD PATTERN.
WHADDAYA SAY, NOMIYA?
Carrying it off with aplomb.
IT SUITS YOU. MY GOD, IT SUITS YOU!
YES, HELLO, IS THIS DANDY HOUSE WADA IN NAGOYA?
I'D LIKE YOU TO SEND ME AN ITEM, TO TOKYO.
YES, I'LL DEPOSIT THE MONEY RIGHT AWAY. IT'LL BE THERE TOMORROW!!
receipt
Your account number please!!
The next day.
ding dong
PARCEL DELIVERY!
IT'S HERE!!
YES!! THIS IS IT! THIS IS THE ONE!! WE SHOULD'VE JUST GONE WITH THIS ONE FROM THE START!!
Joy
NOMIYA... I DON'T KNOW ABOUT THIS.
I KNOW... BUT...
...SHE NEEDS TO GET THIS OUT OF HER SYSTEM...
I'm starting to feel sorry for poor Yamazaki, you know?

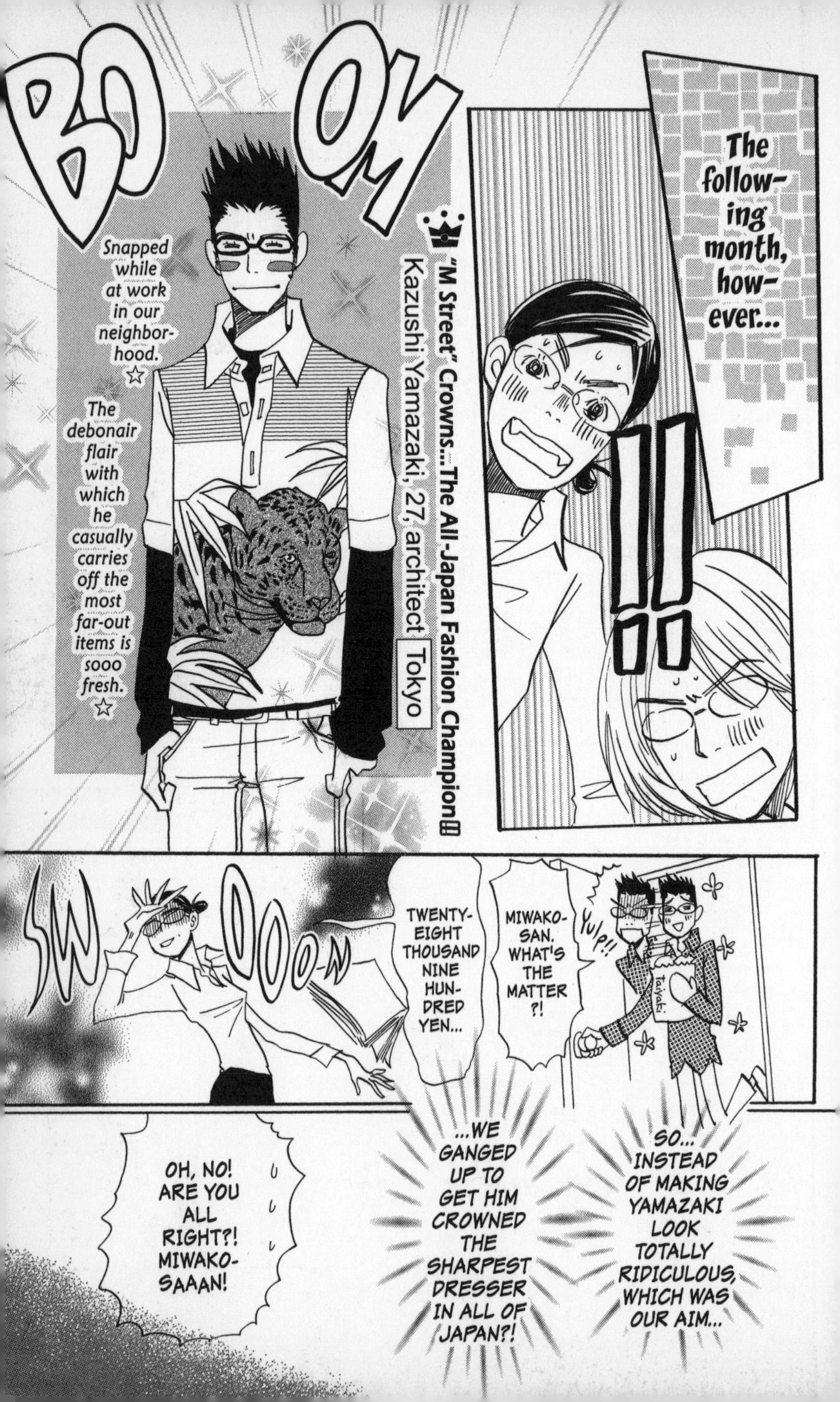
The following month, however...
!!
BOOM
"M Street" Crowns... The All-Japan Fashion Champion!!
Kazushi Yamazaki, 27, architect Tokyo
Snapped while at work in our neighborhood. ☆
The debonair flair with which he casually carries off the most far-out items is sooo fresh. ☆
Yulp!!
Taiyaki
MIWAKO-SAN. WHAT'S THE MATTER?!
TWENTY-EIGHT THOUSAND NINE HUNDRED YEN...
SWOOOON
SO... INSTEAD OF MAKING YAMAZAKI LOOK TOTALLY RIDICULOUS, WHICH WAS OUR AIM...
...WE GANGED UP TO GET HIM CROWNED THE SHARPEST DRESSER IN ALL OF JAPAN?!
OH, NO! ARE YOU ALL RIGHT?! MIWAKO-SAAAN!

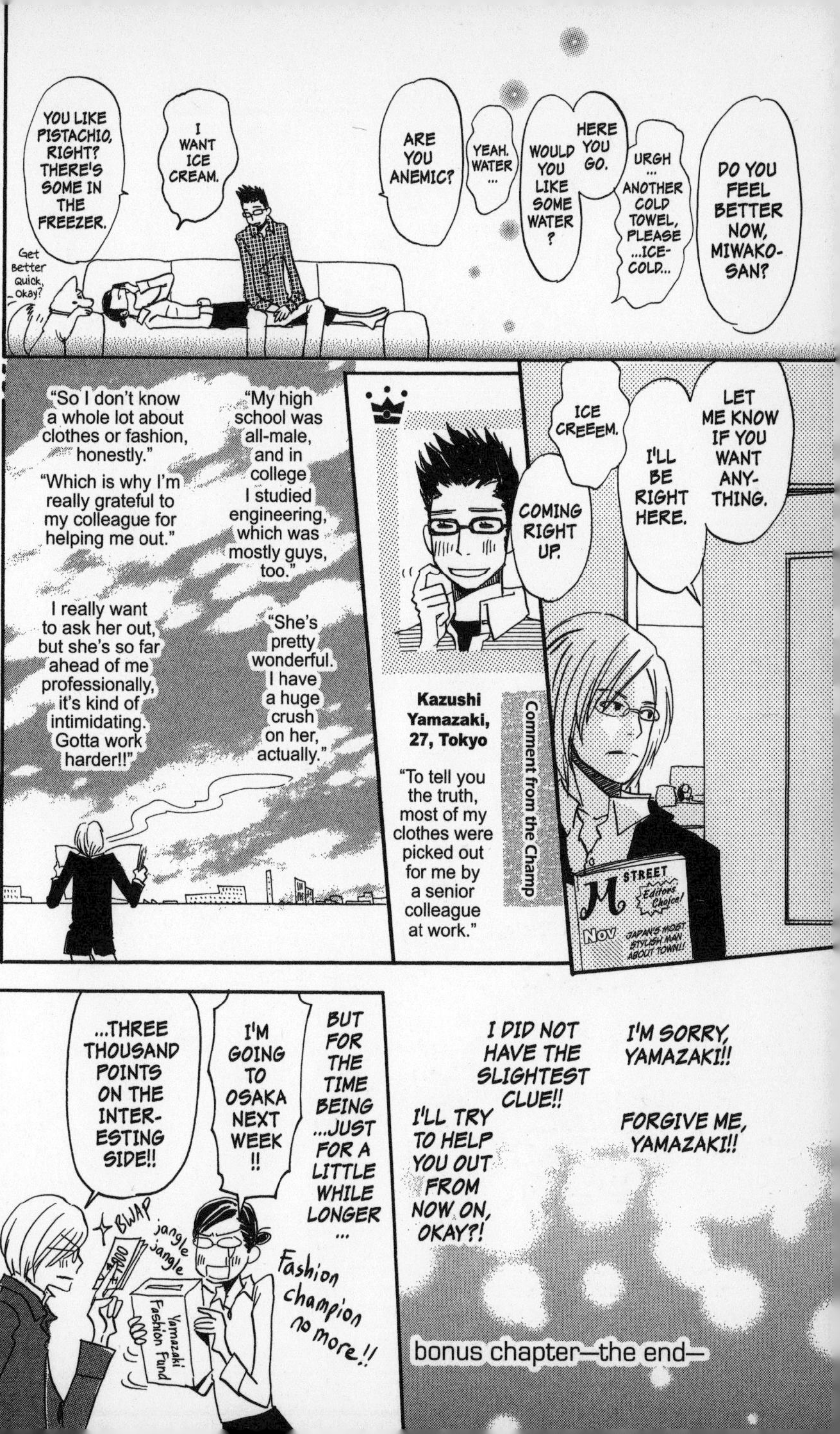
DO YOU FEEL BETTER NOW, MIWAKO-SAN?
URGH ... ANOTHER COLD TOWEL, PLEASE ...ICE-COLD...
HERE YOU GO.
WOULD YOU LIKE SOME WATER?
YEAH. WATER ...
ARE YOU ANEMIC?
I WANT ICE CREAM.
YOU LIKE PISTACHIO, RIGHT? THERE'S SOME IN THE FREEZER.
Get Better Quick, Okay?
LET ME KNOW IF YOU WANT ANY-THING.
I'LL BE RIGHT HERE.
ICE CREEEM.
COMING RIGHT UP.
STREET M Editors' Choice!
Nov JAPAN'S MOST STYLISH MAN ABOUT TOWN!!
Comment from the Champ
Kazushi Yamazaki, 27, Tokyo
"To tell you the truth, most of my clothes were picked out for me by a senior colleague at work."
"My high school was all-male, and in college I studied engineering, which was mostly guys, too."
"So I don't know a whole lot about clothes or fashion, honestly."
"Which is why I'm really grateful to my colleague for helping me out."
"She's pretty wonderful. I have a huge crush on her, actually."
I really want to ask her out, but she's so far ahead of me professionally, it's kind of intimidating. Gotta work harder!!"
I'M SORRY, YAMAZAKI!!
FORGIVE ME, YAMAZAKI!!
I DID NOT HAVE THE SLIGHTEST CLUE!!
I'LL TRY TO HELP YOU OUT FROM NOW ON, OKAY?!
BUT FOR THE TIME BEING ...JUST FOR A LITTLE WHILE LONGER ...
I'M GOING TO OSAKA NEXT WEEK !!
...THREE THOUSAND POINTS ON THE INTER-ESTING SIDE!!
BWAP
jangle jangle
Yamazaki Fashion Fund
Fashion champion no more!!
bonus chapter—the end—

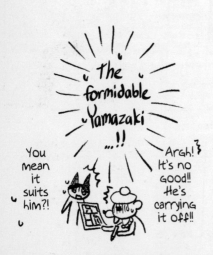

The formidable Yamazaki ...!!
Argh! It's no Good!! He's carrying it off!!
You mean it suits him?!

I wanted to make him look funny, But no matter what screen tone I pasted on him, he looked Great ☆ in it...It was hard work.

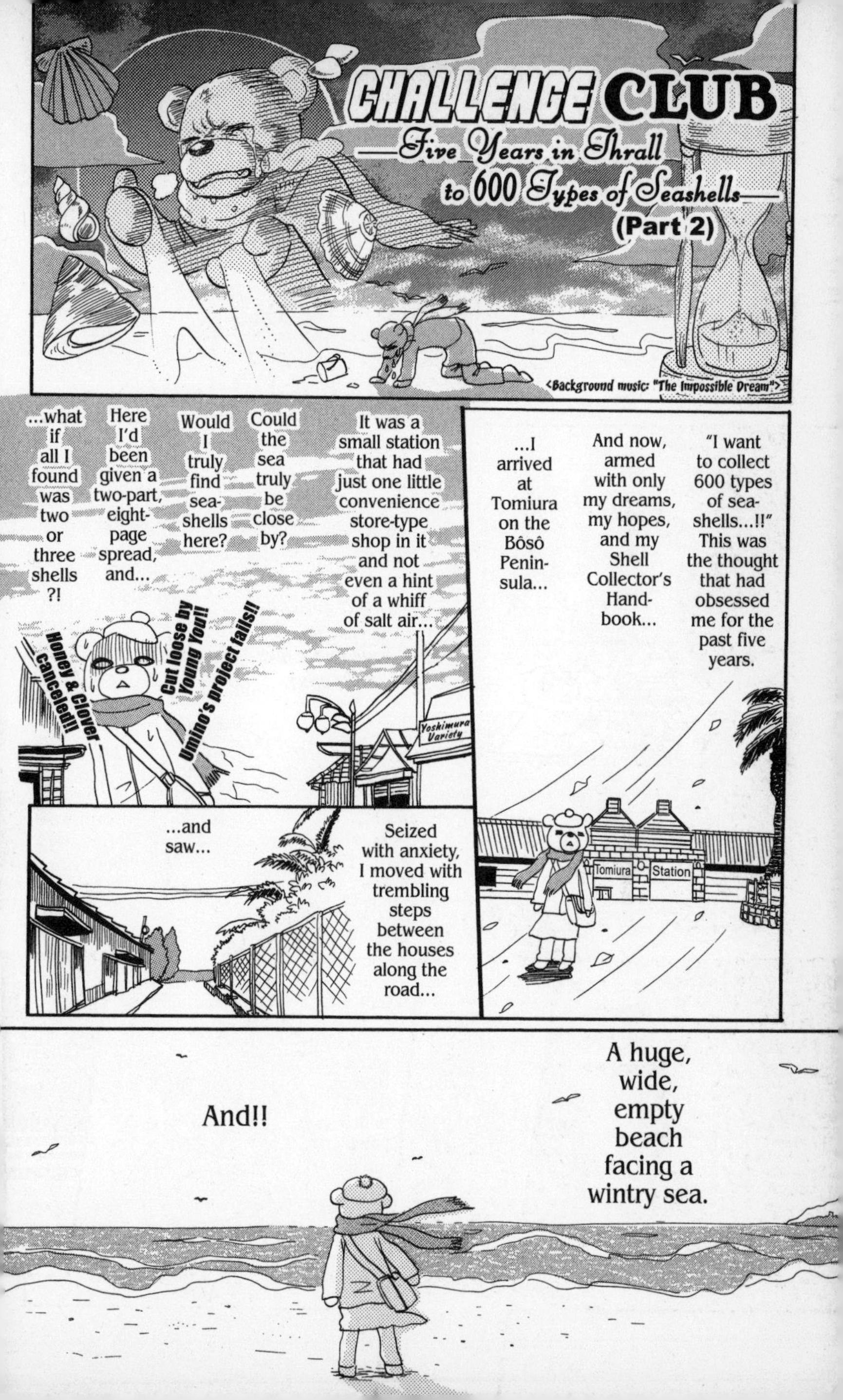

CHALLENGE CLUB
—Five Years in Thrall to 600 Types of Seashells—
(Part 2)
<Background music: "The Impossible Dream">
"I want to collect 600 types of seashells...!!" This was the thought that had obsessed me for the past five years.
And now, armed with only my dreams, my hopes, and my Shell Collector's Handbook...
...I arrived at Tomiura on the Bôsô Peninsula...
Tomiura Station
It was a small station that had just one little convenience store-type shop in it and not even a hint of a whiff of salt air...
Could the sea truly be close by?
Would I truly find seashells here?
Here I'd been given a two-part, eight-page spread, and...
...what if all I found was two or three shells?!
Yoshimura Variety
Cut loose by Young You!!
Umino's project fails!!
Honey & Clover Canceled!!
Seized with anxiety, I moved with trembling steps between the houses along the road...
...and saw...
A huge, wide, empty beach facing a wintry sea.
And!!

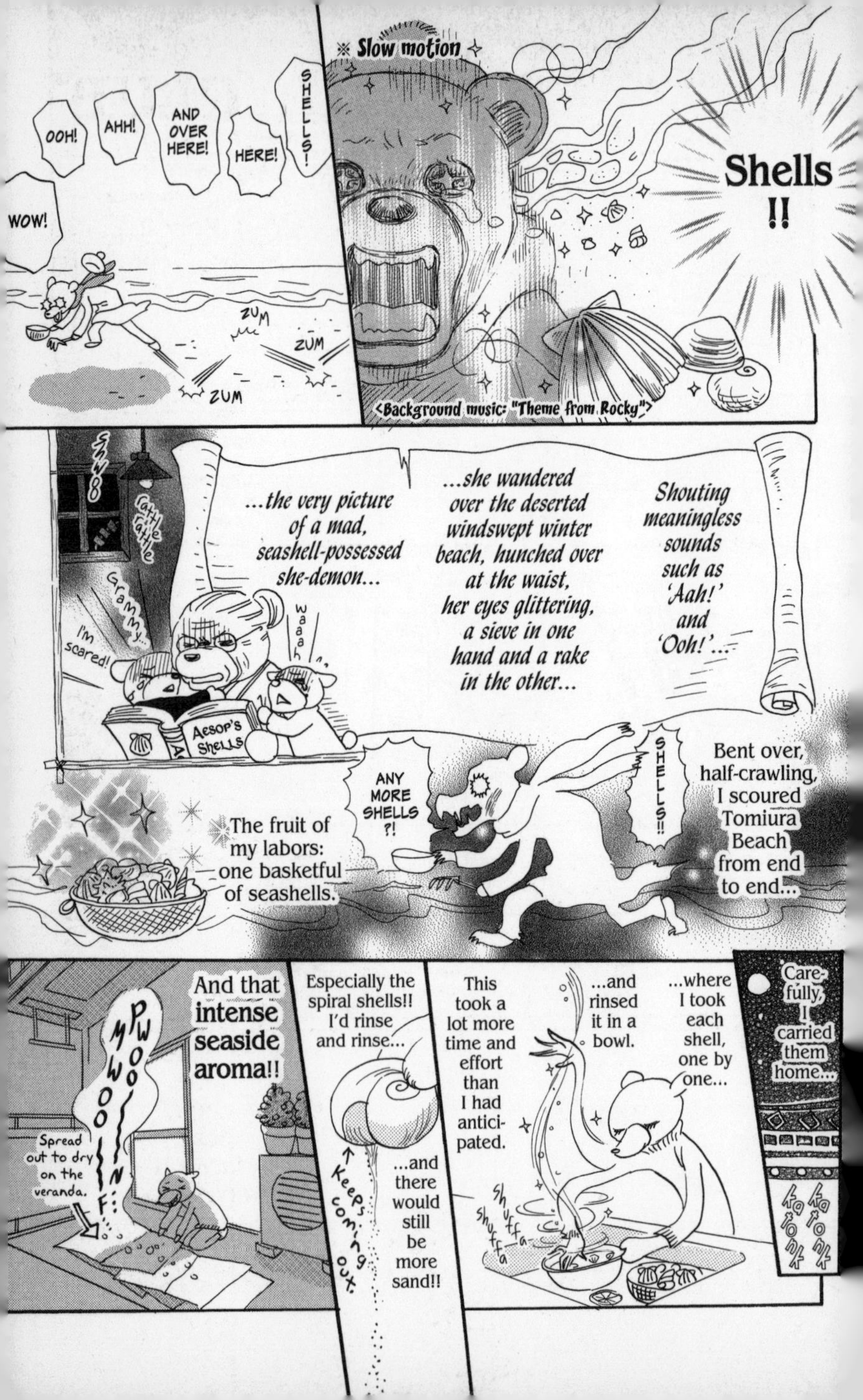
※ Slow motion
Shells!!
<Background music: "Theme from Rocky">
SHELLS!
HERE!
AND OVER HERE!
AHH!
OOH!
WOW!
ZUM
ZUM
ZUM
Shouting meaningless sounds such as 'Aah!' and 'Ooh!'...
...she wandered over the deserted windswept winter beach, hunched over at the waist, her eyes glittering, a sieve in one hand and a rake in the other...
...the very picture of a mad, seashell-possessed she-demon...
rattle rattle
Grammy...
I'm scared!
waaah
AESOP'S SHELLS
Bent over, half-crawling, I scoured Tomiura Beach from end to end...
SHELLS!!
ANY MORE SHELLS?!
The fruit of my labors: one basketful of seashells.
Carefully, I carried them home...
katonk katonk
...where I took each shell, one by one...
...and rinsed it in a bowl.
shuffa shuffa
This took a lot more time and effort than I had anticipated.
Especially the spiral shells!! I'd rinse and rinse...
...and there would still be more sand!!
Keeps coming out.
And that intense seaside aroma!!
PWOOIN...
MWOOOF...
Spread out to dry on the veranda.

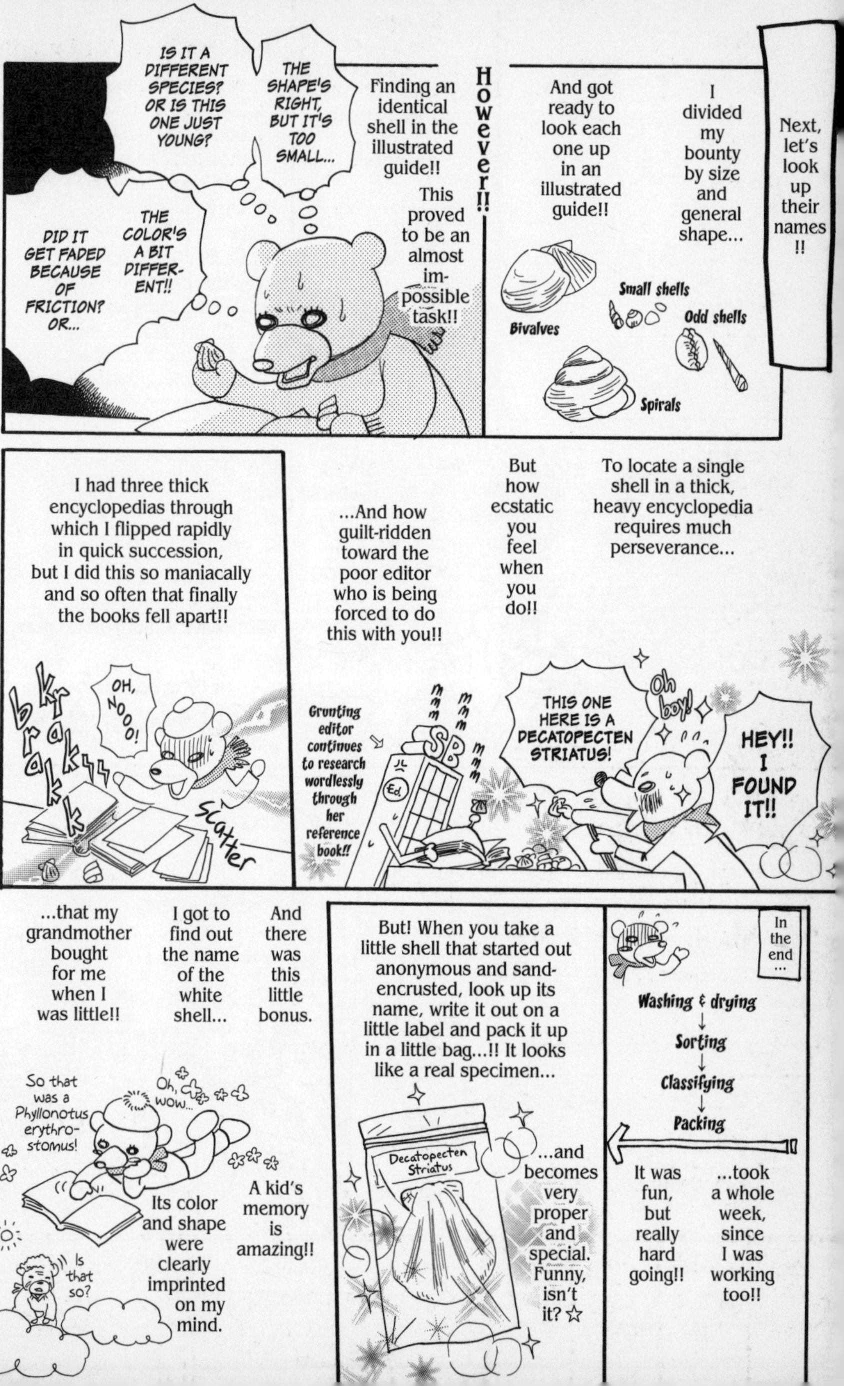

Next, let's look up their names!!
I divided my bounty by size and general shape...
And got ready to look each one up in an illustrated guide!!
Small shells
Odd shells
Bivalves
Spirals
However!!
Finding an identical shell in the illustrated guide!!
This proved to be an almost im-possible task!!
THE SHAPE'S RIGHT, BUT IT'S TOO SMALL...
IS IT A DIFFERENT SPECIES? OR IS THIS ONE JUST YOUNG?
THE COLOR'S A BIT DIFFER-ENT!!
DID IT GET FADED BECAUSE OF FRICTION? OR...
To locate a single shell in a thick, heavy encyclopedia requires much perseverance...
But how ecstatic you feel when you do!!
...And how guilt-ridden toward the poor editor who is being forced to do this with you!!
HEY!! I FOUND IT!!
Oh boy!
THIS ONE HERE IS A DECATOPECTEN STRIATUS!
mmm
mmm
mmm
SB
Ed.
Grunting editor continues to research wordlessly through her reference book!!
I had three thick encyclopedias through which I flipped rapidly in quick succession, but I did this so maniacally and so often that finally the books fell apart!!
OH, NOOOO!
bkrakrak
scatter
In the end...
Washing & drying
Sorting
Classifying
Packing
...took a whole week, since I was working too!!
It was fun, but really hard going!!
But! When you take a little shell that started out anonymous and sand-encrusted, look up its name, write it out on a little label and pack it up in a little bag...!! It looks like a real specimen...
Decatopecten Striatus
...and becomes very proper and special. Funny, isn't it? ☆
And there was this little bonus.
I got to find out the name of the white shell...
...that my grandmother bought for me when I was little!!
Oh, wow...
So that was a Phyllonotus erythro-stomus!
A kid's memory is amazing!!
Its color and shape were clearly imprinted on my mind.
Is that so?

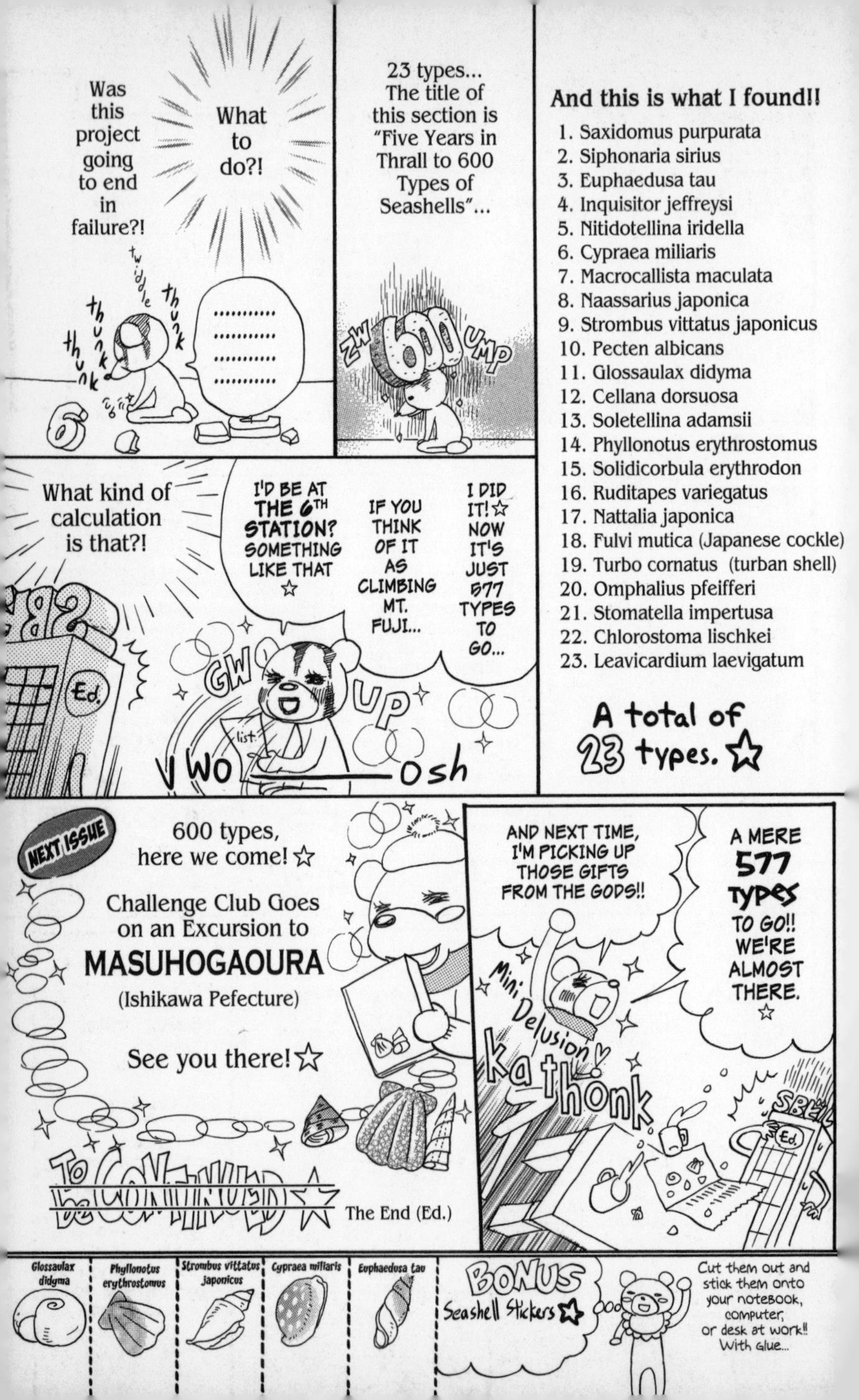

And this is what I found!!
1. Saxidomus purpurata
2. Siphonaria sirius
3. Euphaedusa tau
4. Inquisitor jeffreysi
5. Nitidotellina iridella
6. Cypraea miliaris
7. Macrocallista maculata
8. Naassarius japonica
9. Strombus vittatus japonicus
10. Pecten albicans
11. Glossaulax didyma
12. Cellana dorsuosa
13. Soletellina adamsii
14. Phyllonotus erythrostomus
15. Solidicorbula erythrodon
16. Ruditapes variegatus
17. Nattalia japonica
18. Fulvi mutica (Japanese cockle)
19. Turbo cornatus (turban shell)
20. Omphalius pfeifferi
21. Stomatella impertusa
22. Chlorostoma lischkei
23. Leavicardium laevigatum
A total of 23 types. ☆
23 types... The title of this section is "Five Years in Thrall to 600 Types of Seashells"...
ZWUMP
600
What to do?!
Was this project going to end in failure?!
....
....
....
....
thunk
thunk
thunk
twiddle
6
I DID IT!☆ NOW IT'S JUST 577 TYPES TO GO...
IF YOU THINK OF IT AS CLIMBING MT. FUJI...
I'D BE AT THE 6TH STATION? SOMETHING LIKE THAT ☆
What kind of calculation is that?!
GWUP
list
VWOOSH
Ed.
A MERE 577 TYPES TO GO!! WE'RE ALMOST THERE. ☆
AND NEXT TIME, I'M PICKING UP THOSE GIFTS FROM THE GODS!!
Mini Delusion♥
kathonk
SBE
Ed.
NEXT ISSUE
600 types, here we come! ☆
Challenge Club Goes on an Excursion to
MASUHOGAOURA
(Ishikawa Pefecture)
See you there! ☆
To Be Continued ☆
The End (Ed.)
Glossaulax didgma
Phyllonotus erythrostomus
Strombus vittatus japonicus
Cypraea miliaris
Euphaedusa tau
BONUS Seashell Stickers ☆
Cut them out and stick them onto your notebook, computer, or desk at work!! With Glue...

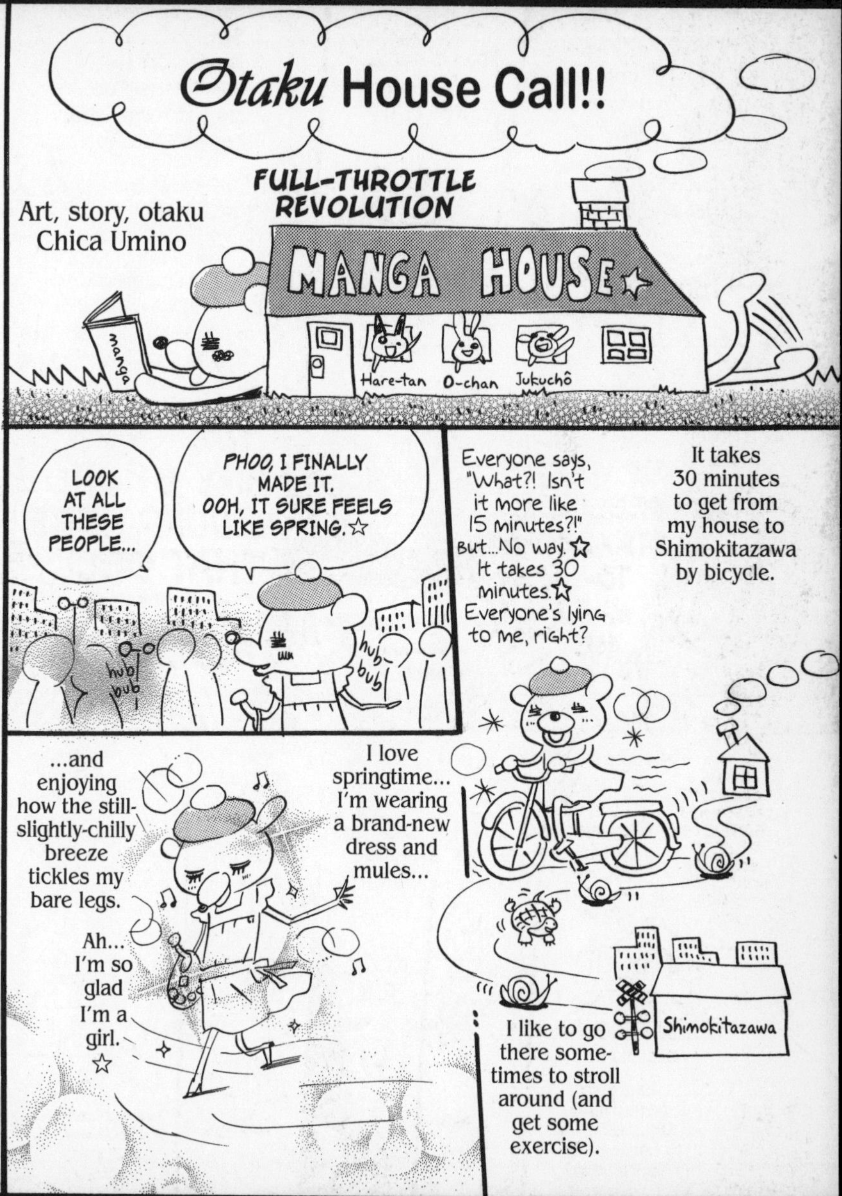
Otaku House Call!!
FULL-THROTTLE REVOLUTION
Art, story, otaku
Chica Umino
MANGA HOUSE
manga
Hare-tan
O-chan
Jukuchô
It takes 30 minutes to get from my house to Shimokitazawa by bicycle.
Everyone says, "What?! Isn't it more like 15 minutes?!" But...No way.☆ It takes 30 minutes.☆ Everyone's lying to me, right?
Shimokitazawa
I like to go there sometimes to stroll around (and get some exercise).
PHOO, I FINALLY MADE IT. OOH, IT SURE FEELS LIKE SPRING.☆
LOOK AT ALL THESE PEOPLE...
hub bub
hub bub
I love springtime... I'm wearing a brand-new dress and mules...
...and enjoying how the still-slightly-chilly breeze tickles my bare legs.
Ah... I'm so glad I'm a girl.☆

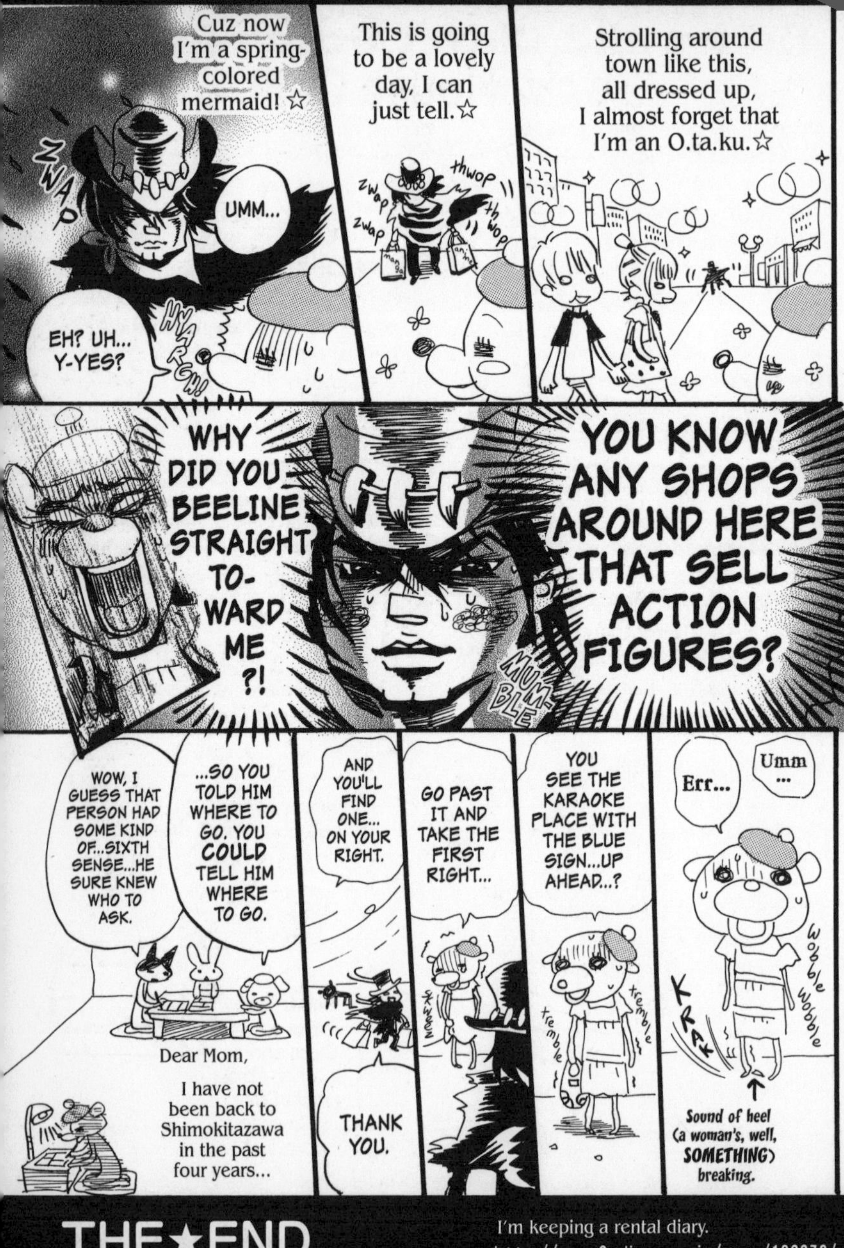

Strolling around town like this, all dressed up, I almost forget that I'm an O.ta.ku.☆
This is going to be a lovely day, I can just tell.☆
thwop thwop
zwap zwap
anime
manga
Cuz now I'm a spring-colored mermaid! ☆
ZWAP
UMM...
HYARGH!!
EH? UH... Y-YES?
YOU KNOW ANY SHOPS AROUND HERE THAT SELL ACTION FIGURES?
MUMBLE
WHY DID YOU BEELINE STRAIGHT TO-WARD ME ?!
Umm ...
Err...
wobble wobble
KRAK
Sound of heel (a woman's, well, SOMETHING) breaking.
YOU SEE THE KARAOKE PLACE WITH THE BLUE SIGN...UP AHEAD...?
tremble tremble
GO PAST IT AND TAKE THE FIRST RIGHT...
skweez
AND YOU'LL FIND ONE... ON YOUR RIGHT.
THANK YOU.
...SO YOU TOLD HIM WHERE TO GO. YOU COULD TELL HIM WHERE TO GO.
WOW, I GUESS THAT PERSON HAD SOME KIND OF...SIXTH SENSE...HE SURE KNEW WHO TO ASK.
Dear Mom,
I have not been back to Shimokitazawa in the past four years...

THE★END

I'm keeping a rental diary.
http://www2.diary.ne.jp/user/162279/

Honey and Clover Study Guide

Page 19, panel 1: Azuki beans
Azuki beans are an ingredient in *osekihan* (red rice), a dish made for celebrations. The other ingredients are mochi rice (smaller grained, sweeter, and stickier than regular Japanese rice) and a garnish of sesame seeds and salt.

Page 34, panel 4: Narazuke
Narazuke are vegetables pickled in sake lees (the sediment left when sake has been pressed). The most common vegetables used are a type of gourd or melon, cucumbers, and eggplants.

Page 49, panel 4: Cosplay
Cosplay is short for costume play and refers to fans dressing up as characters from their favorite manga, anime, video game, movie, etc. In North America, it tends to refer to costumes based on Japanese content, but not exclusively so.

Page 94, panel 1: Fûrinkazan
The kanji 風林火山 literally means "wind, forest, fire, mountain," and adorned the battle standard of the 14th century daimyo Shingen Takeda. It is based on a quote from Sun Tzu's *Art of War*: "Swift as the wind, silent as a forest, fierce as fire and immovable as a mountain."

Page 96, panel 5: Kodama
A Japanese tree spirit. Specifically, Takemoto looks like the *kodama* in Hayao Miyazaki's *Princess Mononoke*.

Page 97, panel 5: Tengu nose
Tengu are mountain spirits, and one type stereotypically has a long nose. People who are vain or boastful are called tengu and are shown with long noses as a visual gag.

Page 104, panel 2: Rakkyo
Pickled shallots used as a condiment and one of Tottori Prefecture's regional specialties. It can also be the name of the specific kind of shallot the pickles are made from.

Page 104, panel 2: Nashi pear
Pyrus pyrifolia. Sometimes also called the Asian pear or apple pear, it is another Tottori specialty.

Pg 108, panel 4: Ebina
Ebina Service Area is one of the famous Japanese Service Areas, and the only one in Kanagawa Prefecture. Japanese Service Areas are similar to highway rest stops but can be very big, and in addition to restrooms they also offer restaurants and gift shops that sell the local specialties.

Page 108, panel 4: Kushi-katsu
Generally breaded and deep-fried meat or vegetables on skewers, but the type Yamazaki bought is the junk food version sold in candy stores and is not freshly fried.

Page 108, panel 4: Sukombu
Slightly sweet, pickled seaweed strips. Like the kushi-katsu, it is a popular item in candy stores.

Page 123, panel 4: Yokozuna
The highest rank in professional sumo wrestling.

Page 139, panel 7: Iwaki
A city in Fukushima Prefecture. It was incorporated in 1966, and was one of the first Japanese cities to be named in hiragana rather than kanji.

Page 139, panel 7: Mito
The capital of Ibaraki Prefecture. It is the sister city of Anaheim, California and the friendship city of Chongqing, China.

Page 148, panel 2: Yôkan
Similar to *anko* (red bean jam), but made firmer by the addition of agar (a seaweed-based gelling agent). It keeps well without refrigeration, so it has a long shelf life.

Page 163, panel 1: Karasu tengu
A type of *yokai* (demon) most often depicted as part tengu and part crow.

Page 165, panel 2: Tanuki udon
A variation of udon (thick noodles in broth) served with *tenkasu* (crumbs left from deep frying tempura), *naruto* (pressed fish cakes with a swirl design in the center), and leeks or green onions.

Page 175, panel 1: Asakusabashi
A neighborhood in Tokyo known for its wholesale shops, traditional doll shops, and bead stores.

It was seven o'clock on the morning of my deadline. I needed to wake up, so I went out to my local Doutor to buy some coffee beans. And somewhere on the way, a distance of not more than 100 meters, I managed to lose my house key. After tracing the route ten times, I gave up and called a locksmith, and by the time he used a drill to let me into my house, I had spent seven hours outside. The new lock cost me ¥40,000 and the coffee beans cost ¥700. So that comes out to ¥40,700 yen for 200 grams of coffee?! My god, was this the most expensive coffee in the entire world???!! I shall savor every drop.

-Chica Umino

Chica Umino was born in Tokyo and started out as a product designer and illustrator. Her beloved *Honey and Clover* debuted in 2000 and received the Kodansha Manga Award in 2003. *Honey and Clover* was also nominated for the Tezuka Culture Prize and an award from the Japan Media Arts Festival.